UNIVERSITY OF WASHINGTON PUBLICATIONS IN LANGUAGE AND LITERATURE
Volume 13   June, 1955

Bibliography of Chaucer

1908-1953

By

DUDLEY DAVID GRIFFITH

University of Washington Press

Seattle : 1955

CONTENTS

INTRODUCTION

This contribution to Chaucerian bibliography is
planned as a supplement to Eleanor Prescott Hammond's
Chaucer, a Bibliographical Manual. Miss Hammond's
Manual is a book remarkable for its accuracy, completeness, and judicious attitudes toward Chaucerian problems
up to the time of its publication in 1908. It should also be
noticed that the section Influence and Allusions is a
supplement to Caroline F. E. Spurgeon's Five Hundred
Years of Chaucer Criticism and Allusions: 1357-1900.
This book is known to all students of Chaucer as the re-
spected collection of Chaucerian references.

The present bibliography contains some items not in
Hammond or Spurgeon, many items not listed in the
partial bibliographies mentioned below in this Introduction, and an extension of the years covered. The purpose
has been to provide a supplement which will make it
necessary for scholars to consult only Hammond, Spurgeon, and the present volume.

The entries in this bibliography are more complete
than those in the aids to be found elsewhere. Each entry
lists the full name or initials of the contributor, the
title, the volume or series, if applicable, the dating and
paging of each book or article. This listing is followed
by reviews and notes which contain cross references and
identification of the entry where such identification is
helpful. As befits a bibliography, these notes are not intended as critical comments but simply to clear the way
for many future investigations. The various added sections on the backgrounds of Chaucer's time are selective.
They form a needed addition to Chaucerian scholarship
which has been recognized in the Modern Humanities Research Association Bibliographies to 1942 and the Cambridge Bibliography of English Literature to 1933.

This volume seeks to bring together all the significant
scholarship of Chaucerian studies during the years from
1908 to 1953. It is intended to facilitate the research of

vii

those interested in the life, writings, and the time of
Geoffrey Chaucer. The activity of Chaucerian scholars
is here recorded. The first edition covering seventeen
years (1908-24) was equaled in number of items by the
additions in Berelson for the eleven years, 1925-35. For
the subsequent seventeen years, this second edition adds
a number of entries almost equal to the twenty-eight
years of the first edition and Berelson. The names of the
contributors to this bibliography are the names of scholars eminent for their studies in this and many other
fields of English language and literature.

  This research by Chaucerian scholars records a con-
tinuous and vigorous interest in the older problems of
manuscripts, text, and literary relations and sources.
The entries in this bibliography indicate, however, an
increased attention to language, style, and word study.
New discoveries have been made in the records of Chaucer's life, even possibly adding to the Chaucer canon.
There has been a large publication of modernizations and
translations, and the texts of the Canterbury Tales and
Troilus and Criseyde have been edited from all the
known manuscripts. Of special importance are the present studies of the Chaucer Group of the Modern Language
Association of America in which the texts that Chaucer
could have used are studies in their relations to his writings.

  Many studies which examine Chaucer's rhetorical
tradition, his independent style, the meaning of the text,
and his methods of characterization have contributed new
materials and have frequently led to lively and informing
controversies. If the added number of entries may be
taken as evidence, these studies indicate a contemporary
interest in the Prologue of the Canterbury Tales and its
backgrounds, the Man of Law's Tale, the Pardoner's
Prologue and Tale, the Wife of Bath's Prologue and Tale,
the Merchant's Tale, the Parlement of Foules, the
Legend of Good Women, and Troilus and Criseyde. Many
documents that are related to Chaucer's religious attitudes and to the activities of his world have been published. Controversies on the theme of courtly love are
voluminous. Some scholars find courtly love everywhere
while others believe that, by Chaucer's time, courtly
love had become a recognized pattern of social graces

which Chaucer approved. The poet embodies these social
graces always in his presentations of good manners, but
when he uses courtly love for narrative effect, he always
reveals his understanding, his humanity, and his wisdom
in regard to social relations. Discussions of chronology
and the order of the Canterbury Tales are frequently offered with great scholarly acumen, but they have won no
generally accepted conclusions. The studies here mentioned are, however, only emphases as many excellent
contributions have appeared on all phases of Chaucerian
research.

In the making of this bibliography some rules of uni-
formity have been observed. Organization has been a
problem because so many entries could properly be
placed in more than one section. Some subdivisions are,
however, necessary in so large a volume. In order that
the competent advanced student may not overlook some
items, selected references, usually from the section:
General Criticism, have been repeated under the various
headings of the sections. Where information might be
missed because an article deals with two or more passages, or has an undescriptive title such as "Chauceriana," the item has been repeated in its appropriate place.
References have been annotated only when the title is
indefinite, or to supplement the title, or to cite the line
when the article concerns only a small part of the text.

It will be noticed that the research value of the dif-
ferent entries varies greatly. This variation results from
the desire to make the bibliography inclusive. The con-
tent of some entries might be called "appreciation," and
other entries repeat well-known information adequate to
their purpose. Both have a bibliographical value. General appreciation of Chaucer's genius has become difficult
because appreciation has become interpretation of particular units of Chaucer's poetry. Chaucer's knowledge
of human character, his wide reading, and his mastery
of various poetic forms and styles make a short and adequate interpretation of his genius almost impossible.
Summaries of well-known facts and abilities, such as
are found in the handbooks and the various introductions,
are important for initiatory studies. In order to make a
contribution to the problems which arise because of the
lack of a variorum Chaucer, all the editions have been

brought together in one section. Almost all of these
editions have short summaries of Chaucer's life and
work.

Several other policies of organization should be listed
here. References to Dorothy Everett's excellent annual
reviews of Chaucerian scholarship published in the Year's
Work in English Studies are listed by page, but omit the
volume and year when the year is the same as that of the
book or article to which the reference is appended. Whole
articles have been cited and special page references in
them have been avoided in the hope that quotations out of
context will be minimized. References to courtly love
are placed in the section: Social Backgrounds, to which
should be added some entries having particular applica-
tion to studies in Troilus and Criseyde. In order to pre-
vent too much duplication, discussions of Lollius are
placed in the section: Literary Relations. Chronology
appears in the sections: General Criticism, and Canterbury Tales: General. In this last section, references on
the order of the tales are also to be found. Studies of
dream poems and their backgrounds are placed in the
section: Works Other than the Canterbury Tales: General.
The research scholar should also keep in mind that the
various general sections contain material which should
be consulted as a supplement to any particular study.
The divisions of this bibliography are almost the same
as those of the first edition except that the sections:
Style and Versification, and Word Study have been re-
arranged from the old classifications of Language and
Metrics, and the descriptions of the persons in the Prologue to the Canterbury Tales have been given separate
listings to facilitate references to them. This change was
first made in Berelson. Because Robinson's text contains both Skeat's numbering and his own, the order of
the tales is changed to that of Robinson. The section:
Backgrounds has been moved from near the center to
the end of the book as these backgrounds provide references applicable to all of Chaucer's work.

The selection of titles for Chaucer's poems has in
general followed Miss Hammond's practice. She modernized these titles when the modernization was a satisfactory translation of the original even when, as in the
cases of the Clerk and the Canon's Yeoman, the four-

teenth-century meanings were infrequent in modern
usage. The authority of Chaucer's text was followed if
the title had no satisfactory modern translation. This
usage applies to Complaint d'Amours, Gentilesse, Merciles Beaute, Parlement of Foules, Stedfastnesse, and
Womanly Noblesse. In this bibliography, Stedfastnesse
has been modernized, and Troilus and Criseyde has re-
placed Miss Hammond's Troilus and Cressida.

From this bibliography some references have been
excluded. Editions which are simply reprints and have no
distinction from type of printing or illustration have been
omitted. Survey books organized for the American standard course in the History of English Literature have usually been given no listing. The selections in these books
from Chaucer's works do not qualify as editions, although
their notes might be taken into account if a variorum
Chaucer were being prepared. Papers read at meetings
of scholarly societies have been omitted unless their published summaries contain suggestions for further research. These papers are not readily obtainable if they
do not become entries in this bibliography because of
later publication. The section: Bibliography contains
only those listings which are concerned directly with
Chaucerian items. On the other hand, the section: Backgrounds seeks to emphasize bibliographical aids for research in the historical, political, philosophic, social,
religious, economic, scientific, and artistic ideas of
Chaucer's time. In this section, the research scholar
will find listed studies of the backgrounds of Chaucer's
world and references to other bibliographies which will
enlarge his investigations. Except for these omissions,
our objective has been to provide all the bibliographical
materials of Chaucerian scholarship to date.

I am under special obligations to many scholars. The
entries of this bibliography have been checked with Bernard R. Berelson's master's thesis, A Bibliography of
Chaucer: 1908-33, which was a careful and accurate
study. Mr. Berelson's professional interest in this subject caused him to contribute items to the year, 1938.
Howell Johnson Heaney of Cornell University sent me his
master's thesis, A Bibliography of Chaucer: 1933-1940,
for which I owe him many thanks. For a long time, all
Chaucerian scholars have consulted the annual bibliog-

raphies of the Modern Humanities Research Association,
Dorothy Everett's reviews of Chaucerian scholarship in
the Year's Work in English Studies, Willard E. Martin's
A Chaucerian Bibliography: 1925-1933, the Progress of
Mediaeval Studies in the United States of America, the
annual bibliographies of PMLA, and John Edwin Wells's
A Manual of Writings in Middle English: 1050-1400 and
its nine supplements. The entries of this bibliography
have been checked against all these books, against general bibliographies, and the footnotes of many articles.

More personally, I wish to express my thanks for
assistance and many courtesies to Miss Madeline Gilchrist and her staff of the Frederick Morgan Padelford
Memorial Library and to the personnel of the other
branches of the University of Washington Libraries. To
the Agnes H. Anderson Research Fund of the University
of Washington, I am grateful for the grant which paid
for the typing and editing of this book.

It is hoped that this publication will be of value to
graduate students and research scholars by presenting
new items, preventing further duplication, and suggest-
ing topics for further study. Corrections and additions
to this bibliography will be very gratefully received.

Dudley D. Griffith

Seattle, Washington
March, 1955

ABBREVIATIONS

A&A	Anelida and Arcite.
AB	Anglia Beiblatt.
Acad	Academy.
AHR	American Historical Review.
AJP	American Journal of Philology.
AL	American Literature.
AM	American Mercury.
Am NQ	American Notes and Queries.
Ang	Anglia.
Ang Bbl	Anglia Beiblatt.
Arch, Archiv	Archiv für das Studium der neueren Sprache und Literaturen.
BD	Book of the Duchess.
Birney	Birney, Earle. The Beginnings of Chaucer's Irony. See section: General Criticism.
Brusendorff	Brusendorff, Aage. The Chaucer Tradition. See section: General Criticism.
CBEL	Cambridge Bibliography of English Literature. See section: Bibliography.
Cbl	Literarisches Centralblatt für Deutschland.
CE	College English.
CHR	Catholic Historical Review.
Clemen	Clemen, Wolfgang. Der junge Chaucer. See section: General Criticism.
ClT	Clerk's Tale.
Com	Commonweal.
CookT	Cook's Tale.
CQR	Church Quarterly Review.
CR	Contemporary Review.
Crit	New Criterion.
CT	Canterbury Tales.
Cummings	Cummings, Hubertis M. The Indebtedness of Chaucer's Works to the Italian Works of Boccaccio. See section: Literary Relations.

Curry	Curry, Walter Clyde. Chaucer and the Medieval Sciences. See section: Scientific Backgrounds.
CW	Catholic World.
CYT	Canon's Yeoman's Tale.
Dempster	Dempster, Germaine. Dramatic Irony in Chaucer. See section: Style.
DL	Deutsche Literaturzeitung.
DNB	Dictionary of National Bibliography.
DUJ	Durham University Journal.
EETS	Early English Text Society.
EHR	English Historical Review.
EJ	English Journal.
ELH	English Literary History.
ES, ESt	Englische Studien.
E Stud	English Studies.
Expl	Explicator.
FrankT	Franklin's Tale.
French	French, Robert Dudley. A Chaucer Handbook. See section: General Criticism.
FriarT	Friar's Tale.
Gerould	Gerould, Gordon Hall. Chaucerian Essays. See section: General Criticism.
GRM	Germanisch-Romanische Monatsschriften.
Hammond	Hammond, Eleanor Prescott. Chaucer: A Bibliographical Manual. See section: Bibliography.
HF	House of Fame.
Hinckley	Hinckley, Henry B. Notes on Chaucer. See section: General Criticism.
Hist	History.
HJ	Hibbert Journal.
HLQ	Huntington Library Quarterly.
Jefferson	Jefferson, Bernard L. Chaucer and the Consolation of Philosophy of Boethius. See section: Literary Relations.
JEGP	Journal of English and Germanic Philology.
JHI	Journal of the History of Ideas.
JRLB	John Rylands Library Bulletin.

Jsb	Jahresbericht über die Erscheinungen auf dem Gebiete der germanischen Philologie.
Kaluza	Kaluza, Max. Chaucer-Handbuch. See section: General Criticism.
Kittredge	Kittredge, George Lyman. Chaucer and his Poetry. See section: General Criticism.
KnT	Knight's Tale.
Koch	Koch, John. Textkritische Bemerkungen zu Chaucers Kleineren Dichtungen. See section: Editions.
Legouis	Legouis, Emile. Geoffrey Chaucer. 1928 edition. See section: General Criticism.
LGRP	Literaturblatt für germanische und romanische Philologie.
LAR	Library Association Record.
LGW	Legend of Good Women.
LL	Life and Letters.
LQR	London Quarterly Review.
MA	Medium Aevum.
Malone	Malone, Kemp. Chapters on Chaucer. See section: General Criticism.
Manly	Manly, John Matthews. Canterbury Tales. See section: Editions.
Manly SNL	Manly, John Matthews. Some New Light on Chaucer. See section: Life.
ManT	Manciple's Tale.
Martin	Martin, Willard E., Jr. A Chaucer Bibliography: 1925-33. See section: Bibliography.
Med Stud	Medieval Studies.
Mel	Melibeus.
MerT	Merchant's Tale.
MilT	Miller's Tale.
MLA	Modern Language Association of America.
MLN	Modern Language Notes.
MLT	Man of Law's Tale.
MLR	Modern Language Review.
MonT	Monk's Tale.
MP	Modern Philology.
NAR	North American Review.

NJWJ	Neue Jahrbücher für Wissenschaft und Jugendsbildung.
Neophil	Neophilologus.
NPT	Nun's Priest's Tale.
NQ	Notes and Queries.
NR	New Republic.
NS	Die Neueren Sprachen.
N St	New Statesman and Nation.
NYHTB	New York Herald-Tribune Books.
NYTBR	New York Times Book Review.
Obs	Observer.
PardT	Pardoner's Tale.
ParsT	Parson's Tale.
Patch	Patch, Howard R. On Rereading Chaucer. See section: General Criticism.
Pbl	Polybiblion.
PF	Parlement of Foules.
PhyT	Physician's Tale.
PMLA	Publications of the Modern Language Association of America.
PQ	Philological Quarterly.
PriorT	Prioress' Tale.
Prol	Prologue.
QJS	Quarterly Journal of Speech.
QQ	Queen's Quarterly.
QR	Quarterly Review.
RAA	Revue Anglo-Américaine.
RBPH	Revue Belge de Philologie et d'Histoire.
Reeve'sT	Reeve's Tale.
RES	Review of English Studies.
Rev	Reviewed.
Rev Crit	Revue Critique d'Histoire et de Littérature.
Rev Germ	Revue Germanique.
Robinson	Robinson, F. N. The Complete Works of Chaucer. See section: Editions.
Rom Rev	Romanic Review.
Root	Root, Robert Kilburn. The Poetry of Chaucer. See section: General Criticism.
RR	Romanic Review; Romaunt of the Rose.
SAQ	South Atlantic Quarterly.
Sat Rev	Saturday Review of Politics, Literature, Science and Art.

Shannon	Shannon, Edgar F. Chaucer and the Roman Poets. See section: Literary Relations.
Shelly	Shelly, Percy Van Dyke. The Living Chaucer. See section: General Criticism.
SHR	Scottish Historical Review.
ShT	Shipman's Tale.
SNT	Second Nun's Tale.
Sources and Analogues	Bryan, W. F., and Germaine Dempster, Eds. Sources and Analogues of Chaucer's Canterbury Tales. See section: Canterbury Tales: General.
SP	Studies in Philology.
SPCK	Society for Promoting Christian Knowledge.
Stud Neophil	Studia Neophilologica.
Spec	Speculum.
Spect	Spectator.
Speirs	Speirs, John. Chaucer, the Maker. See section: General Criticism.
SqT	Squire's Tale.
SRL	Saturday Review of Literature.
SumT	Summoner's Tale.
T&C	Troilus and Criseyde.
TAPA	Transactions of the American Philological Association.
TLS	Times Literary Supplement (London).
Tatlock	Tatlock, John Strong Perry. Development and Chronology of Chaucer's Works. See section: General Criticism.
UTQ	University of Toronto Quarterly.
VQR	Virginia Quarterly Review.
WBT	Wife of Bath's Tale.
Wells	Wells, John Edwin. A Manual of Writings in Middle English. See section: Bibliography.
Willard	Willard, James F. Progress of Mediaeval Studies in the United States of America. See section: Bibliography.
YR	Yale Review.

YWES   Everett, Dorothy. Year's Work in Eng-
                  lish Studies (Chaucer Section).
ZFAAK   Zeitschrift für Aesthetik und Allgemeine
                  Kunstwissenschaft (Stuttgart).
ZFEU   Zeitschrift für französischen und eng-
                  lischen Unterricht.
ZFOG   Zeitschrift für österreichischen Gym-
                  nasion.
ZNU   Zeitschrift für neusprachlichen Unter-
                  richt.

   No references are made to Griffith (1926 edition),
Berelson, or Heaney, as these studies are not easily obtainable. All their items have been included in this bibliography.

BIBLIOGRAPHY OF CHAUCER, 1908-1953

CONCORDANCE AND INDEXES

See CBEL, I, 124-7; also Corson, Index to Proper Names, in section: Canterbury Tales.

BROWN, CARLETON, and ROSSELL ROBBINS. An Index to Middle English Verse. Printed for the Index Society by Columbia Univ Press, 1943. 785 pp.
See index for Chaucer; also Mustanoja below in this section.
Rev: G. D. Willcock, YWES, 71-2, and S. Gibson, 224-5; TLS, 42, Aug 21, 1943, 408; Francis L. Utley, Spec, 20, 1945, 105-11.

CAMPION, ELEANOR E. , Ed. Union List of Microfilms: Revised, Enlarged, and Cumulated Edition. Philadelphia Bibliographical Center and Union Library Catalogue. Ann Arbor: Edwards, 1951.
Listing of films of early printed editions of Chaucer.

DOWNES, ROBERT B. Notable Material Added to American Libraries: 1940-1941. Lib Quart, 12, 1942, 175-220.

JOHNSON, I. Index Criticus Verborum Daretis Phrygii. Vanderbilt Univ Diss, privately printed, 1938.
Rev: Romania, 66:138 (a notice).

MUSTANOJA, TAUNO F. The Index to Middle English Verse: Corrections, Additions, Suggestions. Neuphilologische Mitteilungen, nos. 5-6, 1948, 126-33.

TATLOCK, J. S. P. The Chaucer Concordance. MLN, 38, 1923, 504-6.

---------- and ARTHUR G. KENNEDY. A Concordance to the Complete Works of Geoffrey Chaucer and to the Romaunt of the Rose. Carnegie Institution of Washington, 1927. 1110 pp.
This concordance, based on the Globe text (see Hammond, p. 148), is an important reference work for occurrences of words, the study of their meanings in context, and it may be used as a rhyme index. See page viii for words listed by specimens only.

3

Rev: TLS, Nov 10, 1927, 816; James F. Royster, SP, 25, 1928, 82-9; Clark S. Northup, JEGP, 27, 1928, 236-40; Robert J. Menner, MLN, 43, 1928, 332-6; J. Hoops, ESt, 63, 1928, 86-9; A. Brandl, Arch, 153, 1928, 264-6; Walter Fischer, AB, 39, 1928, 259-62.

THOMPSON, STITH. Motif-Index of Folk Literature: A Classification of Narrative Elements in Folk-Tales, Ballads, Myths, Fables, Medieval Romances, Exempla, Fabliaux, Jest-Books, and Local Legends. 6 vols. Indiana Univ Studies, 19, nos. 96, 97; 20, nos. 100-1; 21, nos. 105-6; 22, nos. 108-10; 23, nos. 111-2. FF Communications, Helsingfors, nos. 106-9, 116-7, 1932-6.

Rev: H. M. Smyser, Spec, 13, 1938, 368.

----------. The Types of the Folk Tale: A Classification and Bibliography. Antli Aarne's Verzeichnis der Märchentypen. Translated and enlarged. FF Communications, 74, Helsingfors, 1928. 279 pp.

Rev: John W. Spargo, MLN, 44, 1929, 482-4.

WELLEIN, LAWRENCE THEODORE. An Index to the Critical Notes of F. N. Robinson's The Poetical Works of Chaucer from the Preface through Fragment IV of the Canterbury Tales. Master's Thesis, Univ of Washington, 1950.

WILLIAMS, HARRY F. An Index to Medieval Studies Published in Festschriften: 1865-1946 with Special Reference to Romanic Materials. Univ of California Press, 1951. 165 pp.

Rev: John Orr, MLR, 47, 1952, 425.

BIBLIOGRAPHY

See Hinckley, 263-86; Wells, 1528, 1639, 1730, and CBEL, I, 208.

BATESON, F. W., Ed. The Cambridge Bibliography of English Literature. 4 vols. New York: Macmillan; Cambridge Univ Press, 1941.

Contains items to 1933 in Chaucer, I, 208-49, by John Edwin Wells and Mrs. J. E. Heseltine (Modernizations and Translations, Early Criticism); English Chaucerians, by Sybil Rosenfeld; Middle Scots Writers, by G. Gregory Smith and D. Hammer. See also the general bibliographies, I, 3-48, and Middle English Period, 113-306; especially The Political Background, 115-9, by M. McKisack; The Social Background, 119-24, by D. C. Douglas; and Education, 124-7, by T. A. Walker, revised by G. R. Potter and J. W. Adamson. Note the alphabetical list of authors, writers' names, and anonymous works in Volume IV. Lists a few items not in Hammond; contains expanded listings of entries before 1870 of those in Hammond or Spurgeon not repeated in this volume.

BAUGH, ALBERT C., and Others. American Bibliography, 1922-. PMLA, 37, 1922, 5-6; PMLA, 38, 1923, 4-5; PMLA, 39, 1924, 6-7; PMLA, 40, 1925, 5-6; PMLA, 41, 1926, 6-7; PMLA, 42, 1927, 9-12; PMLA, 43, 1928, 10-12; PMLA, 44, 1929, 13-16; PMLA, 45, 1930, 21-3; PMLA, 46, 1931, 15-16; PMLA, 46, 1931, 1344-5; PMLA, 47, 1932, 1218-20; PMLA, 48, 1933, 1308-11; PMLA, 49, 1934, 1216-7; PMLA, 50, 1935, 1248-50; PMLA, 51, 1936, 1222-4; PMLA, 52, 1937, 1234-7; PMLA, 53, 1938, 1230-2; PMLA, 54, 1939, 1219-20; PMLA, 55, 1940, 1237-9; PMLA, 56, 1941, 1222-5; PMLA, 57, 1942, 1232-4; PMLA, 58, 1943, 1203-5; PMLA, 59, 1944, 1197-9; PMLA, 60, 1945, 1205-7; PMLA, 61, 1946, 1237-8. To this date, these bibliographies are published in the spring as supple-

ments to the volume of the previous year and are the
bibliographies of the year here indicated. The following bibliographies are listed in the year published and
contain the American bibliography for the previous
year. PMLA, 63, 1948, 31-4; PMLA, 64, 1949, 19-21;
PMLA, 65, 1950, 42-4; PMLA, 66, 1951, 52-3;
PMLA, 67, 1952, 22-4; PMLA, 68, 1953, 106-7.
BAUGH, ALBERT C. Fifty Years of Chaucer Scholarship. Spec, 26, 1951, 659-72.
BERELSON, BERNARD REUBEN. A Bibliography of
Chaucer: 1908-1935. M. A. Thesis, Univ of Washington Libraries, 1937.
   This bibliography contained the items of Griffith
below with additional items and comments to the
year 1937. Its entries are rechecked and included in
this volume.
BUNN, OLENA S. A Bibliography of Chaucer in English
and American Belles-Lettres since 1900. Bull Bibli-
ography, 19, 1949, 205-8.
   Concerns allusions.
COFFMAN, GEORGE RALEIGH. Some Recent Trends
in English Literary Scholarship with Special Reference to Medieval Backgrounds. SP, 35, 1938, 500-14.
COOK, ALBERT S. A Bibliography of Chaucer Compiled
from Various Sources. Univ of California Press, 1886.
ENGLISH ASSOCIATION. The Year's Work in English
Studies, 1920-. Oxford Univ Press, issued annually.
Author of Chaucer Sections: Dorothy Everett.
   Rev: TLS, Mar 17, 1927, 182; R. B. McKerrow,
RES, 3, 1927, 493-4; NQ, 152, 1927, 288; R. W. Zand-
voort, E Stud, 9, 1927, 49; H. Lüdeke, DL, 49, 1928,
1464-6; H. S. V. Jones, JEGP, 27, 1928, 580; NQ,
154, 1928, 234; F. Delattre, RBPH, 7, 1928, 1096-7;
TLS, May 2, 1929, 356 (see Edith Morley, TLS, May
2, 1929, 362); Walter Fischer, AB, 40, 1929, 248;
TLS, June 5, 1930, 474; Walter Fischer, AB, 41,
1930, 271; L. N. Broughton, MLN, 46, 1931, 66; R. B.
McKerrow, RES, 7, 1931, 118; Walter Fischer, AB,
42, 1931, 312-3; C. J. Sisson, MLR, 27, 1932, 112-3;
R. B. McKerrow, RES, 8, 1932, 368-9; E. Gillett,
Mercury, 25, 1932, 411-2; S. B. Liljegren, Litteris,
7, 1931, 243-8; K. M. L. , Oxford Mag, Mar 2, 1933,
509; Walter Fischer, AB, 43, 1932, 277-8; C. J.

Sisson, MLR, 28, 1933, 133-4; R. B. McKerrow,
RES, 10, 1934, 116-7; TLS, Aug 31, 1933, 578;
K. M. L., Oxford Mag, Nov 16, 1933, 237; R. W.
Zandvoort, E Stud, 15, 1933, 177-83; C. J. S(isson),
MLR, 29, 1934, 111; A. B(randl), Arch, 165, 1934,
135-6; TLS, June 28, 1934, 462; K. M. L., Oxford
Mag, Nov 1, 1934, 104; NQ, 173, 1937, 17-18; C. J.
Sisson, MLR, 31, 1936, 411-2; TLS, Oct 10, 1936, 816.
These reviews are not continued as they are usually
only notices. References to this important publication
will in this volume omit volume and year when a
work is reviewed in the year of its publication.
GILCHRIST, DONALD B., Ed. Doctoral Dissertations
Accepted by American Universities. Compiled for
the National Research Council and the American
Council of Learned Societies by the Association of
Research Libraries. H. W. Wilson, 1934.
GRIFFITH, DUDLEY DAVID. A Bibliography of Chaucer,
1908-1924. Univ of Washington Publications in Language and Literature, 4, no. 1, 1926. 148 pp.
    Rev: John Koch, ESt, 61, 1927, 440-1; Martin B.
Ruud, MLN, 42, 1927, 343-4; W. F. Schirmer, NS,
36, 1928, 24-5.
    In this volume, no references are made to this
bibliography because it is out of print. All its items
are included in this bibliography.
HAMMOND, ELEANOR P. Chaucer: A Bibliographical
Manual. Macmillan, 1908. Reprint, P. Smith, 1933.
597 pp.
    Rev: G. C. Macauley, MLR, 4, 1908, 526-9; John
L. Lowes, JEGP, 8, 1909, 619-27; John Koch, AB,
20, 1909, 225-34; Robert K. Root, ESt, 41, 1909, 136-
7; E. Koeppel, DL, 30, 1909, 1191; Rose Abel, MLN,
24, 1909, 159; Athenaeum, 1909, I, 556-7; Jsb, 30,
1908, xv, 275; Jsb, 31, 1908, xvi, 205.
HEANEY, HOWARD JOHNSON. A Bibliography of
Chaucer: 1934-40. Unpublished Thesis, Cornell Univ,
1941.
HUTCHINSON, CECIL G. Chaucer List. School Library
Rev, 3, 1942, 91-5.
    A list for school libraries.
JEWETT. S. English Literature: Chaucer: Selected References. Wellesley, 1911. Revised, M. H. Shackford, 1916.

KENNEDY, ARTHUR G. A Bibliography of Writings on
the English Language from the Beginnings of Printing
to the end of 1922. Yale Univ Press, 1927. 517 pp.
    Rev: George P. Krapp, SRL, 4, 1927, 376; TLS,
June 16, 1927, 428; George T. Flom, JEGP, 27, 1928,
437-40; Louise Pound, Amer Speech, 3, 1928, 239-40;
James F. Royster, MP, 25, 1928, 495-7; Hermann M.
Flasdieck, AB, 39, 1928, 166-74; A. Gabrielson, Stu-
dia Neophilologica, 2, 1930, 117-68; R. B. McKerrow,
RES, 5, 1929, 120-1; A. Brandl, Arch, 161, 1932, 300.
    Subdivided by type and period. Middle English,
159-95; Chaucer, nos. 4371-8, 4455-543.
KOCH, JOHN. Die Chaucerforschung seit 1900. GRM, 1,
1909, 490-507.
----------. Der gegenwartige Stand der Chaucerforsch-
ung. Ang, 49, 1925, 193-243.
----------. Neuere amerikanische Chaucerschriften.
AB, 28, 1917, 152-60.
----------. Neuere Beiträge zur Chaucer-Literatur
aus Amerika. AB, 25, 1914, 327-42.
----------. Neuere Chaucer-Literatur. AB, 22, 1911,
265-82; ESt, 46, 1912, 98-114; ESt, 48, 1914, 251-81.
KORTING, G. Grundriss der Geschichte der englischen
Literatur von ihren Anfangen bis zur Gegenwart. 5th
ed., paragraphs 147-61. Münster, 1910.
LANGHANS, VICTOR. Zu J. Kochs Artikel in Anglia,
(NF) 37, 193. Ang, 49, 1926, 356-60.
    Correction of Koch.
LAWRENCE, W. W. Selected Bibliography of Medieval
Literature in England; from the Beginnings to the
Death of Chaucer. New York, 1930. 23 pp.
    Chaucer, 22-23.
LIBRARY OF CONGRESS. Catalogue Division. A List of
American Doctoral Dissertations Printed. . . .
Government Printing Office, issued each year since
1912.
LOOMIS, ROGER SHERMAN. Introduction to Medieval
Literature Chiefly in England: A Reading List and
Bibliography. 2nd ed. Columbia Univ Press, 1948.
    For undergraduates.
MARTIN, WILLARD E., Jr. A Chaucer Bibliography,
1925-1933. Duke Univ Press, 1935. 97 pp.
    Rev: Walter Fischer, AB, 46, 1935, 322; A.

B(randl), Arch, 168, 1935, 289; J. R. H(ulbert), MP, 34, 1936, 97-8.

MODERN HUMANITIES RESEARCH ASSOCIATION. Annual Bibliography of English Language & Literature, 1920-. Edited (1936) by Mary S. Serjeantson and Leslie N. Broughton. Bowes and Bowes, Cambridge Univ Press, 1921-.

Rev: E. Eckhardt, ESt, 58, 1924, 86-9; G. C. Moore Smith, MLR, 19, 1924, 128-9; Karl Brunner, NS, 32, 1924, 199-201; A. Brandl, Arch, 146, 1924, 261; Walter Fischer, NS, 32, 1924, 164-5; Gustav Binz, AB, 40, 1929, 146-52; H. W. H. , MLR, 25, 1930, 242; A. C. Baugh, MLN, 46, 1931, 207; Walter Fischer, NS, 31, 1931, 69; H. M. Flasdieck, AB, 42, 1931, 380; C. G. S(isson), MLR, 26, 1931, 370-1; A. C. Baugh, MLN, 46, 1931, 351; C. S. Northup, Cornell Alumni News, 33, 1931, 360; Arch, 159, 1931, 134; NS, 39, 1931, 546; H. M. Flasdieck, AB, 43, 1932, 313-4; A. C. Baugh, MLN, 47, 1932, 550-1; TLS, Feb 25, 1932, 136; Arch, 161, 1932, 299-300; C. J. Sisson, MLR, 28, 1933, 133; Walter Fischer, NS, 41, 1933, 116; Amer Speech, 8, 1933, 70; R. W. Zandvoort, E Stud, 15, 1933, 177-83; Walter Fischer, NS, 41, 1933, 190; C. J. S(isson), MLR, 29, 1934, 111; R. B. McK(errow), RES, 10, 1934, 116-7; F. Delattre and P. de Reul, Rev de l'Univ de Bruxelles, 1933-4, no. 1, 135-6; A. B(randl), Arch, 165, 1934, 135; AB, 45, 1934, 63-4; F. Delattre, Chron des Etudes Anglaises, Feb-April, 1935, 358-9; J. Hoops, ESt, 69, 1935, 431; H. M. Flasdieck, AB, 46, 1935, 82; C. J. Sisson, MLR, 32, 1937, 136; B. Engelhardt, NS, 44, 1936, 384; A. B(randl), Arch, 172, 1938, 243; H. M. Flasdieck, AB, 47, 1936, 214-5.

This bibliography was delayed by the war. Volume 24, 1943-4, is ready for the press.

NORTHUP, CLARK SUTHERLAND. A Register of Bibliographies of the English Language and Literature, with Contributions by Joseph Quincy Adams and Andrew Keogh. Yale Univ Press, 1925. 507 pp.

Rev: TLS, Jan 14, 1926, 32; NQ, 151, 1926, 179; A. W. Reed, RES, 2, 1926, 368-9; Arthur Garfield Kennedy, Amer Speech, 1, 1926, 616-8; Ronald S. Crane, MP, 23, 1926, 501-5; H. B. Van Hoesen, Libr

Jour, 51, 1926, 179-82; G. Binz, AB, 37, 1926, 303-
7; Lane Cooper, JEGP, 26, 1927, 410-2; R. W. Zandvoort, ESt, 9, 1927, 45-7; R. B. McKerrow, MLR,
23, 1928, 64-5; T. P. Cross, MLN, 44, 1929, 410-2.
PMLA: RESEARCH IN PROGRESS. PMLA, 63, 1948,
171-2; 64, 1949, 120-1; 65, 1950, 146; 66, 1951, 176-7;
67, 1952, 144-5.
POLLARD, A. W., and G. R. REDGRAVE. A Short
Title Catalogue of Books Printed in England, Scotland
and Ireland, and of English Books Printed Abroad,
1475-1640. The Bibliographical Society, 1926. 609 pp.
Chaucer, 5068-101.
Rev: R. B. McKerrow, RES, 3, 1927, 494-6;
TLS, April 7, 1927, 247.
PRATT, ROBERT A. The Works. (Review of works on
Chaucer's Works). Progress of Medieval and Re-
naissance Studies in the United States and Canada,
15, pp. 19-23. Colorado: Univ of Colorado, 1940.
----------, Comp. Chaucer Research in the United
States in 1937. Mimeographed report of 4 pp. of the
Committee on Bibliography and Research Projects
of the Chaucer group of the MLA. The first six re-
ports to 1942 are compiled by Robert A. Pratt,
Chairman of the Committee on Research and Bibliog-
raphy; 1943-6, 1947, Roland M. Smith, Chairman;
1948-51, Martin M. Crow, Chairman; 1952-3, Thomas
A. Kirby, Chairman.
PURDY, ROB ROY. Chaucer Scholarship in England and
America: A Review of Recent Trends. Ang, 70, 1952,
345-81.
RUUD, M. B. Chaucer Studies, 1928. PQ, 8, 1929, 296-
306.
----------. Chaucer Studies, 1929. MLN, 45, 1930,
288-95.
SAVAGE, HENRY L. Chaucer: The Life. Progress of
Medieval and Renaissance Studies, 15, 1940, 16-18.
Review of publications on Chaucer's Life.
SPEYER, MARION FRANCES. Chaucer Studies, 1920
to 1930, in 5 American periodicals. M. A. Thesis,
Columbia, 1933.
WELLS, JOHN EDWIN. A Manual of the Writings in
Middle English, 1050-1400. Published under the aus-
pices of the Connecticut Academy of Arts and Sci-

ences: Yale Univ Press, 1916. 1st Supplement, Additions and Modifications to September, 1918. 2nd Supplement, Additions and Modifications to January,
1923. 3rd Supplement, Additions and Modifications
to June, 1926. 4th Supplement, Additions and Modifications to July, 1929. 5th Supplement, Additions and
Modifications to July, 1932. 6th Supplement, Additions
and Modifications to July, 1935. 7th Supplement to
1938. 8th Supplement to July, 1941, with cumulative
index of Supplements I-VIII. All published by Yale
Univ Press. (Manual and first three Supplements in
1 vol. , Yale Univ Press, 1926. 1248 pp.)
    Rev: A. G. Kennedy, JEGP, 16, 1917, 321-7;
Athenaeum, 1916, II, 431; John M. Manly, MP, 14,
1916-7, 572-3; John S. P. Tatlock, AJP, 38, 1917,
441-3; and 40, 1920, 324; Seymour de Ricci, Journal
des Savants, 15, 1917, 282-4; Henry N. MacCracken,
YR, 6, 1917, 659-61; W. J. Sedgefield, MLR, 12,
1917, 207; and 15, 1920, 334; Carleton Brown, MLN,
32, 1917, 162; Dial, 61, 1916, 111; Nation, May 3, 1917,
545; Ch. Bastide, Rev Crit, 51, 4; John Koch, LGRP,
42, 1921, 299-306; L. L. Schücking, ESt, 56, 1922,
90-2; H. M. Flasdieck, AB, 33, 1922, 225-30; A. E.
H. Swaen, Neophil, 6, 292; MLR, 19, 1924, 385; A.
Brandl, Arch, 146, 1923, 261; J. R. H. , MP, 25,
1927, 244; NQ, 154, 1928, 162; H. M. Flasdieck, AB,
39, 1928, 28-30; RES, 7, 1931, 246; TLS, April 27,
1933, 296; C. T. Onions, MA, 2, 1933, 245; H. S. V.
Jones, JEGP, 32, 1933, 638; K. M. , MLN, 49, 1934,
138; H. M. Flasdieck, AB, 47, 1936, 136-7; J. Hoops,
ESt, 71, 1936, 86-7; J. S. P. Tatlock, Spec, 11, 1936,
429; J. R. H(ulbert), MP, 33, 1936, 439; H. A. C.
Green, MLR, 31, 1936, 416-7; E. Ekwall, E Stud, 18,
1936, 224-5; TLS, Feb 22, 1936, 165; R. B. McK. ,
RES, 15, 1939, 371; H. A. C. Green, MLR, 34, 1939,
474; H. Flasdieck, Ang Bbl, 50, 1939, 67-9; and 44,
1933, 335, summary of chronology of Manual and
Supplements; J. S. P. Tatlock, Spec, 15, 1939, 397;
Kemp Malone, MLN, 55, 1940, 78; A. Brandl, Arch,
176, 1941, 117; H. S. V. Jones, JEGP, 40, 1941, 564
ff. ; J. S. P. Tatlock, Spec, 17, 1942, 314-5; C. T. O. ,
MA, 12, 1943, 106-8. The 9th Supplement follows.
BROWN, BEATRICE DAW, ELEANOR K. HENINGHAM,

and FRANCIS LEE UTLEY. Ninth Supplement to a
Manual of the Writings in Middle English: 1050-1400.
Additions and Modifications to December, 1945. The
Connecticut Academy of Arts and Sciences, Yale
Univ Press, Sales Agent, 1951. Pp. 1769 to 1938.
   Rev: J. J. Parry, JEGP, 51, 1952, 416-7; P.
Hodgson, MLR, 48, 1953, 367 ff.
WILLARD, JAMES F. Progress of Mediaeval Studies in
the United States of America. Bulletins nos. 1-13,
1923-37. Published by the Univ of Colorado. Bulletins
nos. 13-22 (1953) comp. by S. Harrison Thomson.
See also PMLA, 37, 1922, xvii ff.
   All strictly Chaucerian material has been included
in this bibliography. A list of doctoral dissertations
(in mediaeval studies) in progress or completed is
included in each issue.

LIFE

See Hammond, 1-49; Legouis, 1-43; Kaluza, 5-9; Brusendorff, 13-43; French, 44-74; Manly, 3-44; Robinson, xv-xxiv; Wells, 608, 869, 994, 1027, 1083, 1141, 1186, 1232, 1284, 1322, 1371, 1420, 1530, 1641, 1732, 1926; and CBEL, I, 218-20.

On Thomas Chaucer in addition to notations in this section, see DNB. On Deschamps' Ballade to Chaucer, see the section: Influence and Allusions. Many lives of Chaucer are to be found in the introductions to books listed under General Criticism and Editions with Notes.

ANON. Chaucer and Henry Yevele. Ars Quatuor Coronatorum, 44, 1934, 239-41.
Notes and documents.
----------. A Note about the Oath of the Comptroller of the Petty Customs and Memoranda about Chaucer's Appointment of Deputies. NQ, 18 June, 1927, 434.
ANDERSON, MARJORIE. Alice Chaucer and her Husbands. PMLA, 60, 1945, 24-47.
Life of Alice, daughter of Thomas Chaucer.
Rev: D. Everett, YWES, 59.
ARMITAGE-SMITH, Sir SYDNEY. John of Gaunt, King of Castile and Leon, Duke of Aquitaine and Lancaster, Earl of Derby, Lincoln and Leicester, Seneschal of England. A. Constable and Co., 1904. 490 pp.
----------. John of Gaunt's Register, Edited for the Royal Historical Society from the Original MSS at the Public Record Office. London: Offices of the Society, 1911. 2 vols. Camden, 3rd ser., vols. 20-1.
See also John of Gaunt's Register: 1379-1383. Edited by E. C. Lodge and R. Somerville. Camden, 3rd ser., vol. 56.
Rev: TLS, 1938, 189-90.
BAUGH, ALBERT CROLL. Kirk's Life Records of Thomas Chaucer. PMLA, 47, 1932, 461-515.

-----------. Thomas Chaucer, One Man or Two? PMLA, 48, 1933, 328-39.

See Krauss below in this section: William Chaumbre.

BAYLEY, A. R. A Possible Gloucestershire Origin for Geoffrey Chaucer. NQ, ser. 9, 9, 1902, 134.

BAYNE, THOMAS. Thomas Chaucer. Athenaeum, 1900, I, 146.

BEATTY, JOSEPH M. Johannes de Chause Hauberger. MLN, 34, 1919, 378.

-----------. A Companion of Chaucer. MLN, 35, 1920, 246-8.

See also Beatty, The Genealogist, Oct, 1919.

Reference to Sir Robert de Assheton.

BRADDY, HALDEEN. Froissart's Account of Chaucer's Embassy in 1377. RES, 14, 1938, 63-7.

Rev: D. Everett, YWES, 66.

-----------. Messire Oton de Graunson, Chaucer's Savoyard Friend. SP, 35, 1938, 515-31.

Rev: D. Everett, YWES, 79.

-----------. New Documentary Evidence Concerning Chaucer's Mission to Lombardy. MLN, 48, 1933, 507-11.

-----------. Sir Lewis Clifford's French Mission of 1391. MLN, 52, 1937, 33-4.

Rev: D. Everett, YWES, 87.

-----------. Chaucer and Graunson: The Valentine Tradition. PMLA, 54, 1939, 359-68.

Interprets Mars and Venus by the love intrigue of John of Holland and Isabel of York.

-----------. Three Chaucer Notes. Essays and Studies in Honor of Carleton Brown. New York, 1940, pp. 91-9.

Symbolic Colors. Ceyes and Alcione. Sir Richard d'Angle, A Poitevine Friend.

-----------. Chaucer and Dame Alice Perrers. Spec, 21, 1946, 222-8.

Rev: D. Everett, YWES, 82.

-----------. Chaucer's Philippa, Daughter of Panneto. MLN, 64, 1949, 342-3.

Rev: D. Everett, YWES, 70-1.

BRESSIE, RAMONA. Henry Knighton. TLS, June 26, 1937, 480.

----------. Was Chaucer at the Siege of Paris? JEGP,
    39, 1940, 209-21.
        Evidence on Chaucer's captivity.
BROOKS, E. ST. JOHN. Chaucer and the Duchess of
    Suffolk. NQ, 164, 1933, 357.
----------. Chaucer's Mother. New England Hist and
    Gen Reg, 83, 1929, 391-3.
----------. Chaucer's Mother. TLS, Mar 14, 1929, 207.
----------. The Descendants of Chaucer. NQ, 181, Oct
    4, 1941, 206-7.
BROWN, CARLETON, Ed. Three Chaucer Studies.
    1. Chaucerian Problems: Especially the Petherton
    Forestership and the Question of Thomas Chaucer,
    by Russell Krauss; 2. The Parlement of Foules in its
    Relation to Contemporary Events, by Haldeen Braddy;
    3. Observations on the Shifting Positions of Groups
    G and DE in the Manuscripts of the Canterbury Tales;
    Preface by Carleton Brown. Oxford Univ Press, 1932.
    Separate paging, 182, 101, and 89 pp., respectively.
        Rev: TLS, Dec 29, 1932, 986; NQ, 163, 1932, 449-
    50; G. H. Cowling, MLR, 28, 1933, 501-3; Hugo Lange,
    AB, 44, 1933, 296-9; R. K. Root, MLN, 48, 1933,
    465-70; Nation, 136, 1933, 46; B. J. Whiting, Spec,
    8, 1933, 531-8; Dorothy Everett, YWES, 13, 1932, 80-
    1; 83-5; 92-3; A. J. Barnouw, E Stud, 16, 1934, 220-
    2; J. M. Manly, RES, 10, 1934, 257-73; and RES, 11,
    1935, 209-13; and Mary Chaucer's First Husband, Spec,
    9, 1934, 86-8; J. Koch, ES, 67, 1933, 405-11. See also
    Tupper, The Bearings of the Shipman's Prologue,
    JEGP, 33, 1934, 352. Also YWES, 15, 1934, 89-90.
        Controversial reviews, containing some new mate-
    rial and re-emphasis of material formerly pub-
    lished.
CALL, REGINALD. The Plimpton Chaucer and Other
    Problems of Chaucerian Portraiture. Spec, 22, 1947,
    135-44.
        Contains bibliography and some additions to Spiel-
    mann (Hammond, 49, 539).
CARPENTER, NAN COOKE. A Note on Chaucer's Moth-
    er. MLN, 60, 1945, 382-3.
        Corrects Robinson and Krauss, below in this
    section.
        Rev: D. Everett, YWES, 58.

CHALK, EDWIN S. Chaucer Allusions. NQ, 169, 1935,
241.
>   Mention of a visit to Dartmouth by Chaucer, and
of the ship of the Shipman.
>   Rev: D. Everett, YWES, 99.
CHUTE, MARCHETTE. Geoffrey Chaucer of England.
Dutton, 1946.
>   Rev: TLS, Jan 4, 1952, 12.
COOK, ALBERT S. Chaucerian Papers. Trans Connect-
icut Academy of Arts and Sciences, 23, 1919, 1-63.
Yale Univ Press.
>   Rev: Arch, 141, 1921, 309 ff.
>   Sir Geoffrey Chaucer, 38-39; Chaucer's Mission
to Florence in 1372, 39-44; Katherine Swynford, 44-
55; Sir Paon de Ruet and Chaucer, 55-63.
----------. The Historical Background of Chaucer's
Knight. Yale Univ Press, 1916.
>   Material on Chaucer's life, 161-240.
>   For reviews, see section: General Criticism.
----------. The Last Months of Chaucer's Earliest
Patron. Trans Connecticut Academy of Arts and Sci-
ences, 21. Yale Univ Press, 1916.
>   Rev: F. Liebermann, Arch, 145, 1923, 258.
COPE, E. E. Chaucer and the Duchess of Suffolk. NQ,
164, 1933, 226.
>   Inquiry: What is authority for Alice Chaucer as the
name of the Duke of Suffolk's wife?
>   See Manly, 36-37.
COULTON, GEORGE G. Chaucer's Captivity. MLR, 4,
1908, 234-5.
CROW, MARTIN M. Materials for a New Edition of the
Chaucer Life-Records. Univ of Texas: Studies in
English, 31, 1952, 1-12.
DAVIES, H. W. Chaucer's Name. TLS, Sept 17, 1938,
598.
>   Rev: D. Everett, YWES, 78.
DELACHENAL, R. Histoire de Charles V. (Note, II,
241.) Paris: Picard, 1909.
>   Rev: T. F. Tout, EHR, 25, 1910, 160.
>   See Arch, 148, 1925, 96-7; Emerson, New Chaucer
Item, below in this section.
EMERSON, OLIVER F. Chaucer's First Military Service.
RR, 3, 1912, 321-61.

The possibility of Chaucer's meeting Machaut and
Deschamps during his captivity in France, 354.
----------. Chaucer's Testimony as to his Age. MP,
11, 1913-4, 117-25.
----------. A New Chaucer Item. MLN, 26, 1911, 19-21,
95.
    Chaucer in 1360. For opposing view see Moore, be-
low in this section.
FARNHAM, WILLARD E. John (Henry) Scogan. MLR,
16, 1921, 120-8.
FURNIVALL, F. J. Chaucer's Tomb in Westminster
Abbey. NQ, ser. 10, 1, 1904, 28.
GALWAY, MARGARET. Geoffrey Chaucer, J. P. and
M. P. MLR, 36, 1941, 1-36.
    Chaucer Records: 1384-9: Justice of the Peace:
Clerk of the Works: Knight of the Shire. Also see
Spurgeon, Calendar of Life-Records in Five Hundred
Years of Chaucer Criticism listed under Influence
and Allusions, below.
    Rev: D. Everett, YWES, 67.   .
----------. Chaucer among Thieves. TLS, April 29,
1946, 187.
    Rev: D. Everett, YWES, 81-2.
GAUPP, FRITZ. The Condottiere, John Hawkwood.
Hist, 23, 1939, 305-21.
GOLLANCZ, Sir ISRAEL. The Pearl. London: Chatto,
1921.
    The introduction, xlvi-xlix, discusses Strode and
Chaucer. See also DNB, Vol. 55, pp. 57-9.
GRAHAM, HUGH. Chaucer's Educational Background.
Thought, 9, 1934, 222-35.
GREEN, A. WIGFALL. The Inns of Court and Early
English Drama. Yale Univ Press, 1931. 199 pp.
    Chaucer as member discussed, 3-4, in chapter
on Inns of Court and English Literature.
GYDE, SALLY REEVES. Problems in the Life of
Chaucer. Master's Thesis, Univ of Washington, 1926.
Typewritten, 68 pp.
HALES, J. W. Geoffrey Chaucer. 154-67 in DNB, Vol.
4. Smith, Elder, 1908.
HINCHMAN, WALTER S. , and FRANCIS B. GUMMERE.
Lives of Great English Writers. Houghton, 1908.
Chaucer, 1-21.

HULBERT, JAMES ROOT. Chaucer and the Earl of Ox-
ford. MP, 10, 1912-3, 433-7.
----------. A Chaucer Item. MLN, 36, 1921, 123.
    Supplementary on Henry Gisors, Chaucer's deputy.
----------. Chaucer's Official Life. Doctoral Diss,
Univ of Chicago. Banta, 1912. 75 pp.
    Rev: John Koch, AB, 25, 1914, 79-82; Clark S.
Northup, ESt, 49, 1915, 146-51; Samuel Moore, MLN,
28, 1913, 189-93; Arch, 131, 1913, 249-50.
HUNT, WILLIAM. Thomas Chaucer. 167-8 in DNB, Vol.
4. Smith, Elder, 1908.
HUNTER, JOSEPH. Remarks upon Two Original Deeds
Relating to Sir Thomas Swinford, the Son of Catherine
Swinford who afterwards became the wife of John of
Gaunt. Archaeologia, 36, 1855, 267-9.
HUTTON, EDWARD. Chaucer and Boccaccio. TLS, 34,
1935, 143.
----------. Chaucer and Italy. Nineteenth Century, 128,
1940, 51-9.
----------. Did Chaucer Meet Petrarch and Boccaccio?
Anglo-Italian Review, 1, 1918, 121-35.
JUSSERAND, J. J. The School for Ambassadors and
Other Essays. Fisher Unwin, 1924. 359 pp.
    Rev: TLS, Nov 27, 1924.
    Includes The Tomb of Petrarch, 71-107; On the
Possible Meeting of Chaucer and Petrarch, 327-43.
KERN, ALFRED A. The Ancestry of Chaucer. Johns
Hopkins Diss, 1906.
    Rev: Eleanor P. Hammond, JEGP, 10, 1911, 147-9.
----------. Chaucer's Sister. MLN, 23, 1908, 52.
----------. Deschamps' Thuireval. MP, 6, 1909, 503-9.
----------. New Chaucer Records. MLN, 21, 1906, 224.
KIRK, R. E. G. A Chaucer Tragedy. NQ, ser. 10, 4,
1905, 5-7.
KITTREDGE, GEORGE LYMAN. Chaucer's Envoy to
Bukton. MLN, 24, 1909, 14-15.
    No autobiographical significance in Bukton.
----------. Henry Scogan. Harvard Studies and Notes,
1, 1892, 109-17.
----------. Lewis Chaucer or Lewis Clifford? MP, 14,
1917, 513-8.
    On Lewis Clifford, see also Manly, Rickert, Thou
Vache, and Waugh, below in this section.

KNOTT, THOMAS A. A Bit of Chaucer Mythology. MP,
8, 1910, 135-9.
On the characterization of Chaucer by himself in
the Prologue of Sir Thopas.
KRAUSS, RUSSELL. Chaucerian Problems: Especially
the Petherton Forestership and the Question of
Thomas Chaucer. Doctoral Diss, New York Univ,
1934. Published by Lancaster Press, Inc., Lancaster,
Pennsylvania, 1932. 182 pp. Oxford Univ Press, 1932,
in Three Chaucer Studies.
For reviews, see above in this section, Brown,
Carleton, Ed.
----------. John Heyron of Newton Plecy, Somerset.
Spec, 10, 1935, 187-9.
On Mary Chaucer. Reply to John M. Manly.
Rev: D. Everett, YWES, 116.
----------. Notes on Thomas, Geoffrey, and Philippa
Chaucer. MLN, 47, 1932, 351-60.
Reply to Victor Langhans, below.
----------. William Chaumbre, Kinsman of Thomas
Chaucer. PMLA, 49, 1934, 954-5.
Reply to Baugh's Thomas Chaucer, One Man or
Two?
Rev: D. Everett, YWES, 102.
KUHL, ERNEST PETER. Chaucer and Aldgate. PMLA,
39, 1924, 101-22.
Rev: John Koch, ESt, 59, 1925, 105-6.
----------. Chaucer and the Church. MLN, 40, 1925,
321-38.
Rev: D. Everett, YWES, 6, 1925, 91.
Chaucer's relations to the north country.
----------. Chaucer and Fowle Ok. MLN, 36, 1921,
157-9.
----------. Illustrations of Chaucer from the Life of
the Fourteenth Century. PMLA, 29, 1914, xxiv. MS
Diss, Harvard.
----------. Index to the Life-Records of Chaucer. MP,
10, 1913, 527-52.
----------. My Maistre Bukton. PMLA, 38, 1923, 115-
32.
----------. New Chaucer Items. MLN, 40, 1925, 511-3.
Announcement of these items from the Close Rolls:
1392-6, MLN, 40, 1925, 442.

----------. Some Friends of Chaucer. PMLA, 29, 1914,
270-6.
----------. Chaucer and the Red Rose. PQ, 24, 1945,
33-8.
    HF, RR, LGW, KnT; associates the red rose in
Chaucer with Lancaster.
    Rev: D. Everett, YWES, 82.
----------. Chaucer and Westminster Abbey. JEGP, 45,
1946, 340-3.
    Rev: D. Everett, YWES, 82.
----------. Chaucer the Patriot. PQ, 25, 1946, 277-89.
    Chaucer's relation to his contemporaries in the
Customs, 1376-8.
    Rev: D. Everett, YWES, 28, 1947, 84.
----------. Why Was Chaucer Sent to Milan in 1378?
MLN, 62, 1947, 42-4.
    Rev: D. Everett, YWES, 84.
LAMBORN, E. A. GREENING. The Arms on the Chau-
cer Tomb at Ewelme. Oxoniensia, 5, 1940, 78-93.
----------. The Descendants of Chaucer. NQ, 181,
Sept 20, 1941, 156-7.
----------. Alleged Descents from Chaucer. NQ, 182,
May 16, 1942, 268.
    Rev: D. Everett, YWES, 23, 1942, 68.
----------. A Chaucer Seal. NQ, 184, 1943, 287.
----------. Chaucer in Mythical Pedigrees. NQ, 195,
May 27, 1950, 222-3.
----------. NQ, 193, Oct 2, 1948, 421.
    The arms of Thomas Chaucer.
LANGE, HUGO. Die Bedeutung der Heraldik für die Er-
klärung eines mitteralterlichen Dichters. Ein neuer
Beitrag zur Kenntnis Geoffrey Chaucers. Forschung-
en und Fortschritte, 13, 1937, 59-60.
    Relationship with Michael de la Pole.
----------. Chaucer und Michael de la Pole. Arch, 172,
1938, 214-5.
    Abstract of paper read at the meeting of the Ber-
liner Gesellschaft für das Studium der neueren
Sprachen, Nov 24, 1936.
----------. Geoffrey Chaucer als Hof- und Gelegen-
heitsdichter. Arch, 157, 1930, 36-54.
    Rev: D. Everett, YWES, 80.
----------. Die Kenntnis der Missweisung oder mag-

netischen Deklination bei dem Londoner Geoffrey
Chaucer (1380). Zugleich ein Beitrag zur Lösung
einiger Chaucerprobleme. Forschungen und Fortschritte, 11, 1935, 156-7.

LANGHANS, VICTOR. Chaucers Heirat. Ang, 54, 1930,
297-306.

LAWRENCE, C. E. The Personality of Geoffrey Chaucer. QR, 242, 1924, 315-33.

LEGOUIS, EMILE. Geoffrey Chaucer. (Les Grandes
Ecrivains Etrangers.) Bloud, 1910. Trans by L.
Lailavoix. Dent, Dutton, 1913, 1922, 1928.

   Rev: Ch. Bastide, Rev Crit, 72, 1911, 352-3; A.
J. Barnouw, Museum, 19, 1911, 58-60; G. C. Macau-
ley, MLR, 6, 1911, 532-3; M. H. Shackford, MLN,
27, 1912, 119-21; J. D., Rev Germ, 7, 1911, 478-80;
A. Barbeau, Pbl, 124, 1912, 235; W. H. Hulme,
MLN, 28, 1913, 217.

LETHABY, W. R. Chaucer's Tomb. TLS, Feb 21, 1929, 137.

   See K. A. Esdaile, TLS, Feb 28, 1929, 163; W. H.
Godfrey, TLS, Mar 7, 1929, 186.

LIEBERMANN, FELIX. Lionel, Chaucers Gönner. Arch,
145, 1923, 258.

----------. Zu Chaucers Stellung in Hofämtern. Arch,
140, 1920, 261.

LOOTEN, C. Les Portraits de Chaucer: Leurs Origines.
Rev de Litt Comp, 7, 1927, 397-438.

LUMMIS, E. W. Thomas Chaucer. Athenaeum, 1900, I,
146.

MANLY, JOHN M., and EDITH RICKERT. Chaucer in
a New Setting. TLS, Aug 19, 1926, 549.

   See W. Rye and A. McBain, TLS, Sept 2, 1926,
380.

   An account book yields a new Chaucer item.

MANLY, JOHN MATTHEWS. Chaucer as Controller.
TLS, June 9, 1927, 408.

   See also MP, 25, 1927, 123.

----------. Chaucer's Lady of the Daisies? MP, 24,
1927, 257-9.

   See Tupper, same title, in section: LGW.

   Rev: D. Everett, YWES, 106.

----------. Chaucer's Mission to Lombardy: Reply to
Haldeen Braddy. MLN, 49, 1934, 209-16.

   Rev: D. Everett, YWES, 101-2.

----------. "Litel Lowis My Sone." TLS, June 7, 1928,
430.

　　See W. Rye, TLS, June 28, 1928, 486.

----------. Lowell Lectures on Chaucer, reported in
Boston Evening Transcript, Jan 22, 1924, 7; Jan 24,
4; Jan 31, 20; Feb 5, 5; and Feb 7, 3.

　　These lectures were preliminary studies to Some
New Light, listed below.

----------. Mary Chaucer's First Husband. Spec, 9,
1934, 86-8.

　　See Krauss, John Heron, above in this section.

　　Rev: D. Everett, YWES, 102.

----------. The Prioress of Stratford. TLS, Nov 10,
1927, 817.

----------. Some New Light on Chaucer: Lectures Delivered at the Lowell Institute. Holt, 1926. Reprint,
New York: P. Smith, 1952. 316 pp.

　　Rev: W. F. Schirmer, NS, 36, 1926, 25-8; James
F. Royster, MLN, 42, 1927, 251-6; Frederick Tupper, Nation, 125, 1927, 289-90; Robert K. Root,
NR, 30, 1927, 345-6; George Carver, Commonweal,
5, 1927, 417-8; Gordon H. Gerould, SLR, 3, 1927,
726-7; TLS, Jan 13, 1927, 25; Walter Rye, TLS, Feb
24, 1927, 126; F. Delattre, Humanitas, 2, 1927, 258-
9; John Koch, LGRP, 48, 1927, 263-7; H. S. V.
Jones, JEGP, 27, 1928, 555-7; R. D. French, YR,
17, 1928, 397-400; A. W. Reed, RES, 4, 1928, 217-
20; Dorothy Everett, YWES, 7, 1926, 79-80; John
S. P. Tatlock, AHR, 32, 1927, 913; H. R. Patch,
MP, 25, 1928, 361-6; H. Lüdeke, AB, 39, 1928, 188-
90.

　　Life, 3-69.

----------. Thomas Chaucer, Son of Geoffrey. TLS,
Aug 3, 1933, 525.

　　See Oswald Barron and E. St. John Brooks, TLS,
Aug 10, 1933, 537; O. Barron, TLS, Aug 17, 1933,
549.

----------. A Portrait of Chaucer. TLS, 33, 1934, 229.

----------. Three Recent Chaucer Studies. RES, 10,
1934, 257-73, and 11, 1935, 209-13.

MOGER, Miss O. [Material on the Life of Chaucer.]
West Wales Historical Records, Vol. 4, nos. 4, 5,
6, 8.

See Memorabilia, NQ, 154, 1928, 433, for brief digest.
MOORE, SAMUEL. The New Chaucer Item. MLN, 27,
1912, 79-81.
See Emerson, above in this section.
----------. The New Chaucer Items. MLR, 22, 1927, 435-8.
See Kuhl, above in this section.
----------. New Life-Records of Chaucer. MP, 16, 1918,
49-52.
----------. New Life-Records of Chaucer -- Addendum.
MP, 18, 1921, 497-8.
Items from the Patent Rolls corresponding to
Chancery Warrants in the above article.
----------. Studies in the Life-Records of Chaucer.
Ang, 37, 1913, 1-26.
OLMER, JOHN ARTHUR. Facts and Conjectures on the
Life of Geoffrey Chaucer. Master's Thesis, Univ of
Washington, 1926. 125 pp.
OLSON, CLAIR C. The Emerging Biography of a Poet.
The Third Annual College of the Pacific Research
Lecture, 1953. 20 pp.
ORIGINAL LEASE of "Chawser's house . . . in the
Borough of New Woodstocke," 3 April, 1696, sold
Sotheby and Co., Dec. 20, 1939. Item 687.
For picture of house, see Garnett and Gosse, Eng-
lish Literature: An Illustrated Record, 1903, I, 143.
(Wells)
PARKS, GEORGE B. The Route of Chaucer's First Jour-
ney to Italy. ELH, 16, 1949, 174-87.
Rev: D. Everett, YWES, 69-70.
PLUCKNETT, T. F. T. Chaucer's Escapade. Law Quart
Rev, 64, 1948, 33-6.
Comments on Watts's article on the Cecily Chaum-
paigne episode.
POLLARD, A. W. Chaucer's Pensions in April, 1385.
RES, 4, 1928, 216.
See Wyatt, in this section.
----------. Chaucer's Name. TLS, 37, 1938, 556.
Rev: D. Everett, YWES, 78.
PRATT, ROBERT ARMSTRONG. Chaucer and Boccaccio.
TLS, Feb 28, 1935, 124.
Reply by Edward Hutton, TLS, Mar 7, 1935, 143.
Addendum by R. A. Pratt, TLS, April 11, 1935, 244.

----------. An Introductory Study to Chaucer's Italian
Journeys. Doctoral Diss, Yale.
    Listed as completed in Willard, 12, 1935, 71.
----------. Chaucer and the Visconti Libraries. ELH,
6, 1939, 191-9.
----------. Geoffrey Chaucer, Esq. and Sir John
Hawkwood. ELH, 16, 1949, 188-93.
    Rev: D. Everett, YWES, 69-70.
REDSTONE, VINCENT B. Chaucer, A Norfolk Man.
Acad, 75, 1908, 425.
    Answer to Walter Rye, below.
----------. The Chaucer Seals. Athenaeum, 1908, I, 670.
----------, and LILIAN J. The Heyrons of London:
A Study in the Social Origins of Geoffrey Chaucer.
Spec, 12, 1937, 182-95.
    Map of Heyron and Chaucer tenements in London.
    Rev: D. Everett, YWES, 87-8.
RICKERT, EDITH. Chaucer Abroad in 1368. MP, 25,
1928, 511-2.
----------. Chaucer and the Treasurer at Calais. TLS,
Nov 17, 1932, 859.
----------. Chaucer at St. Paul's School? TLS, Feb 4,
1932, 76.
----------. Chaucer at School. MP, 29, 1932, 257-74.
----------. Chaucer at the Funeral of the Princess of
Wales. TLS, Aug 11, 1927, 548.
----------. Chaucer Called to Account. TLS, Dec 8,
1932, 943.
----------. Chaucer's Debt to John Churchman. MP,
25, 1927, 121-3.
----------. Chaucer's Debt to Walter Bukholt. MP, 24,
1927, 503-5.
----------. Chaucer's Grandfather in Action. TLS,
April 6, 1933, 248.
----------. Elizabeth Chausir a Nun at Barking. TLS,
May 18, 1933, 348.
    See A. H. Fowler, TLS, June 8, 1933, 396.
    Documents and records with suggestion of a mod-
el for Chaucer's Merchant.
----------. Extracts from a 14th-century Account Book.
MP, 24, 1926, 111-9, 249-56.
----------. A Leaf from a Fourteenth-Century Letter
Book. MP, 25, 1927, 249-55.

Relationship to Chaucer of eight personal letters. On p. 255 is the suggestion that Rosamounde was written for the child-wife of Richard II.

----------. More Payments to Chaucer. TLS, Oct 27, 1927, 766.

----------. New Life Records of Chaucer. TLS, Sept 27, 1928, 684; TLS, Oct 4, 1928, 707.

See H. W. Garrod, TLS, Oct 11, 1928, 736; Sir Israel Gollancz, TLS, Oct 25, 1928, 783.

----------. Portrait of an Englishman in the Spanish Chapel, Florence. TLS, Aug 4, 1927, 533.

Edward, Lord le Despenser.

----------. Some English Personal Letters of 1402. RES, 8, 1932, 257-63.

Lady Elizabeth Zouche, and her relationship to Chaucer.

----------. Thou Vache. MP, 11, 1913, 209-25.

Identification of Vache as a friend of Chaucer.

----------. Was Chaucer a Student at the Inner Temple? Manly Anniversary Studies in Language and Literature, 20-31. Univ of Chicago Press, 1923.

Rev: Eleanor P. Hammond, ESt, 60, 1926, 310-4.

ROSS, ALAN S. C. Nicholas Chaucer. TLS, May 23, 1942, 264.

See H. L. Bradfer-Lawrence, TLS, June 6, 1942, 283.

RUUD, MARTIN B. Thomas Chaucer. Research Publications of Univ of Minnesota. Studies of Language and Literature, 9, 1926. 131 pp.

Rev: C. R. D. Young, RES, 3, 1927, 80-3; Frederick Tupper, JEGP, 26, 1927, 407-10; Robert K. Root, MLN, 42, 1927, 56-8; Eleanor P. Hammond, AB, 38, 1927, 54-6; Hugo Lange, ESt, 65, 1931, 393-6; W. F. Schirmer, NS, 36, 1928, 30-3; Dorothy Everett, YWES, 7, 1926, 82.

RYE, WALTER. Chaucer, A Norfolk Man. Athenaeum, 1908, I, 290. Also Acad, 75, 1908, 283-4.

See Redstone, above, same title.

Rev: Jsb, 30, 1908, xv, 276.

----------. Chaucer, A Norfolk Man. Norwich: W. Hunt, 1915.

----------. John of Gaunt and Katherine Swinford. TLS, April 7, 1924, 240.

----------. The Poet Chaucer. TLS, Mar 12, 1925, 223.

----------. New Light on Chaucer. TLS, Feb 24, 1927, 126.

    Chaucer and Lynn.

----------. Some Historical Essays Chiefly Relating to Norfolk. Part 5, 338-70. Part 6, 421-63. Norwich: Hunt, 1929.

SAVAGE, HENRY L. Enguerrand De Coucy VII and the Campaign of Nicopolis. Spec, 14, 1939, 423.

    See note on Chaucer's life.

SCOTT, EDWARD J. L. Chaucer and Westminster Abbey. Athenaeum, 1914, I, 794.

    On the relation of Chaucer's grandparents to the Abbey.

SCOTT, FLORENCE R. Chaucer and the Parliament of 1386. Spec, 18, 1943, 80-6.

    See Loomis, Was Chaucer a Laodicean?, in section: General Criticism.

    Rev: D. Everett, YWES, 51-2.

SHELLY, PERCY VAN DYKE. Geoffrey Chaucer, 1340? - 1400. Scientific Monthly, 51, 1940, 568-70.

SKEAT, WALTER W. Thomas Chaucer. Athenaeum, 1900, I, 116.

SPIELMANN, M. H. A Portrait of Chaucer. TLS, 33, 1934, 244.

STEVENSON, HAZEL ALLISON. A Possible Relation between Chaucer's Long Lease and the Date of his Birth. MLN, 50, 1935, 318-22.

    Rev: D. Everett, YWES, 115.

STEWART-BROWN, R. The Scrope-Grosvenor Controversy. TLS, June 12, 1937, 447.

    Records cancelling the Grosvenor claim.

SYPHERD, W. O. Chaucer's Eight Years' Sickness. MLN, 20, 1905, 240-3.

TATLOCK, JOHN STRONG PERRY. Chaucer and Wyclif. MP, 14, 1916-7, 257-68.

----------. The Duration of Chaucer's Visits to Italy. JEGP, 12, 1913, 118-21.

THOMPSON, C. H. A Note on Nicholas Chaucer. PQ, 14, 1935, 275-8.

    Rev: D. Everett, YWES, 116.

THURSTON, HERBERT. Conversion of Boccaccio and Chaucer. Studies (Educ Co of Dublin), 25, 1936, 215-25.

TOUT, THOMAS F. Review of Delachenal, R., Histoire
de Charles V, Vol. II, 1358-1364. EHR, 25, 1910,
156-61.
    A contribution on Chaucer's captivity and his em-
    ployment in negotiations after his release.
----------. Mission to Calais: 1360. EHR, 25, 1910, 160.
    See indexes of other historical studies by this au-
    thor under the section: General Backgrounds.
TUPPER, FREDERICK. Chaucer and Lancaster. MLN,
32, 1917, 54.
----------. Chaucer and Richmond. MLN, 31, 1916,
250-2.
WAINE, GEORGE W. Scrope-Grosvenor. NQ, 161, 1931,
11.
WARD, A. W. Chaucer. English Men of Letters Series,
Vol. 9. Macmillan, 1909. 199 pp.
    Rev: Jsb, 31, 1909, xvi, 184.
WATTS, P. R. The Strange Case of Geoffrey Chaucer
and Cecilia Chaumpaigne. Law Quart Rev, 63, 1947,
491-515.
    Legal analysis of the case.
    Rev: D. Everett, YWES, 29, 1948, 93-4.
WAUGH, M. T. The Lollard Knights. SHR, 11, 1913,
55-92.
    Lewis Clifford, 58-63.
WHITFORD, HAROLD C. A New Document Concerning
Robert Chaucer. PQ, 14, 1935, 278-82.
    Rev: D. Everett, YWES, 116.
WILLIAMSON, J. BRUCE. The History of the Temple,
London; from the Institution of the Order of the
Knights of the Temple to the Close of the Stuart
Period. Compiled from the honourable societies of
the Temple. John Murray, 1925. 690 pp.
    Chaucer as member discussed, 87-8.
WILSON, S. C. The Name Chaucer. TLS, May 12, 1927,
336.
    See Walter Rye, TLS, May 19, 1927, 355.
WYATT, A. J. Chaucer's Pensions in April, 1385. RES,
4, 1928, 83.
    See Pollard, in this section.
WYLIE, J. HAMILTON. Thomas Chaucer. Athenaeum,
5 Oct, 1901, II, 455.

MANUSCRIPTS

See Hammond, 173-201; Wells, 1536, 1644, 1736, 1931, and CBEL, I, 232-3.

For facsimiles, see especially Spurgeon, C. F. E., Five Hundred Years of Chaucer Criticism, and Manly and Rickert, The Text of the Canterbury Tales.

For much source material directly and indirectly related to Chaucer, see MLA Rotographs of MSS and Rare Printed Books listed complete in PMLA supplement, 1934, and continued additions in subsequent supplements to 1937. Vol. 53, 1938, has complete list to Jan 1, 1939, and the title is changed to Reproductions of Manuscripts and Rare Printed Books. Vols. 1939, 1940, 1942 print additions. Vol. 56, 1941, announces the list as a separate pamphlet. Vol. 59, 1944, 1463-88, American Council of Learned Societies: British Manuscript Project. Vol. 61, 1946, prints additions. Vol. 65, 1950, 289-338, contains complete list with indexes to its date.

ANON. The Cardigan Chaucer. TLS, Mar 19, 1925.
Notes on Sales.
----------. The Ellesmere Chaucer (Reproduced in Facsimile). Manchester Univ Press, 1911. 2 vols.
Rev: Athenaeum, 1911, II, 178-9, 210-1.
----------. The English Novel: An Exhibition of Manuscripts and First Editions, Chaucer to Conrad. Huntington Library Exhibitions, 6. The library, 1934. 26 pp.
Two Chaucer items: Troilus and Criseyde, 1517, with illustrations of the title-page; and Canterbury Tales in MS, c. 1400 -- the Ellesmere Chaucer, 6-7.
----------. A Facsimile of Anelida and Arcite from Unique Copy of Westminster Edition of William Caxton in Cambridge University Library. Cambridge Univ Press, 1905.
----------. Kelmscott Chaucer on Vellum. TLS, July 26, 1928, 556.
Notes on Sales.

----------. Page from Speght's Chaucer: Facsimile.
Library Assn Record, ser. 3, 2, 1932, 222.
----------. The Prioress's Tale. Guildford: Astolat
Press, 1902. Printed and revised from Harl MS 7334.
No critical value. (Martin).
----------. The Lewde Compilator. Time, Mar 10, 1952,
53-4.
On Equatorie of the Planetis with picture of Chau-
cer. See Price, below in this section.
BEVINS, LLOYD EDWARD. Chaucer's Monk's Tale: A
Study of MSS Texts. Univ of Virginia, Abstracts of
Dissertations, 1951, pp. 8-12.
BLISS, A. J. Notes on the Auchinleck MS. Spec, 26,
1951, 652-8.
BOETHIUS. [Boetii De Consolatione Philosophie, with
the English version ascribed to Chaucer in five books,
and Exposicio preclara quam Johannes Theutonicus
prescripsit et finivit A. D. 1306. 8 Idus Junii; a reproduction of MS II. III. 21. in the Cambridge Univ
Library.] 2 vols. , 299 sheets on 150 l. The MLA.
Collection of Photographic Facsimiles, no. 73. 1928.
Deposited in the Library of Congress.
    "The translation attributed to Chaucer alternates
with the Latin text of Boethius. . . . The original is
a 14th century manuscript. . . . Cf. A Catalogue of
the manuscripts preserved in the Library of the University of Cambridge. V. III, 1858, MS II. III. 21."
BONNER, FRANCIS W. The Genesis of Chaucer Apocrypha. SP, 48, 1951, 461-81.
BRESSIE, RAMONA. MS Sloane 3548, Folio 158. MLN,
1939, 246-56.
    A leaf from a medieval catalogue of books.
----------. Manuscript Books. TLS, March 19, 1938,
192.
    On lost manuscripts with list of known MSS.
BROTANEK, RUDOLPH. Me Dichtungen aus der Hs 432
Trinity College, in Dublin. Halle, 1940.
    Rev: Marcus, DL, 61, pts. 27-8; W. Horn, Ar-
chiv, 177, 1940, 120; F. Holthausen, AB, 51, 1940,
97-8; F. Schubel, ES, 75, 1942, 88-91.
    This MS contains Ballade of Stedfastnesse, a de-
fective copy of Gentilesse, and a dialogue on Palamon
and Arcite.

BROWN, CARLETON. Shul and Shal in Chaucer Manu-
scripts. PMLA, 26, 1911, 6-30.
   Rev: John Koch, AB, 22, 1911, 280-2.
BRUSENDORFF, AAGE. The Chaucer Tradition. Mil-
ford, 1925. 509 pp.
   For reviews, see section: General Criticism.
BUHLER, CURT F. A New Lydgate-Chaucer Manuscript.
MLN, 52, 1937, 1-9.
   Edition of Purse from MS 4, Pierpont Morgan Li-
brary.
   Rev: D. Everett, YWES, 73-4, 99.
----------. Notes on the Campsall Manuscript of Chau-
cer's Troilus and Criseyde. Now in the Pierpont
Morgan Library. Spec, 20, 1945, 457-60.
   Rev: D. Everett, YWES, 26, 1945, 55-6.
BULLOCH, J. M. A Chaucer MS. NQ, 162, 1932, 405.
CALDWELL, ROBERT A. Peculiarities of the Cam-
bridge University Library MS, Gg. 4. 27. Unpubl
Diss, Univ of Chicago, 1938. Manly and Rickert, I,
190 ff.
   Rev: D. Everett, YWES, 25, 1944, 53-4.
----------. The Scribe of the Chaucer MS Cambridge
University Library, Gg. 4. 27. MLQ, 5, 1944, 33-44.
   Indicates that the scribe was Dutch or Flemish.
   Rev: D. Everett, YWES, 53-4.
----------. Joseph Holand, Collector and Antiquary.
MP, 40, 1943, 295 ff.
   Cambridge MS Gg. 4. 27. contains an independent
text of Gentilesse.
   Rev: D. Everett, YWES, 51.
CAMPBELL, ROBERT LEE. Extra-textual Data for a
Classification of the Manuscripts of the Canterbury
Tales. Doctoral Diss, Chicago, 1927. Abstract in
Abstracts of Theses: Humanistic Series, Vol. 5,
1926-7, 453-6.
   Rev: D. Everett, YWES, 10, 1929, 110-1.
CHAUCER, GEOFFREY. [Chaucer's Troilus and a few
short poems; reproduced from MS Gg. 4. 27, fol. 5-
132r, in the library of Cambridge University.] 115 neg-
atives mounted on 59 leaves. The MLA. Collection of
Photographic Facsimiles, no. 307. 1935. Deposited in
the Library of Congress.
   Contents: ABC; Litera directa de Scogan; Balade

de bone consele; A parliament of birds; De amico ad
Amicam and Responcio; Troilus; Canterbury Tales,
mutilated page.

----------. The Noble and Amerous Ancyent Hysto-/ry
of Troylus and Cresyde/ in the Tyme of/ the Syege of
Troye. Cŏpyled by Geoffraye/ Chaucer. London, 1517;
San Marino, Calif, 1925. Facsimiles of 141 sheets.
MLA. Collection of Photographic Facsimiles, no. 31.
Reproduced from a copy of the 2nd ed. in the Henry
E. Huntington Library. Negative deposited in the Li-
brary of Congress.

----------. Troilus and Criseyde. n. p. , n. pr. , n. d.
Westminster, William Caxton, 1484? London, 1923.
Facsimile, 234 mounted leaves. The MLA. Collection of Photographic Facsimiles, no. 14. Reproduced
from copy C. 11. c. 10 in the British Museum. Duplicates may be obtained through the Library of Congress.

CHAUCER SOCIETY PUBLICATIONS. Kegan Paul,
Trench, Trübner and Co. , London. Chaucer Society
publications not primarily manuscript studies appear
below under the separate works.

The Six-Text Edition of the Canterbury Tales,
Walter W. Skeat, Editor. Part XI with colored litho-
graphs of six letters of the tales and six emblematic
figures from Cambridge Univ MS, Gg. 4. 27. and
Corson's index, listed below under the section entitled the Canterbury Tales. Six Appendices to the Six
Manuscripts of the Six Text. 1909-11.

Rev: John Koch, ESt, 46, 1912, 98-114.

Specimen Extracts from the Nine Known Unprinted
Manuscripts of Chaucer's Troilus and from Caxton's
and Thynne's First Editions. Sir William McCormick
and Robert K. Root, Editors.

Rev: John Koch, ESt, 48, 1914, 251-9.

The Textual Tradition of Chaucer's Troilus. Robert
K. Root, Editor, 1916.

Rev: J. Douglas Bruce, MLN, 34, 1919, 37-40.

The Romance of the Rose, from Thynne's Print,
1532. F. J. Furnivall, Editor, 1911.

Rev: John Koch, ESt, 46, 1912, 98-114.

Harleian Manuscript 7334 and Revision of the Canterbury Tales. John S. P. Tatlock, Editor, 1907.

Rev: Eleanor P. Hammond, JEGP, 9, 1910, 564-5;

Jsb, 31, 1909, xvi, 200; Arch, 124, 1910, 212; AB, 22,
1911, 266.

    The Eight-Text Edition of the Canterbury Tales
with Especial Reference to Harleian MS 7334. Walter
W. Skeat, Editor, 1908.

    Rev: MLR, 5, 1910, 246; AB, 22, 1911, 267.

    The MSS of Chaucer's Troilus and Criseyde with
23 Collotype Facsimiles of all the MSS. Robert K.
Root, Editor.

CHAYTOR, HENRY JOHN. The Medieval Reader and
Textual Criticism. John Rylands Library Bulletin,
26, 1941, 49-56.

CROW, MARTIN MICHAEL. Corrections in the Paris
Manuscript of Chaucer's "Canterbury Tales": A
Study in Scribal Collaboration. Univ of Texas: Studies
in English, 15, 1935, 5-18.

    See Halfmann, below in this section.

    Rev: D. Everett, YWES, 103-4.

----------. Scribal Habits: Illustrated in the Paris
Manuscript of Chaucer's "Canterbury Tales." Doctoral Diss, Univ of Chicago, 1935. Reprints of items
directly above and below issued as abstract of diss
under title: Corrections and Unique Variants in the
Paris Manuscript of Chaucer's Canterbury Tales.

    Rev: Hermann Heuer, AB, 48, 1937, 297-8.

----------. Unique Variations in the Paris Manuscript
of Chaucer's "Canterbury Tales." Univ of Texas
Studies in English, 16, 1936, 17-41.

----------. The Reeve's Tale in the Hands of a North
Midland Scribe. Univ of Texas Publ: Studies in English, 18, 1938, 14-24.

----------. John of Angoulême and his Chaucer Manuscript. Spec, 17, 1942, 86-99.

    Rev: D. Everett, YWES, 51-2.

D'ARDENNE, SIMONNE R. T. O. The Editing of Middle
English Texts. In English Studies Today, C. L.
Wrenn and G. Bullogh, Editors, Oxford, 1951, 74-
84.

    A charming essay for Middle English editors.

DEMPSTER, GERMAINE. A Chapter in the Manuscript
History of the Canterbury Tales: The Ancestor of
Group d, the Origin of its Texts, Tale-order, and
Spurious Links. PMLA, 63, 1948, 456-84.

Rev: D. Everett, YWES, 72-4; rejoinder by A. E.
Hartung, PMLA, 67, 1952, 1173-81.
----------. On the Significance of Hengwrt's Change of
Ink in the Merchant's Tale. MLN, 63, 1948, 325-30.
Rev: D. Everett, YWES, 74-5.
----------. The Fifteenth-Century Editors of the Can-
terbury Tales and the Problem of Tale Order. PMLA,
64, 1949, 1123-42.
Rev: D. Everett, YWES, 56-7.
DE RICCI, SEYMOUR, and W. J. WILSON, Comps.
Census of Medieval and Renaissance Manuscripts in
the United States and Canada. 2 vols. H. W. Wilson,
1935-7. Vol. 3, index, 1940.
Rev: Charles H. Beeson, MP, 34, 1937, 425-7.
DUNN, THOMAS F. The Manuscript Sources of Caxton's
Second Edition of the Canterbury Tales. Chicago, 1940.
Rev: D. Everett, YWES, 23, 1942, 52-3.
EVERETT, DOROTHY. Another Collection of the Elles-
mere Manuscripts of the "Canterbury Tales." MA, 1,
1932, 42-55.
EVERETT, VIRGINIA THORNTON. A Study of the Scri-
bal Editing in Twelve MSS of the Canterbury Tales.
Unpubl Diss, Univ of Chicago Library, 1940.
GOLSON, EVA OLIVIA. The Spelling System of the Glas-
gow Manuscript of Canterbury Tales. Diss, Univ of
Chicago, 1942.
GREG, W. W. The Calculus of Variants: An Essay on
Textual Criticism. Clarendon Press, 1927. 64 pp.
Rev: R. A. Williams, AB, 40, 1929, 178-83.
General discussion of textual reconstruction.
----------. Chaucer Attributions in MS R. 3. 19 in the
Library of Trinity College, Cambridge. MLR, 8, 1913,
539-40.
Discussion of authorship of notes in this MS.
----------. Early Printed Editions of the Canterbury
Tales. PMLA, 39, 1924, 737-61.
Comparison of the first six printed editions with
the manuscripts, with listings of variants.
----------. Facsimiles of Twelve Manuscripts in the
Library of Trinity College, Cambridge. Oxford, 1913.
----------. The MS Sources of Caxton's Second Edition
of the Canterbury Tales. PMLA, 44, 1929, 1251-3.
See Kilgour, below in this section.

HALFMANN, JOHANNES. Das auf der Bibliothèque Na-
tionale zu Paris befindliche Manuscript der Canter-
bury Tales. Doctoral Diss, Kiel, 1898. 57 pp.
        See Crow, above in this section.
HAMMOND, ELEANOR PRESCOTT. A Burgundian Copy
of Chaucer's Troilus. MLN, 26, 1911, 32.
----------. On the Editing of Chaucer's Minor Poems.
MLN, 23, 1908, 20-1.
        Value of Oxford group of MSS.
----------. Chaucer and Dante and their Scribes. MLN,
31, 1916, 121.
----------. A Scribe of Chaucer. MP, 27, 1929, 27-33.
Three pages of facsimile plates.
        Rev: D. Everett, YWES, 10, 1929, 108-9.
HARRISON, FREDERICK. Treasures of Illumination;
English Manuscripts of the Fourteenth Century (c.
1250 to 1400). Studio, 1937. 48 pp. and 24 plates.
HARTUNG, ALBERT E. The Clerk's Endlink in the d
Manuscripts. PMLA, 67, 1952, 1173-7.
        See Dempster, A Chapter on the Manuscript His-
tory, above, and her reply here, 1177-81.
HAWKINS, LAURENCE F. The Place of Group F in the
Canterbury Chronology. Diss, New York Univ, 1937.
HENCH, ATCHESON L. Printer's Copy for Tyrwhitt's
Chaucer. Stud in Bibl, 3, 1950, 265-6.
        Rev: D. Everett, YWES, 31, 1950, 56.
HERMANN, HERMAN JULIUS. Englische und französische
Handschriften des 14. Jahrhunderts. Hiersemann,
1937. 211 pp.
IRVINE, ANNIE S. A Manuscript Copy of "The Plow-
man's Tale." Univ of Texas Studies in English, 12,
1932, 27-56.
KASE, C. ROBERT. Observations on the Shifting Posi-
tions of Groups G and DE in the Manuscripts of the
Canterbury Tales. In Three Chaucer Studies, Carle-
ton Brown, Ed, Oxford Univ Press, 1932.
        For reviews, see the section: Life.
KER, NEIL R. Migration of Manuscripts from the Eng-
lish Medieval Libraries. Library, 23, 1942, 1-11.
KERBY-MILLER, WILMA ANDERSON. Scribal Dialects
in the C and D MSS of the Canterbury Tales. Unpubl
Diss, Univ of Chicago, 1939.
KILGOUR, MARGARET. The Manuscript Source of Cax-

ton's Second Edition of the Canterbury Tales. PMLA,
44, 1929, 186-201.
    Rev: D. Everett, YWES, 10, 1929, 109; Martin B.
Ruud, MLN, 45, 1930, 290.
    See Greg, above in this section.
KLETSCH, ERNEST, Comp. A Union Catalog of Photo-
Facsimiles in North American Libraries. Material
so far received by the Library of Congress. Unedited.
F. S. Cook, 1929.
    Rev: Colbert Searles, MLN, 44, 1929, 547-8.
KOCH, JOHN. Neuere Chaucer-Literatur. AB, 22, 1911,
265-82; ES, 46, 1912, 98-114; ES, 48, 1914, 251-81.
----------. Berichtigungen. ESt, 69, 1934, 318-20.
    Readings of the Naples MS of the Clerk's Tale.
----------. A Detailed Comparison of the Eight Manu-
scripts of the Canterbury Tales as Printed by the
Chaucer Society, Second Series 43. Anglistische
Forschungen, 36, 1913. 422 pp.
    Rev: E. Eckhardt, ESt, 50, 1916, 323-35; Eleanor
P. Hammond, AB, 25, 1914, 234-9; John Koch, ESt,
48, 1914, 259-60.
LOOMIS, LAURA HIBBARD. Chaucer and the Auchinleck
MS: Thopas and Guy of Warwick. 111-28, in Essays and
Studies in Honor of Carleton Brown. New York, 1940.
    Presents parallels between Chaucer and the Auch-
inleck MS.
----------. Chaucer and the Breton Lays of the Auchin-
leck MS. SP, 38, 1941, 14-33.
    Argues for Chaucer's use of this MS in FrankT,
WBT, MerT, and Sir Thopas.
    Rev: D. Everett, YWES, 60.
----------. The Auchinleck Manuscript and a Possible
London Bookshop of 1330-1340. PMLA, 57, 1942, 595-
627. Footnote bibliography.
LOSSING, M. L. S. The Order of the Canterbury Tales,
a Fresh Relation between A and B Types of MSS.
JEGP, 37, 1938, 153-63.
McCORMICK, Sir WILLIAM, with the assistance of
JANET E. HESELTINE. The Manuscripts of Chaucer's
Canterbury Tales: A Critical Description of their
Contents. Clarendon Press, 1933. 561 pp.
    Rev: TLS, July 27, 1933, 509; A. W. P., Library,
14, 1933, 236-8; Dorothy Everett, RES, 11, 1935, 342-

4; Dorothy Everett, YWES, 14, 1933, 106-7; John M.
Manly, MLR, 29, 1934, 182-6; H. Heuer, AB, 45,
1934, 204-6.
MacCRACKEN, HENRY N. The Laborer and the Bochour
and the Smyth. MLN, 28, 1913, 230.
----------. More Odd Texts of Chaucer's Troilus. MLN,
25, 1910, 126-7.
----------. A New Manuscript of Chaucer's Monk's
Tale. MLN, 23, 1908, 93.
----------. Notes Suggested by a Chaucer Codex. MLN,
23, 1908, 212-4.
----------. An Odd Text of Chaucer's Purse. MLN, 27,
1912, 228-9.
     Truth and Lak of Stedfastnesse.
MANLY, JOHN MATTHEWS. A Portrait of Chaucer.
TLS, Mar 29, 1934, 229.
     See M. H. Spielmann, TLS, April 5, 1934, 244.
----------, and EDITH RICKERT. The Text of the
Canterbury Tales. 8 vols. Univ of Chicago Press,
1940.
     For full description and reviews, see section:
Canterbury Tales: General.
----------. The Hengwrt MS of the Canterbury Tales.
Nat Lib Wales Jour, 1, 1939, 59-75.
     A preview of materials for the Text of the Canter-
bury Tales with facsimiles.
     Rev: The Library, 25, 1945, 201.
MARBURG, CLARA. Notes on the Cardigan Chaucer
Manuscript. PMLA, 41, 1926, 229-51.
     Includes Doctor-Pardoner link, and Pardoner's
Prologue and Tale as supplementary to the Chaucer
Society Parallel Text specimens, 236-51.
MILLAR, ERIC G. English Illuminated Manuscripts of
the Fourteenth and Fifteenth Centuries. Paris and
Brussels, Les Editions G. van Oest, 1928. 107 pp.
and 100 plates.
     Report on a paper containing material in the book
is in Library, ser. 4, Vol. 6, 1926, 42-5. Facsimile
of MS Corpus Christi College, Cambridge. 61 f. lv.,
plate 94.
     Rev: TLS, Feb 23, 1928, 124; G. F. Warner, Antiq
Jour, 8, 1928, 376-9; W. W. Greg, Library, 8, 1928,
482-7; Kingsley Porter, SRL, 5, 1928, 1111.

MOORE, SAMUEL. The Position of Group C in the Canterbury Tales. PMLA, 30, 1915, 116-23.

MORSBACH, LORENZ. Mittelenglische Originalurkunden
von der Chaucerzeit bis zur des 15. Jahrhunderts.
Alt- und mittelenglische Texte, hg. v. Morsbach und
Holthausen. Vol. x, Heidelberg, 1923.

Rev: Richard Jordan, ESt, 58, 1924, 245-7; Fritz
Karpf, NS, 32, 1924, 443-4; Eilart Ekwall, AB, 35,
1924, 225-6; F. Liebermann, Arch, 148, 1924, 112-5.
See also Morsbach, Korrekturen zu meinen Urkunden.
ESt, 58, 1924, 129.

ONIONS, C. T. The Equatorie of the Planetis. TLS, Mar
7, 1952, 173.

PACE, GEORGE B. Four Unpublished Chaucer Manuscripts. MLN, 63, 1948, 457-62.

Truth: B. M. Add. MS. 36983, f. 262^a, and Magd.
Coll. Camb. Pepys MS. 2006, pp. 389-90; Lak of
Stedfastnesse: Trin. Coll. Dublin MS. 432, f. 59^a;
Complaint of Chaucer to his Purse: Caius Coll. Camb.
MS. 176, p. 12.

Rev: D. Everett, YWES, 29, 1948, 92-3.

----------. Otho A XVIII. Spec, 26, 1951, 306-16.

A new Chaucer manuscript.

PIPER, EDWIN F. The Miniatures of the Ellesmere
Manuscript. PQ, 3, 1924, 241-56.

----------. The Royal Boar and the Ellesmere Chaucer.
PQ, 5, 1926, 330-40.

Rev: D. Everett, YWES, 78.

PLIMPTON, GEORGE ARTHUR. The Education of
Chaucer, Illustrated from the School-Books in Use
in his Time. Oxford, 1935. 176 pp.

Excellent reproductions of 14th century MSS.

Rev: T. M., CW, 143, 1936, 240-1; M. W., Com-
monweal, 23, 1936, 558; S. A. Coblentz, NYTBR,
Feb 23, 1936, 14; H. S. Canby, SRL, 13, 1926, 26;
Derek Verschoyle, Spect, 156, 1936, 268; Martin B.
Ruud, MLN, 52, 1937, 464-5; TLS, June 13, 1936,
495; K. Brunner, AB, 47, 1936, 262; F. S. Boas, Obs,
Feb 2, 1936; E. Rickert, NR, 88, 1936, 53; E. L.
Getchell, Education, 56, 1936, 319.

PRATT, ROBERT A. The Importance of Manuscripts
for the Study of Medieval Education as Revealed by
the Learning of Chaucer. Progress of Medieval and

Renaissance Studies, Bull no. 20, 1949, 43-51.
Rev: D. Everett, YWES, 54-5.

PRICE, DEREK J. The Equatorie of the Planetis, Pe-
terhouse MS (1) Attributed to Simon Bredon Now Suggested as an Unknown Work of Chaucer? TLS, Feb
29, 1952, 164, and Mar 7, 1952, 180.

REPRODUCTIONS OF MANUSCRIPTS AND RARE
PRINTED BOOKS. PMLA, 65, 1950, 289-338.
These reproductions are now on deposit in the
Library of Congress, Washington, D. C. See especially nos. 14, 15, 31, 62, 67, 73, 77, 100, 109, 110, 111,
112, 124, 128, 140, 145, 162, 307, 311, 299 and 744,
854F-861F, 863F, 868F-870F, 885F, 888F, 889,
966F, 968F-984F.
These reproductions are listed in more detail with
the appropriate works in this bibliography.

RICKERT, EDITH. Are There More Chaucer Manuscripts? TLS, Dec 17, 1931, 1028.

RICKERT, MARGARET. The Reconstructed Carmelite
Missal: An English Manuscript of the Late Fourteenth
Century in British Museum, Add. 29704-5; and 44892.
Faber and Faber, 1952.
A very ingenious reconstruction from picture
fragments.
Rev: A. Mayor, Library, 5th ser. , 7, 215-7.

ROBBINS, ROSSELL HOPE. The Speculum Misericor-
die. PMLA, 54, 1939, 935-66.
Description and notes on the Delamere-Penrose
MS, Manly and Rickert, I, 108.

ROOT, ROBERT KILBURN, Ed. The Book of Troilus
and Criseyde. Edited from all the known MSS.
Princeton Univ Press, 1926. 573 pp.
Rev: D. Everett, YWES, 7, 1926, 77-8; TLS, Aug
19, 1926, 547; F. N. Robinson, Spec, 1, 1926, 461-7;
John S. P. Tatlock, SRL, 3, 1926, 362; Karl Young,
MLN, 41, 1926, 537-45; E. Einenkel, AB, 37, 1926,
265-8; John M. Manly, NR, 50, 1927, 26; George N.
Shuster, Commonweal, 5, 1926, 220-1; A. J. Wyatt,
RES, 3, 1927, 240-1; Eleanor P. Hammond, AB, 38,
1927, 315-8; John Koch, ESt, 64, 1929, 84-100; Wal-
ter F. Schirmer, NS, 36, 1928, 33-5; J. R. Hulbert,
MP, 24, 1926, 243-4.

ROSENBACH COLLECTION, NEW YORK CITY. Manly
and Rickert's Nos. Ph^2, Ph^3, Ox. , and Ph^1. Catalogue of Exhibition by Rosenbach Co, Mar 25-April

and Rickert's Nos. Ph^2, Ph^3, Ox., and Ph^1. Cata-
logue of Exhibition by Rosenbach Co, Mar 25-April
30, 1940, Nos. 156-9. Has one page facsimile from
Oxford MS.
SCHULZ, H. C. Thomas Hoccleve, Scribe. Spec, 12,
1937, 71-81.
SCIENCE, MARK. A Suggested Correction of the Text of
Chaucer's Boethius. TLS, Mar 29, 1923, 199-200.
SILK, EDMUND T. An Edition of Chaucer's Boethius in
the Cambridge MS II. 3. 21. Doctoral Diss, Yale.
Listed as completed in Willard, 9, 1931, 102.
SKEAT, WALTER W. Chaucer: A Curious Misplacement
of Lines. NQ, ser. 11, 1, 1910, 201-2.
----------. Chaucer: The Shipman's Prologue. MLR, 5,
1910, 430.
STROUD, THEODORE A. A Chaucer Scribe's Concern
with Page Format. Spec, 23, 1948, 683-7.
• Rev: D. Everett, YWES, 76.
----------. The MS Fitzwilliam: An Examination of
Miss Rickert's Hypothesis. MP, 46, 1948, 7-17.
See also Stroud's dissertation, The Problem of the
Fitzwilliam MS of the Canterbury Tales, Chicago, 1948.
Rev: D. Everett, YWES, 75-6.
TATLOCK, JOHN STRONG PERRY. The Development
and Chronology of Chaucer's Works. Chaucer Society,
ser. 2, 37. London, 1907.
Rev: Robert K. Root, ESt, 41, 1910, 405-11; Nation,
86, 1908, 220; John Koch, AB, 20, 1909, 129-45.
----------. Notes on Chaucer. MLN, 29, 1914, 140-4.
The Plimpton Fragment of the Canterbury Tales,
140-1.
----------. The Canterbury Tales in 1400. PMLA, 50,
1935, 100-39.
Rev: D. Everett, YWES, 101-3.
THOMPSON, DANIEL V., Jr., and GEORGE HEARD
HAMILTON, Trans. De Arte Illuminandi. The Tech-
nique of Manuscript Illumination. An anonymous 14th
century treatise, translated from the Latin of Naples
MS xii. E. 27. Yale Univ Press, 1933. 67 pp.
TYSON, MOSES. Handlists of the Collection of English MSS
in John Rylands Library, 1928. JRLB, 13, 1, 1929, 152-219.
Nos. 63 and 113 describe MSS containing fragments
of Chaucer material.

VINE, GUTHRIE. The Miller's Tale. A Study of an Un-
   recorded Manuscript in the John Rylands Library in
   Relation to the First Printed Text. Reprinted from
   JRLB. Manchester Univ Press, 1933. 17 pp.
      Also JRLB, 17, 1933, 333-47; contains facsimiles.
WILD, FREDERICK. Die sprachlichen Eigentumlich-
   keiten der wichtigeren Chaucer-Handschriften und
   die Sprache Chaucers. Leipzig, 1915.
      Rev: Eilert Ekwall, AB, 27, 1915, 164; Erik Björk-
   man, ESt, 51, 1917, 84-94; John Koch, LGRP, 39,
   1916, 233-7; Arch, 134, 1916, 465; Rudolf Imelmann,
   NS, 24, 1916, 181-2.

EDITIONS WITH NOTES

Hammond, 114-49; Wells, 1514-5, 1528, 1644, 1735, 1936, and CBEL, I, 233. Some editions, as indicated below, are listed because of illustrations or typography.

ABEL, ROSE. Cumberland's Edition of Chaucer. MLN, 24, 1909, 59.
ANON. Complete Works, in Poetry and Prose; with Introduction, Aids to Chaucer's Grammar, Versification and Pronunciation. Boston: Cornhill, 1930. 890 pp.
----------. The Works of Geoffrey Chaucer. Shakespeare Head Edition. Complete in 8 vols. Oxford: Blackwell, Vols. 1-4, 1929; Vols. 5-8, 1930. Vols. 1-3, The Canterbury Tales; Vol. 4, The Parson's Tale and Minor Poems; Vol. 5, Boece de Consolacione Philosophie; Vol. 6, Troilus and Criseyde; Vol. 7, the House of Fame and Minor Poems; Vol. 8, The Romaunt of the Rose.
    Rev: TLS, April 4, 1929, 273; TLS, Aug 15, 1929, 639; TLS, May 8, 1930, 388.
----------. Geoffrey Chaucer: The Canterbury Tales. With wood engravings by Eric Gill. Golden Cockerel Press, 1929-30. 2 vols.
    Globe text.
    Rev: TLS, Jan 2, 1937, 13, with reproduction of one of Gill's drawings.
----------. Chaucer's Wyf of Bathe. London: Mandrake Press, 1929. Ill by Pearl Binder and printed in black letter.
    Prologue and tale.
----------. Geoffrey Chaucer: The Frankeleyn's Tale. Pittsburgh: Bentley Press, 1931. Limited ed. 2nd ed, revised and enlarged.
AUDEN, WYSTAN H., and N. H. PEARSON. Poets of the English Language. The Viking Press, 1950.
    Vol. 1: RR, 47-59; T&C, 74-159; CT, 160-224.
BONNARD, GEORGES. Troilus and Criseyde: Extracts

Selected and Edited. Bibliotheca Anglicana, 4. Berne:
Francke, 1943. 104 pp.
    Rev: D. Everett, YWES, 25, 1944, 48-9; T. A.
Kirby, MLN, 64, 1949, 213-4; W. Fischer, AB, 54-5,
1943, 108-9.
BROWN, CARLETON, Ed. Pardoner's Tale. Oxford
Univ Press, 1935, 1942. 63 pp.
    Rev: Martin B. Ruud, MLN, 52, 1937, 379-81; H.
S. V. J(ones), JEGP, 36, 1937, 269-70; Robert K.
Root, Spec, 4, 1936, 523-4; Dorothy Everett, MA, 6,
1937, 144-51, and YWES, 16, 1937, 112.
BURRELL, ARTHUR, Ed. Chaucer's Canterbury Tales.
No. 307, Everyman Library for the Modern Reader.
Dent; Dutton, 1908, 1910. Rev ed, Coniston Classics,
1912. English Literature for Schools Series, 1914. Pro-
logue of the Canterbury Tales. Portland, Maine: South-
worth-Athenaeum Press, 1937. Ill by Thomas Thorne.
    See introductions.
CHAUCER, GEOFFREY. Canterbury Tales: Prologue;
Nun's Priest's Tale; Squire's Tale. Masterpieces of
English. Nelson, 1938. 96 pp.
CHILD, CLARENCE G. Selections from Chaucer Includ-
ing his Earlier and his Later Verse and an Example of
his Prose. Heath, 1912.
    Rev: MLN, 27, 1912, 264.
COWLING, GEORGE H., Ed. The Prologue to the Can-
terbury Tales, the Prioress's Tale, the Nun's
Priest's Tale, the Pardoner's Tale. Ginn, 1934.
221 pp.
CUNLIFFE, R. J. The Knight's Tale. Blackie, 1915.
DAVIES, R. T., Ed. Prologue to the Canterbury Tales.
Harrap, 1953. 160 pp.
DELCOURT, JOSEPH. Chaucer: Contes de Cantorbéry.
Bibliothèque de Philologie Germanique, 10. Paris:
Aubier, 1946. 329 pp.
    General Prol, FrankT, ClT -- the last having
Petrarch's Latin version and a French version. In-
troductions and notes.
    Rev: D. Everett, YWES, 71-2; A. Basil Cottle,
MLR, 43, 1938, 129; H. R. Patch, MLN, 63, 1948,
140-1; R. M. Smith, JEGP, 47, 1948, 92.
DRENNAN, C. M. The House of Fame. London: Univ
Tutorial Press, 1921.

----------, and A. J. WYATT. The Pardoner's Tale.
London: Clive, 1911.
DRENNAN, C. M. The Parlement of Foules. London:
Clive, 1911.
----------. The Prioress's Tale. London: Clive, 1914.
DUNN, CHARLES W., Ed. Chaucer Reader: Selections
from the Canterbury Tales. 225 pp. Harcourt, 1952.
EMERSON, OLIVER F. Poems of Chaucer: Selections
from his Earlier and his Later Works Edited with In-
troduction, Bibliographical Notes and Glossary. Mac-
millan, 1911.
    Contains discussion of chronology of Chaucer's
works.
    Rev: John Koch, ESt, 48, 1914, 260-73.
FRENCH, R. D. The Canterbury Tales: Selected and
Edited. Crofts Classics. Appleton, 1948.
FUNKE, OTTO, Ed. A Middle English Reader: Texts
from the 12th to the 14th Century. Bibliotheca Angli-
cana, 7 and 7a. Berne: Francke, 1941.
GEROULD, GORDON HALL, Ed. Old English and Medi-
eval Literature. Nelson's English Readings, Vol. 1.
Rev and enl ed, Nelson, 1933. 445 pp.
    Book of selections with notes and introduction.
Chaucer, 152-275.
----------. The Prologue and Four Canterbury Tales.
Nelson's English Series. Thomas Nelson and Co.,
1935. Pp. 197-335.
GOFFIN, R. C., Ed. Troilus and Criseyde, Abridged
and Edited. Oxford Univ Press, 1935. 166 pp.
    Rev: English, 1, 1936, 70; Dorothy Everett, MA,
6, 1937, 144-51.
GREENLAW, EDWIN A. Selections from Chaucer. Scott,
Foresman, 1908.
GREG, W. W. Early Printed Editions of the Canterbury
Tales. PMLA, 39, 1924, 737-61.
    Comparison of the first six printed editions with
the manuscripts, with listings of variants.
GUNTHER, R. T. Chaucer and Messahalla on the Astro-
labe: Now Printed in Full for the First Time with the
Original Illustrations. Oxford Univ Press, 1930, 1932.
234 pp.
    Rev: TLS, Mar 27, 1930, 263.
----------, Ed. Chaucer on the Astrolabe. With the

Original Illustrations. 2nd and abbreviated ed, rev.
Oxford: The editor, 1932. 92 pp.
HOWARD, EDWIN J. , and GORDON D. WILSON, Eds.
The Canterbury Tales by Geoffrey Chaucer. Selected
and edited. Rev and corr ed. Oxford, Ohio: The
Anchor Press, 1942. 2nd ed, Prentice-Hall, 1947.
Rev: H. Patch, MLN, 59, 1944, 217.
INNES, A. D. Squieres Tale. Blackie, 1905.
JELIFFE, ROBERT ARCHIBALD, Ed. Chaucer: Canter-
bury Tales: Selections Together with Selections from
the Shorter Poems. Modern Student's Library. Scrib-
ners, 1952. 377 pp.
KALUZA, MAX. Chaucer-Handbuch für Studierende;
ausgewählte Texte mit Einleitungen, einem Abriss
von Chaucers Versbau und Sprache und einem Wörter-
verzeichnis. Leipzig, 1915. 248 pp. 2nd ed, 1927.
Rev: F. Karpf, NS, 30, 1922, 86-8; J. H. Kern,
Neophil, 5, 1919, 87-8; E. Ekwall, AB, 31, 1920, 50-
4; E. Appel, ZFEU, 18, 372-4; E. Eckhardt, ESt, 54,
1920, 311; John Koch, LGRP, 41, 1920, 18-23; Arch,
140, 1920, 314-5.
KASHKIN, I. A. , and O. B. RUNNER. Geoffrey Chaucer: Canterbury Tales. With an Introduction and
Commentary by I. A. Kashkin, Engravings on Wood
by F. Konstantinov. Moscow: State Publ Co for Artis-
tic Literature, 1943.
Rev: D. Everett, YWES, 28, 1947, 74.
KOCH, JOHN. Chaucer: Canterbury Tales: Nach dem
Ellesmere MS mit Lesarten, Anmerkungen, und einem
Glossar. Heidelberg, 1915. 475 pp.
Rev: E. Eckhardt, ESt, 50, 1916, 322; Jsb, 36,
1915, xvi, 148; Arch, 134, 1916, 465; R. Imelmann,
NS, 24, 1917, 177-80; Heinrich Mutschmann, AB, 27,
1916, 224-6; Neophil, 2, 1917, 234-6; Zsf für Bücherfr
7, Beibl, 551; Max Kaluza, ZFEU, 15, 234; John Koch,
GRM, 8, 1920, 115.
----------. Textkritische Bemerkungen zu Chaucers
Canterbury Tales. ESt, 47, 1913, 338-414.
Notes preliminary to the above edition.
----------. Geoffrey Chaucer: Kleinere Dichtungen.
Heidelberg: Winter, 1928, 1947. 360 pp.
Texts edited; chronology discussed; notes.
LEGOUIS, EMILE, et al. Les Contes de Canterbury:

Traduction Française avec une Introduction et Notes
par Th. Bahans, J. Banchet, Ch. Bastide, P. Berger,
L. Bourgogne, M. Castelain, L. Cazamain, Ch. Ces-
tre, Ch. Clermont, J. Delcourt, J. Deroquigny, C-M.
Garnier, R. Huchon, A. Koszol, L. Levault, E. Le-
gouis, L. Morel, Ch. Petit, W. Thomas, G. Vallod,
E. Wahl. Paris: Felix Alcan, 1908. 527 pp.
    Introduction by Emile Legouis.
LIDDELL, MARK H. The Prologue to the Canterbury
    Tales; the Knight's Tale; and the Nun's Priest's Tale.
    Macmillan, 1910, 1926.
LLOYD, L. J., Ed. Chaucer Selections. Life, Litera-
    ture, and Thought Library. Harrap; Clarke, Irwin,
    1952.
MacCRACKEN, HENRY N. The College Chaucer. Yale
    Univ Press, 1913. College Edition. Milford, 1914.
    Glossary in collaboration with T. Goddard Wright.
MALONE, KEMP. The Works of Chaucer. In Literary
    Masterpieces of the Western World, Francis Horn,
    Ed. Johns Hopkins Press, 1953.
MANLY, JOHN MATTHEWS, Ed. Canterbury Tales by
    Geoffrey Chaucer. With an Introduction, Notes and a
    Glossary. Holt, 1928. 721 pp.
    Rev: TLS, April 4, 1929, 273; John Koch, ESt, 64,
    1929, 100-13; Kemp Malone, JEGP, 28, 1929, 137-8;
    Martin B. Ruud, MLN, 44, 1929, 541-3; A. W. Pol-
    lard, MLR, 25, 1930, 101-2; P. N. U. Harting, E Stud,
    14, 1932, 138-41; Dorothy Everett, YWES, 83-5.
MATHER, FRANK J. The Prologue, the Knight's Tale,
    and the Nun's Priest's Tale from Chaucer's Canter-
    bury Tales. Houghton, 1908.
    Rev: John Koch, AB, 20, 1909, 166.
NEILSON, WILLIAM A., and HOWARD R. PATCH. Se-
    lections from Chaucer. Harcourt, 1921.
    Rev: Frederick Wild, AB, 35, 1924, 137-41.
NEILSON, WILLIAM A., and K. G. T. WEBSTER. The
    Chief Poets of the Fourteenth and Fifteenth Centuries.
    Houghton, 1916.
    Chaucer, 95-198.
OSGOOD, CHARLES GROSVENOR, and MARVIN T. HER-
    RICK. Eleven British Writers: Beowulf to Arnold.
    Houghton, 1940. 1396 pp.
    Chaucer, 136 pp.

PATTERSON, R. F. Chaucer: The Nonne Preest his
   Tale. Blackie, 1920.
----------, Ed. Six Centuries of English Literature. In
   6 vols. Vol. 1, Chaucer to Spenser, with Introductory
   Essay by W. L. Renwick. Blackie, 1933. 383 pp.
      Rev: TLS, July 6, 1933, 460; G. Sampson, Obs,
   May 28, 1933.
      Chaucer, 1-28; contains MS portrait of Chaucer and
   facsimile of an illustrated MS of CT.
POLLARD, A. W. Chaucer. 2nd ed, Macmillan, 1931.
   1st ed in Hammond.
----------, and Others. Chaucer's Works. Macmillan,
   1923, 1929, 1953. Reprint of the Globe Edition.
      See Hammond, 148.
----------. The Nun's Priest's Tale. Macmillan, 1907,
   1924.
----------, and G. R. REDGRAVE. A Short Title Catalogue of Books Printed in England, Scotland, and
   Ireland and of English Books Printed Abroad: 1475-
   1640. The Bibliographical Society, 1926. 609 pp.
      Chaucer, 5068-101.
      Rev: R. B. McKerrow, RES, 3, 1927, 494-6; TLS,
   April 7, 1927, 247.
----------, and M. M. BARBER, Eds. The Pardoner's
   Tale, Edited with Introduction and Notes. English
   Classics. Macmillan, 1929.
----------, Ed. Works of Geoffrey Chaucer. Limited
   ed. 8 vols. Basil Blackwell, 1928-9.
ROBINSON, F. N., Ed. The Complete Works of Chaucer.
   Oxford Univ Press, 1933. 1133 pp.
      Rev: NQ, 165, 1933, 287; A. Brandl, Arch, 164, 1933,
   266-8; H. N. MacCracken, SRL, 10, 1933, 311; M. Day,
   RES, 11, 1935, 346-7; D. Everett, YWES, 103-5; H.
   Lange, DL, 55, 1934, 448-52; H. Heuer, AB, 45, 1934,
   201-4; TLS, Feb 22, 1934, 123; J. S. P. Tatlock, Spec, 9,
   1934, 459-64; A. H. Marckwardt, EJ, 23, 1934, 433-4;
   M. B. Ruud, MLN, 50, 1935, 329-32; Herbert Drennon,
   ESt, 69, 1935, 406-7; D. Everett, MA, 7, 1938, 204-13;
   F. Tupper, JEGP, 39, 1940, 503-26.
ROOT, ROBERT KILBURN, Ed. The Book of Troilus
   and Criseyde. Edited from All the Known MSS.
   Princeton Univ Press, 1926. 573 pp.
      For reviews, see section: Manuscripts.

SISAM, KENNETH. The Clerkes Tale of Oxenford. Ox-
ford, 1923.
   Contains also MerT.
   Rev: F. Wild, AB, 35, 1924, 70-1; E. Kruisinga, E
   Stud, 6, 1924, 35-6; H. R. Patch, MLN, 40, 1925, 53-5;
   P. G. Thomas, YWES, 58-9;Arch, 147, 1924, 146.
- - - - - - - - - -, Ed. The Nun's Priest's Tale. Oxford, 1926,
1940. 82 pp.
   Rev: Eleanor P. Hammond, AB, 38, 1927, 314-5;
   Paull F. Baum, MLN, 43, 1928, 206-7; George H.
   Cowling, MLR, 22, 1927, 448.
SKEAT, WALTER W. The Complete Works of Chaucer.
Oxford: Clarendon Press, 1909, 1912, 1925. 3 vols.
The World's Classics.
   Rev: H. T. Price, AB, 24, 1914, 50; H. M. Flas-
   dieck, AB, 36, 1925, 208.
- - - - - - - - - -. Complete Works, Edited from Numerous
Manuscripts. Oxford Standard Authors. School ed.
Oxford Univ Press, 1929, 1933. 881 pp.
- - - - - - - - - -. The Prologue of the Canterbury Tales and
Minor Poems. Oxford, 1907.
- - - - - - - - - -. Tale of the Man of Lawe, with Pardoneres
Tale, Second Nonnes Tale, Chanoun's Yemannes
Tale. Reissue. Oxford, 1952.
   See Hammond, 215.
SMITH, M. BENTINCK. The Prologue and the Knight's
Tale. Cambridge Univ Press, 1908.
   Rev: A. Mawer, MLR, 4, 1909, 420-1.
STEPHENSON, HAROLD. Chaucer Explored. Use of
English, 4, 1952, 91-3.
   Study of the Prologue in secondary modern schools.
VAN DYKE, A. M. Prologue and the Knight's Tale.
American Book Co. , 1909.
VAN WYCK, WILLIAM, Ed. and Tr. The Canterbury
Tales of Geoffrey Chaucer, Together with a Version
in Modern English Verse. Ill by Rockwell Kent. 2 vols.
Covici, Friede, 1930. Limited ed.
   Original and modernization in parallel columns.
   Rev: Robert K. Root, SRL, 7, 1931, 545-6.
WILLOUGHBY, E. F. Chaucer. The Prologue. Chicago:
Educational Publishing Co, 1907. Prologue of the Can-
terbury Tales. Blackie's Standard English Classics.
Blackie, 1940.

WINSTANLEY, LILIAN. Chaucer's The Clerkes Tale
and The Squieres Tale. Cambridge Univ Press; Put-
nam, 1908.
    Rev: Erik Björkman, ESt, 42, 1910, 111; John Koch,
AB, 20, 1909, 166-9.
----------. Nonne Prestes Tale. Cambridge Univ Press;
Putnam, 1915.
----------. The Prioress's Tale, the Tale of Sir Thopas.
Cambridge Univ Press, 1922. Macmillan, 1922.
    Rev: NQ, ser. 12, 11, 1922, 300.
WYATT, A. J., Ed. The Links of the Canterbury Tales
and the Wife of Bath's Prologue. With a Preface by
A. A. Coulton. London: Sidgwick and Jackson, 1930.
110 pp.
    Rev: TLS, Nov 6, 1930, 914; F. Karpf, AB, 41,
1930, 367-8.
----------. The Nun's Priest's Tale. London: Clive,
1915.
----------, and C. M. DRENNAN, Eds. Prioress's
Tale; Tale of Sir Thopas; Monk's Tale. London: Univ
Tutorial Press, 1933. 48 pp.
WYATT, A. J., Ed. Prologue to the Canterbury Tales.
2nd ed. London: Univ Tutorial Press, 1927.
----------, Ed. The Prologue to the Canterbury Tales
and the Nun's Priest's Tale. London: Sidgwick and
Jackson, 1930. 94 pp.
    Rev: TLS, Nov 6, 1930, 914; F. Karpf, AB, 41,
1930, 367-8.
ZUPITZA, J. The Book of the Tales of Canterbury. Prolog mit Varianten zum Gebrauch bei Vorlesungen her-
ausgegeben. Berlin, 1935. 3rd ed.
    See Hammond, 213, for first two editions.

MODERNIZATIONS AND TRANSLATIONS

See Hammond, 220-37; Wells, 1529, 1644, 1735; Heseltine, J. E., CBEL, I, 209-11. Some reprints with notable illustrations are included as indicated below.

BARNOUW, A. J. Die Kantelberg-vertellingen van Geoffrey Chaucer. Onze Eeuw, 16, 1916, 1-37, 161-95. Dutch translation of KnT.

----------. The Miller's Tale, van Chaucer. Handelingen van het zesde nederlandische Philologencongres, 1910.

    Rev: John Koch, AB, 22, 1911, 271.

----------. De Prolog tot de Kantelberg-Vertellingen van Geoffrey Chaucer. Onze Eeuw, 12, 1912, 375-411.

    Rev: ESt, 46, 1912, 110-2.

----------. De Vertelling van der Nonnen-priester. Onze Eeuw, 16, 1916, 330-52.

    Dutch translation of NPT.

----------. De Vertellingen van de Pelgrims naar Kantelberg. Vertold door A. J. Barnouw. Haarlem: Willink and Zoon, 1930-3. 3 vols.

    Metrical translation of CT; no prose sections; brief notes; foreword by J. Huizinga.

    Rev: P. Fijn van Draat, ESt, 66, 1931, 76-81; TLS, Feb 16, 1933, 108; TLS, Jan 18, 1934, 44; O. K. S., MLR, 29, 1934, 229; Germaine Dempster, MP, 35, 1937, 103.

BATES, KATHERINE LEE. The Story of Chaucer's Canterbury Pilgrims: Retold for Children. Rand, 1909, 1914, 1921.

----------. Canterbury Pilgrims: Retold by Katherine Lee Bates; ill by Angus Macdonall. Rand, McNally, 1914. 305 pp.

BIRKEDAL, UFFE. Af Chaucers og Langlands Digtning. Paa Dansk ved Uffe Birkedal. Studier fra Sprog- og Oldtidsforskning, 90. Pio, 1913. 56 pp.

BOOK, FREDRIK, PER HALLSTROM, and MARTIN
    LAMM. Världslitteraturen: De Stora Mästerverken.
    Stockholm: Bonnier, 1929. Vol. 10, Medeltidsdiktning,
    2: Chaucer, v. d. Vogelweide, Boccaccio. 358 pp.
BURRELL, ARTHUR, Ed. Chaucer's Canterbury Tales
    for the Modern Reader. Everyman Library, no. 307.
    Dent; Dutton, 1908, 1910. Rev ed, Coniston Classics,
    1912. English Literature for School Series, 1914.
    Prologue, Southworth-Athenaeum Press, 1937, ill.
CARPENTER-JACOBS, W. E. W., Ed. First Chaucer.
    Wheaton, 1952.
CARR, W., Tr. Merciless Beauty. Trans. Golden Book,
    II, 1930, 43.
CHIARINI, CHINO. Goffredo Chaucer: I Racconti di
    Canterbury. Firenze: Sansoni, 1912.
CLARKE, CHARLES COWDEN. Tales from Chaucer.
    Everyman ed. Dent; Dutton, 1911.
        See E. B., NQ, 194, Aug 6, 1949, 348, Cowden
    Clarke and Chaucer, where review of Clarke's The
    Riches of Chaucer by Leigh Hunt is mentioned.
----------. Tales from Chaucer, with a Chinese
    Note by C. K. Ke. Shanghai: Commercial Press,
    1929.
----------. Tales from Chaucer, Told by Cowden
    Clarke. Illustrated Children's Classics. William
    Collins Sons and Co, 1931. 336 pp.
COGHILL, NEVILL. Geoffrey Chaucer: The Canterbury
    Tales Translated into Modern English. Baltimore and
    Harmondsworth, Middlesex, England: Penguin Books,
    1952.
        Introduction: Chaucer's Life; Chaucer's Works;
    The Present Translation (on translating Chaucer).
        Rev: R. H. Llewellyn, Spec, 27, 1952, 538-40;
    Time, Aug 11, 1952, 94 (Lollipop Chaucer), with por-
    trait of Chaucer.
COLLINGSWOOD, S. D. The Prioress's Tale Adapted
    by S. D. C. Herder, 1923.
CURRY, SARAH J. The Devil's Gold. 25-38 in Frank
    Shay, A Treasury of Plays for Men. Little, Brown,
    1928.
        Dramatization of the Pardoner's Tale.
DARTON, F. J. HARVEY. Pilgrim Tales from Chaucer.
    Darton and Co, 1928.

----------. Pilgrim's Tales from the Tales of the Canterbury Pilgrims: Told for Children. Dodge, 1909.

----------. The Story of the Canterbury Pilgrims: Retold from Chaucer and Others. Stokes, 1908, 1914,
1932. Lippincott, 1952, ill by M. G. Kirk.

DELATTRE, F., L. CAZAMIAN, et al. Les Contes de
Canterbury. Paris, 1942.

 Introduction; trans of the Prologue, Clerk's Tale,
Miller's Tale, and Nun's Priest's Tale.

DEL RE, ARUNDELL, Ed. Troilus and Criseyde. Gold-
en Cockerel Press, 1927. 310 pp. Ill by Eric Gill.

 Globe text; not a translation.

DRYDEN, JOHN. Dryden's Chaucer. Being Part of
Fables, ed by W. Roy Macklin. A. and C. Black, Ltd,
1927. The Socrates Booklets, VIII.

 Dryden's version of Knight's Tale, Nun's Priest's
Tale, and character of Parson.

FARJEON, ELEANOR. Tales from Chaucer. The Canterbury Tales Done into Prose. Ill by W. Russell
Flint. Cape and Smith, 1930. 245 pp. Reprint, 1934.
Hale, Cushman, and Flint, 1932. 257 pp. Medici Society; Clarke, Irwin, 1948.

GLIMT af Verdensliteraturn (for dansk Ungdom i Skole
og Hjem). Udg. af Margrethe Thunbo. Nr. 2: Canterbury Fortaellingen af Geoffrey Chaucer. Harck, 1929.
c32 pp.

HALES, ADA. Stories from Chaucer. Methuen, 1911.

HERTZBERG, W. Chaucers Canterbury-geschichten.
Berlin, 1925.

 Introduction by J. Koch.

HILL, FRANK ERNEST. Verses from Chaucer: Before
the Tournament: Emely. Commonweal, 11, 1930, 656.

----------. The Canterbury Tales. The Prologue and
Four Tales with the Book of the Duchess and Six Lyr-
ics. Translated into Modern English Verse. Ill by
Hermann Rosse. Longmans, 1930, 1940. 190 pp.
School ed, 1931. 227 pp.

 Rev: TLS, July 24, 1930, 610; M. Day, RES, 7,
1931, 112; H. S. Canby, SRL, 6, 1930, 1085-6.

----------. Canterbury Tales, Rendered into Modern
English Verse. 2 vols. Folio. Limited Editions Club,
1935. Newly rev and ill by Arthur Szyk. Heritage,
1946.

----------. Canterbury Tales, Translated into Modern
English. Longmans, 1935. 583 pp.
    Rev: D. F. B., AL, 7, 1935, 240; H. S. Canby,
Book-of-the-Month-Club News, Mar, 1935, 14.
    English ed, The Canterbury Tales. A Rendering
for Modern Readers. Allen & Unwin, 1936. 583 pp.
    Rev: TLS, Aug 15, 1936, 661; H. Wolfe, Obs, Aug
16, 1936.
----------, Tr. Chanticleer and Pertelote. Trans.
Golden Book, 20, 1934, 556-9.
----------, Tr. Prologue to the Canterbury Tales.
Trans. Golden Book, 11, 1930, 85-8.
----------. The Unknown Poet. SRL, 6, 1930, 889-90.
    Argument on the value of modernizing Chaucer.
HITCHINS, H. L., Ed. Canterbury Tales: Chaucer for
Present Day Readers. 128 pp. London: J. Murray,
1946; 2nd enl ed, ill by Laurie Tayler, 1950. The same
as above adapted for schools by Frank Mosby, 1949.
HOPPER, VINCENT F. Chaucer's Canterbury Tales: In-
terlinear Translation. Barron's Educational Series,
1948. 463 pp.
    Contains General Introduction, Prologue, Knight's
Tale, Prioress' Prologue, Invocation and Tale, Pro-
logue, Tale, and Epilogue Nun's Priest's Tale, Par-
doner's Prologue and Tale, Wife of Bath's Prologue
and Tale, and the Franklin's Prologue and Tale. The
book is intended for introductory courses.
JERNSTROM, HARALD. Chaucerdikt i Svenks Drakt, av
Harald Jernstrom. Tiden, 1933. 99 pp.
JOHNSON, R. B. Tales from Chaucer. Gowans, 1909, 1911.
JONES, CLAUDE. Chaucer's "Truth" Modernized. NQ,
171, 1936, 455.
JONES, C. W. Mediaeval Literature in Translation.
Longmans, Green, 1950.
KASHKIN, I. Russian Translation of the Prologue of the
Canterbury Tales. Krasnaia, Nov 4, 1940, 143.
KOCH, JOHN. Ausgewählte kleinere Dichtungen Chaucers;
im Versmass des Originals in Deutsche Übertragen.
ESt, 69, 1934, 35-105.
    Chronology discussed with notes.
----------. Chaucerproben. ESt, 53, 1919, 161-7.
    Newfangelnesse, To Rosamounde, and Merciles
Beautee translated into German.

----------. Geoffrey Chaucers Canterbury-Erzählungen
nach Wilhelm Hertzbergs Ubersetzung neu herausgegeben. Berlin: Herbert Stübenrauch, 1925. 579 pp.

Rev: T. F. Crane, MLN, 41, 1926, 64-7; Alfons
Hilka, LGRP, 49, 1928, 1-3; Schroer, Kölner Zeitung,
1925, no, 104, Beilage.

----------. Geoffrey Chaucers Kleinere Dichtungen.
Heidelberg: Winter, 1928. 260 pp.

Rev: E. Eckhardt, ESt, 63, 1929, 422-3; Mabel
Day, RES, 5, 1929, 336-9; W. F. Schirmer, NS, 37,
1929, 335-6; F. Wild, LGRP, 50, 1929, 102-4; Muriel
B. Carr, MLN, 44, 1929, 538-41; H. S. V. Jones,
JEGP, 28, 1929, 417-21; T. D., Leuvensche Bijdragen,
23, 1931, 98 (Bijblad); M. S. Serjeantson, E Stud, 15,
1933, 97-8; H. Lüdeke, AB, 42, 1931, 149-52; Deu-
schle, Neophil, 16, 1931, 215-6; Dorothy Everett,
YWES, 9, 1928, 82-3; YWES, 10, 1929, 117.

----------. Textkritische Bemerkungen zu "Chaucers
Kleineren Dichtungen." Ang, 53, 1929, 1-101.

Notes explaining method of determining readings
for the edition.

KRAPP, GEORGE PHILIP. Troilus and Criseyde: Eng-
lished Anew. Wood engravings by Eric Gill. The
Modern Library. Random House, 1932, 1940, 1947,
1949. Limited Editions Club, 1940.

Rev: Robert K. Root, SRL, 10, 1933, 204; F. E.
Hill, Nation, 136, 1933, 45-6.

LEGOUIS, EMILE, and Others. Les Contes de Canterbury. Paris: Alcan, 1908. 530 pp.

For list of editors, see section: Editions with
Notes, above.

Rev: A. Barbeau, Pbl, 118, 1909, 520; Ch. Bastide,
Rev Crit, 67, 1909, 485-8.

LEGOUIS, EMILE. Geoffrey Chaucer. Bloud, 1910. Trans
by L. Lailavoix. Dent; Dutton, 1913, 1922, 1928.

Translation of Chaucer selections into French, 205-15.

For reviews, see section: General Criticism.

----------. Oeuvres Choisies. Introduction and Notes.
Renaissance du Livre, Paris, 1924.

French translation.

LUMIANSKY, ROBERT MAYER. The Canterbury Tales
of Geoffrey Chaucer. A New Modern English Prose
Translation, Published Together with the Original

Middle English Text of the General Prologue and the
Nun's Priest's Tale. Preface by Mark Van Doren.
Ill by H. Lawrence Hoffman. New York: Simon and
Shuster, 1948. 346 pp.
    Rev: H. R. Patch, MLN, 64, 1949, 500-1; Haldeen
Braddy, MLQ, 11, 1950, 246-7.
----------. Geoffrey Chaucer's Troilus and Criseyde:
Rendered into Modern English Prose. Ill by H. Law-
rence Hoffman. 217 pp. Columbia, S. C.:Univ of
South Carolina Press, 1952.
MACAULAY, MARGARET C. Stories from Chaucer.
Cambridge Univ Press, 1911, 1912, 1926. Putnam,
1912.
McSPADDEN, J. WALKER. Stories from Chaucer. Told
Through the Ages Series. New Ed. Harrap, 1932, 1949.
232 pp.
----------. Tales from Chaucer. Harrap, 1909. Crowell,
1922.
MATHESIUS, V. , Tr. and Ed. Vybor z Canterburskych
providek Geofreye Chaucers. Obecny prolog a Vyra-
veni Kneze jeptiscina. A Selection from Chaucer's
Canterbury Tales: The Prologue and the Nun's Priest's
Tale. A Czech translation with Introduction and Com-
mentary. Prague, 1927. 62 pp.
MORRISON, THEODORE. The Portable Chaucer. Viking
Press, 1949.
    Translation and interesting introduction on trans-
lation of Chaucer.
    Rev: R. H. Llewellyn, Spec, 25, 1950, 287-90.
NICHOLS, DORIS JEAN. Twentieth-Century Translations
of Geoffrey Chaucer: Canterbury Tales. Southern
Methodist Univ Abstracts of Theses, 7, 1940, 46.
NICHOLSON, J. U. The Canterbury Tales; Rendered
into Modern English. With Illustrations by Rockwell
Kent and Introduction by Gordon Hall Gerould. Co-
vici, Friede, 1934. 627 pp. Harrap, 1935. Garden
City Publ Co, 1936, 1943, 1950.
    Rev: F. Thompson, Commonweal, 21, 1934, 240-1;
H. S. Canby, Book-of-the-Month Club News, Nov,
1934, 14; R. Church, Spect, 154, 1935, 576-7.
PARKER, WILLIS L. The Three Cuckolds out of Chaucer
in Modern Prose Rendering. Privately printed, New
York, 1932.

Prose versions of Merchant's, Miller's, and
Reeve's Tales.

PEREZ y del RIO-COSA, MANUEL. Los Cuentos de
Cantarbery, Versión Directa del Ingles Antiguo con
una Introducción y Notas. Prólogo de Adolfo Bonilla
y San Martin. Biblioteca Literaria de Autores Es-
pañoles y Extranjeros, Vols. I-II. Madrid: Reuss (a. a.),
1921. 2 vols.
Prose version.

PHILLIPS, ADDISON LEROY. Chaucer's Good Counsel
to a Friend Deflated. Poet Lore, 48, 1942, 268-71.
Modernization of Truth.

PINSSEAU, PIERRE. Les Contes de Canterbury. Tra-
duction Juxtalineaire du Prologue. Paris: Libraire
Louis Arnette, 1921.
Translation of Prologue and condensation of KnT.

PLESSOW, G. Des Haushalters Erzählung aus den Can-
terbury-Geschichten Gottfried Chaucers. Berlin:
de Gruyter, 1929. 169 pp.
Rev: TLS, April 3, 1930, 299; K. Brunner, DL,
51, 1930, 1027-9; H. Lange, AB, 42, 1931, 149-52;
John Koch, ESt, 65, 1931, 384-93; Martin B. Ruud,
MLN, 45, 1930, 288; Arch, 157, 1930, 147-8; Dorothy
Everett, YWES, 10, 1929, 119-20.

ROBERTS, DONALD A. Chaucer in Translation. SRL,
6, 1930, 1180. See A. Colton, SRL, 6, 1930, 1210;
F. E. Hill, S. O'Sheel, SRL, 7, 1930, 26; H. S.
Davis, SRL, 7, 1930, 171; D. A. Roberts, SRL, 7,
1930, 256.
Arguments on value of modernizing Chaucer.

ROBERTSON, STUART. Chaucer and Wordsworth.
MLN, 43, 1928, 104-5.

SEYMOUR, MARY. Chaucer Stories. Für d. Schulgebr.
ausgew. u. erke. v. Clemens Klopper. 6 Aufl.
Leipzig, Rengersche Buchl. , 1928. 87 pp. Franzö́s.
u. engl. Schulbibliothek. Reihe A. Bd. 109. Also,
1929. 95 pp. Wörterbuch, 27 pp.
Chaucer version for children. 1st ed in Hammond,
234.

SHAVER, CHESTER LINN. Two Eighteenth-Century
Modernizations of Chaucer. Harvard Studies and
Notes, 16, 1934, 199-201.

SIMONS, SARAH E. , and C. I. ORR. Dramatization of

the Prologue of the Canterbury Tales. Scott, Foresman, 1913.

SKEAT, WALTER W. The Legend of Good Women Done
into Modern English. King's Classics. Chatto, 1907.

----------. The Parlement of Birds and the House of
Fame Done into Modern English. King's Classics.
Chatto, 1908.

----------. The Prologue to the Canterbury Tales and
Minor Poems Done into Modern English. King's
Classics. Chatto, 1909.

STEAD, WILLIAM T. Stories from Chaucer: The Canterbury Tales. Penn, 1908.

STORR, F., and H. H. TURNER. Canterbury Chimes,
or Chaucer Tales Retold for Children. Dutton, 1915.

STURT, MARY, and ELLEN G. OAKPEN. Canterbury
Pilgrims, Being Chaucer's Canterbury Tales Retold
for Children. Dutton, 1913.

TAPPAN, EVA M. The Chaucer Story Book. Houghton,
1908.

TATLOCK, JOHN S. P., and PERCY MACKAYE. Complete Poetical Works of Geoffrey Chaucer. Macmillan,
1912. Modern Reader's Chaucer, 1914. Reprints, 1926,
1931, 1938, 1943, 1951.
       Abridged by C. W. Ziegler, see below in this sec-
tion.
       Rev: Nation, 95, 1912, 427-8; Clark S. Northup,
Dial, 53, 1912, 436-9; H. S. V. Jones, JEGP, 12,
1913, 343-4.

THOLEN, WILHELM. Stories. Canterbury Tales. Ausgew. von Dr. Wilhelm Tholen. Schoningh; Furlinger;
Gotschmann, 1938. 96 pp.

TOWNSEND, ANSELM M., Tr. Hymn to the Blessed
Virgin; the A B C Called La Priere de Nostre Dame,
Done in Modern English. Milwaukee: Bruce Publ Co,
1935. 50 pp.

UNDERDOWN, EMILY, and Others. The Approach to
Chaucer. Thomas Nelson and Sons, London, 1925,
1938. 190 pp.
       Prose and verse modernizations of part of the
Prologue and some tales. Modified from the volume
formerly known as The Gateway to Chaucer, following.
Modern verse renderings by R. B. Horne, Leigh Hunt,
and Thomas Powell, 1938.

UNDERDOWN, EMILY. The Gateway to Chaucer. Sully
and Kleinteich, 1913.
----------. Stories from Chaucer. Nelson, 1913.
VALLESE, TARQUINIO. Le Novelle di Canterbury. Mi-
lan, Rome, Naples: Albrighi, Segati, e c., 1926.
Vol. 1, Italian verse translation of Group A.
----------. Le Novelle di Canterbury, Tradatte e Cor-
redate di Note e Introduzione. Milan: Società Anonima
Editrice Dante Alighieri; Albrighi, Segati, e c., 1928.
----------. Le Novelle di Canterbury. Milan: Società
Anonima Editrice Dante Alighieri; Albrighi, Segati,
e c., 1931.
Italian verse translation of Groups B (without Meli-
beus) and C, and WBT.
VAN NAME, WARREN MESEREAU. The Modernization
of Chaucer. Master's Thesis, Columbia, 1905.
VAN WYCK, WILLIAM, Tr. Canterbury Tales, Trans-
lated into Modern English Verse. Covici, Friede,
1928. 2 vols.
----------. The Canterbury Tales of Geoffrey Chaucer,
Together with a Version in Modern English Verse.
Ill by Rockwell Kent. Covici, Friede, 1930. 2 vols.
Limited ed.
Original and modernizations in parallel columns.
WARRINGTON, JOHN, Ed. Troilus and Criseyde. Every-
man Library. Dutton; Dent, 1952. 337 pp.
WATTS, NEVILLE HUNTER. Love Songs of Sion; a
Selection of Devotional Verse from Old English
Sources. Benziger, 1924. 167 pp.
Modern rendering of Prioress' Tale, 117.
WHITMORE, FREDERIC. Canterbury Tales by Geoffrey
Chaucer: A Selective Version. Dorrance, 1939; Van-
tage, 1949.
Modernized and selective version.
WIGHT, DOUGLAS. Under the Oak. Short Plays for
Modern Players, 123-47, ed by Glenn Hughes. New
York, 1931.
Modern dramatic version of Pardoner's Tale.
ZIEGLER, CARL W. Chaucer's Canterbury Tales. Mac-
millan, 1922.
Selections from the edition of Tatlock and Mackaye.

GENERAL CRITICISM

See Manly, SNL, 265-95; Robinson, xxiv-xxv; and
Wells, The Chaucer Canon, CBEL, I, 213, 1531, 1641,
1732, 1926-7; Chronology of Chaucer's Works, CBEL,
I, 213, 1641, 1733; General Studies and Miscellaneous,
CBEL, I, 213-15, 1529, 1639-40, 1730-1, 1924-5; J. E.
Heseltine, Early Criticism and Scholarship, CBEL,
I, 211-3.

ALEXANDER, HENRY. Chaucer after Six Centuries.
Queen's Quarterly, 47, 1940, 400-10.
AMOS, FLORA ROSS. Early Theories of Translation.
Doctoral Diss, Columbia, 1919. Columbia Univ Press,
1920. 184 pp. Columbia Univ Studies in English and
Comparative Literature.
Several references to Chaucer in chapter on The
Medieval Period, 3-46.
ANDERSON, GEORGE K. Old and Middle English Litera-
ture from the Beginnings to 1485. In A History of Eng-
lish Literature, by Anderson, George K., Hardin
Craig, Louis Bredvold, and J. W. Beach, 1-172. New
York: Oxford University Press, 1950.
ANON. Nature in Medieval Poetry. TLS, Aug 1, 1929,
597.
----------. Romanticism in the Dock. TLS, Jan 8, 1938,
17-18.
APPERSON, G. L. Chaucerian Reference Wanted. NQ,
149, 1925, 445.
To a proverb listed by Hazlitt.
ARNOULD, E. J. Taine et le Moyen-Age Anglais. Rev
Litt Comp, 16, 1936, 494-520.
ATKINS, J. W. H. English Literary Criticism: The
Medieval Phase. Cambridge Univ Press, 1943. 211 pp.
Appendix contains listing of Geoffrey de Vinsauf's
figures.
Rev: D. Everett, YWES, 57-8; J. F. Lockwood,
MLR, 39, 1944, 399-401; R. McKeon, MP, 42, 1944,

59-60; F. M. Powicke, EHR, 60, 1945, 111; Tillotson,
English, 5, 1944, 57-8; G. H. Gerould, MLN, 60,
1945, 65-7; A. A. Gilbert, JEGP, 44, 1945, 212-5;
NQ, 186, 1948, 235; Sweeting, RES, 21, 1945, 63-4;
Durham Univ Journal, 36:101; TLS, Feb 12, 1944, 82.

ATKINSON, DOROTHY FRANCES. Chaucer's Religious
Satire. Master's Thesis, Univ of Washington, 1927.
Typewritten, 74 pp.

----------. Some Notes on Heraldry and Chaucer. MLN,
51, 1936, 328-31.

AUSTIN, ALFRED. Chaucer, Modern Eloquence. Vol. 7,
45-8. Philadelphia: Morris, 1900. Lecture delivered
in the Collegiate Church of St. Saviour, Southwark,
Oct 29, 1900.

BAILEY, JOHN. Poets and Poetry, 18-27. Oxford:
Clarendon Press, 1911.

BALDWIN, CHARLES SEARS. Three Medieval Centuries
of Literature in England, 1100-1400. Little, Brown,
1932. 274 pp.
     Chaucer, 203-25.
     Rev: Dorothy Everett, YWES, 13, 1932, 125-6;
Kemp Malone, MLN, 52, 1937, 378-9.

BARNOUW, ADRIAAN JACOB. Chaucer. In National
Encyclopedia, Collier and Son, 1933, Vol. 2, 549-50.

BAUGH, ALBERT C. Chaucer: I, Chaucer: II, and Other
Contemporaries of Chaucer. Chapters in A Literary
History of England, Appleton-Century-Crofts, 1948,
249-72.
     Rev: D. Everett, YWES, 69-70; John J. Parry,
JEGP, 48, 1949, 147-9; Robert Alger Law, MLN, 67,
1951, 560-3.

BENHAM, ALLEN R. English Literature from Widsith
to Chaucer: A Source Book. Yale Univ Press, 1916.
     Chaucer, 605-13.
     Rev: William Lawrence, JEGP, 16, 1917, 316-21;
James R. Hulbert, MP, 15, 1917, 575-6; Raleigh
State Journal (Raleigh, N.C.), Oct 16, 1916.

BENNETT, H. S. Chaucer and the Fifteenth Century.
Oxford History of English Literature, Vol. II, pt. 1.
Oxford Univ Press, 1947. 326 pp.
     Rev: D. Everett, YWES, 29, 1948, 68-9; John E.
Houseman, English, 7, 1948, 76-7; DUJ, 40, 1948,
60-1; J. R. Hulbert, MP, 46, 1949, 203-4; J. A. W. Ben-

net, MLR, 45, 1950, 78-9; Neville Coghill, RES, n. s. 1,
1950, 155-6; Francis Utley, Spec, 26, 1951, 370-5; H.
Lüdeke, E Stud, 34, 1953, 83-4; G. L. Brook, MA,
18, 1949, 32-3.

BERNDT, ELSA. Dame Nature in der englischen Literatur bis herab zu Shakespeare. Leipzig, 1923. Palaestra, 110.
    Particularly 38-9.

BJORKMAN, ERIK. Geoffrey Chaucer: Englands storste
medeltida Skald. Stockholm: Bonnier, 1906.

BLAND, D. S. Chaucer and his Critics. Jour of the
South-West Technical College and School of Art, Dec,
1947:
    Rev: D. Everett, YWES, 74. Not seen.

BLOOMFIELD, MORTON W. Chaucer's Sense of History.
JEGP, 51, 1952, 301-13.

BOYCE, BENJAMIN. The Theophrastan Character in
England to 1642. With the Assistance of Notes by
Chester Noyes Greenough. Harvard Univ Press, 1947.
324 pp.
    Discussions of medieval rhetoric; considers char-
acters of the Prologue not Theophrastan. See index.

BREGY, KATHERINE. The Inclusiveness of Chaucer.
CW, 115, 1922, 304-13.

----------. Poets and Pilgrims, from Geoffrey Chaucer
to Paul Claudel. Beinziger Bros, 1925.
    Chapter I, The Inclusiveness of Chaucer.

BRETT-JAMES, NORMAN G. Introducing Chaucer. Harrap, Clarke, Irwin, 1949. 126 pp.
    Emphasizes geographic and social conditions of
Chaucer's time.
    Rev: D. Everett, YWES, 53-4; History, 34, 1949,
304.

BROWN, W. N. The Sixth Centenary of Chaucer's Birth.
Millgate, April, 1940, 389-91.

BRUSENDORFF, AAGE. The Chaucer Tradition. Copenhagen: V. Pio, Poul Branner; Milford, 1925. 509 pp.
    Rev: Hugo Lange, AB, 39, 1928, 70-4; TLS, Jan
14, 1926, 25; A. W. Pollard, Library, 7, 1926, 229-
32; NQ, 150, 1926, 431-2; Ernest Kuhl, MLN, 41,
1926, 402-6; A. Brandl, Arch, 151, 1926, 115-6; Robert K. Root, JEGP, 26, 1927, 258-62; C. R. D.
Young, RES, 3, 1927, 80-3; Mario Praz, MLR, 22,

1927, 202-8; John Koch, LGRP, 48, 1927, 101-8; G. Hübener, DL, 48, 1927, 559-61; Howard R. Patch, MP, 25, 1928, 361-6; Walter F. Schirmer, NS, 36, 1928, 29-35; Dorothy Everett, YWES, 83-6; V. Langhans, Ang, 51, 1927, 323-53 (review article).

BUTT, FERDINAND H. Chaucer's Types of Literature: A Partial Study of the Poet's Critical Theory. Master's Thesis, Univ of Washington, 1925. Typewritten, 29 pp.

CALLAHAN, Sister MARY D. Chaucer as a Traditional Figure. Master's Thesis, Iowa, 1933.

CAMP, LEO LEONARD. Studies in the Rationale of Medieval Allegory. Unpubl Doctoral Diss, Univ of Washington Library, 1942.

CANBY, HENRY SEIDEL. Chaucer Renewed. SRL, 6, 1930, 1085-6.
    Long review of F. E. Hill's translation of Chaucer, with general appreciation.

‒‒‒‒‒‒‒‒‒‒. The Short Story in English. Holt, 1909.
    Part 2, Chaucer to the Elizabethans, 57-100.

CASTELLI, ROBERTO. Geoffrey Chaucer. Brescia, 1946. 175 pp.
    Rev: D. Everett, YWES, 69-70.

CATE, ALICE E. Housemaids and Chaucer. Lit Digest International Book Review, 4, 1926, 258.
    General appreciation; no critical value.

CAZAMIAN, LOUIS. The Development of English Humor. Macmillan, 1930. 160 pp.
    Humor in Middle English Literature before Chaucer, 63-99; Chaucer's Humor, 100-29; English and Scottish Humor after Chaucer, 130-60.
    Rev: J. B. Allin, AB, 72, 1930, 328; TLS, Jan 15, 1931, 38; C. W. Wells, Univ Calif Chron, 33, 1931, 482-9; S. Strahan, Commonweal, 14, 1931, 118-20; F. Delattre, RAA, 8, 1931, 534-7.

‒‒‒‒‒‒‒‒‒‒. The Development of English Humor. Parts I & II. Duke Univ Press, 1952. 421 pp.
    Rev: Joseph Jones, JEGP, 52, 1953, 108-10; Stewart M. Tave, MP, 50, 1953, 206-8.

CHAMBERS, R. W. Geoffrey Chaucer: Springtide of English Poetry. TLS, 39, April 20, 1940, 194, 195, 198.

CHESTERTON, GILBERT KEITH. Chaucer. Farrar,

1932. 302 pp. Reprint, Faber, 1934; new ed, 1948. Tr
de l'anglais par Roland Bourdariat. Nouvelle Revue
Française, 1937. 281 pp.

    Rev: Dorothy Everett, YWES, 13, 1932, 76-7; TLS,
April 14, 1932, 266; H. R. Patch, SRL, 9, 1932, 87-8;
C. Wright, Nation, 135, 1932, 315; M. Praz, E Stud,
14, 1932, 198-201; T. E. Welby, Week End Review, 5,
1932, 490; D. Cecil, N St, 3, 1932, 590; G. Rylands,
Spect, 148, 1932, 631-2; H. E. Joyce, VQR, 9, 1933,
127-30; K. Garvin, JEGP, 32, 1933, 95-7; E. Rickert,
NR, 73, 1933, 303-4; Hugh Ross Williamson, Book-
man (London), 82, 1932, 94-6; Speer Strahan, Cath
Educ Rev, 31, 1933, 211-6.

----------. On Mr. Geoffrey Chaucer. 209-14, in All I
Survey; a Book of Essays. Dodd, Mead, 1933.

CHRISTY, J. Z. Queen Philippa in Chaucer. NQ, 145,
1923, 451.

    Request for information.

CHUBB, E. W. Chaucer. 10-30, in Masters of English
Literature. McClurg, 1914.

CLEMEN, WOLFGANG. Der junge Chaucer; Grundlagen
und Entwicklung seiner Dichtung. Kölner anglistische
Arbeiten, 33. Bochum-Langendreer, 1938. 243 pp.

    Rev: Germaine Dempster, MP, 38, 1940, 215; W.
Héraucourt, ES, 74, 1940, 116-8; D. Everett, YWES,
64-8; A. Brandl, Arch, 175, 1939, 248; W. Schmidt,
AB, 50, 1939, 7-9; H. Lange, Lit Beibl, 61, 1939, 311.

COFFMAN, GEORGE RALEIGH. Two Masters of Comedy.
TLS, Aug 25, 1927, 565-6.

    Chaucer and Jane Austen. Coffman's definition of
satire: "A literary manner which blends a critical
attitude with humor and wit to the end that human in-
stitutions may be improved."

COGHILL, NEVILL. The Poet, Chaucer. Home University Library. Oxford Univ Press, 1949. 185 pp.

    Rev: TLS, May 20, 1949, 332; D. Everett, YWES,
52-3, and RES, 2 n. s., 1951, 159-61; Garland Ethel,
MLQ, 12, 1951, 361-3; R. H. Llewellyn, Spec, 25,
1950, 259-61; DUJ, 42, 1950, 77-8; NQ, 194, 1949,
506.

COLBY, ELBRIDGE. Geoffrey Chaucer. 1-22, in English
Catholic Poets, Chaucer to Dryden. Bruce, 1936.

    Rev: T. M. , CW, 144, 1936, 245-6.

COLVIN, I. Geoffrey Chaucer. Outlook (London), 60,
    1927, 542.
CONNER, MARGARET. Some Renaissance Aspects of
    Chaucer. Master's Thesis, Iowa, 1933.
CONNOLLY, TERENCE L. Chaucer. Fordham Univ
    Press, 1936.
COOK, ALBERT S. Chaucerian Papers. Trans Connec-
    ticut Academy of Arts and Sciences, 23, 1919, 1-63.
        Rev: Arch, 141, 1921, 309.
----------. The Historical Background of Chaucer's Knight.
    Trans Conn Acad of Arts and Sciences, 2 0, 1916, 161-240.
        Rev: J. Koch, AB, 28, 1917, 156-60; E. Eckhardt,
    ESt, 50, 1916, 430-1; G. G. Coulton, MLR, 12, 1917,
    369-70; Arch, 134, 1916, 466; Nation, 102, 1916, 653.
COWLING, GEORGE H. Chaucer. Methuen; Dutton, 1927.
    223 pp.
        Contains discussion of chronology of Chaucer's
    works. See also RES, 2, 1926, 311.
        Rev: Barrington Gates, Nation-Athen, 41, 1927, 5,
    160; N St (Lit Suppl), May 21, 1927, 29; H. Lüdeke,
    AB, 39, 1928, 187-8; Paull F. Baum, MLN, 43, 1928,
    206-7; J. H. Lobban, MLR, 23, 1928, 229; Dorothy
    Everett, YWES, 101-3.
CURRY, WALTER C. Chaucer and the Mediaeval Sci-
    ences. Oxford, 1926. 268 pp.
        Chapters: The Doctor of Physic and Mediaeval
    Medicine; The Summoner and the Cook; The Pardon-
    er's Secret; The Reeve and the Miller; The Wife of
    Bath; The Knight's Tale; The Man of Law's Tale;
    Mediaeval Dream Lore; Chauntecleer and Pertelote
    on Dreams; Notes.
        Rev: Frederick Tupper, Nation, 124, 1927, 720-1;
    James J. Walsh, Commonweal, 5, 1927, 695; Eleanor
    P. Hammond, AB, 39, 1928, 185-7; R. D. French,
    YR, 17, 1928, 397-400; Paull F. Baum, MLN, 43,
    1928, 206-7; Robert K. Root, Spec, 3, 1928, 114-6;
    Allan H. Gilbert, JEGP, 27, 1928, 400-2.
----------. Chaucer's Science and Art. Texas Review,
    8, 1923, 307-22.
DAHLBERG, CHARLES R. The Secular Tradition in Chau-
    cer and Jean de Meun. Doctoral Diss, Princeton, 1953.
DAICHES, DAVID. Literature and Society. Gollancz, 1938.
    Chaucer, 53-64, and other references.

DAVIDS, E. I. GOSE. A Fourteenth Century Dickens.
Dickensian, 38, 1943, 70-4.

DE SELINCOURT, ERNEST. Chaucer. 24-49, in Oxford
Lectures on Poetry. Oxford Univ Press, 1934.
Rev: James R. Sutherland, RES, 12, 1936, 233-4.

DISRAELI, ISAAC. Amenities of Literature. Warne, 1881.
Chaucer, 158-76; Occleve, the Scholar of Chaucer,
191-5. Not in Hammond.

DRINKWATER, JOHN. Chaucer: The Poet of Spring.
66-73, in Prose Papers. Mathews, 1917.

DRYDEN, JOHN. Preface to the Fables. 206-36, in E.
D. Jones, Ed, English Critical Essays (sixteenth,
seventeenth, and eighteenth centuries). World's
Classics. Oxford, 1922.

EBERGARD, OSCAR. Der Bauernaufstand vom Jahre
1381 in der englische Poesie. Angl Forsch, 51, 1917.
133 pp.
Chaucer, 43-7. Attitude toward the Peasants' Revolt.

EDMUNDS, E. W. Chaucer and his Poetry. London:
Harrap, 1915.

ELIAS, EDITH L. Great Names in English Literature:
Chaucer to Bunyan. Harrap, 1913.

ELLIS, CONSTANCE B. The Humour of Geoffrey Chaucer. Holborn Rev, 22, 1931, 375-8.

EMERSON, OLIVER F. Chaucer Essays and Studies.
Selections from Writings of 1860-1927. Western Re-
serve Univ Press, 1930. 456 pp.
Rev: TLS, June 19, 1930, 518; Mabel Day, RES, 6,
1930, 464; H. W. H. , MLR, 25, 1930, 381-2; Paull F.
Baum, SAQ, 29, 1930, 221; C. S. Northup, Cornell
Alumni News, 32, 1930, 221; R. F. Russell, Mercury,
23, 1931, 293-7; John Koch, ESt, 66, 1931, 81-94; F.
Mossé, Rev Crit, 65, 1931, 13; M. Gouron, Moyen
Age, 40, 1930, 223-4; Dorothy Everett, YWES, 11,
1930, 74-5.

----------. Some Notes on Chaucer and Some Conjectures. PQ, 2, 1923, 81-96.
Contains: Book of the Duchess, 309-11, 866-9; Complaint of Mars, 113-4; Parlement of Foules, 204-10;
Troilus and Criseide II, 1228-9; Knight's Tale, A.
979-80; Prologue to Canterbury Tales, 164, "and
preestes thre."

ERDMANN, A. Chaucer. In Nordisk Familjebok; Kon-
versationslexikon och Realencyklopedi, Stockholm,
1906, Vol. 5, 118-22.
EVANS, B. I. Tradition and Romanticism: Studies in
English Poetry from Chaucer to W. B. Yeats. Long-
mans, 1940.
    Chaucer to Shakespeare, 23-43.
FANSLER, DEAN S. Chaucer and the Roman de la Rose.
Columbia Univ Press, 1914. 269 pp.
    Contains material on several of Chaucer's works.
For reviews, see section: Romaunt of the Rose.
FRENCH, ROBERT DUDLEY. A Chaucer Handbook.
Crofts, 1927. 394 pp. 2nd ed, Crofts; G. Bell, 1947.
402 pp.
    Rev: Cortlandt van Winkle, Commonweal, 6, 1927,
586; Paull F. Baum, MLN, 43, 1928, 206-7; Dorothy
Everett, YWES, 8, 1927, 100-1, and 28, 1949, 184.
GEROULD, GORDON HALL. Chaucerian Essays.
Princeton Univ Press; Oxford, 1952.
    Chapters: Chaucer's Calendar of Saints; The Social
Status of the Franklin; The Vicious Pardoner; Some
Dominant Ideas of the Wife of Bath; The Serious Mind
of Chaucer; The Limitations of Chaucer.
GETTY, AGNES K. The Mediaeval-Modern Conflict in
Chaucer's Poetry. PMLA, 47, 1932, 385-402.
    Rev: Dorothy Everett, YWES, 77-8.
GILCHRIST, M. E. Uncritical Appreciation. Poet Lore,
30, 1919, 304-8.
GILLETE, DOROTHEA. Literary Criticism in Chaucer.
Master's Thesis, Columbia, 1920.
GLUNZ, H. H. Die Literarästhetik des europäischen
Mittel-Alters. Wolfram; Rosenroman; Chaucer;
Dante. Boschum-Langendreer, 1937.
    Rev: Rudolph Metz, AB, 48, 1937, 290-7; B. E. C.
Davis, MA, 7, 1938, 151-2; D. Everett, YWES, 70-1;
TLS, Aug, 1937, 608; Hittmair, ES, 73, 1938, 72-83;
R. Woesler, ZFAAK, 32, 1939, 90-2; M. Praz, E
Stud, 21, 1939, 166-9; H. O. Burger, DL, 59, 1938,
600-4; H. Rüdiger, Geistige Arbeit, 1938, v. 2; Karl
Hammerle, Archiv, 176, 1939, 85-92.
----------. Nationale Eigenart in mittelalterlichen
Schriften Englands. Grundformen der englischen
Geistesgeschichte, 97-189. Stuttgart, 1941.

GREY, PAMELA WYNDHAM, Viscountess. Chaucer.
    79-92, in Shepherd's Crown, a Volume of Essays.
    Appleton-Century, 1923.
GRIERSON, Sir H. J. C., and J. C. SMITH. Critical
    History of English Poetry. Oxford, 1946.
    Chaucer, Gower, and Langland, 23-42.
GWYNN, STEPHEN LUCIUS. Chaucer. 1-20, in Masters
    of English Literature. Macmillan, 1904.
HADOW, GRACE E. Chaucer and his Times. Holt;
    Williams and Norgate, 1914. 2nd ed, Holt, 1926.
    Rev: Arch, 150, 1926, 286.
HALES, J. W. Geoffrey Chaucer. 154-67, in DNB, Vol.
    4. Smith, Elder, 1908.
HALL, JAMES NORMAN. Flying with Chaucer. Hough-
    ton, 1930. 56 pp.
    General appreciation.
HAMILTON, MARIE P. The Utterances of Chaucer on
    Literary Art. Abstract of Doctoral Diss, Cornell
    Univ, 1932. 7 pp.
HAMMOND, ELEANOR P. Chaucer: A Bibliographical
    Manual. Macmillan, 1908. Reprint, P. Smith, 1933.
    597 pp.
    For reviews, see section: Bibliography.
HAYES, J. A Study in Chaucer: An English Poet's Nature
    Lore. Cork: Shandon Printing Co, 1917.
HECHT, HANS, and LEVIN L. SCHUCKING. Die eng-
    lische Literatur im Mittelalter. In Walzel, Handbuch
    der Literaturwissenschaft. Wildpark-Potsdam, 1930.
    191 pp.
    Rev: Gerard Buck, NS, 41, 1933, 28-34.
HELMEKE, TH. Beteuerungen und Verwünschungen bei
    Chaucer. Kiel Diss, 1913.
HENDRICKS, D. Geschichte d. englischen Autobiographie
    v. Chaucer bis Milton. Berlin Diss. Leipzig: Mayer
    and Müller, 1925. 48 pp.
    Rev: Karl Arna, ZFEU, 26, 1927, 308-9.
HERAUCOURT, WILL. Die Wertwelt Chaucers: Die Wert-
    welt einer Zeitwende. Heidelberg, 1939.
    Rev: S. B. Liljegren, AB, 51, 1940, 127-31; W.
    Schmidt, NS, 48, 1941, 129-33; MacDonald, MLR,
    36, 1941, 121.
HERBEN, STEPHEN J., Jr. Arms and Armor in Chau-
    cer. Spec, 12, 1937, 475-87.

HERRICK, JAMES B. Why I Read Chaucer at Seventy.
Annals of Medical History, 5, 1933, 62-72.
HOWELLS, WILLIAM D. Wordsworth, Lowell, Chaucer.
79-85, in My Literary Passions. Harpers, 1891.
HUNT, L. Fine Days in January and February. 374-6,
in Rosalind Vallance, Ed, Hundred English Essays.
Nelson, 1936.
HUXLEY, ALDOUS L. Chaucer. 206-28, in Essays New
and Old. Limited ed, Chatto & Windus, 1926. Trade
ed, George H. Doran, 1927; H. W. Wilson, 1932.
Same essay, 194-218, in Huxley's On the Margin;
Notes and Essays. Doran, 1923.
IIJIMA, IKUZO. Langland and Chaucer. A Study of the
Two Types of Genius in English Poetry. Boston: Four
Seas Co, 1925. 256 pp.
    Rev: Walter F. Schirmer, NS, 36, 1928, 28-9.
JACK, ADOLPHUS A. A Commentary on the Poetry of
Chaucer and Spenser. Maclehose and Jackson; Mac-
millan, 1920. 369 pp.
    Rev: TLS, April 22, 1920; Evening Post Book Re-
view, Sept 4, 1920, 13; George Saintsbury, Acad, 1920,
I, 698-9.
JAMES, STANLEY B. Happy Warriors. Month, 160, 1932,
109-112.
JELLIFFE, R. A. Chaucer; 1340-1940. College English,
2, 1941, 750-4.
JOHNSON, ADELE REMSEN. Womanhood and Women in
Chaucer. Master's Thesis, Columbia, 1903.
K., E. Chaucer and Modernity. Acad, 76, 1909, 712-4.
KALUZA, MAX. Chaucer-Handbuch. Leipzig, 1919. 248 pp.
    For reviews, see section: Editions with Notes.
KASHKIN, I. Realizm Chaucera. Literaturny Kritik, nos.
9/10, p. 73.
----------. Geoffrey Chaucer. Intern Lit, U.S.S.R.,
1940, pts. 5-6, 276-83.
KER, WILLIAM PATON. English Literature: Medieval.
Holt, 1912. 256 pp.
    Chaucer, 220-52.
----------. Chaucer. 76-100, in Essays on Medieval
Literature. Macmillan, 1905.
KIRBY, THOMAS A., and HENRY BOSLEY WOOLF, Eds.
Philologica: The Malone Anniversary Studies. Johns
Hopkins Press, 1949. 382 pp.

This festschrift contains three articles in the
Chaucer field which are noted in the proper sections
below.

Rev: D. Everett, YWES, 54-5; Elliot V. K. Dobbie,
MLN, 67, 1951, 555-60; D. C. Fowler, JEGP, 50,
1951, 257-8; Norman Davis, MA, 20, 1951, 56-60;
Millet Hinshaw, MLQ, 14, 1953, 217-8; H. M. Smyser,
Spec, 26, 1951, 719-24.

KITTREDGE, GEORGE L. Chaucer and his Poetry. Harvard Univ Press, 1915; 9th printing, 1946.

Rev: John L. Lowes, MLN, 31, 1916, 316-8; H. S.
V. Jones, JEGP, 17, 1918, 622-5; T. A. Knott, MP,
14, 1916, 61-4; Nation, 101, 1915, 121-2; Sewanee Review, 23, 1915, 494-8; YR, 5, 1916, 426-30; W. P.
Ker, MLR, 11, 1916, 509-10; E. Koeppel, Arch, 134,
1916, 175-8.

----------. Chauceriana. MP, 7, 1910, 465-83.

Contains: The Book of the Duchess and Guillaume
de Machaut; "Make the Metres of hem as thee leste";
The Wife of Bath; "A Finch eek coude he pulle";
Chaucer and "L'Intelligenza"; "No man caste his pilch
away": "Cast up the Gates"; "Drede fond first Goddes";
Chaucer and Geoffrey de Vinsauf; "Marcia Catoun";
Chaucer and Alanus de Insulis.

KNOWLTON, E. C. Nature in Middle English. JEGP, 20,
1921, 186-207.

Especially 187-8.

----------. An Outline of World Literature from Homer
to the Present Day. Nelson, 1929. 397 pp.

Chaucer, 67-70.

KOCH, JOHN. Alte Chaucerprobleme und neue Lösungs-
versuche. ESt, 55, 1921, 161-225.

Contains discussion of chronology.

----------. Chaucers Boethiusübersetzung: Ein Beitrag
zur Bestimmung der Chronologie seiner Werke. Ang,
46, 1922, 1-51.

----------. Kleinere Dichtungen. Heidelberg, 1928.

Chronology of Chaucer's works.

KORSCH, HEDWIG. Chaucer als Kritiker. Berlin Diss,
1916.

Rev: John Koch, LGRP, 38, 1917, 86-91; E. Björk-
man, AB, 28, 1917, 235-6; Arch, 135, 1916, 467.

KROG, F. Studien zu Chaucer und Langland. Heidelberg:

Winter, 1928. 174 pp. Anglistische Forschungen, Vol. 65.

    Chaucer's attitude toward contemporary affairs.

    Rev: Hugo Lange, ESt, 64, 1929, 82-4; Mabel Day, RES, 5, 1929, 212-3; John Koch, LGRP, 1929, 19-24; M. B. Carr, MLN, 44, 1929, 538-41; E. Blackman, MLR, 25, 1930, 344-5; H. Lüdeke, AB, 42, 1931, 152-3; J. Vriend, E Stud, 11, 1929, 72-3; Dorothy Everett, YWES, 93-4; F. Mossé, Rev Crit, 64, 1930, 45.

KUHL, ERNEST P. Chaucer and the Church. MLN, 40, 1925, 321-38.

LA DRIERE, CRAIG. Chaucer's Place. Commonweal, 20, 1934, 584.

LANGE, HUGO. Chaucer und das Wilton House Diptychon. Nachricht von der Gesellschaft der Wissenschaften zu Göttingen; Philol. -hist. Kl. Fachgr. 4, N. F. Bd. 1, No. 2, 1934, 31-40. Berlin: Weidmann.

LANGENFELT, GOSTA. Englands Boccaccio. Finsk Tidskrift, 110, 1931, 30-45.

LAWRENCE, WILLIAM WITHERLE. Chaucer and the Canterbury Tales. Columbia Univ Press; Oxford (Toronto), 1950. 182 pp.

    Chapters: Realism and Artifice; The Fabliau Tales; The Sequence of Tales; The Discussion of Marriage; The Ending of the Tales; Bibliography.

    Rev: TLS, Jan 5, 1951, 8; D. Everett, YWES, 56-7; G. Kane, MLR, 46, 1951, 473-5; Robert K. Root, Spec, 26, 1951, 170-1; D. Everett, RES, n. s. 3, 1952, 377-9; W. Clemen, Arch, 189, 1952, 61; S. B. Liljegren, Stud Neophil, 25, 1953, 40-1; Etud Angl, 5, 1952, 353-5; Howard R. Patch, MLN, 66, 1951, 484-7.

LEGOUIS, EMILE. Geoffrey Chaucer. Bloud, 1910. Trans by L. Lailavoix. Dent; Dutton, 1913, 1922, 1928.

    For reviews see section: Life.

----------. The Middle Ages and the Renascence (650-1660). Trans by H. D. Irvine. Macmillan, 1926; Dent, 1933. 387 pp.

    Geoffrey Chaucer, 82-98.

    Rev: Allardyce Nicoll, Nation-Athen, 39, 1926, 104-5; Charles Sears Baldwin, Dial, 81, 1926, 348-51; Willis Fletcher Johnson, NAR, 223, 1926, 551-6; Jacob Zeitlin, Nation, 123, 1926, 109-10; Karl Young, SRL, 3, 1926, 20; Outlook, 144, 1926, 26-7; TLS,

Aug 3, 1933, 526; B. De Selincourt, Obs, July 23,
1933; L. Abercrombie, Spect, 151, 1933, 130.
LEVY, H. L. "As Myn Auctour Seith." MA, 12, 1943,
25-9.
   Attitude toward historical truth.
   Rev: D. Everett, YWES, 49.
LEWIS, CLIVE STAPLES. The Allegory of Love; A
Study in Medieval Tradition. Oxford, 1936. Reprint,
1948. 378 pp.
   Courtly love, 1-43; Romance of the Rose, 112-56;
Chaucer, 157-97.
   Rev: SRL, 14, 1936, 23; S. A. Coblentz, N. Y.
Times Book Review, July 5, 1936, 12; TLS, June 6,
1936, 474; Kathleen Tillotson, RES, 13, 1937, 477-9;
G. L. Brook, MLR, 32, 1937, 287-8; Edgar C. Knowl-
ton, JEGP, 36, 1937, 124-6; Fr. Krog, AB, 48, 1937,
333-8; Mona Wilson, English, 1, 1937, 344-6; Gray
C. Boyce, AHR, 43, 1937, 103-4; Howard R. Patch,
Spec, 12, 1937, 272-4; Thomas A. Kirby, MLN, 52,
1937, 515-8; W. Empson, Spect, 157, 1936, 389; NQ,
171, 1936, 250-1; B. Ifor Evans, Obs, Aug 23, 1936;
O. Elton, MA, 6, 1937, 34-40; B. Ifor Evans, YWES,
12-13; V. S. M. Fraser, New Criterion, 16, 1937,
383-8; C. L. W., Oxford Mag, 55, 1937, 449-50; C.
F., Studi Danteschi, 21:195; G. R. Coffman, SP, 35,
1938, 511; G. Bonnard, E Stud, 21, 1938, 78-82.
LOOMIS, ROGER S. Was Chaucer a Laodicean: Essays
and Studies in Honor of Carleton Brown. New York,
1940, 129-48.
   Chaucer's attitude toward war, the Peasants' Revolt, Wyclif, and questions of the day.
LONG, E. HUDSON. Chaucer as a Master of the Short
Story. Delaware Notes, 16th ser., 1943, 11-29.
LOOTEN, C. Chaucer, ses Modèles, ses Sources, sa
Religion. Economat des Facultés Catholiques de Lille,
1931. 260 pp.
   Rev: M. Praz, E Stud, 14, 1932, 198-201; E. Le-
gouis, RAA, 10, 1932, 51-4; F. Delattre, Rev de Litt
Com, 12, 1932, 453-9; A. Koszul, Rev Crit, 66, 1932,
322-4.
LOUNSBURY, THOMAS R. Geoffrey Chaucer. In War-
ner's Library, The World's Best Literature, 1917,
Vol. 6, 3551-600. Same in Columbia Univ Course in

Literature, Columbia Univ Press, 1929, Vol. 4, 552-
95.

LOWES, JOHN LIVINGSTON. The Art of Geoffrey Chaucer. 75-118, in Essays in Appreciation. Houghton-
Mifflin, 1936.

    Rev: C. Gauss, SRL, 14, Sept 12, 1936, 12-13.

----------. The Art of Geoffrey Chaucer. Sir Israel
Gollancz Memorial Lecture, 1930. Oxford Univ Press,
1931. 32 pp.

    Rev: C. J. S. , MLR, 27, 1932, 114; NQ, 161, 1931,
36; Dorothy Everett, YWES, 12, 1931, 81-2; W. F.
Schirmer, AB, 43, 1932, 304-6.

----------. The Art of Geoffrey Chaucer. Abstracted
from the Sir Israel Gollancz Memorial Lecture. SRL,
7, 1931, 937-9. Comment by the author, SRL, 8, 1931,
46.

----------. Geoffrey Chaucer and the Development of
his Genius. Lectures at Swarthmore College on the
William J. Cooper Foundation. Houghton-Mifflin,
1934. 246 pp. English ed: Geoffrey Chaucer. Oxford
Univ Press, 1934, 1944, 1949. 210 pp.

    Rev: Percy Hutchison, N. Y. Times Book Rev,
Feb 25, 1934, 5; W. Fischer, AB, 46, 1935, 65-7;
G. P. Krapp, Nation, 138, 1934, 335-6; A. H. Marck-
wardt, EJ, 23, 1934, 790-1; B. R. Redman, Scrib-
ner's, 95, 1934, 11; A. J. Barnouw, E Stud, 16, 1934,
148-9; R. D. French, YR, 23, 1934, 646-8; H. L.
Binsse, Amer Rev, 3, 1934, 101-6; J. M. Manly, SRL,
10, 1934, 703; H. R. Patch, Spec, 9, 1934, 337-9;
W. G. Leonard, AM, 32, 1934, 373-4; E. Rickert,
NR, 79, 1934, 188-9; C. Van Winkle, Commonweal,
20, 1934, 51-2; H. E. Joyce, VQR, 10, 1934, 624-6;
C. Morley, Book-of-the-Month-Club News, Feb,
1934, 11; Dorothy Everett, YWES, 15, 1934, 83-5; E.
C. , America, 51, 1934, 91; S. C. Chew, N. Y. Herald
Tribune Books, April 1, 1934, 6; E. VR. W. , CW,
139, 1934, 501; G. W. Stonier, New Statesman and
Nation, 7, 1934, 917; George Rylands, Spect, 153,
1934, 138; TLS, June 21, 1934, 438; NQ, 167, 1934,
35-6; A. B(randl), Arch, 166, 1934, 138; R. A. Pratt,
MLN, 50, 1935, 111-3; E. V. Gordon, MA, 6, 1937,
125-30; Edwin Cuffe, Thought, 25, 1950, 119-20.

MACAULAY, ROSE. Some Religious Elements in English

Literature. Hogarth Lectures, no. 14. Harcourt, 1931.
160 pp.

A few references to Chaucer.

Rev: K. Arns, ESt, 71, 1936, 137-8; TLS, Aug 6,
1931, 607; Hugh Kingsmill, Eng Rev, 53, 1931, 511-2;
Oxford Mag, Nov 5, 1931, 151; Amer Mercury, 24,
1931, xii; B. Dobree, Spect, 147, 1931, 360; E. C.
Batho, RES, 9, 1933, 357-8.

McCULLY, BRUCE. Chivalry in Chaucer. TAPA, 44,
1913, lxv-lxvi.

Abstract of paper.

MacKAIL, J. W. Chaucer. 1-69, in The Springs of
Helicon: A Study in the Progress of English Poetry
from Chaucer to Milton. Longmans, 1909.

McNABB, VINCENT JOSEPH. Geoffrey Chaucer: A
Study in Genius and Ethics. Stones from the Brook,
Vol. 1. Limited ed. St. Dominic's Press, 1934.
Haesocks, Sussex, 1935.

Rev: TLS, Nov 15, 1934, 798.

McNALLY, FRANCIS EVELYN. The Aristocratic Home
in Chaucer. Master's Thesis, Stanford, 1930.

MAGNUS, LAURIE. European Literature in the Centuries of Romance. London: Paul, 1918.

----------. A History of European Literature. W. W.
Norton, 1934. 318 pp.

Beginning Notes on the Renascence in Chaucer,
55-8.

Rev: TLS, Feb 15, 1934, 104; AM, 32, 1934, New
Books, iv; Commonweal, 19, 1934, 616; J. W. Gass-
ner, N. Y. Herald Tribune Books, May 13, 1934, 12;
New Statesman & Nation, 7, 1934, 424; Harold Strauss,
N. Y. Times Book Rev, April 8, 1934, 10; Sat Rev,
157, 1934, 329; Ernest Boyd, SRL, 10, 1934, 769.

MAGOUN, FRANCIS P., Jr. Chaucer's Ancient and
Biblical World. Med Stud, 15, 1953, 107-36.

Chaucer's acquaintance with the ancient world
viewed through his use of geographic terms.

MALONE, KEMP. Chapters on Chaucer. Johns Hopkins
Press; Oxford, 1951. 240 pp.

Chapters: Geoffrey Chaucer and the Fourteenth
Century; The Book of the Duchess; The House of Fame;
The Parliament of Fowls; The Legend of Good Women;
Troilus and Criseyde; The General Prolog; The

Canterbury Pilgrims; Index to Proper Names and
Pilgrims.
    Rev: TLS, Sept 21, 1951, 598; Heinrich Ch. Matthes,
Archiv, 189, 1953, 226; W. W. Lawrence, Spec, 27, 1952,
235-6; James Sledd, MP, 50, 1952, 59-60; Karl Brunner,
Ang, 70, 1952, 442-4; M. Galway, MLR, 48, 1953, 61-4;
Etud Angl, 5, 1952, 353-5; James Kinsley, MA, 21, 1952,
46-8; S. B. Liljegren, Stud Neophil, 25, 1953, 40-1.
MARCUS, HANS. Chaucer, der Freund des einfachen
    Mannes. Arch, 171, 1937, 174-82; 172, 1937, 28-41.
    Cited passages translated into German.
    Rev: D. Everett, YWES, 70.
MARTIN, DOROTHY. A First Book about Chaucer.
    Routledge, 1929; Dutton, 1930. 120 pp.
MASEFIELD, JOHN. Chaucer. Leslie Stephen Lecture,
    1931. Cambridge Univ Press, 1931. 36 pp.
    Rev: A. Porter, Amer Bookman, 73, 1931, 552;
    LL, 7, 1931, 226-7; H. Lange, AB, 44, 1933, 294-5.
----------. Chaucer. 199-223, in Recent Prose. Mac-
    millan, 1933.
MAYNARD, THEODORE. Chaucer's Literary Develop-
    ment. CW, 138, 1933, 65-75.
MEYER, EMIL. Die Charakterzeichnung bei Chaucer.
    Halle: Niemeyer, 1913. 95 pp. Studien zur englischen
    Philologie, 48.
    Contains studies of important characters in Chau-
    cer's works.
    Rev: Heinrich Mutschmann, AB, 26, 1915, 309-12;
    ESt, 48, 1914, 273-81; O. Glöde, LGRP, 35, 1914,
    245-6; Arch, 131, 1913, 494; DL, 36, 1915, 2351.
MINERS, TOM. Chaucer and the Cornish Cottage. Old
    Cornwall, 2, no. 6, 1933, 34-6; 2, no. 7, 1934, 18-19.
MONROE, HARRIET. Chaucer and Langland. 157-61, in
    Poets and their Art. Revised ed, Macmillan, 1932.
    141-5 in 1st ed, 1926.
MONTMORENCY, J. E. G. de. Gardens in Chaucer and
    Shakespeare. CR, 99, suppl 44, 1911, 1-8; Living Age,
    269, 1911, 625-9.
MOORE, ARTHUR K. Chaucer's Lost Songs. JEGP, 48,
    1949, 198-208.
    Suggests that the lost songs may be included in
    Chaucer's other writings.
    Rev: D. Everett, YWES, 30, 1949, 68-9.

MURRY, JOHN MIDDLETON. Heroes of Thought. New
    York: J. Messner, 1938.
        Chaucer, Chap. I.
NEWBOLT, H. The Poetry of Chaucer. English Review,
    15, 1913, 170-89.
NORTHUP, CLARK S. Chaucer in Prose. Dial, 53, 1912,
    436-9. See also Nation, 95, 1912, 427-8.
NOYES, ALFRED. Chaucer. Bookman (London), 76,
    1929, 191-5; 78, 1930, 216-9.
----------. Eye of Day. 222-34, in Opalescent Parrot:
    Essays. Sheed, 1929.
----------. Chaucer. 1-13, in Pageant of Letters. Sheed,
    1946.
PALMER, G. H. Formative Types in English Poetry.
    Houghton, 1916. 310 pp.
        Geoffrey Chaucer, 31-61.
PATCH, HOWARD R. Characters in Medieval Literature.
    MLN, 40, 1925, 1-14.
----------. Chaucer and the Common People. JEGP, 29,
    1930, 376-84.
        Rev: Dorothy Everett, YWES, 11, 1931, 79-80.
----------. Chaucer and Lady Fortune. MLR, 22, 1927,
    377-88.
----------. Chaucer and Medieval Romance. 93-108, in
    Essays in Memory of Barrett Wendell, by his assist-
    ants. Harvard Univ Press, 1926.
----------. Chauceriana. ESt, 65, 1931, 351-9.
        Contains: Prologue of the Canterbury Tales, A.
    658; Knight's Tale, A. 1096-7; Tale of Sir Thopas, B.
    2047 ff.; Nun's Priest's Tale, B. 4584; Franklin's
    Tale, F. 932; House of Fame, 742-6; Troilus and
    Criseyde, V, 1907-27.
----------. Desiderata in Middle English Research.
    MP, 22, 1925, 27-34.
----------. On Rereading Chaucer. Harvard Univ Press,
    1939. Reprint, 1949. 269 pp.
        Rev: Haldeen Braddy, RES, 16, 1940, 198-201; Mar-
    garet Galway, MLR, 35, 1940, 228-9; H. S. V. Jones,
    JEGP, 39, 1940, 398; Martin B. Ruud, MLN, 56, 1941,
    69-72; R. M. Estrich, Spec, 16, 1941, 504-5; NQ,
    177, Sept 2, 1939, 180; M. M. Colum, Forum, 102,
    1939, 160-1; Edgar C. Knowlton, SAQ, 39, 1940, 116;
    W. F. Bryan, College English, 1, 1940, 463-4.

----------. Geoffrey Chaucer and Youth. CE, 11, 1949,
    14-22.
PECK, MARGARET ELEANOR. Types of Women in
    Chaucer. Univ of Washington, Abstracts of Theses,
    5, 1941, 87-9.
PHILIP, Brother C., F.S.C. A Further Note on Old
    Age in Chaucer's Day. MLN, 53, 1938, 181-2.
POLLARD, ALFRED WILLIAM. Chaucer. Encyclopaedia
    Britannica. 11th ed, 1910, Vol. 6, 13-17. Same in 14th
    ed, 1929, Vol. 5, 326-30.
----------. The Development of Chaucer's Genius. Acad,
    1906, I, 227-9.
POWYS, LLEWELYN. Geoffrey Chaucer. The Freeman,
    6, 1923, 535-7.
----------. Geoffrey Chaucer. 13-27, in Amer Library
    Service, 1923; Grant Richards, 1924.
PRAZ, MARIO. Chaucer. In Enciclopedia Italiana, Isti-
    tuto Giovanni Trecanni, 1931, Vol. 9, 952-5.
PRESTON, RAYMOND. Chaucer. Sheed and Ward, 1952.
        Rev: Neville Braybrooke, English, 9, 1953, 140-1;
    James Kinsley, MA, 22, 1953, 34-7.
PROKOSCH, FREDERIC. Geoffrey Chaucer. 1-16, in The
    English Novelists, ed by Derek Verschoyle. Harcourt,
    1936.
        Rev: TLS, May 9, 1936, 395; K. Arns, ESt, 71, 1936,
    284-5; H. S. C(anby), SRL, 15, Nov 21, 1936, 24; H. T.
    M., NR, 88, 1936, 361; B. de Selincourt, Obs, May 10,
    1936; Commonweal, 25, 1936, 228; E. Sackville West,
    Spect, 156, 1936, 892, 894; L. Kronenberger, NYTBR,
    Dec 6, 1936, 36; Q. D. Leavis, Scrutiny, 5, 1936, 93-
    9; L. E. Cannon, Christian Cent, 53, 1936, 1465;
    Raymond Mortimer, N St, 11, 1936, 730; G. Hopkins,
    London Times, May 17, 1936.
QUILLER-COUCH, Sir ARTHUR T. A Gossip on Chaucer,
    and After Chaucer. 206-45, in Studies in Literature,
    2nd ser. Putnam's, 1922.
RALEIGH, Sir WALTER A. On Chaucer. 103-19, in On
    Writing and Writers: Being Extracts from his Note-
    books, Selected and Edited by G. Gordon. Longmans,
    Green, 1926.
RASCOE, BURTON. Chaucer and the English Spirit. 240-
    9, in Titans of Literature, from Homer to the Present.
    Putnam, 1932.

RICKERT, EDITH. King Richard II's Books. Library,
    ser. 4, 13, 1932, 144-7.
ROOT, ROBERT K. The Poetry of Chaucer. Houghton,
    1906. Rev ed, 1922. Reprint, P. Smith, 1950. 306 pp.
        Rev: John M. Manly, School Review, 16, 1908, 59-
    61; Gustav Binz, AB, 21, 1910, 161-3; A. A. Kern,
    JEGP, 8, 1909, 282-6; Howard R. Patch, JEGP, 22,
    1923, 168-70.
SAINTSBURY, GEORGE. Chaucer. Vol. 2, 156-96, in
    Cambridge History of English Literature. 3rd im-
    pression. Macmillan, 1920.
SALTER, F. M. Chaucer: A Character Analysis. Univ
    Rev (Univ of Kansas City), 4, 1938, 264-70.
SCHINNAGEL, MARGRET. Schmuck als Lebensäusser-
    ung in den Werken Chaucers. Doctoral Diss, Bres-
    lau. Würzburg: Triltsch, 1938. 68 pp.
        Rev: Hans Marcus, AB, 49, 1938, 361-2; K. Brun-
    ner, LGRP, 60, 249.
SCHIRMER, W. F. Chaucer. Die Literatur, 39, 1937,
    733-5.
SCHLAUCH, MARGARET. Chaucer's Doctrine of Kings
    and Tyrants. Spec, 20, 1945, 133-56.
        Survey of political theory of the good and bad rul-
    er; Wyclif; illustrated notably from Legend of Good
    Women, Knight's Tale, Parlement of Foules, Former
    Age, Purse, Lak of Stedfastnesse, Monk's Tale,
    Physician's Tale, Clerk's Tale, Boethius, and con-
    temporary documents.
        Rev: D. Everett, YWES, 53-4.
SCHOFIELD, WILLIAM H. Chivalry in English Litera-
    ture: Chaucer, Malory, Spenser, Shakespeare. Har-
    vard Studies in Comparative Literature, 2. Harvard
    Univ Press, 1912. 294 pp.
        Especially 11-72.
        Rev: Th. Mühe, AB, 30, 1919, 158-61; R. Acker-
    mann, LGRP, 35, 1914, 283-4.
SCHUTT, J. H. A Guide to English Studies. The Study
    of the History of Old and Middle English Literature.
    E Stud, 9, 1927, 140-8.
SEDGWICK, HENRY DWIGHT. Dan Chaucer: An Intro-
    duction to the Poet, his Poetry and his Times.
    Bobbs, Merrill, 1934. 374 pp.
        Rev: B. R. Redman, N.Y. Herald Tribune Books,

Oct 14, 1934, 18; P. H. , N. Y. Times Book Rev, Sept
16, 1934, 2; D. Everett, YWES, 85.
SELLARDS, CORA KIRBY. Color in Chaucer. Master's
Thesis, Kansas, 1897.
SHELLY, PERCY VAN DYKE. The Living Chaucer.
Univ of Pennsylvania Press, 1940. 331 pp.
    Chapters: Chaucer and the Critics; Development
of Chaucer's Art: Book of the Duchess, House of Fame
and after; On Chaucer's Borrowings: Troilus and Criseyde, Legend of Good Women; Chaucer, the Classics
and the Renaissance; Canterbury Tales; "Well of English Undefiled"; This Green Earth.
    Rev: H. S. Bennett, RES, 17, 1941, 338-40; Mar-
garet Galway, MLR, 36, 1941, 518-20; H. S. V. Jones,
JEGP, 40, 1941, 284-5; Thomas A. Kirby, MLQ, 2,
1941, 151-5; H. R. Patch, Spec, 16, 1941, 258-60; Edgar C. Knowlton, SAQ, 40, 1941, 193-4; Robert A.
Pratt, AHR, 47, 1942, 324-5.
SHUMAKER, WAYNE. Alisoun in Wanderland: A Study
in Chaucer's Mind and Literary Method. ELH, 18,
1951, 77-89.
SMITH, J. H. , and E. W. PARKS, Eds. Great Critics:
An Anthology of Literary Criticism. 3rd ed. Norton,
1951.
    See 361-81, Dryden, Preface to Fables Ancient
and Modern.
SMITH, ROLAND M. Two Chaucer Notes. MLN, 51,
1936, 314-7.
    Unlucky days in the Chaucer tradition, 316-7.
SNELL, F. J. The Age of Chaucer. London: Bell, 1901.
    242 pp.
    Rev: ESt, 32, 1903, 117-24.
SPEIRS, JOHN. Chaucer, the Maker. London: Farrar
and Faber, 1951. 222 pp.
    Rev: Dorothy Everett, RES, 3 n. s. , 1952, 377-9;
James Sledd, MP, 49, 1951, 135-6; Etud Angl, 5,
1952, 353-5; TLS, Mar 9, 1951, 150.
----------. Chaucer: The Canterbury Tales. Scrutiny,
11, no. 3, 1942-3, 189-211; and 12, no. 1, 1943-4, 35-
57.
SPEYER, MARION FRANCES. Chaucer Studies, 1920 to
1930, in Five American Periodicals. Master's Thesis,
Columbia, 1933.

STAPLETON, CHRISTOPHER R. Chaucer the Catholic.
    CW, 127, 1928, 186-93.
STEWART, GEORGE R., Jr. The Moral Chaucer. 89-
    109, in Essays in Criticism, by members of the De-
    partment of English, Univ of California. Univ of Cal-
    ifornia Publications in English, I. 1929.
        Rev: Dorothy Everett, YWES, 106-7.
STRAHAN, SPEER. The Largeness of Chaucer. Cath
    Educ Rev, 31, 1933, 395-411.
TATLOCK, JOHN S. P. Chaucer. In Encyclopedia Amer-
    icana, Vol. 6, 361-6. Americana Corporation, 1936.
----------. Chaucer and Wyclif. MP, 14, 1916-7, 257-68.
----------. The Development and Chronology of Chau-
    cer's Works. Chaucer Society, 1907. 233 pp.
        Rev: Robert K. Root, ESt, 41, 1910, 405-11; Nation,
    86, 1908, 220; John Koch, AB, 20, 1909, 129-45; M.
    C. Macaulay, MLR, 4, 1909, 415.
----------. Interpreting Literature by History. Spec,
    12, 1937, 390-5.
----------. The Mind and Art of Chaucer. Introd by
    Germaine Dempster, Ed with Sanford B. Meech.
    Syracuse University Press, 1950. 114 pp.
        Chapters: London, Chaucer, and his English Gen-
    eration; Chaucer and the French Tradition; Troilus
    and Criseyde; Anelida and Arcite; The Hous of Fame;
    The Parliament of Fowls; The Legend of Good Women;
    Less Conspicuous Works; The Canterbury Tales
    (Group A (I)). General bibliography and bibliography
    of the writings of the author.
        Rev: T. A. Kirby, Thought, 27, 1952, 311-2; Doro-
    thy Everett, YWES, 53-4; J. R. Hulbert, MP, 48,
    1951, 214-5; Howard R. Patch, MLN, 66, 1951, 484-
    7.
THOMPSON, NESTA M. A New Way with Chaucer. Univ
    Calif Chron, 29, 1927, 366-79.
        The "new way" is to choose intriguing single lines,
    then hunt them up in context.
        Rev: E. Trauschke, NS, 37, 1929, 652-3.
THOMPSON, W. H. Chaucer and his Times. A. Brown,
    1936. 136 pp.
THURSTON, HERBERT. Conversion of Boccaccio and
    Chaucer. Studies (Educ Co of Dublin), 25, 1936, 215-
    25.

TOUT, THOMAS FREDERICK. Literature and Learning
in the English Civil Service in the Fourteenth Century.
Spec, 4, 1929, 365-89.
        Chaucer, 381-8.
TUPPER, FREDERICK. Wilful and Impatient Poverty.
Nation, 99, 1914, 41.
----------. Chaucer and the Cambridge Edition. JEGP,
39, 1940, 504-26.
        1. Ille Vates Chaldeorum Trophee; 2. Chaucer and
the Ormondes; 3. Sins and Sinners; 4. The Sequence
of Tales.
        Reargues views rejected by Robinson. See Robin-
son under heading: Editions with Notes. (Trophee,
Monk's Tale, *3307, 2117.)
TUVE, ROSEMOND. Seasons and Months: Studies in a
Tradition of Middle English Poetry. 232 pp. Paris:
Librairie Universitaire, 1933.
        Chapter on Chaucer, 170-92.
        Rev: H. R. Patch, MLN, 52, 1937, 462-3; H. A.
C. Green, MLR, 33, 1938, 277-8; D. Everett, YWES,
162-4; H. S. V. J(ones), JEGP, 37, 1938, 277-8.
----------. Spring in Chaucer and before Him. MLN,
52, 1937, 9-16.
        Rev: D. Everett, YWES, 81-2.
UNTERMEYER, LOUIS. Introduction to Skeat edition of
the Canterbury Tales. Modern Library, 1929.
VALLESE, TARQUINIO. Geoffrey Chaucer Visto da un
Italiano. Roma: Albrighi e Segati, 1930. 140 pp.
VAN DYKE, H. Morning Star. 1-26, in The Man Behind
the Book: Essays in Understanding. Scribner, 1929.
VIGLIONE, FRANCESCO. Genova nella Storia della
Letteratura Inglese. Genova, 1937.
        "Gives a few pages to Chaucer."
VOGT, G. M. Gleanings for History of a Sentiment:
Generositas Virtus, non Sanguis. JEGP, 24, 1925,
102-23.
WALKER, HUGH. English Satire and Satirists. Dent;
Dutton, 1925.
        Langland and Chaucer, 9-23; The English and
Scottish Chaucerians and Skelton, 24-38.
        Rev: TLS, Dec 10, 1925; Ernest Boyd, Independent,
116, 1926, 106; SRL, 2, 1926, 499; Robert C. Whitford,
MLN, 43, 1928, 187-90.

WARD, A. W. Chaucer. English Men of Letters Series.
Macmillan, 1909, Vol. 9, 1-199.
For review, see section: Life.
WELLS, WHITNEY H. Chaucer as a Literary Critic.
MLN, 39, 1924, 255-68.
WILKINS, ERNEST H. Petrarch's Coronation Oration.
PMLA, 68, 1953, 1241-50.
Important as early Renaissance literary criticism.
Professor Wilkins translates the oration into English.
A poet's study of his work and his position in society
-- a critical attitude accepted by Boccaccio.
WILLIAMS, BLANCHE COLTON, and JOHN MACY. Do
You Know English Literature? A Book of Questions
and Answers for Students and General Readers. Ap-
pleton, 1930. 597 pp.
Chaucer, 52-74.
Rev: TLS, Sept 25, 1930, 761.
WILLY, MARGARET. Life Was their Cry. Evans, 1950.
Chaucer, 11-51.
WILSON, P. W. He Was a Veray Parfit Gentil Poet.
N. Y. Times Mag, May 12, 1940, 8, 19.
WILSON, S. C. Scottish Canterbury Pilgrims. SHR, 24,
1927, 258-64.
WOLFE, HUMBERT. Notes on English Verse Satire.
Hogarth Lectures, no. 10. Harcourt, Brace, 1929.
158 pp.
Chaucer to Skelton, 34-9.
Rev: TLS, Oct 31, 1929, 866; H. E. A. Northcutt,
RES, 7, 1931, 114.
WOOLF, VIRGINIA S. Pastons and Chaucer. 13-38, in
Common Reader. Harcourt, Brace, 1925.
WORK, JAMES A. Echoes of the Anathema in Chaucer.
PMLA, 47, 1932, 419-30.
Rev: Dorothy Everett, YWES, 79-80.

LITERARY RELATIONS AND SOURCES

See Hammond, 73-105; Legouis, 48-61, 109-21,
157-61; Kaluza, 11-12; Wells, Sources, CBEL, I, 216-
7, 1529, 1640, 1732, 1926; Shelly, 94-193. See also
the separate works for particular source studies.

AIKEN, PAULINE. The Influence of Vincent of Beauvais
on Chaucer. Doctoral Diss, Yale, 1934. Publ in part:
Spec, 10, 1935, 281-7, as Vincent of Beauvais and
Dame Pertelote's Knowledge of Medicine.
----------. The Summoner's Malady. SP, 33, 1936, 40-4.
----------. Arcite's Illness and Vincent of Beauvais.
PMLA, 51, 1936, 316-9.
----------. Chaucer's Legend of Cleopatra and the Specu-
lum Historiale. Spec, 13, 1938, 232-6.
----------. Vincent of Beauvais and the Green Yeoman's
Lecture on Demonology. SP, 35, 1938, 1-9.
----------. Vincent of Beauvais and Chaucer's Monk's
Tale. Spec, 17, 1942, 56-68.
ALLEN, RALPH K. The Point of View of John Gower.
Master's Thesis, Univ of Washington, 1928. 70 pp.
AYRES, HARRY M. Chaucer and Seneca. RR, 10, 1919,
1-15.
BARDELLI, M. Qualche Contributo agli Studi sulle Re-
lazioni del Chaucer col Boccaccio. Firenze, 1911.
BARRY, RAYMOND WALKER. The Sententiae in Chau-
cer. Doctoral Diss, Stanford, 1925. Abstract in Ab-
stracts of Dissertations, 1, 1924-6, 91-4.
BECK, NEMIAS BRAMLETTE. Chaucer and Boccaccio's
Decamerone: A Study of Influence. Master's Thesis,
Univ of Washington, 1925. Typewritten, 81 pp.
BELLEZZA, PAOLO. Irradiazioni e Riverberi dell'
Anima Italiana. Saggi Culturali. Il Presunto Convegno
del Chaucer col Petrarca. . . . Milan: Risorgimento,
1926. 319 pp.
BENHAM, ALLEN R. Three Chaucer Studies: II. Chau-
cer and Ovid. SAQ, 20, 1921, 330-48.

BENNETT, J. A. W. Chaucer, Dante, and Boccaccio.
MA, 22, 1953, 114-5.
   Boccaccio's verses calling to Chaucer's mind
Dante's.
BENNETT, JOSEPHINE WATERS. Chaucer and Mande-
ville's Travels. MLN, 68, 1953, 531-4.
BETHEL, JOHN PERCEVAL. The Influence of Dante on
Chaucer's Thought and Expression. Summaries of
Theses, 1927, Harvard Univ, 1931, 145-8.
BONASCHI, ALBERTO C. Italian Currents and Curiosi-
ties in the English Literature from Chaucer to Shake-
speare. Correnti e Curiosità Italiane nella Letteratura
Inglese da Chaucer a Shakespeare. N. Y. Italian Cham-
ber of Commerce, 1937. 25 pp.
   English and Italian text. Chaucer, 6-10.
BRADDY, HALDEEN. Messire Oton de Graunson, Chau-
cer's Savoyard Friend. SP, 35, 1938, 515-31.
----------. Sir Oton de Graunson -- "Flour of hem that
make in Fraunce." SP, 35, 1938, 10-24.
----------. Chaucer and Graunson: The Valentine Tra-
dition. PMLA, 54, 1939, 359-68.
----------. Chaucer and the French Poet Graunson.
Louisiana State Univ Press, 1947. 100 pp.
   Rev: D. Everett, YWES, 70-1; M. Galway, 43,
1948, 101-2; H. R. Patch, MLN, 67, 1952, 268-9; G.
Stillwell, JEGP, 47, 1948, 293-5; T. A. Kirby, Spec,
22, 1947, 628-9; Etud Angl, 3:259; J. A. W. Bennett,
MA, 1949, 35-7; A. Basil Cottle, RES, 24, 1948,
150-1.
BRIDGES, JOHN ELBERT. Studies in the Aeneas Story
in English Literature. Doctoral Diss, Duke, 1941.
BROWN, HUNTINGTON. The Classical Tradition in
English Literature: A Bibliography. Harvard Studies
and Notes, 18, 1935, 7-46.
   Middle Ages, 21-5; Chaucer, 25-6.
BRUSENDORFF, AAGE. The Chaucer Tradition. Mil-
ford, 1925. 509 pp.
   Chaucer and Deschamps, 485-93.
   For reviews, see section: General Criticism.
BRYAN, WILLIAM FRANK, and GERMAINE DEMPSTER,
Eds. Sources and Analogues of Chaucer's Canterbury
Tales. Univ of Chicago Press, 1941. 765 pp.
   In this bibliography, the names of the contributors

to this volume are entered under the separate tales.
 Rev: W. E. Garrison, The Christian Century, 58,
1941, 721; Com, 34, 1941, 213; George R. Coffman,
SP, 38, 1941, 571-83 (review article under title:
Chaucer's Library and Literary Heritage for the
Canterbury Tales); D. Everett, YWES, 51; and MA,
12, 1943, 78-84; Germaine Dempster, MP, 38, 1940,
205-14; Earl Daniels, College English, 3, 1942, 603-
4; Francis L. Utley, Spec, 17, 1942, 274-83; Mar-
garet Galway, MLR, 37, 1942, 493-5; Boas, English,
4, 1942, 56; W. G. Clawson, JEGP, 42, 1943, 118-
20; Howard R. Patch, MLN, 57, 1942, 383-5.
BUCHANAN, DOROTHY A. The Love Complaint: A
 Study of a Literary Type. Diss, Bryn Mawr, 1939.
CALLAN, NORMAN. Thyn Owne Book: A Note on Chau-
 cer, Gower, and Ovid. RES, 22, 1946, 269-91.
 A comparison of Chaucer's and Gower's handling
of materials from Ovid.
 Rev: D. Everett, YWES, 27, 1946, 66-7, and G.
D. Willcock, 94.
CAMPBELL, J. M. Patristic Studies and the Literature
 of Medieval England. Spec, 8, 1933, 465-78.
 Points out strong influence on medieval literature
from Latin fathers. Some passages from Chaucer
are explained by recourse to patristic study.
CARSWELL, CATHERINE. "Lollius Myn Autour." TLS,
 Dec 28, 1935, 899.
CHAPMAN, COOLIDGE O. Chaucer and Dante. TLS,
 Aug 29, 1952, 565.
 Suggests LGW, 924-7, echoes the words of
Statius in Purgatorio 22, 64-9.
CHAYTOR, H. J. The Troubadours and England. Cam-
 bridge Univ Press, 1923.
 Rev: J. P. Strachey, Modern Languages, 5, 1923,
57; N St, 22, 1923, 58, 60; Spect, 131, 1923, 323; NQ,
Sept 1, 1923, 179-80; A. M. Richie, Nation-Athen, 33,
1923, 691; John J. Parry, JEGP, 23, 1924, 610-1;
Grace Frank, MLN, 39, 1924, 318; L. E. Kastner,
MLR, 19, 1924, 353-54; Walter Fischer, AB, 36,
1925, 67-70; SP, 22, 1925, 554.
CLARK, JOHN W. Dante and the Epilogue of Troilus.
 JEGP, 50, 1951, 1-10.
 Influence of Paradiso 14 and 22.

COFFMAN, GEORGE R. Old Age from Horace to Chau-
cer: Some Literary Affinities and Adventures of an
Idea. Spec, 9, 1934, 249-77.
  Rev: D. Everett, YWES, 99-100.
----------. Old Age in Chaucer's Day. MLN, 52, 1937,
25-6.
  See Phillip, below in this section.
  Rev: D. Everett, YWES, 68.
COGHILL, NEVILL. Two Notes on Piers Plowman. MA,
4, 1935, 83-94.
  Chaucer's debt to Langland, 89-94.
COHEN, HELEN LOUISE. The Ballade. Columbia Univ
Press, 1915. 397 pp.
  Rev: L. E. Kastner, MLR, 11, 1916, 240-3; Arch,
134, 1916, 466; Nation, 101, 1915, 332; Spect, 115, 1915,
407; Dial, 59, 1915, 117.
COOK, ALBERT S. Chauceriana II. RR, 8, 1917, 353-82.
  Chaucer's Linian.
COOKE, JOHN DANIEL. Euhemerism: A Mediaeval In-
terpretation of Classical Paganism. Spec, 2, 1927,
396-410.
  Notes that Chaucer nowhere subscribes to an eu-
hemeristic interpretation.
  Rev: Dorothy Everett, YWES, 8, 1927, 126.
CORNOG, W. H. Alain de Lille: The Anticlaudianus.
Univ of Pennsylvania Diss, 1935.
  Prologue, Argument, and nine books translated
into English.
CRAIGIE, Sir WILLIAM. The Northern Element in Eng-
lish Literature. Univ of Chicago Press, 1933. 135 pp.
  Rev: TLS, Aug 24, 1933, 558; NQ, 165, 1933, 90;
R. Brunner, AB, 45, 1934, 284-5.
CUMMINGS, HUBERTIS M. The Indebtedness of Chau-
cer's Works to the Italian Works of Boccaccio. Univ
of Cincinnati Studies, 10, pt. 2, 1916.
  Chaucer and "myn auctour called 'Lollius, ' " 153-
75.
  Rev: Eleanor P. Hammond, MLN, 32, 1917, 302-4;
Hugo Lange, AB, 29, 1918, 138-40; Howard R. Patch,
AJP, 39, 1918, 83-6; Arch, 137, 1918, 126-7; John L.
Lowes, MP, 15, 1918, 689-728; John S. P. Tatlock,
MP, 18, 1920-1, 657 n; Arch, 135, 1916, 467.
DODD, WILLIAM GEORGE. Courtly Love in Chaucer and

Gower. Harvard Studies in English, 1. Ginn; Milford,
1913.
> Rev: Karl Young, JEGP, 15, 1916, 154-61; George
L. Hamilton, AJP, 35, 1914, 87-90.

EDWARDS, AUBREY C. Chaucer and Italian Humanism.
Univ of Iowa: Doctoral Dissertations: Abstracts and
References, 4, 1944, 200-2.

EMERSON, OLIVER F. Seith Trophee. MLN, 31, 1916,
142-6.

ENGEL, HILDEGARD. Structure and Plot in Chaucer's
Canterbury Tales. Diss, Bonn, 1931.
> Brief discussion of the tales, classified according
to the type of source. (Martin)

EPSTEIN, HANS J. The Identity of Chaucer's Lollius.
MLQ, 3, 1942, 391-400.
> Suggests Lollius Bassus.
> Rev: D. Everett, YWES, 63-4.

EVERETT, DOROTHY. A Characterization of the English Medieval Romances. 98-121, in Essays and Studies, Vol. 15, ed by Sir Herbert Warren. Milford, 1929.
> Study of the romance as a poetic form.

FANSLER, DEAN S. Chaucer and the Roman de la Rose.
Columbia Univ Press, 1914.
> See Index of Borrowings, 240-7.
> Rev: E. Koeppel, AB, 25, 1914, 203-5; John Koch,
ES, 49, 1915, 431-7; Grace E. Hadow, MLR, 11, 1916,
90-2; Arch, 134, 1916, 466.

FARNHAM, WILLARD E. England's Discovery of the
Decameron. PMLA, 39, 1924, 123-39.

FARRAR, CLARISSA P., and AUSTIN P. EVANS. Bibliography of English Translations from Medieval
Sources. Records of Civilization: Sources and Studies,
39. Columbia Univ Press, 1946.

FLESCHENBURG, O. SCHISSEL von. Daresstudien.
Halle: Niemeyer, 1908.

FORSTER, MAX. Boccaccios De Casibus Virorum Il-
lustrium in englischer Bearbeitung. DL, 27, 1924,
1943-6.

FORSMANN, JULIUS. Einiges über französische Ein-
flüsse in Chaucers Werken. Program, St. Peters-
burg. Deutsche Studien, Annenschule, 1909.

FRIEND, ALBERT C. Chaucer's Version of the Aeneid.
Spec, 28, 1953, 317-23.

GASELEE, STEPHEN. The Transition from the Late
Latin Lyric to the Medieval Love Poem. Bowes, 1931.
34 pp.
Rev: C. F. , MA, 1, 1932, 141.
GEROULD, GORDON H. Saints' Legends. Houghton, 1916.
393 pp.
Rev: H. S. Canby, YR, 6, 1917, 436-8; Dial, 61,
1916, 402; Rev of Revs, 54, 1916, 565.
GOFFIN, R. C. Chaucer's Lollius. TLS, Aug 26, 1926,
564; TLS, April 21, 1927, 280.
GRANSON, OTON DE. Complainte amoureuse de Sainct
Valentin [by] Granson [reproduced from MS français
1131, Fol. 69-71 (recto) in the Bibliothèque nationale,
Paris.] 5 sheets on 3 l. The MLA. Collection of Pho-
tographic Facsimiles, no. 67. 1927. Deposited in the
Library of Congress.
"The original is a 15th century manuscript."
GRIFFIN, NATHANIEL, E. Dares and Dictys. Johns
Hopkins Diss. Baltimore: Furst, 1907. 121 pp.
Rev: George L. Hamilton, MLN, 24, 1909, 16-21;
Cbl, 59, 1908, 656; Jsb, 29, 1907, xv, 85.
HAMMOND, ELEANOR P. Two Chaucer Cruces. MLN,
22, 1907, 51-2.
On Lollius.
HARRINGTON, KARL P. Catullus and his Influence. Our
Debt to Greece and Rome. Marshall Jones, 1923. 245
pp.
Rev: Edmund Wilson, Dial, 78, 1925, 145-52.
HART, WALTER M. The Narrative Art of the Old French
Fabliaux. 209-16, in Anniversary Papers . . . for
George Lyman Kittredge. Ginn, 1913.
HARVEY, Sir PAUL, Ed. The Oxford Companion to Eng-
lish Literature. Clarendon Press, 1932. 866 pp.
Brief encyclopedia of English literature. Entries
for Chaucer and Chaucer Society.
Rev: TLS, Dec 1, 1932, 918; NQ, 164, 1933, 34; NR,
74, 1933, 111; AL, 5, 1933, 97; SRL, 9, 1933, 524;
R. E. C. H. , Oxford Mag, Feb 2, 1933, 378; R. B.
McK(errow), RES, 10, 1934, 367-9.
HARVEY, S. W. Chaucer's Debt to Sacrobosco. JEGP,
34, 1935, 34-8.
Rev: D. Everett, YWES, 94.
HASKINS, CHARLES HOMER. The Renaissance of the

Twelfth Century. Harvard Univ Press, 1927. 437 pp.
An important work on Chaucer's humanistic back-
ground.
Rev: George R. Coffman, MLN, 43, 1928, 336-8.
HATHAWAY, CHARLES M. Chaucer's Lollius. ESt, 44,
1911, 161-4.
HECHT, HANS, and LEVIN L. SCHUCKING. Die eng-
lische Literatur im Mittelalter. Walzel, Handbuch der
Literatenwissenschaft. Wildpark-Potsdam, 1930. 191
pp.
Rev: Gerhard Buck, NS, 41, 1933, 28-34.
HENKIN, LEO J. The Apocrypha and Chaucer's House
of Fame. MLN, 56, 1941, 583-8.
"On similarities between details in the third part
of the poem and those in the Book of Revelation --
i. e. , the Apocalypse, not the Apocrypha." (PMLA)
HIBBARD, LAURA ALANDIS. Mediaeval Romance in
England. A Study of the Sources and Analogues of the
Noncyclic Metrical Romances. Oxford Univ Press,
1924. 342 pp.
Rev: Cyril Brett, MLR, 20, 1925, 339-40; SP, 22,
1925, 554; SRL, 1, 1924, 419.
HIGHET, GILBERT. Classical Tradition: Greek and Ro-
man Influences on Western Literature. Oxford Univ
Press, 1949. 763 pp.
Towards the Renaissance: Petrarch, Boccaccio,
Chaucer, 81-103.
Rev: James Hutton, AJP, 73, 1952, 79-87; Jacob
Hammer, Thought, 27, 1952, 579-82.
HINCKLEY, HENRY B. Chaucer and Ywaine and Gawin.
Acad, 1906, II, 640-1. Skeat's criticism, 1906, II,
647. Hinckley's reply, 1907, I, 99.
----------. Chauceriana, PQ, 6, 1927, 313-4.
Three parallels between Chaucer and Roman lit-
erature.
HOLZKNECHT, KARL J. Literary Patronage in the Mid-
dle Ages. Univ of Pennsylvania Diss. Banta, 1923.
258 pp.
Rev: Erna Fischer, AB, 36, 1925, 102-7; G. G.
Coulton, MLR, 20, 1925, 478-9.
HORNSTEIN, LILLIAN H. Petrarch's Laelius Chaucer's
Lollius? PMLA, 63, 1948, 64-84.
Rev: D. Everett, YWES, 86-7.

HUTTON, EDWARD. Did Chaucer Meet Petrarch and
Boccaccio? Anglo-Italian Rev, 1, 1918, 121-35.
----------. Giovanni Boccaccio: A Bibliographical
Study. Lane, 1909.
     Rev: George L. Hamilton, RR, 3, 1912, 125-7.
----------. Chaucer and Boccaccio. TLS, 34, 1935, 143.
     See also Pratt, below.
IMELMANN, RUDOLF. Chaucers Haus der Fama. ESt,
45, 1912, 397-431.
     Contains material on Lollius.
JEFFERSON, BERNARD L. Chaucer and the Consolation
of Philosophy of Boethius. Princeton Univ Press, 1917.
Milford, 1920.
     Discussion of source material.
     Rev: Howard R. Patch, JEGP, 16, 1917, 620-4.
KELLETT, E. E. Chaucer as a Critic of Dante. Mer-
cury, 4, 1921, 282-91.
KITCHEL, ANNA T. Chaucer and Machaut's Dit de la
Fontaine Amoreuse. 217-31, in Vassar Mediaeval
Studies. Yale Univ Press, 1923.
KITTREDGE, GEORGE L. Chaucer and Alanus de Insulis.
MP, 7, 1910, 483.
----------. Chaucer's Lollius. Harvard Studies in Class-
ical Philology, 28, 1917, 47-133.
     Rev: Hugo Lange, Ang, 42, 1918, 345-51; G. G.
Coulton, MLR, 13, 1918, 240-1; Nation, 105, 1917, 181.
----------. The Date of Chaucer's Troilus and Other
Chaucer Matters. Chaucer Society, 2nd ser., 42, 1909.
     Lollius, 57-9.
----------. The Pillars of Hercules and Chaucer's Tro-
phee. 545, in Putnam Anniversary Volume. Cedar
Rapids, Iowa: Torch Press, 1909.
     Rev: Arch, 124, 1910, 428; John Koch, AB, 22,
1911, 271.
KOCH, JOHN. Chaucers Belesenheit in den römischen
Klassikern. ESt, 57, 1923, 8-84.
KOEPPEL, EMIL. Chaucer and Cicero's Laelius de Ami-
citia. Arch, 126, 1911, 180-2.
----------. Chaucer und Innocenz der Dritten Traktat
De Contemptu Mundi. Arch, 84, 1890, 405-18. Nach-
trag, Arch, 85, 1890, 48.
KORTEN, HERTHA. Chaucers literarische Beziehungen
zu Boccaccio: Die künstlerische Konzeption der

Canterbury Tales und das Lolliusproblem. Rostock:
Hinstorff, 1920.
  Rev: Walther Fischer, NS, 20, 1921, 172-3.
KRAEMER, CASPER J., Jr. The Influence of the Class-
  ics on English Literature. Class Jour, 22, 1927, 485-
  97.
    Middle English period, 489.
LANDRUM, GRACE W. Chaucer's Use of the Vulgate.
  PMLA, 39, 1924, 75-100.
LANGE, HUGO. Chaucers "Myn Auctor Called Lollius"
  und die Datierung des Hous of Fame. Ang, 42, 1918,
  345-51.
----------. Chaucer and Mandeville's Travels. Archiv,
  174, 1938, 79-81.
    Summoner's Tale, 2079-84; Troilus and Criseyde,
    V, 379-85; Legend of Good Women, 1114-22; Friar's
    Tale, 6 notations.
LANGHANS, VICTOR. Chaucers angebliche Ubersetzung
  des Traktates "De Contemptu Mundi" von Innozenz
  III. Ang, 52, 1928, 325-49.
    Rev: Dorothy Everett, YWES, 10, 1929, 111-2.
LEGOUIS, EMILE. Geoffrey Chaucer. Trans by L. Lai-
  lavoix. Dent; Dutton, 1913.
    Chaucer's relation to French poetry and to
  Boccaccio.
LERCH, EUGEN. Zu einer Stelle bei Eustache Des-
  champs. Romanische Forschungen, 62, 1950, 67-8.
    "Pandras" in Deschamps' ballade to Chaucer sug-
    gested as a reference to Pandarus.
    Rev: D. Everett, YWES, 70.
LOCKE, EVALEEN, II. Satire of the Thirteenth and
  Fourteenth Centuries, with Especial Reference to the
  Seven Deadly Sins. Master's Thesis, Univ of Southern
  California, 1932. 148 pp.
    "A study of the extant satiric pieces in the English
    vernacular, between 1200 and 1399, to show the devel-
    opment in language, character, content and tone."
LOOTEN, CHANOINE C. Chaucer et Dante. Rev de Litt
  Comp, Oct, 1925, 545-71.
----------. Chaucer, ses Modèles, ses Sources, sa
  Religion. Economat des Facultés Catholiques de Lille,
  1931. 260 pp.
    For reviews, see section: General Criticism.

LOSSING, MARIAN. The Prologue of the Legend of Good
    Women and the Lai de Franchise. SP, 39, 1942, 15-35.
        Denies Lowes's contention that the Lai is an un-
    doubted source of the Legend. Also see Brown, The
    Date of Prol. F, etc.
        Rev: D. Everett, YWES, 65-6.
LOWES, JOHN L. Chaucer and Dante. MP, 14, 1917, 705-35.
        Chaucer remembering Dante's verses while read-
    ing Boccaccio. See also MP, 12, 1915, 19.
----------. Chaucer and Ovide Moralisé. PMLA, 33,
    1918, 302-25.
----------. Chaucer and the Classics. N.Y.: Nation,
    103, 1916, 2-3.
----------. Chaucer and the Miroir de Mariage. MP, 8,
    1910-1, 165-86, 305-34.
        The influence of the Miroir discussed with attention
    to chronology.
----------. Chaucer's Etik. MLN, 25, 1910, 87-9.
        Has bearing on Lollius problem.
----------. The Franklin's Tale, Teseide, and the Fi-
    locolo. MP, 15, 1918, 689-728.
        Includes also CT, Prol, 1-7; KnT, A. 2431-3; T&C,
    III, 1427-9, 1437-40; LGW, 1894-9, 1639-43.
----------. Illustrations of Chaucer Drawn Chiefly from
    Deschamps. RR, 2, 1911, 113-28.
        Rev: John Koch, ESt, 46, 1912, 114.
----------. Simple and Coy: A Note on Fourteenth Cen-
    tury Poetic Diction. Ang, 33, 1910, 440-51.
MacCALLUM, M. W. Chaucer's Debt to Italy. Sydney,
    Australia, 1931; Angus, 1934.
MacCRACKEN, HENRY N. Dant in English: A Solution.
    Nation, 89, 1909, 276-7.
        See also G. C. Macaulay, MLR, 4, 1908, 528.
McGALLIARD, JOHN C. Chaucer's Merchant's Tale and
    Deschamps' Miroir de Mariage. PQ, 25, 1946, 193-
    220.
        Rev: D. Everett, YWES, 28, 1947, 80-1.
McNEAL, THOMAS H. Chaucer and The Decameron.
    MLN, 53, 1938, 257-8.
        Rev: D. Everett, YWES, 75.
McPEEK, JAMES A. S. Did Chaucer Know Catullus?
    MLN, 46, 1931, 293-301.
        Rev: Dorothy Everett, YWES, 85-6.

MAGNUS, LAURIE. A Dictionary of European Literature.
Designed as a Companion to English Studies. Dutton,
1926. 594 pp.
> Chaucer, 94-5.
> Rev: Brander Matthews, Lit Digest International
> Book Rev, 4, 1926, 563-4; TLS, Mar 18, 1926, 212.
----------. English Literature in its Foreign Relations,
1300-1800. Dutton, 1927. 290 pp.
> Chaucer, 1-23.
> Rev: H. B. Fuller, N. Y. Times Book Rev, April
> 8, 1928, 2; SRL, 4, 1928, 689.
----------. A History of European Literature. W. W.
Norton, 1934. 318 pp.
> Beginning Notes of the Renaissance in Chaucer,
> 55-8.
> For reviews, see section: General Criticism.
MAKAREWICZ, Sister M. DELPHINE. The Patristic
Influence on Chaucer. Doctoral Diss, Catholic Univ,
1953.
MEECH, SANFORD B. Chaucer and an Italian Transla-
tion of the Heroides. PMLA, 45, 1930, 110-28.
> Rev: Dorothy Everett, YWES, 11, 1930, 78-9.
----------. Chaucer and Medieval Ovidiana. Doctoral
Diss, Yale. Listed as completed in Willard, 8, 1930,
75.
----------. Chaucer and the Ovide Moralisé -- a Fur-
ther Study. PMLA, 46, 1931, 182-204.
> Rev: Dorothy Everett, YWES, 85.
MEOZZI, ANTERO. Il Petrarchismo Europeo. Parte
Prima. Pisa: Vallerini, 1934. 326 pp.
> On Petrarch in England.
> Not seen.
MONROE, HARRIET. Chaucer and Langland. Poetry, 7,
1915, 297-302.
MOORE, ARTHUR K. Chaucer and Matheolus. NQ, 190,
1946, 245-8.
> Rev: D. Everett, YWES, 78-9.
MOORE, JOHN R. Literary Paganism in the Poetry of
France and England from Hildebert of Tours to
Chaucer. Doctoral Diss, Harvard, 1931. Summary in
Harvard Univ Summaries of Theses, 1931, 235-9.
MOSSE, F. Chaucer et la Liturgie. Rev Germ, 14, 1923,
283-9.

NITCHIE, ELIZABETH. Vergil and the English Poets.
   Doctoral Diss, Columbia, 1919. Columbia Univ Studies
   in English and Comparative Literature. Columbia
   Univ Press, 1919. 251 pp.
      The Mediaeval Tradition, 13-38; Chaucer, his Con-
   temporaries and his Imitators, 39-65.
NORRIS, DOROTHY MacBRIDE. The Saints in English
   Poetry from Chaucer to Milton. Doctoral Diss, Iowa,
   1932.
OSGOOD, CHARLES G. , Ed. Boccaccio on Poetry. Be-
   ing the Preface and the 14th and 15th Books of the
   "Genealogia Deorum Gentilium" in English with Intro-
   ductory Essay and Commentary. Princeton Univ Press,
   1931. 214 pp.
      For reviews, see section: Style.
PAGE, CURTIS C. Chaucer's Testimony Concerning his
   Sources. Diss, Yale, 1947.
PARRY, JOHN J. The Art of Courtly Love of Andreas
   Capellanus with Introduction, Translation and Notes.
   Columbia Univ Press; London: Milford, 1941.
      For reviews, see section: Backgrounds: Social.
PATCH, HOWARD R. Chaucer and Lady Fortune. MLR,
   22, 1927, 377-88.
----------. The Goddess Fortune in Medieval Literature.
   Harvard Univ Press, 1927. 215 pp.
      Expansion of the next entry.
      Rev: E. C. Knowlton, JEGP, 27, 1928, 408-12;
   Dorothy Everett, YWES, 126-7; Beatrice D. Brown,
   AHR, 33, 1928, 627-9; Stanley L. Galpin, MLN, 43,
   1928, 563; J. S. P. Tatlock, Spec, 3, 1928, 406; Mar-
   garet Schlauch, RR, 19, 1928, 354-5; Willard Farn-
   ham, Univ of California Chron, 30, 1928, 476-8.
----------. The Tradition of the Goddess Fortuna in
   Roman Literature and in the Transition Period; in
   Medieval Philosophy and Literature. Smith College
   Studies in Modern Language, 3, 1922, nos. 3 and 4.
      See entry above.
      Rev: F. Wild, ESt, 60, 1926, 304-16.
PATTERSON, WARNER FOREST. Three Centuries of
   French Poetic Theory. A Critical History of the Chief
   Arts of Poetry in France (1328-1630). Univ of Michi-
   gan Publications, Language and Literature, 14-15.
   Univ of Michigan Press, 1935. 2 vols.

PATZER, OTTO. Eustache Deschamps as a Commentator upon the Events and Conditions of his Time. Doctoral Diss, Univ of Wisconsin, 1907. Abstract published in Univ of Wisconsin, Abstracts of Theses, 1, 1917, 151-68.

PETERSEN, HALGAR. Note sur une Ballade Adressée par Eustache Deschamps à Chaucer. Neuphilologische Mitteilungen, 27, 1926, pts. 3-4, 95-7.

PHILIP, Brother C. A Further Note on Old Age in Chaucer's Day. MLN, 53, 1938, 181-2.

    Rev: D. Everett, YWES, 62.

PIAGET, ARTHUR. Oton de Granson, sa Vie et ses Poésies. Mémoires et Documents Publiés par la Societé d'Histoire de la Suisse Romande. Troisième série, I. Lausanne, 1941.

POWELL, LAWRENCE F. Boccaccio's "Decamerone." NQ, Jan 27, 1923, 72-3; Corrigenda, 100.

    List of some editions of the Decameron in English.

POWER, EILEEN, Ed. Goodman of Paris (Le ménagier de Paris); a Treatise on Moral and Domestic Economy by a Citizen of Paris (c. 1393). Now first translated into English with an introduction and notes. Broadway Medieval Library. Harcourt; Routledge, 1928. 348 pp.

PRATT, ROBERT A. Karl Young's Work on the Learning of Chaucer. In A Memoir of Karl Young, 45-55, New Haven, 1946. Privately printed.

    Rev: D. Everett, YWES, 67-9.

----------. Chaucer's Claudian. Spec, 22, 1947, 419-29.

    Concerns passages in LGW, G. 267-80; T&C, V, 1020; PF, 99-105, 176 ff. ; HF, 71-2, 445-50, 1507-12; MerchT, E. 2038-41.

    Rev: D. Everett, YWES, 67-8.

----------. A Note on Chaucer and the Policraticus of John of Salisbury. MLN, 65, 1950, 243-6.

    Parallel to WB Prol, 765-71.

    Rev: D. Everett, YWES, 64-5.

----------. A Note on Chaucer's Lollius. MLN, 65, 1950, 183-7.

    Excerpt from a MS referring to Lollius as historian of Troy.

    Rev: D. Everett, YWES, 68.

PRAZ, MARIO. Chaucer and the Great Italian Writers
of the Trecento. New Criterion, 6, 1927, 18-39, 131-
57, 238-42. Report of this as lecture: Chaucer and
Italy, E Stud, 9, 1927, 43, 81-2.

PRESTAGE, EDGAR, Ed. Chivalry: A Series of Studies
to Illustrate its Historical Significance and Civilizing
Influence, by members of King's College, London.
Kegan Paul; Knopf, 1928. 231 pp.

Includes the following relevant chapters: The Beginnings of Medieval Chivalry, by E. F. Jacob, 37-
55; Chivalry in Middle English Poetry, by Sir Israel
Gollancz, 167-81; Medieval Courtesy Books and the
Prose Romances of Chivalry, by A. T. B. Byles,
183-206; Chivalry and the Idea of a Gentleman, by
A. W. Reed, 207-28.

Rev: TLS, Nov 22, 1928, 882 (answered by A. T.
B. Byles, TLS, Dec 13, 1928, 991); Georgiana P.
McEntee, Commonweal, 9, 1929, 409-10.

PRESTON, RAYMOND. Chaucer and the Ballades Notées
of Guillaume de Machaut. Spec, 26, 1951, 615-23.

PURDY, ROB R. The Friendship Motif in Middle English
Literature. Vanderbilt Studies in Humanities, 1, 1951,
113-41.

----------. The Platonic Tradition in Middle English
Literature. Bull of Vanderbilt Univ, Abstracts of
Theses, 47, 1947, 15-16.

RAITH, JOSEF. Boccaccio in der englischen Literatur
von Chaucer bis Painters Palace of Pleasure. Ein
Beitrag zur Geschichte der ital. Novelle in England.
Leipzig: Noske, 1936. 167 pp.

Rev: Herbert G. Wright, MLR, 32, 1937, 288-9;
A. Brandl, Arch, 171, 1937, 82-3; Karl Brunner,
LGRP, 58, 1937, 164-5; H. Marcus, AB, 47, 1936,
294-6; Kemp Malone, MLN, 55, 1940, 241; Stamm,
E Stud, 20, pt. 6.

RAMSAY, J. H. Chaucer and Wycliffe's Bible. Acad,
1882, II, 435-6.

RAND, EDWARD KENNARD. Ovid and his Influence.
Our Debt to Greece and Rome. Marshall Jones, 1925.
184 pp.

Chaucer, 145-9.

Rev: TLS, July 1, 1926, 442; Henry W. Prescott,
NR, 47, 1926, 69.

RASIN, Sister MARY EUNICE. Evidences of Romanticism in Poetry of Medieval England. Doctoral Diss, Notre Dame, 1929. Publ by the Slater Co, Louisville, Kentucky, 1929. 202 pp. Also by Univ of Notre Dame library, 1930.

REPRODUCTIONS OF MANUSCRIPTS AND RARE PRINTED BOOKS. Now on deposit on the Library of Congress. Les Cent Ballades; Oton de Granson, Complainte Amoureuse de Saint Valentin. 110 sheets. Paris: Bibl Nat, MS. fr. 2201 fols. 1-104 and MS. fr. 1131 fols. 69-71.

RICKERT, EDITH. King Richard II's Books. Library, ser. 4, 13, 1932, 144-7.

ROORDA, P. Chaucer and Italy. E Stud, 9, 1927, pts. 2-3.

ROOT, ROBERT K. Chaucer and the Decameron. ESt, 44, 1911, 1-7.

----------. Chaucer's Dares. MP, 15, 1917, 1-22.

ROSENBERG, MELRICH V. Eleanor of Aquitaine, Queen of the Troubadours and of the Courts of Love. Houghton Mifflin, 1937. 303 pp.
    Rev: Sidney Painter, Spec, 12, 1937, 411-2; Arpad Steiner, Commonweal, 25, 1937, 676; G. M., SRL, 15, Mar 13, 1937, 22; Thomas A. Kirby, MLN, 53, 1938, 477-8; Curtis H. Walker, AHR, 43, 1938, 358-9.

ROUTH, H. V. God, Man, and Epic Poetry: A Study in Comparative Literature. Cambridge Univ Press, 1927. Vol. 2, Medieval, 283 pp.
    Religious elements in medieval literature.
    Rev: TLS, Sept 22, 1927, 640; John A. Scott, Class Journ, 23, 1927, 74-6; NQ, 152, 1927, 323-4; F. P. Magoun, Jr., Spec, 3, 1928, 124-7; C. H. Herford, MLR, 23, 1928, 255-9; Oxford Mag, May 31, 1928, 587.

RUIZ, JUAN. The Book of Good Love. Translated into English Verse by Elisha K. Kane. Privately printed for the translator by William Edwin Rudge, 1933. 320 pp.
    Some resemblances to Chaucer noted.

RUTTER, GEORGE McKELVY. The Influence of Guillaume de Machaut's Dit dou Lion on Chaucer. Master's Thesis, Columbia, 1924.

SCHAAR, CLAES. Notes on Thomas Usk's Testament of
    Love. Lund: G. W. K. Gleerup, 1950. 64 pp.
        Rev: J. S. , Neophilologus, 35, 1951, 182-3.
SCHINNERL, HUBERT. Die Belesenheit Chaucers in der
    Bibel und der antiken Literatur. MS Diss, München,
    1921. Summary, München, 1923. 4 pp.
SCHIRMER, W. F. Boccaccios Werke als Quelle G.
    Chaucers. GRM, 12, 1924, 288-305.
----------. Chaucer, Shakespeare und die Antike. 83-102,
    in England und die Antike. Vorträge der Bibliothek War-
    burg, 1930-1931. Berlin and Leipzig: Teubner, 1931.
SCHLEICH, G. Die me. Umdichtung von Boccaccios De
    claris mulieribus nebst der lateinischen Vorlage zum
    erstmal hg. Palaestra, 144. Mayer and Müller, 1924.
        Rev: F. Holthausen, AB, 36, 1925, 235-6; F. Wild,
    ES, 60, 1926, 327-30.
SEIBERT, HARRIET. Chaucer and Horace. MLN, 31,
    1916, 304-7.
SHANNON, EDGAR F. Chaucer and Lucan's Pharsalia.
    MP, 16, 1919, 609-14.
----------. Chaucer and the Roman Poets. Harvard
    Studies in Comparative Literature, no. 7. Harvard
    Univ Press, 1929. 401 pp.
        Rev: TLS, Sept 26, 1929, 740; Mabel Day, RES, 6,
    1930, 334-6; S. B. Meech, JEGP, 29, 1930, 435-9;
    M. Y. Hughes, Univ Calif Chron, 32, 1930, 140-2;
    H. R. Patch, Spec, 5, 1930, 332-5; E. H. Haight,
    AJP, 51, 1930, 81-3; M. Praz, E Stud, 12, 1930, 68-
    9; H. Lüdeke, AB, 42, 1931, 12-17; P. F. Baum,
    SAQ, 30, 1931, 108-10; M. B. Ruud, MLN, 45, 1930,
    290; Dorothy Everett, YWES, 103-6.
----------. Notes on Chaucer. MP, 11, 1913, 227-36.
SMITH, GEORGIANA E. The Influence of the English
    Queen Consorts on English Literature. Doctoral
    Diss, Iowa, 1927.
SMITH, Sister MARY FRANCES. Wisdom and Personi-
    fication of Wisdom Occurring in Middle English Lit-
    erature before 1500. Diss of the Catholic Univ of
    America, Washington, D. C. , 1935. 199 pp.
SMITH, ROBERT METCALF. Froissart and the English
    Chronicle Play. Columbia Univ Studies in English and
    Comparative Literature. Doctoral Diss, Columbia,
    1915. Columbia Univ Press, 1915. 165 pp.

SMITH, ROLAND M. Five Notes on Chaucer and Frois-
    sart. MLN, 66, 1951, 27-32.
        1. Dane and Diane, KnT, 2862-4; 2. Actaeon, KnT,
    2065-8; Candace, PF, 288; 4. The "Absolon" Balade,
    LGW, F. 249-69; 5. Conquerour of Brutes Albyon,
    Purse, 22.
SPENCER, THEODORE. Chaucer's Hell: A Study in
    Mediaeval Convention. Spec, 2, 1927, 177-200.
STEVENSON, J. H. Chaucer and Theodulus. Athen, 1902,
    I, 338.
STILLWELL, GARDINER B. Chaucer Studies: 1. The Po-
    litical Meaning of the Tale of Melibee; 2. Chaucer's
    Plowman and the Contemporary English Peasant;
    3. Important Analogues to the Manciple's Tale in the
    Ovide Moralisé and Machaut's Voir-dit. Programs
    Announcing Candidates for Higher Degrees, Univ of
    Iowa, 1940.
TATLOCK, JOHN STRONG PERRY. Notes on Chaucer:
    Earlier or Minor Poems. MLN, 29, 1914, 97-101.
        Dante.
        Rev: John Koch, AB, 25, 1914, 339-42.
----------. Chaucer and Dante. MLN, 30, 1906, 367-72.
        Concerns T&C, V, 743-9; LGW, A (G) 206-7; B
    (F) 252-3, and passages on Fortune.
----------. Chaucer and the Legenda Aurea. MLN, 45,
    1930, 296-8.
----------. Interpreting Literature by History. Spec,
    12, 1937, 390-5.
        The tradition of the Middle Ages with significant
    references to Chaucerian scholarship.
----------. The Mind and Art of Chaucer. Syracuse
    Univ Press, 1950. 114 pp.
        Concerns Chaucer and the French tradition.
        For reviews and list of chapters, see section:
    General Criticism.
THOMPSON, A. HAMILTON. Classical Echoes in Medi-
    eval Authors. History, 33, 1948, 29-48.
        Influence of John of Salisbury and Alanus on Chau-
    cer.
THOMSON, J. A. K. The Classical Background of Eng-
    lish Literature. Allen and Unwin, 1948. 272 pp.
TORRACA, F. Scritti Vari. Soc Dante, 1928. 523 pp.
        On Chaucer and Boccaccio.

TOYNBEE, PAGET. The Author of Chaucer's "Book
    Cleped Valerie." Acad, 40, 1891, 588-9.
----------. Dante in English Literature from Chaucer
    to Cary. Macmillan, 1908. 2 vols.
        Rev: Nation, 89, 1909, 161-3. See also Edinburgh
    Rev, 207, 1908, 398-420.
----------. The Liber de Nuptiis of Theophrastus in
    Medieval Literature. Acad, 42, 1892, 616.
TRAVERSARI, GUIDO. Bibliografia Boccaccesca. Città
    di Castello, 1907. 272 pp.
TRIGONA, F. PRESTIFILIPPO. Chaucer Imitatore del
    Boccaccio. Studio Editoriale Moderno, 1923.
        Rev: TLS, Aug 16, 1923.
TUPPER, FREDERICK. Chaucer's Bed's Head. MLN,
    30, 1915, 5-12.
        Chaucer and Ambrose; Jerome and the Summoner's
    Friar; Chaucer and the Prymer; a Parallel to the
    Parson's Tale.
----------. Chaucer's Trophee. MLN, 31, 1916, 11-14.
----------. The Envy Theme in the Prologue and Epi-
    logues. JEGP, 16, 1917, 555-7.
----------. Twelfth Century Scholarship and Satire. In
    Essays and Studies in Honor of Carleton Brown, New
    York Univ Press, 1940, 46-61.
VOIGHT, MAX. Beiträge zur Geschichte der Vision-
    literatur im Mittelalter. Palaestra, 146. Mayer and
    Müller, 1924.
WILCOX, LELAND FORD. An Index of Analogues in
    Fourteenth-Century English Literature to Gower's
    Tales in Confessio Amantis. Master's Thesis, Stan-
    ford, 1931.
WILSON, R. M. The Lost Literature of Medieval
    England. New York: The Philosophical Library,
    1952.
        Rev: Robt. A. Caldwell, JEGP, 52, 1953, 399-400;
    C. E. Wright, RES, n. s. 4, 1953, 151-3.
WIMSATT, W. K. , Jr. Vincent of Beauvais and Chau-
    cer's Cleopatra and Croesus. Spec, 12, 1937, 375-81.
        Rev: D. Everett, YWES, 76.
WISE, B. A. The Influence of Statius upon Chaucer.
    Johns Hopkins Diss, 1911. Jsb, 33, 1911, xvi, 204a.
WOLFERS, THEODORE. Geschichte der englischen

Marienlyrik im Mittelalter. Anglia, 69, 1950, 3-88.
For Chaucer, see 28-37.
Rev: G. D. Willcock, YWES, 83-4.

WRENN, C. L. Chaucer's Knowledge of Horace. MLR,
18, 1923, 286-92.

YOUNG, KARL. Chaucer and Peter Riga. Spec, 12, 1937,
299-303.
Rev: D. Everett, YWES, 74-5.

----------. Chaucer and Aulus Gellius. MLN, 52, 1937,
347-51.
Rev: D. Everett, YWES, 71-2.

----------. Chaucer and the Liturgy. MLN, 30, 1915,
97-99.

----------. Chaucer's Aphorisms from Ptolemy. SP,
34, 1937, 1-7.
Rev: D. Everett, YWES, 84.

----------. The Plan of the Canterbury Tales. Anniversary Papers (Kittredge). 405 ff. Ginn, 1913.
Chaucer and Sercambi.

----------. Machaut's Dit de la Harpe. In Essays in
Honor of Albert Feuillerat, ed by Henri M. Peyre.
Yale Romanic Studies, 22. Yale Univ Press; London:
Milford, 1943. 294 pp.
An editing of the Dit.
Rev: A. Lytton Sells, MLR, 40, 1945, 141.

----------. Chaucer and Geoffrey de Vinsauf. MP, 41,
1944, 172-82.
Prints parts of a version of Nova Poetrie and certain glosses hitherto unpublished.
Rev: D. Everett, YWES, 45-6.

INFLUENCE AND ALLUSIONS

See Hammond, 50, 237-8; Speirs, 15-25; Wells, 1529, 1640, 1731, 1925, and CBEL, I, 215-7; also The English Chaucerians, CBEL, I, 250-4 (Sybil Rosenfeld), and The Middle Scotch Writers, 254-60 (G. G. Smith; Rev by D. Hamer).

ADAMS, JOHN Q. Willyam Goddard. MLN, 32, 1917, 187.

AINGER, ALFRED. The Influence of Chaucer upon his Successors. 136-51, in Lectures and Essays, Vol. 2, Macmillan, 1905.

ALDERSON, WILLIAM L. A Check-List of Supplements to Spurgeon's Chaucer Allusions. PQ, 32, 1953, 418-27.

  Corrects some references in Spurgeon and notes duplication of references published.

ALLEN, DON C. A Chaucer Allusion. TLS, May 23, 1936, 440.

ANDRAE, AUGUST. Zu Longfellows und Chaucers Tales. AB, 27, 1916, 56-62, 84-7. See also AB, 17, 1906, 70 ff.

ANON. For Geoffrey Chaucer. Poem. Literary Digest, 110, 1931, 23.

----------. Song of Troilus, by Francesco Petrarch, trans by G. Chaucer. Golden Book, 15, Feb, 1932, 112.

----------. Whan That Aprille --. Atlantic, 145, 1930, 568.

ASHTON, J. W. Three Sixteenth Century Allusions to Chaucer. PQ, 13, 1934, 82-3.

  Rev: D. Everett, YWES, 103.

ATKINSON, DOROTHY F. Chaucer Allusions. NQ, 169, 1935, 116; NQ, 169, 1935, 205; E. S. Chalk, NQ, 169, 1935, 241; NQ, 170, 1936, 207.

----------. References to Chaucer. NQ, 168, 1935, 313.

  Rev: D. Everett, YWES, 117.

----------. Some Notes on Heraldry and Chaucer. MLN,
    51, 1936, 328-31.
        See Alderson, above in this section, 421.
----------. Some Further Chaucer Allusions. MLN, 55,
    1940, 361-2.
        From 16th and 17th century books of heraldry and
    dictionaries.
----------. Some Further Chaucer Allusions. MLN, 59,
    1944, 568-70.
        Rev: D. Everett, YWES, 54.
ATWOOD, E. BAGBY. Some Minor Sources of Lydgate's
    Troy Book. SP, 35, 1938, 36-42.
AURNER, NELLIE SLAYTON. Caxton: Mirrour of Fif-
    teenth-Century Letters: A Study of the Literature of
    the First English Press. Houghton, 1926. 304 pp.
        Chaucer, Gower, Lydgate, 163-75.
BALE, JOHN E. The Place of Chaucer in Sixteenth
    Century Literature. Doctoral Diss, Illinois, 1953.
    Microfilmed.
BASHE, E. J. The Prologue of the Tale of Beryn. PQ,
    12, 1933, 1-16.
BENHAM, ALLEN R. Three Chaucer Studies: I, Chaucer
    and the Renaissance; III, Chaucer and Molière. SAQ,
    20, 1921, 330-48.
BENNETT, JOSEPHINE WATERS. The Evolution of The
    Faerie Queene. Univ of Chicago Press, 1942.
        Influence of WBT, KnT, SqT, MerT, and Sir Tho-
    pas.
        Rev: D. J. Gordon, YWES, 23, 1942, 137-8; TLS,
    1943, 270.
BENSUSAN, S. L. The Bee in Literature. QR, 241, 1924,
    270-92.
        Chaucer, 278.
BERDAN, JOHN M. Early Tudor Poetry. Macmillan,
    1920.
        See 48 ff. and other references.
BERKELMAN, ROBERT G. Chaucer and Masefield. EJ,
    16, 1927, 698-705.
BETHURUM, D. Shakespeare's Comment on Medieval
    Romance in Midsummer Night's Dream. MLN, 60,
    1945, 85-94.
        Influence of Sir Thopas.
        Rev: Allardyce Nicoll, YWES, 92.

BOAS, GUY. Chaucer and Spenser Contrasted as Narra-
tive Poets. Thomas Nelson and Sons, 1926.
BOND, RICHMOND P. , JOHN W. BOWYER, C. B.
MILLICAN, and G. HUBERT SMITH. A Collection of
Chaucer Allusions. SP, 28, 1931, 481-512.
    Passages quoted.
BOND, RICHMOND P. Some Eighteenth Century Chaucer
Allusions. SP, 25, 1928, 316-39.
BONNER, FRANCIS W. Chaucer's Reputation during the
Romantic Period. Bull of Furman Univ, 34, 4, 1951, 1-21.
----------. A History of the Chaucer Apocrypha. Doc-
toral Diss, Univ of North Carolina, 1949.
BOSWELL, ELEANORE. Chaucer, Dryden, and the
Laureateship. RES, 7, 1931, 337-9.
BOWERS, R. H. Thomas Randolph Alludes to Chaucer.
PQ, 12, 1933, 314.
    See Alderson, above in this section, 422.
----------. R. H. Brathwaite's "Comments" upon Chau-
cer. NQ, 196, 1951, 558-9.
BOYS, RICHARD C. Some Chaucer Allusions, 1705-1799.
PQ, 17, 1938, 263-70.
    Bibliography of allusions since last supplement of
Spurgeon, below. See also Alderson, 422.
    Rev: D. Everett, YWES, 79.
----------. Some Modern Variations of "January and
May." NQ, 172, 1937, 8.
BRADNER, LEICESTER. References to Chaucer in
Campion's Poemata. RES, 12, 1936, 322-3.
BRESSIE, RAMONA. The Date of Thomas Usk's Testa-
ment of Love. MP, 26, 1928, 17-29.
BROWN, CARLETON. Lydgate and the Legend of Good
Women. ESt, 47, 1913, 59-62.
BUDD, F. E. Shakespeare, Chaucer, and Harsnett. RES,
11, 1935, 421-9.
BUNN, OLENA S. A Bibliography of Chaucer in English
and American Belles-Lettres since 1900. Bull Bibli-
ography, 19, 1949, 205-8.
    Lists allusions, including Vallens, with notes.
CAMDEN, CARROLL, Jr. Chaucer and Elizabethan
Astrology. MLN, 45, 1930, 298-9.
----------. Chaucer and Greene. RES, 6, 1930, 73-4.
CAMPBELL, GERTRUDE H. Chaucer's Prophecy in
1586. MLN, 29, 1914, 195-6.

CANBY, HENRY S. The Short Story in English. Holt, 1909.
     See 78-100.
CARPENTER, FREDERICK I. A Reference Guide to
     Edmund Spenser. Univ of Chicago Press, 1923.
          See 141 ff.
          Rev: MLR, 19, 1924, 258-9.
CAWLEY, ROBERT R. A Chaucerian Echo in Spenser.
     MLN, 41, 1926, 313-4.
CHALK, EDWIN S. Chaucer Allusions. NQ, 169, 1935,
     241, and 170, 1936, 207.
          Rev: D. Everett, YWES, 99.
CHAPPELL, LOUIS W. Another Canterbury Tale. MLN,
     50, 1935, 87-8.
          An allusion by William Byrd.
          Rev: D. Everett, YWES, 117.
CHUTE, MARCHETTE. Chaucer and Shakespeare. CE,
     12, 1950, 15-19.
COLERIDGE, EDITH. Sara Coleridge: Memoir and Letters.
     Harpers, 1874.
          Chaucer and Dryden compared, 80-1, 90-1. Con-
     tributed by Professor Garland Ethel.
COOK, ALBERT S. Skelton's Garland of Laurel and
     Chaucer's House of Fame. MLR, 11, 1916, 9-14.
DANDRIDGE, EDMUND P., Jr. An Eighteenth-Century
     Theft of Chaucer's Purse. MLN, 68, 1953, 237-8.
DART, JOHN. The Complaint of the Black Knight. 1718, 1720.
DENNIS, LEAH. "Blandamour" in the Percy-Ritson
     Controversy. MP, 29, 1931, 232-4.
          See Magoun, below in this section.
DE SELINCOURT, E., Ed. The Poetical Works of
     William Wordsworth. Oxford: Clarendon Press, 1947.
          Wordsworth's Englishing of Chaucer, Vol. IV,
     209-33, 358-65, and notes, 443-5.
DE VOCHT, H. Chaucer and Erasmus. ES, 41, 1910, 385-92.
DICKINS, BRUCE, Ed. The Testament of Cresseid, by
     Robert Henryson. Porpoise Press, 1925. 46 pp. Lim-
     ited ed. Revision, 1943.
          Rev: Dorothy Everett, YWES, 103.
DOBBINS, AUSTIN C. The Employment of Chaucer by
     Dryden and Pope. Doctoral Diss, North Carolina,
     1951. Abstract publ.
----------. More Seventeenth-Century Chaucer Allu-
     sions. MLN, 68, 1953, 33-4.

DODDS, M. H. A Chaucer Allusion of 1610. NQ, 159,
    1930, 258.
----------. Chaucer: Spenser: Milton in Drama and
    Fiction. NQ, 176, Jan 28, 1939, 69, and T. O. M.,
    176, Feb 4, 1939, 89.
DRYDEN, JOHN. Dryden's Chaucer. Being Part of
    "Fables," ed by W. Roy Macklin. The Socrates Book-
    lets, VIII. A. & C. Black, Ltd, 1927.
EMERSON, FRANCIS W. Why Milton Uses Cambuscan
    and Camball. MLN, 47, 1932, 153.
----------. The Spenser in John Lane's Chaucer. SP,
    29, 1932, 406-8.
ERDMANN, AXEL, and EILERT EKWALL, Eds. Lyd-
    gate's Siege of Thebes. Oxford Univ Press for
    EETS, 1930. 220 pp.
        Contains comparisons between Lydgate and Chaucer.
ERICSON, ESTON E. Chaucer in Fiction. NQ, 180, Feb
    22, 1941, 134.
        Chaucer as a character in an anonymous short
    story in Brother Jonathan, New York, 1843, Vol. IV.
FARNHAM, WILLARD. The Merchant's Tale in Chaucer
    Junior. MLN, 41, 1926, 392-6.
        The Merchant's Tale and the Miller's Tale retold
    in a 17th century jest book.
FORSE, EDWARD J. G. Chaucer in Fiction. NQ, 190,
    Mar 8, 1941, 178.
        From Willard B. Nichols, Deputy for Youth. Ward,
    Lock, 1935.
FURNISS, W. TODD. Gascoigne and Chaucer's "Pesen."
    MLN, 68, 1953, 115-8.
GEBHARDT, E. R. Ben Jonson's Appreciation of Chau-
    cer as Evidenced in the English Grammar. MLN, 49,
    1934, 452-4.
        Rev: D. Everett, YWES, 103.
GEROULD, GORDON H. Deschamps as Eustace. MLN,
    33, 1918, 437-8.
        See Jenkins in this section.
GOLDING, LOUIS. The Scottish Chaucerians. Sat Rev,
    Nov 25, 1922, 782-3.
GOLDSMITH, THEODORA. Chaucer in the Drama of the
    Sixteenth Century. Master's Thesis, Columbia, 1907.
GOUGHENHEIM, G. Une Mention de Chaucer en France
    au XVIe Siècle. RAA, 11, 1934, 330-1.

GRAVES, THORNTON S. Some Chaucer Allusions. SP,
   20, 1923, 469-78.
GREEN, HENRY, Ed. Whitney's Choice of Emblems.
   London, 1866.
      Facsimile reprint with introductory dissertation,
   essays literary and bibliographical, and explanatory
   notes. Parallels from Chaucer, Spenser, and
   Shakespeare.
HALL, VERNON, Jr. Sherlock Holmes and the Wife of
   Bath. Baker Street Jour, 3, 1948, 84-93.
      Holmes "discovers" that the Wife of Bath is respon-
   sible for the murder of her fourth husband.
HAMMOND, ELEANOR P. Lydgate's Prologue to the
   Story of Thebes. Ang, 36, 1912, 360-76.
----------. Chaucer and Lydgate Notes. MLN, 27, 1912,
   91-2.
      Reference to Chaucer in Thomson's Seasons.
HARRIS, BRICE. Some Seventeenth Century Chaucer
   Allusions. PQ, 18, 1939, 395-405.
      Bibliography of allusions since last supplement of
   Spurgeon. See Alderson, above in this section, 422.
HART, WALTER M. The Pardoner's Tale and Der Dot
   im Stock. MP, 9, 1911, 17-22.
      Chaucer and Hans Sachs.
HEILMAN, ROBERT B. Three Modern Chaucer Allusions.
   NQ, 176, 1939, 117.
      Bliss Perry, T. S. Eliot, Dos Passos.
HENCH, ATCHESON L. Dunmow Bacon, 1949. CE, 11,
   1950, 350.
      Recent instance of contest referred to in WB Prol,
   217-8.
----------. The Dunmow Flitch Trials of 1949. South-
   ern Folklore Quart, 16, 1952, 128-31.
HERTWIG, DORIS. Der Einfluss von Chaucers Canterbury
   Tales auf die englische Literatur. Marburg Diss, 1908.
HILLYER, ROBERT. For Maistre Geoffrey Chaucer.
   A Poem. Outlook, 131, 1922, 491.
HOLMES, OLIVER WENDELL. At the Pantomime, lines
   34-6. Page 85 in Oliver Wendell Holmes: Represent-
   ative Selections, S. I. Hayakawa and Howard Mum-
   ford Jones, Eds, American Book Co, 1929.
HOOKER, EDWARD NILES. Johnson's Understanding of
   Chaucer's Metrics. MLN, 48, 1933, 150-1.

HORN, ANGIE. Chaucer and Morris. M. A. Diss, Kan-
sas, 1904.
HORNSBY, ESTELLE MAY. A Project in High-School
English. EJ (High School ed), 20, 1931, 668-9.
Class set first lines of Prologue to music and gave
pageant.
HORNSTEIN, LILLIAN H. Some Chaucer Allusions by
Sir Edward Coke. MLN, 60, 1945, 483-6.
Rev: D. Everett, YWES, 59-60.
HOUSMAN, A. E. The Name and Nature of Poetry. Mac-
millan, 1933. 50 pp.
Some comments on Dryden's translations of Chau-
cer, 20-3.
Rev: E. L. Walton, NYHTB, June 4, 1933, 5; L. A.
MacKay, Canadian Forum, 13, 1933, 431; CW, 137, 1933,
753; Nation, 136, 1933, 685; G. W. Stonier, NSt, 5, 1933,
856; P. H. , NYTBR, June 4, 1933, 2; R. Humphries,
Poetry, 43, 1933, 52; A. Sampson, Sat Rev, 155, 1933,
600; B. Davenport, SRL, 9, July 1, 1933, 673; SRL, 10,
Sept 23, 1933, 128; TLS, June 1, 1933, 369; C. B. Tinker,
YR, 23, 1933, 167.
HUNTER, ALFRED C. Le Conte de la Femme de Bath en
Français au XVIIIe Siècle. Rev Litt Comp, 9, 1929, 117-40.
INQUIRER. A XVII-Century Chaucer Allusion. NQ, 174,
1938, 174.
Criticizes Sloane, below in this section.
JACK, ADOLPHUS A. A Commentary on the Poetry of
Chaucer and Spenser. Glasgow: Maclehose and Jack-
son; Macmillan, 1920.
See 117 ff. , Apocrypha and Imitations.
For reviews, see section: General Criticism.
JENKINS, T. ATKINSON. Deschamps' Ballade to Chau-
cer. MLN, 33, 1918, 268-87.
See Gerould, above in this section.
JONES, CLAUDE E. Poetry and the Critical Review:
1756-1785. MLQ, 9, 1948, 17-36.
See note on p. 32.
KELLETT, E. E. Chaucer and his Influence. 1-31, in
Reconsiderations. Literary Essays. Cambridge Univ
Press, 1928.
Rev: TLS, June 28, 1928, 482.
KIPLING, RUDYARD. The Justice's Tale: Chaucer.
P. 119 in Muse among the Motors, bound with The

Years Between and Parodies. The Mandalay Edition.
Doubleday, 1925. Also in Rudyard Kipling's Verse,
682-3, with Consolations of Memory Done Out of
Boethius by Geoffrey Chaucer. Doubleday, 1940.
KIRBY, THOMAS A. Further Seventeenth-Century
Chaucer Allusions. MLN, 64, 1949, 81-2.
    Rev: D. Everett, YWES, 71.
----------. Carlyle on Chaucer. MLN, 61, 1946, 184-5.
----------. J. Q. Adams and Chaucer. MLN, 61, 1946,
185-6.
----------. The Pardoner's Tale and The Treasure of
Sierra Madre. MLN, 66, 1951, 269-70.
    A modern analogue.
----------. A Twentieth-Century Wife of Bath. MLN,
67, 1952, 321-5.
    Nedra Tyre, Red Wine First, "The Woman Who
Had Five Husbands," 1947.
----------. Theodore Roosevelt's Comments on Chau-
cer and a Chaucerian. MLN, 68, 1953, 34-7.
    Comment on Loundsbury, Studies in Chaucer.
----------. Browning on Chaucer. MLN, 68, 1953, 552-3.
    Browning in a letter to Edward Moxon.
KOLLER, KATHRINE. A Chaucer Allusion. MLN, 52,
1937, 568-70.
    Norden's Labyrinth of Man's Life.
    Rev: D. Everett, YWES, 88.
KUHL, ERNEST P. Chaucer and Thomas Nash. TLS,
Nov 5, 1925, 739.
----------. Chaucer in Tennessee. TLS, Nov 27, 1937, 911.
    Also mentioned in Quercus' column, SRL, 17, Jan
8, 1938, 24.
----------. Francis Beaumont and Chaucer. TLS, Sept
23, 1926, 632.
    Identification of the Francis Beaumont who defend-
ed Chaucer in 1597, before Speght.
LAM, GEORGE L., and WARREN H. SMITH. George
Vertue's Contributions to Chaucer Iconography. MLQ,
5, 1944, 303-22.
    Rev: D. Everett, YWES, 54-6.
LERCH, EUGEN. Zu eine Stelle bei Eustace Deschamps.
Rom Forsch, 62, 1950, 67-8.
    On Deschamps' Balade to Chaucer, especially the
word "pandras."

LINTHICUM, M. CHANNING. Three Chaucer Allusions
    in Sixteenth Century Libraries. PQ, 12, 1933, 409-10.
LONG, PERCY W. From Troilus to Euphues. Anniver-
    sary Papers (Kittredge), 367 ff. Ginn, 1913.
LONG, RICHARD A. John Heywood, Chaucer, and Lyd-
    gate. MLN, 64, 1949, 55-6.
    Rev: D. Everett, YWES, 71.
MACKERNESS, E. D. A Chaucer Allusion of 1598. NQ,
    194, Dec 24, 1949, 554.
    Rev: D. Everett, YWES, 71.
McMANAWAY, JAMES G. A Chaucerian Fisherman (?).
    MLN, 53, 1938, 422-3.
    Rev: D. Everett, YWES, 79.
McNEAL, THOMAS H. The Influence of Chaucer on the
    Works of Robert Greene. Doctoral Diss, Univ of
    Texas, 1937.
----------. The Clerk's Tale as a Possible Source for
    Pandosto. PMLA, 47, 1932, 453-60.
MAGOUN, F. P., Jr. The Chaucer of Spenser and Mil-
    ton. MP, 25, 1927, 129-36.
    See Leah Dennis, above in this section.
MARKINO, Y. Chaucer and the Chinese Odes. English
    Rev, 27, 1918, 29-38.
MAURY, ANNE FONTAINE. May Day in Canterbury: A
    Chaucerian Festival Celebrated at Wheaton College,
    May 23, 1926. Walter H. Baker Co, 1925. 69 pp.
MEECH, S. B., and H. E. ALLEN, Eds. The Book of
    Margery Kempe. Vol. I, The Text of the Unique Ms
    Owned by Colonel W. Butler-Bowden. EETS, original
    series, 212. London: Milford, 1940. 441 pp.
    Rev: G. R. Coffman, Spec, 17, 1942, 138-41.
MILLER, MILTON. Definition by Comparison: Chaucer,
    Lawrence, and Joyce. In Essays in Criticism, III,
    369-81.
MITCHELL, P. BEATTIE. An Allusion to Chaucer in
    the Seventeenth Century. MLN, 51, 1936, 437.
    Mercurius Britanicus, no. 103.
    Rev: D. Everett, YWES, 86.
----------. A Chaucer Allusion in a 1644 Pamphlet.
    MLN, 51, 1936, 435-7.
    Rev: D. Everett, YWES, 85.
MOON, A. R. Two References to Chaucer Made by
    Nicholas Udall. MLR, 21, 1926, 426-7.

MORLEY, CHRISTOPHER. Ballade of an Old Friend.
New Yorker, May 22, 1937, 27.
----------. The Trojan Horse. Lippincott, 1937. 248 pp.
See also Morley's explanation of the theme of the
book, SRL, 17, Nov 27, 1937, 16-17.
Rev: P. M. Jack, N. Y. Times Book Rev, Nov 28,
1937, 4; Edward Weeks, SRL, 17, Dec 4, 1937, 6;
John Patton, N. Y. Herald-Tribune Books, Nov 28,
1937, 4; TLS, Mar 5, 1938, 155-6.
MOUNTS, C. E. The Place of Chaucer and Spenser in
the Genesis of Peter Bell. PQ, 23, 1944, 108-15.
Refers to the House of Fame and the Squire's Tale.
NADAL, THOMAS W. Spenser's Daphnaida and Chaucer's
Book of the Duchess. PMLA, 23, 1908, 646-61.
----------. Spenser's Muiopotmos in Relation to Chau-
cer's Sir Thopas and the Nun's Priest's Tale. PMLA,
25, 1910, 640-56.
NICHOLS, PIERREPONT HERRICK. Lydgate's Influence
on the Aureate Terms of the Scottish Chaucerians.
PMLA, 47, 1932, 516-22.
Such terms due to Lydgate's influence, not Chaucer's.
Rev: Dorothy Everett, YWES, 123-4.
OLIVE, W. J. A Chaucer Allusion in Jonson's Bartholo-
mew Fair. MLQ, 13, 1952, 21-2.
OLIVER, ANNA M. Chaucer Allusions in Eighteenth
Century Minor Poetry. NQ, 174, Feb 5, 1938, 97-8.
See Alderson, above in this section, 421.
ORD, HUBERT. Chaucer and the Rival Poet in Shake-
speare's Sonnets. Everyman Library. Dent; Dutton,
1921. 64 pp.
Rev: CR, 121, 1922, 134-5; TLS, May 4, 1922
(Ord's reply, TLS, May 18, 1922); Literary Rev, Feb
18, 1922, 435.
PARKER, W. R. Chaucer Theme Topics. EJ, 21, 1932,
146-8.
PARR, JOHNSTONE. Chaucer and Partonope of Blois.
MLN, 60, 1945, 486-7.
See R. M. Smith, below in this section.
PARSONS, C. O. A Scottish Sequel to the Wife of Bath's
Prologue. Scottish Notes and Queries, Mar, 1933, 33-5.
PATCH, HOWARD R. Notes on Spenser and Chaucer.
MLN, 33, 1919, 177-80.
Also Dekker.

PERCIVAL-KAYE, GEORGE. Chaucer in Fiction. NQ,
   190, Mar 29, 1941, 233.
   Desmond, The Golden Quill, 1926.
PETERSEN, OTTOMAR. Two Noble Kinsmen. Ang, 38,
   1914, 213-26.
POPE, EMMA FIELD. The Critical Background of the
   Spenserian Stanza. MP, 24, 1926, 31-53.
   Mention of Chaucer as a Spenser model.
POTTS, ABBIE FINDLAY. A Letter from Wordsworth
   to Thomas Powell. MLN, 45, 1930, 215-8.
PRATT, ROBERT A. Two Chaucer Allusions: 1819 and
   1899. MLN, 63, 1948, 55-6.
   Rev: D. Everett, YWES, 94.
PRIESTLY, F. E. L. Keats and Chaucer. MLQ, 5, 1944,
   439-47.
RATHBORNE, ISABEL E. The Meaning of Spenser's
   Fairyland. Columbia Univ Press, 1937. 275 pp.
   See 41-8.
   Rev: TLS, Feb 12, 1938, 105; R. E. Keighton,
   Crozer Quart, 15, 1938, 145.
RIBNER, IRVING. A 1576 Allusion to Chaucer. NQ, 195,
   1950, 24.
   Ulpian Fulwell, Ars Adulandi.
   Rev: D. Everett, YWES, 69-70.
RINGLER, WILLIAM. An Early Chaucer Allusion Re-
   stored. NQ, 174, Feb 12, 1938, 120.
   Rev: D. Everett, YWES, 79.
ROBERTSON, STUART. Chaucer and Wordsworth. MLN,
   43, 1928, 104-5.
ROLLINS, HYDER E. The Troilus-Criseyde Story
   from Chaucer to Shakespeare. PMLA, 32, 1917, 383-
   429.
ROOT, ROBERT K. Shakespeare Misreads Chaucer.
   MLN, 38, 1923, 346-8.
   Merchant of Venice.
ROSENTHAL, BRUNO. Spensers Verhältnis zu Chaucer.
   Kiel Diss, Berlin, 1911.
SACKTON, ALEXANDER H. A Note on Keats and Chau-
   cer. MLQ, 13, 1952, 37-40.
   Lamia and opening lines of WBT.
SAINTSBURY, GEORGE. The English Chaucerians. Vol.
   2, 197-222, in Cambridge History of English Litera-
   ture. 3rd impression. Macmillan, 1920.

SALE, ARTHUR. Chaucer in Cancer. English, 6, 1947, 240-4.

Influence of Chaucer on Crabbe.

SANDISON, HELEN E. An Elizabethan Economist's Method of Literary Composition. HLQ, 6, 1943, 205-11.

The curious use to which the Elizabethan, Gerald de Malynes, put his knowledge of Chaucer.

Rev: D. Everett, YWES, 52, and D. J. Gordon, 139.

SCHOECK, R. J. "Goe Little Book": A Conceit from Chaucer to William Meredith. NQ, 197, 1952, 370-2, and 413.

SCHULTZ, J. R. Sir Walter Scott and Chaucer. MLN, 28, 1913, 246-7.

SCHULZE, K. Zu Chaucers Weib von Bath und Shakespeares Kaufmann von Venedig. GRM, 8, 1920, 103-5.

SCOTT-THOMAS, H. F. A Chaucerian (?) Fisherman. MLN, 54, 1939, 448-9.

SEATON, ETHEL. "That Scotch Copy of Chaucer." JEGP, 47, 1948, 352-6.

Rev: D. Everett, YWES, 76.

SELLS, A. LYTTON. Boccaccio, Chaucer, and Stendhal. Rivista di Letterature Moderne, Settembre-Decembre, 1947. Astrl: Casa Editrice Arethusa.

Rev: D. Everett, YWES, 77-8. Not seen.

SHAVER, CHESTER LINN. Two Eighteenth-Century Modernizations of Chaucer. Harvard Studies and Notes, 16, 1934, 199-201.

SLOANE, WILLIAM. A XVII-Century Chaucer Allusion. NQ, 173, 1937, 226.

In schoolboy exercises and quite inaccurate, 1672.

Rev: D. Everett, YWES, 88.

SMITH, LOUISE. The Indebtedness of William Morris to Chaucer. M.A. Diss, Kansas, 1903.

SMITH, G. GREGORY. The Scottish Chaucerians. Vol. 2, 223-38 in Cambridge History of English Literature. 3rd impression. Macmillan, 1920.

SMITH, ROLAND M. Two Scottish Chaucerians: Modern Versions in Rime Royal of the King's Quair and the Testament of Cressid. Wesleyan Univ, 1935. 100 pp.

----------. Chaucer Allusions in the Letters of Sir Walter Scott. MLN, 65, 1950, 448-55.

Rev: D. Everett, YWES, 70.

SNELL, F. S. Chaucer's Canterbury Tales: Early
Reference. NQ, ser. 11, 2, 1910, 26.
SNYDER, FRANKLIN B. Sir Thomas Norray and Sir
Thopas. MLN, 25, 1910, 78-80.
On Chaucer and Dunbar.
SPURGEON, CAROLINE F. E. Chaucer devant la Cri-
tique en Angleterre et en France depuis son Temps
jusqu'à nos Jours. Paris, 1911.
Rev: Cbl, 63, 1035-6; Rev Germ, 7, 605, and 8,
75-6; Arch, 128, 449-50; DL, 33, 870-2.
----------. Five Hundred Years of Chaucer Criticism
and Allusion, 1357-1900. Cambridge Univ Press, 1925.
3 vols.
See pt. 4, appendix A, for index.
Rev: H. S. V. Jones, JEGP, 27, 1928, 555-7; R.
D. French, YR, 17, 1928, 397-400; G. Saintsbury,
Nation-Athen, 38, 1925, 6, 218; D. S. Mirsky, Mercury, 14, 1926, 96; TLS, Nov 5, 1925; NQ, 150, 1926,
71-2; Spect, 135, 1925, 1192; A. W. Reed, RES, 2,
1926, 232-5; G. A. Auden, Antiquaries Jour, 6, 1926,
204; John Manly, NR, 46, 1926, 117-8; J. R. H., MP,
23, 1926, 494-5; Mark Van Doren, Nation, 122, 1926,
234; B. Fehr, AB, 37, 1926, 309-11; John M. Manly,
MLN, 42, 1927, 401-4; Dorothy Everett, YWES, 93-4.
STARNES, D. T. Chaucer, John Lyly, and Sphaera Ci-
vitatis (1588). NQ, 171, 1936, 95.
Rev: D. Everett, YWES, 86.
STEARNS, MARSHALL W. Robert Henryson. Columbia
Univ Press, 1949. 156 pp.
Contains chapter: Henryson and Chaucer.
Rev: H. M. Smyser, MLN, 66, 1951, 409-11; Fran-
cis Lee Utley, MLQ, 12, 1951, 493-7 (see reply to
Utley, 498-9).
----------. Henryson and Chaucer. MLQ, 6, 1945, 271-
84.
Relation of the Testament of Cresseid to Troilus
and Criseyde.
----------. Planet Portraits of Robert Henryson in the
Testament of Cressid. PMLA, 59, 1944, 911-27.
Henryson following Chaucer's example.
STILLWELL, GARDINER. Chaucer in Tartary. RES,
24, 1948, 177-88.
Spenser, Warton, and Milton on the Squire's Tale.

SULLIVAN, FRANK. Allusions to Chaucer. TLS, Sept
   19, 1952, 613.
TATLOCK, JOHN S. P. The Welsh Troilus and Cressida
   and its Relation to Elizabethan Drama. MLR, 10, 1915,
   265-82.
THORP, MARGARET FARRAND. William Allan Neilson.
   Word Study, 13, Feb, 1938, 2-4.
TOBLER, A. Chaucer's Influence on English Literature.
   Zürich Diss. Berne: Haller, 1905.
VINSON, E. Chaucer and the Seniors. EJ, 20, 1931, 813-
   6.
VOGT, GEORGE M. The Wife of Bath's Tale, Women
   Pleased, and La Fée Urgele: A Study in the Trans-
   formation of Folklore Themes in Drama. MLN, 37,
   1922, 339-42.
W., A. T. A XVI Century Allusion to Chaucer. NQ, 159,
   1930, 231.
WAGGONER, GEORGE R. Allusions to Chaucer. TLS,
   Nov 21, 1952, 761.
      John Selden's The Duella, 1610.
WARREN, C. HENRY. The Pilgrim's Way. Spect, 137,
   1926, 513.
      Plea to keep the road to Canterbury "hallowed."
WARTER, JOHN W. Selections from the Letters of Robert Southey. London: Longmans, Brown, 1856, IV, 213.
      "If I were to edit the works of Chaucer, I should
   not think it right to castrate them, because whoever
   buys Chaucer knows what he has to expect. But in
   making selections, it was my duty to be careful that
   nothing should be admitted which might deter a parent
   from putting the volume into the hands of his children.
   This I owe both to myself and you." (Contributed by
   Professor Garland Ethel.)
WATKINS, W. B. C. Johnson and English Poetry before
   1660. Princeton Studies in English, Vol. 13. Princeton
   Univ Press, 1936. 120 pp.
      Rev: Doris B. Saunders, MP, 34, 1937, 326-9.
WELLS, WHITNEY. A New Analogue to the Pardoner's
   Tale. MLN, 40, 1925, 58-9.
      Jack London's use of the plot.
WHITEBREAD, L. Two Chaucer Allusions. NQ, 183,
   Sept 12, 1942, 157-8.
      On Hogge and Roger, Clerk's Prologue.

See M. H. Dodds, NQ, 183, Oct 24, 1942, 266.

WHITFORD, HAROLD C. An Uncollected Sixteenth-
Century Allusion to the House of Fame. MLN, 52,
1937, 31-2.

Rev: D. Everett, YWES, 88.

WHITING, B. J. Some Chaucer Allusions: 1923-42. NQ,
187, 1944, 288-91.

----------. Emerson, Chaucer, and Thomas Wharton.
AL, 17, 1945, 75-8.

The source of an Emerson misquotation from Chaucer.

----------. A Fifteenth Century English Chaucerian: The
Translator of Partonope de Blois. Med Stud, 7, 1945,
40-54.

WILLIAMS, FRANKLIN B., Jr. Unnoted Chaucer Allusions, 1550-1650. PQ, 16, 1937, 67-71.

See Alderson, above in this section, 422.

WILLOUGHBY, EDWIN E. A Chaucer Allusion of 1608.
NQ, 159, 1930, 225.

----------. A Sixteenth Century Allusion to Chaucer.
NQ, 159, 1930, 134-5, 367.

WILSON, ELKIN CALHOUN. Chaucer Allusions. NQ,
173, Dec 25, 1937, 457-8.

See Alderson, above in this section, 421.

WISTER, OWEN. Fifty Years of the Virginian. Univ of
Wyoming Library Associates, 1952.

Several references and observations on Chaucer
in Owen Wister's letters.

WOOLF, HENRY BOSLEY. Thomas Godfrey: Eighteenth
Century Chaucerian. AL, 12, 1941, 486-90.

The first American poet to show definite Chaucerian influence. Shows extent and type of influence of
Chaucer on Godfrey.

----------. Chaucer in Colonial America. Am NQ, 3,
1942, 71-2.

Allusions to Chaucer.

----------. An Eighteenth Century Allusion to Chaucer.
NQ, 192, 1947, 60.

Rev: D. Everett, YWES, 84.

----------. Chaucer Redivivus. MLN, 62, 1947, 258-60.

G. H. Vallins' imitations of Chaucer with list.

----------. Chaucer and Vallins Again. MLN, 67, 1952,
502.

Chaucerian portraits by G. H. Vallins in Punch.

WOOLF, V. S. Pastons and Chaucer. 708-27, in Critical Reader: Poems, Stories, Essays, ed by Wallace Douglas, Roy Lamson, Hallet Darius Smith. Norton, 1949.

WRENN, C. L. On Rereading Spenser's Shepheardes Calendar. Essays and Studies, 29, 1943, 30-49.

    Rev: D. J. Gordon, YWES, 25, 1944, 117-8; Husbands, MLR, 40, 1945, 230; MacDonald, RES, 21, 1945, 339.

WRIGHT, HERBERT G. An Early Allusion to Chaucer? TLS, April 18, 1935, 257.

WRIGHT, LOUIS B. A "Character" from Chaucer in a Seventeenth Century Satire. MLN, 44, 1929, 364-8.

----------. William Painter and the Vogue of Chaucer as a Moral Teacher. MP, 31, 1933, 165-74.

YOUNG, KARL. Chaucer and Aulus Gellius. MLN, 52, 1937, 347-51.

    On Deschamps' Balade to Chaucer with references to literary habits expressed in LGW, HF, and PF.

ZIMANSKY, CURT A. Chaucer and the School of Provence: A Problem in Eighteenth Century Literary History. PQ, 25, 1946, 321-42.

    Rymer's influence in promoting the idea that Chaucer's poetry derived from Provençal poetry; accepted by Dryden, Pope, and others.

    Rev: D. Everett, YWES, 28, 1947, 74.

STYLE
INCLUDING VERSIFICATION

See Legouis, 191-9; Kaluza, 209-15; French, 339-67; Manly, 122-32; Hammond, 464-504; Robinson, xxv-xxxii; Wells, CBEL, I, 218, 1529-30, 1640, 1732, 1926; Speirs, 25-7; Shelly, 39-93. See also sections: Language and General Criticism.

AMOS, FLORA ROSS. Early Theories of Translation. Doctoral Diss, Columbia, 1919. Columbia Univ Studies in English and Comparative Literature. Columbia Univ Press, 1920. 184 pp.

Several references to Chaucer in chapter: The Medieval Period, 3-46.

ATKINS, J. W. H. English Literary Criticism: The Medieval Phase. Cambridge Univ Press, 1943. 211 pp.

For reviews, see section: General Criticism.

BABCOCK, CHARLOTTE F. A Study of the Metrical Use of the Inflectional "E" in Middle English with Particular Reference to Chaucer and Lydgate. PMLA, 29, 1914, 59-92.

BALDWIN, CHARLES S. Cicero on Parnassus. PMLA, 42, 1927, 106-12.

A discussion of Chaucer's various remarks on "colours of rethoryk," especially in the Franklin's Prologue.

----------. Medieval Rhetoric and Poetic (to 1400). Interpreted from Representative Works. Macmillan, 1928. 321 pp.

Medieval Verse Narrative in Chaucer, 280-301.

Rev: Edmond Faral, SRL, 5, 1928, 540; W. B. Sedgwick, Spec, 3, 1928, 599-600; G. Saintsbury, Dial, 85, 1928, 246-8; Theodore Stenberg, Sewanee Rev, 37, 1929, 121-2; Morris W. Croll, MLN, 44, 1929, 63-4; M. W. Bundy, JEGP, 29, 1930, 288-9; E. L. H., QJS, 17, 1931, 120-2.

BARRY, RAYMOND WALKER. The Sententiae in Chau-

cer. Doctoral Diss, Stanford, 1925. Abstract in Abstracts of Dissertations, 1, 1924-6, 91-4.

BENSON, MARIAN E. The Uses of Metaphor and Simile
in The Canterbury Tales. Master's Thesis, Columbia,
1931.

BESCHORNER, FRANZ. Verbale Reime bei Chaucer. Studien zur englischen Philologie, 60. Halle:Niemeyer, 1920.
    Rev: W. Preusler, Cbl, 72, 1921, 396-7; John Koch,
LGRP, 43, 1922, 102-5.

BIHL, J. Die Wirkungen des Rhythmus in der Sprache
von Chaucer und Gower. Anglistische Forschungen,
50. Heidelberg, 1916.
    Rev: E. Björkman, AB, 28, 1917, 10-18; E. Eck-
hardt, ESt, 52, 1918, 94-7; Rudolf Imelmann, NS, 24,
1916, 561-2; John Koch, LGRP, 38, 1917, 312-9; Arch,
135, 1916, 467; K. Brunner, Arch, 138, 1919, 243-4.

BIRNEY, EARLE. Chaucer's Irony. Abstracts of Dissertations, Univ of Toronto, 1936.

----------. English Irony before Chaucer. UTQ, 6, 1937,
538-57.

----------. The Beginnings of Chaucer's Irony. PMLA,
54, 1939, 637-55.

----------. The Two Worlds of Geoffrey Chaucer. Ma-
nitoba Arts Rev, 2, 1941, 3-16.

----------. Is Chaucer's Irony a Modern Discovery?
JEGP, 41, 1942, 303-19.
    Rev: D. Everett, YWES, 66-7.

BLAND, D. S. Chaucer and the Art of Narrative Verse.
English, 7, 1949, 216-20.
    Rev: D. Everett, YWES, 54.

BOAS, GUY. Chaucer and Spenser Contrasted as Narrative Poets. Nelson, 1926.

BOWERS, R. H. A Middle English Treatise on Herme-
neutics. PMLA, 65, 1950, 590-600.
    The four interpretations of scripture and story ex-
plained in an edited manuscript.

BRADDY, HALDEEN. Three Chaucer Notes. 91-9, in
Essays and Studies in Honor of Carleton Brown. New
York, 1940.
    Symbolic colors.

BRADLEY, Sister RITAMARY. Self Revelation in Chaucer's Characters: A Study in Technique. Doctoral
Diss, St. Louis, 1953. Abstract publ.

BRONSON, BERTRAND H. Chaucer's Art in Relation to
his Audience. In Five Studies in Literature, Univ of
California Press, 1940.
  Rev: Morris W. Croll, MLN, 57, 1942, 76; Gal-
way, MLR, 36, 1941, 148-9.
BUCK, HOWARD. Chaucer's Use of Feminine Rhyme.
MP, 26, 1928, 13-14.
CALLAHAN, JOHN LEONARD. A Theory of Esthetic Ac-
cording to the Principles of St. Thomas Aquinas. Doc-
toral Diss, Catholic Univ of America, 1927. Catholic
Univ of America, Washington, D. C. , 1927. 132 pp.
CAPLAN, HARRY. Classical Rhetoric and the Medieval The-
ory of Preaching. Classical Philology, 28, 1933, 73-96.
----------. The Four Senses of Scriptural Interpreta-
tion and the Medieval Theory of Preaching. Spec, 4,
1929, 282-90.
  These four senses were applied by Boccaccio to
story in general.
CLINE, JAMES MASON. A Study in the Prose of Chaucer's Boethius. Doctoral Diss, Princeton. Listed as
completed in Willard, 6, 1928, 69.
COHEN, HELEN LOUISE. The Ballade. Columbia Univ
Press, 1915. 397 pp.
  For reviews, see section: Literary Relations and
Sources.
COOPER, RUSSELL. The English Question Patterns
from 1100 to 1600. Diss, Michigan, 1948.
CORSON, HIRAM. Index of Proper Names and Subjects
to Chaucer's Canterbury Tales Together with Com-
parisons and Similes, Metaphors and Proverbs, Max-
ims, etc. , in the Same. Oxford Univ Press, Chaucer
Society, 1911. 1st ser., no. 72. 121 pp.
  Rev: ESt, 48, 1912, 98-114.
COWLING, G. H. A Note on Chaucer's Stanza. RES, 2,
1926, 311-7.
  See Lineberger, below in this section. Also dis-
cusses chronology.
  Rev: Dorothy Everett, YWES, 7, 1926, 85.
COX, SIDNEY H. Chaucer's Cheerful Cynicism. MLN,
36, 1921, 475-81.
CROSBY, RUTH. Chaucer and the Custom of Oral Deliv-
ery. Spec, 13, 1938, 413-32.
  Rev: D. Everett, YWES, 61-2.

----------. Oral Delivery in the Middle Ages. Spec, 11,
     1936, 88-110.
CURRY, WALTER C. Chaucer's Science and Art. Texas
     Rev, 8, 1923, 307-22.
CUTLER, JOHN L. A Manual of Middle English Stanzaic
     Patterns. Ohio State Univ, Abstracts of Dissertations,
     1948-9, 61-6.
DE BRUYNE, E. Etudes d'Esthétique Médiévale. Brugge,
     1946.
     Includes studies of medieval symbolism.
DEMPSTER, GERMAINE. Dramatic Irony in Chaucer.
     Stanford Univ Publ in Language and Literature, Vol.
     4. Stanford Univ Press, 1932. 104 pp.
        Rev: TLS, Feb 2, 1933, 78; G. Bullough, MLR, 28,
     1933, 503-5; Mabel Day, RES, 9, 1933, 470; Dorothy
     Everett, YWES, 78-9; A. J. Barnouw, E Stud, 16,
     1934, 147-8; Hugo Lange, AB, 47, 1936, 10; H. R.
     Patch, ESt, 71, 1937, 87-8.
EITLE, HERMANN. Die Satzverknüpfung bei Chaucer.
     Anglistische Forschungen, 44. Heidelberg: J. Hoops,
     1914.
        Rev: E. Björkman, ESt, 51, 1917, 84-94; J. Koch,
     LGRP, 35, 1914, 332-6; K. Brunner, Arch, 133, 1915, 460.
EMERSON, OLIVER F. The Old French Diphthong EI
     (EY) and Middle English Metrics. RR, 8, 1917, 68-76.
ERSKINE, JOHN. Chaucer's Narrative Method. Master's
     Thesis, Columbia, 1901.
EVERETT, DOROTHY. Chaucer's Good Ear. RES, 23,
     1947, 201-8.
        Rev: D. Everett, YWES, 71-2.
----------. Some Reflections on Chaucer's "Art Poeti-
     cal." Proc of the Brit Acad, 1950. Oxford, 1950.
        Refers to HF, PF, Prol CT, T&C, BD, PriorT,
     MerT, KnT, PardT, ManT, and NPT.
EWER, MARY A. A Survey of Mystical Symbolism. Lon-
     don SPCK. New York: Macmillan, 1933.
FARAL, EDMUND. Les Arts Poétiques du XIIe et du
     XIIIe Siècle. Paris: Edouard Champion, 1924.
     Source book of medieval rhetoric.
FRANCIS, W. NELSON. Chaucer Shortens a Tale.
     PMLA, 68, 1953, 1126-41.
        Analysis of Chaucer's use of abbreviation with
     tables comparing Chaucer and Gower.

FRIESHAMMER, JOHANN. Die sprachliche Form der
chaucerischen Prosa: Ihr Verhältnis zur Reimtechnik
des Dichters sowie zur Sprache der älteren Londoner-
Urkunden. Göttingen Diss. Studien zur englischen
Philologie, 42. Halle: Niemeyer, 1910.
   Rev: John Koch, AB, 22, 1911, 278.
GEISMAN, ERWIN W. The Style and Technique of Chau-
cer's Translations from the French. Doctoral Diss,
Yale, 1952.
GLUNZ, H. H. Die Literarästhetik des europäischen
Mittelalters. Wolfram, Rosenroman, Chaucer, Dante.
Poppinghaus, 1937. 608 pp.
   Rev: B. E. C. Davis, MA, 7, 1938, 151-3.
GOFFIN, R. C. Chaucer and Elocution. MA, 4, 1935, 127-42.
----------. Chaucer and "Reason." MLR, 21, 1926, 13-18.
GORDON, R. K. Chaucer's Imagery. Trans Royal Soc
of Canada, 33, ser. 3, sec. 2, 81-90.
HAMILTON, MARIE PADGETT. Notes on Chaucer and
the Rhetoricians. PMLA, 47, 1932, 403-9.
   Rev: Dorothy Everett, YWES, 78.
HAMMOND, ELEANOR P. English Verse between Chau-
cer and Surrey; Being Examples of Conventional Sec-
ular Poetry, Exclusive of Romance, Ballad, Lyric
and Drama, in the Period from Henry IV to Henry
VIII. Duke Univ Press, 1927. 591 pp.
   Chaucer, 11-12, 18-21, and many references in the
notes and introductions. See index.
   Rev: A. W. Reed, RES, 8, 1932, 93-4; H. N. Mac-
Cracken, SRL, 4, 1928, 1051; F. P. Magoun, Spec, 3,
1928, 269-70; Albert Eichler, AB, 40, 1929, 330-2;
TLS, Feb 16, 1928, 109; Brie, DL, 51, 1930, 455.
----------. The Nine Syllabled Pentameter Line in
Some Post-Chaucerian MSS. MP, 23, 1924-5, 129-52.
HARRISON, B. S. Medieval Rhetoric in the Book of the
Duchesse. PMLA, 49, 1934, 428-42. From Doctoral Diss,
Yale, 1932, entitled The Colors of Rhetoric in Chaucer.
----------. The Rhetorical Inconsistency of Chaucer's
Franklin. SP, 32, 1935, 55-61.
HARRISON, TINSLEY CARTER. Chaucer's Mesure: A
Study in Moderation. Master's Thesis, Univ of Vir-
ginia, 1929.
HART, WALTER M. The Reeve's Tale: A Comparative
Study of Chaucer's Narrative Art. PMLA, 23, 1908, 1-44.

See also this author's The Narrative Art of the Old
French Fabliaux, Anniversary Papers (Kittredge),
209 ff.

HASELMAYER, LOUIS A. Chaucer and Medieval Verse
Portraiture. Doctoral Diss, Yale, 1937.

----------. The Portraits in Chaucer's Fabliaux. RES,
14, 1938, 310-4.

HASWELL, RICHARD ELLIS. The Heroic Couplet before Dryden (1550-1675). Doctoral Diss, Univ of Illinois, 1931. Abstract publ at Urbana, Illinois, 1932.
12 pp.

HERAUCOURT, WILL. Das Hendiadyoin als Mittel zur
Hervorhebung des Werthaften bei Chaucer. ESt, 73,
1939, 190-201.

HILL, MARY A. Rhetorical Balance in Chaucer's Poetry.
PMLA, 42, 1927, 845-61.

HINCKLEY, HENRY B. Chauceriana. MP, 16, 1918-9,
39-48.

Note on rime royal, 39-40.

HOMAN, ELIZABETH R. Kinesthetic Imagery in Chaucer. Abstract in the Program of Final Examination,
Univ of California, 1948.

HONOUR, MARGARET C. The Metrical Derivation of
the Middle English Lyric. Doctoral Diss, Yale, 1949.

HOOKER, EDWARD NILES. Johnson's Understanding of
Chaucer's Metrics. MLN, 48, 1933, 150-1.

JOERDAN, OTTO. Das Verhältnis von Wort-, Satz-, und
Vers-Akzent in Chaucers Canterbury Tales. Studien
zur englischen Philologie, 55. Halle: Niemeyer, 1915.

Rev: A. Eichler, AB, 27, 1916, 298-303; E. Björk-
man, ESt, 51, 1917, 84-94; John Koch, LGRP, 38,
1917, 312-9; DL, 38, 1917, 647; Arch, 134, 1916, 466;
K. Brunner, Arch, 137, 1918, 127-8.

KALUZA, MAX. A Short History of English Versification. Macmillan, 1911.

KAR, GANGACHARAN. Thoughts on the Mediaeval Lyric. Blackwell, 1933. 98 pp.

Chaucer and the Troubadours, 29 ff.

KER, WILLIAM P. Form and Style in Poetry. Ed by R.
W. Chambers. Macmillan, 1928.

Includes Chaucer and the Middle Ages, 49-63;
Chaucer and the Renaissance, 64-79, in chapter on
Chaucer, and the Scottish Chaucerians, 49-91.

Rev: TLS, Nov 8, 1928, 826; C. S. L., Oxford
Mag, Dec 6, 1928, 283; W. Kramer, De Nieuwe Taal-
gid, 23, 1928, 65-80; Criterion, 8, 1928, 505-8; Engl
Rev, 48, 1928, 120-1; R. Mortimer, Amer Bookman,
69, 1928, 102-3; C. H. Herford, MLR, 24, 1928, 209-
12; L. Solomon, Hibbert Jour, 27, 1928, 371-3; Bar-
rington Gates, Nation-Athen, 44, 1928, 557-8; L.
Jones, Poetry, 34, 1928, 161-7.

KLEE, FR. Das Enjambement bei Chaucer. Diss, Halle,
1913.

KNOWLTON, E. C. Notes on Early Allegory. JEGP, 29,
1930, 159-81.

KOZIOL, HERBERT. Grundzüge der Syntax der mittelenglischen Stabreimdichtungen. Braumüller, 1935.
172 pp.

Rev: C. L. W., RES, 12, 1936, 246; J. Koch, ESt,
68, 1933, 249-50; W. Franz, DL, 54, 1933, 1606-9;
H. C. Matthes, GRM, 22, 1934, 409; M. Callaway,
Jr., Language, 10, 1934, 212-7; H. Marcus, Arch,
165, 1934, 254-5; H. Heuer, LGRP, 56, 1935, 17-19;
K. Jost, AB, 46, 1935, 363-4; C. S. Northup, JEGP,
34, 1935, 440-1.

----------. Die Anredeform bei Chaucer. ESt, 75, 1942,
170-4.

----------. "He was whit so the flur, Rose Red was his
Color." Arch, 181, 1942, 44-5.

Note on color in description of heroes.

LANGHANS, VICTOR. Der Reimvokal "E" bei Chaucer.
Ang, 45, 1921, 221-82, 297-392.

LEVY, M. L. "As Myn Auctor Seith." MA, 12, 1943,
25-9.

Chaucer's consciousness of the poetic imagination.
Rev: D. Everett, YWES, 49.

LEWIS, C. S. The Fifteenth Century Heroic Line. Essays and Studies, 24, 1930, 28-41.

Many references to Chaucer's verse.

LICHLIDER, A. H. Chapters on the Metric of the Chaucer Tradition. Diss, Johns Hopkins. Baltimore, 1910.

LINEBERGER, JULIA E. An Examination of Professor
Cowling's New Metrical Test. MLN, 42, 1927, 229-
31.

See Cowling, above in this section. Also discusses
chronology.

LONG, EUGENE HUDSON. Chaucer as Master of the
Short Story. Univ of Delaware: Notes, 1943, 11-29.
LOOTEN, C. Chaucer et la Dialectique. RAA, 7, 1930,
193-214.
See this author's Chaucer, ses Modèles, etc. , in
section: General Criticism, where this article is in-
cluded in revision and summary.
Rev: Dorothy Everett, YWES, 77-8.
LUDEKE, H. Die Funktionen des Erzählers in Chaucers
epischer Dichtung. Stud Eng Phil, 1928, no. 72. 157
pp.
Rev: Heinrich Straumann, DL, 48, 1928, 2375-7;
Mabel Day, RES, 5, 1929, 463-5; E. Eckhardt, ESt,
64, 1929, 120-4; J. Koch, LGRP, 50, 1929, 104-8; W.
F. Schirmer, NS, 37, 1929, 236-7; Eleanor P. Hammond, AB, 40, 1929, 321-4; M. B. Carr, MLN, 44,
1929, 538-41; J. Koch, Arch, 157, 1930, 278-83; H.
S. V. Jones, JEGP, 30, 1931, 273-6; Fr. de Backer,
RBPH, 10, 1931, 240-1; Dorothy Everett, YWES, 8,
1927, 103; F. Mossé, Rev Crit, 64, 1930, 45; J.
Vriend, E Stud, 11, 1929, 72-3; J. Farens, RAA, 6,
1929, 356-7; GRM, 17, 238.
McKEON, RICHARD. Rhetoric in the Middle Ages. Spec,
17, 1942, 1-32.
A general study of the classical influence on the
rhetoric of the Middle Ages with large footnote bibliography.
Rev: G. P. Willcock, YWES, 23, 1942, 69-70.
MALONE, KEMP. A Poet at Work: Chaucer Revising
his Verses. LGW, 27-39. Proc Amer Philos Soc, 94,
1950, 317-21.
Compared in both versions for style.
MANLY, JOHN M. Chaucer and the Rhetoricians. Warton Lecture on English Poetry, 17. Milford, 1926. 21
pp.
Rev: NQ, 152, 1927, 126; H. Lüdeke, AB, 39, 1928,
190; H. S. V. Jones, JEGP, 27, 1928, 555-7; Dorothy
Everett, YWES, 80-1; H. R. Patch, ESt, 67, 1932,
264-6.
----------. The Stanza-Forms of Sir Thopas. MP, 8,
1910, 141-4.
MAYNARD, THEODORE. The Connection between the
Ballade, Chaucer's Modification of It, Rime Royal,

and the Spenserian Stanza. Doctoral Diss, Catholic
Univ of America, 1934. 139 pp.

    Rev: TLS, Dec 6, 1934, 878; Josef Raith, AB, 48,
1937, 13-14; H. S. V. J(ones), JEGP, 37, 1938, 126;
Gordon, MLR, 34, 1939, 429.

MOORE, ARTHUR K. Chaucer's Use of Lyric as an Or-
nament of Style. Comp Lit, 3, 1951, 32-46.

-----------. The Secular Lyric in Middle English. Univ
of Kentucky Press, 1951. 255 pp.

    Rev: R. M. Wilson, RES, 3 n. s., 1952, 379-80;
Phyllis Hodgson, MLR, 47, 1952, 215-7; R. J.
Schoeck, Spec, 27, 1952, 114-6; A. A. Prins, E Stud,
33, 1952, 219-20.

MORGAN, MARGERY M. A Treatise in Cadence. MLR,
47, 1952, 156-64.

    Footnote bibliography.

MUSCATINE, CHARLES S. The Form of Speech in Chaucer: A Study in the Style and Function of Direct Dis-
course in Medieval Narrative Poetry. Diss, Yale,
1948.

NAUNIN, TRAUGOTT. Der Einfluss der mittelalterlichen
Rhetorik auf Chaucers Dichtung. Bonn Diss, 1930. 65 pp.

    Rev: A. Eichler, AB, 44, 1933, 144-6; Dorothy
Everett, YWES, YWES, 75-7.

OAKDEN, JAMES PARKER, and E. R. INNES. Alliterative Poetry in Middle English. Manchester Univ Publ:
English ser., nos. 19, 22. Manchester Univ Press,
1930, 1935. 2 vols.

    See Vol. 2, p. 372.

OMOND, T. S. English Metrists. Oxford, 1907.

OSGOOD, CHARLES G., Ed. Boccaccio on Poetry. Being the Preface and the 14th and 15th Books of the
"Genealogia Deorum Gentilium" in English with Introductory Essay and Commentary. Princeton Univ
Press, 1931. 214 pp.

    Rev: J. M. Berdan, SRL, 8, 1931, 113-4; R. Al-
trocchi, Spec, 6, 1931, 624-5; W. P. Mustard, AJP,
52, 1931, 93; J. W. Draper, PQ, 11, 1932, 220-1.

OWEN, CHARLES A. The Crucial Passages in Five of
the Canterbury Tales: A Study in Irony and Symbol.
JEGP, 52, 1953, 294-311.

    PardT, VI(C), 772, 448; NPT, VII, 3157-71; WBT, III(D),
925, 1066; MerT, IV(E), 1319-36; FrankT, V(F), 988-98.

PATTISON, BRUCE. Music and Poetry in the English
 Renaissance. London, 1948.
  Refers to KnT, 1510-6.
PAYNE, ROBERT O. The Function of Rhetoric in Chau-
 cer's Style. Doctoral Diss, Johns Hopkins, 1953.
PERRY, MARY AGNES. Chaucer's Use of Proverbs.
 Master's Thesis, Univ of Washington, 1927. Type-
 written, 38 pp.
POPE, EMMA FIELD. The Critical Background of the
 Spenserian Stanza. MP, 24, 1926, 31-53.
  Mention of Chaucer as a Spenser model.
PRATT, ROBERT A. Chaucer Borrowing from Himself.
 MLQ, 7, 1946, 259-64.
  Invocations to the Virgin in SNT and PriorT and
 Invocations to Venus in HF and PF.
  Chaucer's method of composition.
  Rev: D. Everett, YWES, 69.
PYLE, FITZROY. A Metrical Point in Chaucer. NQ, 170,
 1936, 128.
  Rev: D. Everett, YWES, 78.
REGER, HANS. Die epische Cäsur in der Chaucerschule.
 München Diss. Bayreuth: Ellwanger, 1910.
ROBERTSON, D. W., Jr. The Doctrine of Charity in
 Medieval Gardens: A Topical Approach through Sym-
 bolism and Allegory. Spec, 26, 1951, 24-49.
  See also Stroud, MP, 49, 1951, 1-9, on double
 meaning in medieval style.
ROBERTSON, STUART. Old English Verse in Chaucer.
 MLN, 43, 1928, 234-6.
RUBEL, V. L. Poetic Diction in the English Renaissance
 from Skelton through Spenser. MLA Revolving Fund,
 ser. 12, 1941.
  Attitude of early Tudor writers toward Chaucer.
SAINTSBURY, GEORGE. A History of English Prose
 Rhythm. Macmillan, 1912. Reprint, 1922. 489 pp.
  From Chaucer to Malory, 56-101.
----------. A History of English Prosody from the
 Twelfth Century to the Present Day. 2nd ed. Macmil-
 lan, 1923.
  Especially, Vol. 1, 143-78.
----------. The Prosody of Old and Middle English.
 Vol. 1, 372-8, of Cambridge History of English Lit-
 erature. 3rd impression. Macmillan, 1920. Also,

Prosody from Chaucer to Spenser, Vol. 3, 273-88.

SCHLAUCH, MARGARET. Chaucer's Prose Rhythms.
PMLA, 65, 1950, 568-89.
    HF, 623 (in cadence); Boethius, Melibeus, Astro-
labe, Parson's Tale, Retractions.
    Rev: D. Everett, YWES, 31, 1950, 55-6.

----------. Chaucer's Colloquial English: Its Structural
Traits. PMLA, 67, 1952, 1103-16.
    An important analysis of Chaucer's style.

SEEBERGER, ALFRED. Fehlende Auftakt und fehlende
Senkung nach der Cäsur in der Chaucerschule. München Diss. Bayreuth: Ellwanger, 1911.

SHANNON, EDGAR. Chaucer's Use of Octosyllabic
Verse in the Book of the Duchess and the Hous of
Fame. JEGP, 12, 1913, 277-94.

SNELL, ADA L. F. Chaucer's Comments on his Method
of Composition. EJ, 2, 1913, 231-4.

STEVENS, JAMES W. A Classification of Amplification
and Addition in Troilus and Criseyde. Master's Thesis, Univ of Washington, 1936. Typewritten, 107 pp.

SULLIVAN, FRANK. Finished Fragments in Chaucer.
SRL, 26, Oct 16, 1943, 27.
    On the Cook's Tale, Squire's Tale, and Anelida
and Arcite as intentional interruptions and artistically
completed compositions.

TATLOCK, JOHN STRONG PERRY. Chaucer's "Dremes:
Lemes." MLN, 20, 1905, 126.
    On rhyming of closed and open "e."

----------. Origin of the Classical Closed Couplet in
English. Nation, 98, 1914, 310.

----------. The Hermaphrodite Rhyme. MLN, 32, 1917, 373.
    Influence of misreading Chaucer.

----------. Hermaphrodite Rhyme (in Chaucer). SRL,
9, 1932, 161. See also G. Fraser, Chaucer's Accents,
SRL, 9, 1932, 242.

----------. Puns in Chaucer. Flügel Memorial Volume,
228-32. Stanford, 1916.

TEAGER, FLORENCE E. Chaucer's Eagle and the Rhetorical Colors. PMLA, 47, 1932, 410-8.

----------. Chaucer's Poetry in the Light of Rhetorical
Tradition. Doctoral Diss, Iowa, 1931. Abstract in
Iowa Univ Studies, Series on Aims and Progress of
Research, no. 36, Feb 1, 1932.

TEN BRINK, BERNHARD. Chaucers Sprache und Vers-
kunst. Dritte Auflage bearbeitet von Ed. Eckhardt.
Leipzig: Tauchnitz, 1920.
    Rev: Richard Jordan, ESt, 54, 1920, 400-3; J. W.
Bright, MLN, 36, 1921, 123-7; F. Wild, Arch, 142,
1921, 281-3; G. Binz, LGRP, 42, 1921, 306-7; J. H.
Kern, Neophil, 6, 1921, 4; Max Kaluza, AB, 32, 1921,
265-7; F. Karpf, NS, 29, 1921, 228-31; E. Appel,
ZFEU, 20, 216-7; John Koch, LGRP, 41, 1920, 374-9,
and ES, 37, 1907, 131 ff. See also Jiriczek, Skeat's
Debt to Ten Brink, AB, 33, 1922, 120.

THOMPSON, E. N. S. The Octosyllabic Couplet. PQ, 18,
1939, 257-68.

TROUNCE, A. McI. The English Tail-Rhyme Romances.
MA, 1, 1932, 87-108, 168-82.

VERRIER, PAUL. Essai sur les Principes de la Mé-
trique Anglaise. Vol. 2, Théorie Générale du
Rythme. Paris, 1909.

VOCKRODT, G. Reimteknik bei Chaucer als Mittel zur
chronologischen Bestimmung seiner im Reimpaar geschriebenen Werke. Halle, 1914.

WATSON, MELVIN R. Wyatt, Chaucer, and Terza Rima.
MLN, 68, 1953, 124-5.

WEESE, WALTER E. Word Order as a Factor in Chaucer's Poetry. Doctoral Diss, Yale, 1951.

WESTERN, AUG. Aphesis, Syncope, and Apocope in
Middle and Early Modern English. 133-43, in Grammatical Miscellany Offered to Otto Jesperson, 1930.

WHITING, BARTLETT JERE. Chaucer's Use of Proverbs. Harvard Studies in Comparative Philology and
Literature, 11. Harvard Univ Press, 1934. 297 pp.
    Rev: Mabel Day, RES, 11, 1935, 344-5; TLS, Aug
9, 1934, 550; NQ, 167, 1934, 18; A. H. Krappe, Spec,
9, 1934, 456-8; J. P. Oakden, MLR, 30, 1935, 358-9;
Margaret Galway, MLN, 50, 1935, 332-5; H. S. V.
Jones, JEGP, 34, 1935, 594-5; A. T., MP, 32, 1935,
431-2; Dorothy Everett, YWES, 85-7.

WILSON, GEORGE P. Chaucer and Oral Reading. SAQ,
25, 1926, 283-99.

WORCESTER, DAVID. The Art of Satire. Harvard Univ
Press, 1940.

LANGUAGE

See Hammond, 464-504; Legouis, 44-8; Kaluza, 216-30; French, 339-67; Manly, 88-121; Robinson, xxv-xxxii; Wells, the same references as those under Style and Versification, above; Shelly, 284-308.

As there is no Variorum Chaucer, attention should be called here to the glossaries and the numerous notes to be found in the editions listed in the section: Editions with Notes.

AHLGREN, A. The Use of the Definite Article with "Nouns of Possession" in English. Appelbergs Boktryckeriaktiebolag. Upsala, 1946. 221 pp.

   The use of the definite article in all periods of English.

   Rev: R. M. Wilson, YWES, 40.

ATKINS, J. W. H. The Language from Chaucer to Shakespeare. Vol. 3, 439-465 of Cambridge History of English Literature. 3rd impression. Macmillan, 1920.

   See Henry Bradley, below in this section.

BABCOCK, CHARLOTTE FARRINGTON. A Study of the Metrical Use of the Inflectional "E" in Middle English, with Particular Reference to Chaucer and Lydgate. PMLA, 29, 1914, 59-92.

BAUGH, ALBERT CROLL. A History of the English Language. Appleton-Century, 1935.

   For Chaucer, see index.

BAXTER, J. H., and CHARLES JOHNSON. Medieval Latin Word-List. From British and Irish Sources. Oxford, 1935. 482 pp.

   Rev: M. S. Serjeantson, MLR, 31, 1936, 558-9; TLS, Feb 28, 1935, 125; N. D. -Y., MA, 4, 1935, 218-21; A. H. Thompson, Antiq Jour, 15, 1935, 363-5; NQ, 168, 1935, 251.

BOND, GEORGE D. The Factors Governing the Pronunciation of Chaucer's Final -e. Diss, Michigan, 1947. 109 pp.

BORNAND, -----. The Subjunctive in Chaucer. Thesis
    for Diplome d'Etudes Supérieures, Sorbonne. Univ of
    Paris, 1922.
BORST, EUGEN. Zur Stellung des Adverbs bei Chaucer.
    ESt, 42, 1910, 339-62.
        Rev: John Koch, AB, 22, 1911, 280.
BRADLEY, HENRY. Changes in the Language to the Days
    of Chaucer. Vol. 1, 379-406, of Cambridge History of
    English Literature. 3rd impression. Macmillan, 1920.
BRADLEY, RUTH J. The Use of Cockney Dialect by
    Chaucer. Quart Jour of Speech, 29, 1943, 74-6.
        Sounding of initial "h" in Chaucer.
BRANDL, A., and O. ZIPPEL. Mittelenglische Sprache-
    und Literaturproben. Mit etymologischen Wörterbuch
    zugleich f. Chaucer. Neuausgabe von Mätzners alt-
    englischen Sprachproben. Berlin: Weidmann, 1927.
BROWN, CARLETON. Shul and Shal in the Chaucer
    Manuscripts. PMLA, 26, 1911, 6-30.
        Rev: John Koch, AB, 22, 1911, 280-2.
BRUNNER, K. Abriss der mittelenglischen Grammatik.
    Halle: Niemeyer, 1938.
BUCHHOLZ, ERICH. Das Verbum Substantivum im Mit-
    telenglischen. Diss, Berlin, 1936. 70 pp.
        Rev: Herbert Koziol, ESt, 72, 1938, 272-3.
CALDWELL, ROBERT A. An Elizabethan Chaucer
    Glossary. MLN, 58, 1943, 374-5.
        By Joseph Holand in MS Gg. 4. 27.
        Rev: D. Everett, YWES, 51.
CALDWELL, ROBERT PAUL. Chaucerian Graphemics
    and Phonemics: A Study in Historical Methodology.
    Univ of Virginia, Abstracts of Dissertations, 1952,
    11-13.
CALLAWAY, MORGAN, Jr. Recent Works in the Field
    of English Linguistics (1921-1927). Univ of Texas
    Studies in English, 8, 1928, 5-41.
        Middle English, 26-30.
CHAMBERS, R. W., and MARJORIE DAUNT, Eds. A
    Book of London English, 1384-1425. With an Appendix
    on English Documents in the Record Office by M. M.
    Weale. Oxford Univ Press, 1931. 395 pp.
        Rev: H. T. Price, JEGP, 34, 1935, 115-6; TLS,
    Oct 8, 1931, 767; NQ, 161, 1931, 198; P. H. Reaney,
    RES, 8, 1932, 463-5; A. Brandl, Arch, 161, 1932,

110-2; H. M. Flasdieck, AB, 44, 1933, 40-4.

CLOYD, MANIE G. Chaucer's Romance Element. PQ,
11, 1932, 89-91.

> Study of "varying percentages of words of Romance
> origin in four selections from Chaucer's poetry."

CROSS, J. E. A Point of Chaucer's Syntax. NQ, Oct 25,
1952, 468.

> Preposition "of" with noun used as an adjective.

CROSLAND, JESSIE. The Conception of "Mesure" in
Some Middle English Poets. MLR, 21, 1926, 380-4.

> BD, 872; Prol, A435; also see Concordance for
> uses in Melibeus.

DEVELIN, JOSEPH C. Gummere and the Chaucerian
Short E. Privately printed by the author, 1950. 8 pp.

> See the Southworth-Donaldson controversy, below.

DEW, R. Tamarside Dialect and the Language of Chaucer. Cornhill, 63, 1927, 179-85.

DOLLE, ERNST. Zur Sprache Londons vor Chaucer.
Studien zur englischen Philologie, 32. Halle: Niemeyer, 1913.

> Rev: E. Ekwall, AB, 26, 1915, 37-8.

DONALDSON, E. TALBOT. Chaucer's Final -e. PMLA,
63, 1948, 1101-24.

> See Southworth, below in this section.
> Rev: D. Everett, YWES, 71-2.

EICHORN, ERNST. Partizipium bei Gower im Vergleich
mit Chaucers Gebrauch. Kiel Diss, 1912.

EKWALL, EILERT. The Middle English a/o Boundary.
E Stud, 20, 1938, 147-68.

----------. Variation in Sur-names in Medieval London.
Lund: Gleerup, 1945. 56 pp.

> Rev: Simeon Potter, MLR, 41, 1946, 344.

EMERSON, O. F. Some Notes on Chaucer and Some Conjectures. PQ, 2, 1923, 85.

FEIST, R. Studien zur Rezeption des französischen Wortschatzes im Mittelenglischen. München Diss. Beitr.
zur engl. Philologie, 25. Tauchnitz, 1934. 87 pp.

FETTIG, ADOLF. Die Gradaverbien im Mittelenglischen.
Anglistische Forschungen, 79. Winter, 1934. 222 pp.

> Rev: Herbert Koziol, ESt, 71, 1936, 244-7; Olöf
> Anderson, E Stud, 19, 1937, 176-7; Kemp Malone,
> MLN, 53, 1938, 34; F. M(ossé), Rev Germ, 28, 1937,
> 181-2.

FLASDIECK, H. M. Studien zur mittelenglischen Grammatik. AB, 36, 1925, 240-9.

FLUGEL, EWALD. Prolegomena and Side-Notes of the Chaucer Dictionary. Ang, 34, 1911, 354-422.

----------. Specimen of the Chaucer Dictionary -- Letter "E." Ang, 37, 1913, 497-532.

FORD, H. C. Observations on the Language of Chaucer's House of Fame. Lexington, Virginia, 1908. (Rev of 1899 ed.)

FORSSTROM, GOSTA. The Verb "to Be" in Middle English: A Survey of Forms. Lund: G. W. K. Gleerup, 1948.
    Rev: Alarik Rynell, Stud Neophil, 21, 1949, 305-10; Marg. McD. Long, Spec, 25, 1950, 130-1; Randolph Quirk, MLR, 44, 1949, 438; Heinrich Ch. Matthes, Archiv, 189, 1952, 59, and Ang, 71, 1953, 237-42.

FOSTER, C. H. Chaucer's Pronunciation of ai, ay, ei, ey. MLN, 26, 1911, 76-7.

FOWLER, G. HERBERT. Notes on the Pronunciation of Medieval Latin in England. Hist, 22, 1937, 97-109.

FRIDEN, G. Studies in the Tenses of the English Verb from Chaucer to Shakespeare. Uppsala: Almqvist & Wiksells Boktryckeri AB, 1948. 222 pp.
    Rev: Sherman M. Kuhn, JEGP, 49, 1950, 104-6; James Sledd, MP, 47, 1950, 208-9; Simeon Potter, MLR, 45, 1950, 77-8; Friedrich Schubel, Stud Neophil, 21, 1949, 300-2; F. Mossé, Etud Angl, 5, 1952, 69-70.

FRIEDERICI, HANS. Der Lautstand Londons um 1400. Diss, Jena. Forsch. z. engl. Phil., 6. Jena: Frommann, 1937. 95 pp.
    Rev: H. Koziol, ES, 73, 1938, 62-5.

FUNKE, OTTO, Ed. Grammatica Anglicana. Wiener Beiträge, 60. Wien and Leipzig, 1938. Ed of MS dated 1594.

GERIKE, FRITZ. Das Partizipium Präsentis bei Chaucer. Kiel Diss, 1911.

GROSSE, EGINHARD. Die neuenglische ea-Schreibung: Ein Beitrag zur Geschichte der englischen Orthographie. Palaestra, 208. Leipzig: Mayer and Müller, 1937.
    Rev: G. Lenke, Archiv, 173, 1938, 85-7; Karl Brunner, AB, 49, 1938, 330-1.

HARE, C. E. The Language of Field Sports. Country Life, 1949. 276 pp.
    Rev: R. M. Wilson, YWES, 30, 1949, 29.

HELMEKE, TH. Beteuerungen und Verwünschungen bei
  Chaucer. Kiel Diss, 1913.
HEUER, HERMANN. Studien zur syntaktischen und sti-
  listischen Funktion des Adverbs bei Chaucer und im
  Rosenroman. Anglistische Forschungen, 75. Winter,
  1932. 168 pp.
      Rev: Herbert Koziol, DL, 40, 1933, sp. 1089-90;
  Dorothy Everett, YWES, 90-1; H. C. Matthes, GRM,
  22, 1934, 409; O. Funke, AB, 45, 1934, 141-7; C. S.
  Northup, JEGP, 34, 1935, 105-7; John Koch, ESt, 67,
  1933, 391-5; H. C. Matthes, LGRP, 56, 1935, 164-6;
  H. Heuer, LGRP, 56, 1935, 286-8.
HITTMAIR, RUDOLF. Das Zeitwort "Do" in Chaucers
  Prosa. Wiener Beiträge, 51, 1923.
      Rev: G. C. Moore Smith, MLR, 19, 1924, 256.
HOFFMANN, F. Das Partizipium bei Spenser mit Be-
  rücksichtigung Chaucers und Shakespeares. Berlin
  Diss, 1909.
HORTON BURCH, J. C. Notes on the Language of John
  Gower. E Stud, 16, 1934, 209-15.
HULBERT, JAMES R. Chaucer's Romance Vocabulary.
  PQ, 26, 1947, 302-6.
      See Mersand, below in this section.
HUTTMANN, ERNST. Das Partizipium Präsentis bei
  Lydgate im Vergleich mit Chaucers Gebrauch. Doc-
  toral Diss, Könige Christian-Albrechts Universität
  zu Kiel, 1914. 92 pp.
JESPERSEN, OTTO. Growth and Structure of the English
  Language. 4th ed. Teubner, 1923. 8th ed, 1935.
      Also for many other studies of the English language,
  see Jespersen's other works, and for review see R.
  W. Zandvoort, A Critique of Jespersen's English
  Grammar, Etud Angl, 5, 1952, 2-10.
      Rev: E. Björkman, AB, 24, 1913, 193-5; Fritz
  Karpf, NS, 32, 1924, 441-3; A. E. H. Swaen, Neo-
  phil, 21, 1936, 169-71; E. Zellmer, ZNU, 35, 1936,
  280.
JORDAN, RICHARD. Handbuch der mittelenglische
  Grammatik. Lautlehre. Heidelberg: Winter, 1925.
  273 pp.
      Rev: Robert J. Menner, JEGP, 25, 1926, 415-8;
  Eilert Ekwall, Litteris, 3, 1926, 153-8; Kemp Malone,
  MLN, 41, 1926, 400-1; Cyril Brett, MLR, 21, 1926,

78; F. Klaeber, ESt, 60, 1926, 317-22; K. Luick, AB, 37, 1926, 193-8; Dorothy Everett, YWES, 106-7.

----------. Handbuch der mittelenglischen Grammatik. Lautlehre, durchgesehene Auflage, bearbeitet von H. Chr. Matthes. Heidelberg: Winter, 1934. 294 pp. 2nd ed, 1937.

    Rev: G. Eckhardt, ESt, 69, 1934, 240-2; A. B(randl), Arch, 166, 1934, 137-8; W. v. d. G. , E Stud, 18, 1936, 236; C. L. W. , RES, 12, 1936, 374-5; O. Boerner, NS, 44, 1936, 485; C. T. O. , MA, 7, 1938, 159-61.

----------. Die mittelenglische Mundarten. GRM, 2, 1910, 124-34.

JUHL, HUGO. Der Syntaktische Gebrauch des Infinitivs bei John Lydgate im Vergleich zu dem bei Chaucer und Occleve. Kiel Diss, 1921. Summary, Kiel, 1921. 4 pp.

KAISER, ROLF. Zur Geographie des mittelenglischen Wortschatzes. Palaestra, 205. Mayer and Müller, 1936. 318 pp.

    Rev: George T. Flom, JEGP, 36, 1937, 569-72; G. Linke, Arch, 171, 1937, 80-2; Karl Brunner, AB, 49, 1938, 7-10; Sanford B. Meech, Spec, 13, 1938, 107-10; E. Ekwall, E Stud, 20, 1938, 257-9; E. L. Deuschle, Museum, 45, 1938, 147-8.

----------. Zur geographischen Verteilung des mittelenglischen Wortschatzes. Diss, Berlin, 1936. 65 pp.

    Rev: H. M. , Arch, 169, 1936, 297-8; E. Ekwall, E Stud, 20, 1938, 257-9; S. B. Meech, Spec, 13, 1938, 107-10.

KARPF, FRITZ. Studien zur Syntax in den Werken Geoffrey Chaucers. Teil 1. Wiener Beiträge, 55. Braumüller, 1930. 148 pp.

    Rev: A. H. Smith, MLR, 27, 1932, 98-9; K. Brunner, NS, 40, 1932, 240; W. van der Goof, E Stud, 15, 1933, 38-43; H. Heuer, LGRP, 54, 1933, 10-14; Dorothy Everett, YWES, 80-1; John Koch, ESt, 67, 1933, 391-5; C. L. W. , RES, 12, 1936, 246.

----------. Zur Kontamination bei Chaucer. ESt, 64, 1929, 252-60.

----------. Nachträge zur Kontamination bei Chaucer. ESt, 66, 1932, 467-8.

KENNEDY, ARTHUR G. Bibliographical Guides for the

Study of English. Papers of the Bib Soc of America,
25, 1931, 130-80.

Chaucer, 157.

----------. A Bibliography of Middle English Language.
MLN, 36, 1921, 304-7.

Announcement.

----------. A Bibliography of Writings on the English
Language from the Beginnings of Printing to the End
of 1922. Yale Univ Press, 1927. 517 pp.

Middle English, 159-95. Chaucer, nos. 4371-8,
4455-543.

For reviews, see section: Bibliography.

KENYON, JOHN S. Syntax of the Infinitive in Chaucer.
Chaucer Society, 2nd ser., 44. London, 1909.

Rev: John Koch, AB, 22, 1911, 279-80; Jacob Zeitlin, JEGP, 12, 1913, 496-503.

KNOTT, THOMAS A. The Middle English Dictionary.
Michigan Alumnus Quart Rev, 48, 1942, 127-32.

KOKERITZ, HELGE. The Reduction of Initial Kn and Gn
in English. Language, 21, 1945, 77-86.

KOZIOL, HERBERT. Der Abfall des nachtönigen -e im
Mittelenglischen. AB, 48, 1937, 307-9.

----------. Handbuch der englischen Wortbildungslehre.
Winter, 1937. 260 pp.

Rev: S. B. Liljegren, AB, 49, 1938, 37-47.

----------. Die romanischen Lehnwörter in Chaucers
Werken: Im Anschluss an das Buch, Chaucer's Romance Vocabulary von J. Mersand. ESt, 74, 1940,
270-1.

KRUISINGA, E. A Guide to English Studies: Introduction,
E Stud, 7, 1925, 1-4; The Study of Old and Middle
English, E Stud, 7, 1925, 129-36; The Study of the
History of English, E Stud, 8, 1926, 97-105.

See also J. H. Schutt, in section: General Criticism.

KUHN, SHERMAN McA. The Grammar of the Mercian
Dialect. Doctoral Diss, Univ of Chicago, 1936.

KURATH, HANS, and SHERMAN M. KUHN, Eds. Middle
English Dictionary. E to "fered" published and being
continued. Univ of Michigan Press; London: Oxford
Univ Press, 1952.

Rev: Kemp Malone, Lang, 29, 1953, 204-8; notice,
E Stud, 34, 1953, 23.

LANGENFELT, GOSTA. Select Studies in Colloquial
English of the Late Middle Ages. Gleerupska Univ
Bokhandeln, Lund, Sweden, 1933. 129 pp.
　　Rev: Herbert Koziol, ESt, 69, 1934, 243-7; F.
M(ossé), Rev Germ, 28, 1937, 396-7; W. van der
Gaaf, E Stud, 17, 1935, 96-100.
LOFVENBURG, MATTIAS T. Studies in Middle English
Local Surnames. Lund Studies in English. Lund, 1942.
　　Rev: O. Arngart, Stud Neophil, 16, 1943, 144-6.
----------. Contributions to Middle English Lexicogra-
phy and Etymology. Lund: C. W. K. Gleerup, 1946.
110 pp.
　　Notes many words not in OED and earlier occur-
rences not there listed.
　　Rev: R. M. Wilson, YWES, 27, 1946, 34-5; Hilda
Hulme, MLR, 44, 1949, 292; G. V. Smithers, RES,
2 n. s. , 1951, 67-8.
LONG, MARY McDONALD. The English Strong Verb
from Chaucer to Caxton. Menasha, Wis: Banta, 1944.
314 pp.
　　Rev: Simeon Foster, MLR, 40, 1945, 134-5; E. J.
Bashe, PQ, 24, 1945, 94; Herbert Meritt, MLQ, 6,
1945, 495-6; F. P. Magoun, Jr. , Spec, 20, 1945,
250-1; Hereward T. Price, JEGP, 45, 1946, 108.
McJIMSEY, RUTH B. Chaucer's Irregular -e: A Demon-
stration among Monosyllabic Nouns of Exceptions to
Grammatical and Metrical Harmony. New York:
Crown Press (lithograph), 1942. 248 pp.
　　Rev: D. Everett, YWES, 234; Arthur G. Kennedy,
MLQ, 4, 1943, 113-4; H. Patch, MLN, 59, 1944, 188;
Potter, MLR, 38, 1943, 138-9.
MACKENZIE, BARBARA ALIDA. The Early London Dia-
lect. Contributions to the History of the Dialect of
London during the Middle English Period. Clarendon
Press, 1928.
　　Rev: TLS, Sept 20, 1928, 665; NQ, 155, 1928, 288;
P. H. Reaney, RES, 5, 1929, 470-1.
MADELEVA, Sister MARY (MARY EVALINE WOLFF).
A Lost Language and Other Essays on Chaucer. New
York: Sheed, 1951.
MAGOUN, FRANCIS P. , Jr. Colloquial Old and Middle
English. Harvard Studies and Notes, 19, 1936, 167-
73.

MALONE, KEMP. Studies in English Phonology. MP, 23,
    1926, 483-90.
        Mainly Chaucerian phonology; on diphthong "ai, "
    "ay. "
MARCKWARDT, ALBERT H. Origin and Extension of
    the Voiceless Preterit and Past Participle Inflections
    of the English Irregular Verb Conjugation. Essays
    and Studies in Comparative Literature. Univ of Mich-
    igan Press, 1935, 151-328.
        Important bibliography.
MARCUS, HANS. Zum neuen mittelenglischen Wörter-
    buch. Arch, 169, 1936, 30-5.
MERSAND, JOSEPH. Scientific Studies in Chaucer's
    Romance Vocabulary. Doctoral Diss, New York Univ,
    1934. Published as: Chaucer's Romance Vocabulary.
    Comet Press, 1937. 2nd ed, 1939. 173 pp.
        Rev: John S. P. Tatlock, RR, 28, 1937, 274; Her-
    bert Koziol, ESt, 72, 1938, 270-2, and ES, 74, 1940,
    270-1; W. Héraucourt, AB, 49, 1938, 231-2, and E-
    tud Angl, 3, 1939, 259; J. R. Hulbert, PQ, 26, 1947,
    302-6 (review article); EJ, 27, 1938, 877; Delattre,
    Rev Belg, 18, pt. 1; Oakden, MLR, 33, 1938, 576-7;
    S. H. B. , PQ, 18, 1939, 91-2; Rolf Kaiser, Arch,
    176, 1939, 117-8; TLS, Sept 18, 1937, 677; Martin B.
    Ruud, MLN, 54, 1939, 140-2; R. G. Kent, Lang, 14,
    1938, 301-2; Brunner, LGRP, 61, 1939, 213; West-
    chester Co Times, Jan 14, 1938; YWES, 18, 1937, 66-
    8; E. L. Deuschle, E Stud, 22, 1940, 119-21; Will
    Héraucourt, Etud Angl, 3, 1939, 259.
MOORE, SAMUEL. Historical Outlines of English Pho-
    nology and Middle English Language for Courses in
    Chaucer, Middle English, and the History of the Eng-
    lish Language. Ann Arbor: George Wahr, 1919. Rev
    ed, 1925. Revised by Albert H. Marckwardt, 1951,
    under title, Historical Outlines of English Sounds and
    Inflections. 179 pp.
        Rev: Hermann M. Flasdieck, AB, 33, 1922, 230-2,
    and 36, 1925, 263-4; James R. Hulbert, MP, 18, 1920-
    1, 63-4; Arch, 145, 1923, 154; E. G. Ingram, RES, 2,
    1926, 240-1.
----------, SANFORD BROWN MEECH, and HAROLD
    WHITEHALL. Middle English Dialect Characteristics
    and Dialects Boundaries: Preliminary Report of an

Investigation Based Exclusively on Localized Texts and
Documents. Essays and Studies in English and Com-
parative Literature, Univ of Michigan, 13, 1935, 1-60.
    Rev: A. G. Kennedy, Amer Speech, 11, 1936, 173-
5; J. R. H., MP, 34, 1936, 96.
----------, SANFORD BROWN MEECH, and HAROLD
WHITEHALL. The Middle English Dictionary. PMLA,
48, 1933, 281-8.
    Methods of compiling, checking, etc.
MOSSE, FERDINAND. A Handbook of Middle English.
Trans by James A. Walker. Baltimore: Johns Hop-
kins Press, 1952.
    Contains selections from BD, T&C, LGW, and the
Pardoner's Tale.
NAKAYAMA, TAKEJIRO. On Some Features of Chau-
cer's Language. Studies in English Literature: A
Quarterly Review Compiled and Issued by The English
Literary Society of Japan, 18, 1938, 577-89.
NOJD, R. The Vocalism of Romanic Words in Chaucer.
Diss, Uppsala, 1919.
    Rev: Arch, 146, 1923, 286; H. Kalen, ESt, 59,
1925, 102.
NOYES, GEORGE RAPALL. Analyses of the Sources of
the Accented Vowels in Chaucer's Canterbury Tales:
B 4011-4060. Univ of California Press, 1909.
OHLANDER, URBAN. Studies on Coordinate Expressions
in Middle English. Lund Stud Engl, V. Lund: Gleerup;
London: Williams and Norgate, 1936. 213 pp.
    Use of "and" in Middle English.
    Rev: G. L., Arch, 171, 1937, 259-60; Herbert Ko-
ziol, LGRP, 58, 1937, 394-6; A. Sale, MLR, 33,
1938, 276-7; Frank Behre, E Stud, 20, 1938, 140-4;
George William Small, JEGP, 37, 1938, 291-5; Will
Héraucourt, AB, 48, 1937, 264-6; W. Preusler, Indo-
germanische Forsch, 55, 1937, 319.
----------. A Study on the Use of the Infinitive Sign in
Middle English. Stud Neophil, 14, 1941, 58-66.
ORR, J. The Impact of French upon English. The Taylor-
ian Lecture. Oxford Univ Press, 1948. 28 pp.
    Rev: R. M. Wilson, YWES, 32.
PASCHKE, E. Der Gebrauch des bestimmten Artikels in
der spätmittelenglischen Prosa (1380-1500). Münster
Diss, 1934. 272 pp.

PATCH, HOWARD R. , and R. J. MENNER. A Bibliography of Middle English Dialects. SP, 20, 1923, 479-
95.

PEITZ, A. Der Einfluss des nordlichen Dialektes im
Mittelenglischen auf die entstehende Hochsprache.
Bonner Studien z. engl. Philologie, 20. Hanstein,
1933. 133 pp.
    Rev: A. B. , Arch, 164, 1933, 294-5; H. C.
Matthes, GRM, 22, 1934, 409-10; George T. Flom,
JEGP, 33, 1934, 468-70; F. Fiedler, ZNU, 35, 1936,
201-2; F. Wilde, LGRP, 57, 1936, 311-3; O. Boerner,
NS, 44, 1936, 308-10.

PRAZ, MARIO. The Italian Element in English. 20-66,
in Essays and Studies, Vol. 15, ed by Sir Herbert
Warren. Milford, 1929.
    Study of Italian influence on English vocabulary.

PRICE, H. T. Foreign Influences on Middle English.
Univ of Michigan Contributions in Modern Philology,
no. 10, 1947. 45 pp.
    Uses of words under influence of translation from
foreign languages, especially "at." Many references
to Chaucer.
    Rev: R. M. Wilson, YWES, 33-4, and G. D. Will-
cock, 105; G. Stillwell, JEGP, 47, 1948, 190-1; A. W.
Read, RES, 43, 1948, 247-8.

PRINS, A. A. French Phrases in English: I and II. Neophil, 32, 1948, 28-39 and 73-83.
----------. French Influence on English Phrasing. Lei-
den: Universitaire Pers, 1952. 320 pp.

REED, DAVID W. The History of Inflectional N in English Verbs before 1500. Doctoral Diss, Michigan,
1949. Univ of California Publications in English, 7,
1951, no. 4. 172 pp.
    Rev: R. M. Wilson, YWES, 31, 1950, 29; K. R.
Brooks, MLR, 47, 1952, 99-100.

REMUS, HANS. Die kirchlichen und speziellwissen-
schaftlichen romanischen Lehnworte Chaucers. Studien zur englischen Philologie, 14. Niemeyer, 1906.
    Rev: Eilert Ekwall, ESt, 41, 1910, 97-9; also,
Museum, 14, 292; DL, 28, 25-89.

RETTGER, JAMES F. The Development of Ablaut in the
Strong Verbs of the East Midland Dialects of Middle
English. Doctoral Diss, Yale. Language Dissertations,

published by Linguistic Society of America, no. 18, 1934. 186 pp.

Rev: K. Jost, Indogerm Forsch, 54, 1936, 308-9; Mary S. Serjeantson, E Stud, 20, 1928, 42-4; A. B(randl), Arch, 167, 1935, 300-1.

ROBERTS, W. F. J. Ellipsis of the Subject-Pronoun in Middle English. London Mediaeval Studies, 1, 1937, 107-15.

ROBERTSON, STUART. The Development of Modern English. 3rd printing with additions and revisions. Prentice-Hall, 1941.

For Chaucer, see index.

ROOTH, ERIK. Zur Geschichte der englischen Partizip-Präsens Form auf -ing. Stud Neophil, 14, 1941, 71-85.

ROSEBOROUGH, MARGARET M. An Outline of Middle English Grammar. Doctoral Diss, Univ of Toronto, 1937. Macmillan, 1938.

SAUERBREY, GERTRUD. Die innere Sprachform bei Chaucer. Diss, Halle, 1917.

SCHLAUCH, MARGARET. The Gift of Tongues. Modern Age Books, 1942.

For Chaucer, see index and especially 209 ff.

----------. Chaucer's Colloquial English: Its Structural Traits. PMLA, 67, 1952, 1103-16.

SCHLEPPER, ERICH. Die Neubildung von Substantiven in den Ubersetzungen König Alfreds mit einem Ausblick auf Chaucer. Diss, Münster, 1936. 137 pp.

Rev: D. Everett, YWES, 66.

SERJEANTSON, MARY S. The Dialects of the West Midlands in Middle English. RES, 3, 1927, 54-67, 186-203, 319-31.

Examination, discussion, assignments of texts by dialect tests.

----------. Distribution of Dialect Characters in Middle English. Amsterdam: Swets and Zeitlinger, 1925. 34 pp.

Rev: Eilert Ekwall, AB, 38, 1927, 46-8.

SKEAT, WALTER W. English Dialects. Cambridge Univ Press, 1911.

----------. Hit: Tense in Chaucer. NQ, ser. 11, 5, 1912, 465-6.

SLETTENGREN, E. Contributions to the Study of French Loanwords in Middle English. I. Orebo, 1934.

Rev: E. Fischer, LGRP, 55, 1934, 100-2. Not seen.

SOUTHWORTH, JAMES G. Chaucer's Final -E in Rhyme. PMLA, 62, 1947, 910-35.

Argues that final "-e" is inorganic and need not be pronounced in rhyme.

Rev: D. Everett, YWES, 72-3.

----------. Chaucer's Final -E. PMLA, 64, 1949, 601-9.

Reply to Donaldson, above in this section, followed by rejoinder by Donaldson, 609, and re-rejoinder by J. G. S., 609.

Rev: D. Everett, YWES, 55.

STIDSTON, RUSSELL OSBORNE. The Use of Ye in the Function of Thou in Middle English Literature from MS. Auchinleck to MS. Vernon; a Study of Grammar and Social Intercourse in Fourteenth-Century England. Doctoral Diss, Stanford, 1914. Publ by Stanford Univ, 1917. Stanford Publ, Univ Series, 28. 95 pp.

STOCKWELL, ROBERT P. Chaucerian Graphemics and Phonemics: A Study in Historical Methodology. Doctoral Diss, Virginia, 1952.

STUMPFE, O. Der Befreier der englischen Sprache. Berliner Börsenzeitung, Nr. 559, 1937.

TAYLOR, ARCHER. Investigations of English Proverbs, Proverbial and Conventional Phrases, Oaths, and Clichés. Jour Amer Folklore, 65, 1952, 255-65.

A bibliography.

TEN BRINK, BERNHARD. Chaucers Sprache und Verskunst. Dritte Auflage bearbeitet von Ed. Eckhardt. Tauchnitz, 1920.

For reviews, see section: Style.

THURESEN, BERTIL. Middle English Occupational Terms. Lund Studies in English, 19. Lund: Gleerup; Copenhagen: Munksgaard, 1950. 285 pp.

Rev: Sherman M. Kuhn, Lang, 28, 1952, 135-9; B. M. H. Carr, RES, 3 n. s., 1952, 65-7; F. P. Magoun, Jr., Spec, 27, 1952, 431-2.

TOLKIEN, J. R. R. Chaucer as a Philologist: The Reeve's Tale. Philological Soc Trans, 1934, 1-70.

Rev: Dorothy Everett, YWES, 98-9.

TROUNCE, A. McI. Chaucer's Imperative with As. MA, 2, 1933, 68-70.

TUCKER, EMMA CURTISS. The Later Version of the
Wycliffite Epistle to the Romans, Compared with the
Latin Original: A Study of Wycliffite English. Doctoral
Diss, Yale, 1913. Yale Studies in English, Vol. 49.
Holt, 1914. 177 pp.
    Study of Wycliffite versions, "with a view to dis-
covering the resources and capacities of the English
language in the last quarter of the 14th century."
VAN DER GAAF, W. The Split Infinitive in Middle Eng-
lish. E Stud, 15, 1933, 15-20.
VON GROSS, ERNA. Bildung des Adverbs bei Chaucer.
Berlin Diss. Uschmann, Vol. 21, 1921.
WALCUTT, CHARLES CHILD. The Pronoun of Address
in Troilus and Criseyde. PQ, 14, 1935, 282-7.
WALKER, HAZEL PEARL. Chaucer's Use of Proverbs
in Troilus and Criseyde. Master's Thesis, Univ of
Iowa, 1932.
WARDALE, E. E. An Introduction to Middle English.
Kegan, Paul, 1937. 130 pp.
    Rev: R. M. Wilson, MLR, 33, 1938, 317 (short
notice).
WEHRLE, OTTO. Die hybriden Wortbildungen des
Mittelenglischen (1050-1400): Ein Beitrag zur eng-
lischen Wortgeschichte. Diss, Freiburg, 1935. 62 pp.
WEISE, H. Die ei (ee) -Schreibung im Englischen und
ihre Geschichte. Diss, Berlin, 1937. 189 pp.
    Rev: G. Linke, Archiv, 173, 1938, 263-4.
WEYMOUTH, R. F. On Early English Pronunciation with
Especial Reference to Chaucer. London, 1874.
WILD, FREDERICK. Die sprachlichen Eigentumlichkeit-
en der wichtigeren Chaucer-Handschriften und die
Sprache Chaucers. Wiener Beiträge, 44. Leipzig,
1915.
    Rev: Eilert Ekwall, AB, 27, 1916, 164-7; E. Björk-
man, ESt, 51, 1917, 84-94; John Koch, LGRP, 39,
1916, 233-7; Arch, 134, 1916, 465; Rudolf Imelmann,
NS, 24, 1916, 181-2.
WINKLER, G. Das Relativum bei Caxton und seine Entwicklung von Chaucer bis Spenser. Berlin Diss, 1933.
82 pp.
WRIGHT, JOSEPH and ELIZABETH MARY. An Elementary Middle English Grammar. Milford, 1923. 2nd ed,
1928. 226 pp.

Rev: J. M. Toll, Arch, 149, 1925, 108-9; F. Wild,
ESt, 59, 1925, 96-9; Eilert Ekwall, AB, 35, 1924,
226-8; F. Holthausen, LGRP, 45, 1924, 302-5; E.
Kruisinga, E Stud, 6, 1924, 162 ff.; G. B. H., RES,
5, 1929, 246-7; F. Wild, ESt, 63, 1929, 401-2; F.
Holthausen, LGRP, 50, 1929, 346-8.

WYLD, HENRY CECIL. A Short History of English,
with a Bibliography of Recent Books on the Subject
and Lists of Texts and Editions. 3rd ed, rev and enl.
London: John Murray, 1927.

See index for Chaucer. See also London Dialect,
p. 9, bibliography.

WORD STUDY

See Hammond, 504-9.

For the phrase, "Under the sonne he looketh, "
see Hustvedt, Klaeber, Patch, Savage, Smith (2),
Tatlock, Van Roosbroeck in the section: Knight's
Tale. For words that interpret particular passages,
see the section in which the word occurs.

ACKERMAN, R. W. Tester: Knight's Tale, 2499. MLN,
49, 1934, 397-400.
ALLEN, HOPE E. The Mystical Lyrics of the Manuel
des Pechiez. RR, 9, 1918, 187.
Meaning of "cadence." See also Hammond, English
Verse from Chaucer to Surrey, 457n.
ANON. The Study of Words in Chaucer. Word Study, 7,
1931, 1-2.
BAXTER, EDNA. Chaucer's Use of Literary Terms.
M. A. Thesis, Univ of Washington, 1946.
BLAU, ERNST. Zu Chaucers Tale of Sir Thopas. AB,
31, 1920, 237.
Meaning of "payndemayn." See Patterson, below
in this section.
BONNARD, G. A Note on Chaucer's "Troilus and Cri-
seyde," V, 1637. RES, 5, 1929, 323-4.
Meaning of "love. "
BOYS, RICHARD C. An Unusual Meaning of "Make" in
Chaucer. MLN, 52, 1937, 351-3.
BROOKS, CLEANTH. Chaucer: Saturn's Daughter. MLN,
49, 1934, 459-61.
Meaning of "doughter. "
BROWN, DAVID. Solas in the Miller's Tale. MLN, 48,
1933, 369-70.
See Collins in this section.
BRUCE, J. DOUGLAS. Prologue to the Canterbury Tales.
MLN, 34, 1919, 118-9.
"Purchas" and "rente. " See Greenlaw and Kit-
tredge, below in this section.

CAMDEN, CARROLL, Jr. Chauceriana. MLN, 47, 1932,
    360-2.
        Word studies: "Worthy," "sangwyn," "moral ver-
    tu," and on images.
CASSIDY, FREDERIC G. Chaucer's "Broken Harm."
    MLN, 58, 1943, 23-7.
        Meaning of "broken" in Merchant's Tale, 1425.
        Rev: D. Everett, YWES, 24, 1943, 46.
COLLINS, FLETCHER. Solas in the Miller's Tale. MLN,
    47, 1932, 363-4.
        See Brown in this section.
COOK, ALBERT S. Chaucer's Fraknes. MLN, 31, 1916, 315.
----------. Note on Mormal. MLN, 33, 1918, 379.
CURRY, WALTER C. Two Notes on Chaucer. MLN, 36,
    1921, 272-6.
DAHL, THORSTEN. Middle English Seint, Seinte. Stud
    Neophil, 22, 1949, 14.
DAY, MABEL. Chaucer's "Troilus and Criseyde," V,
    1637. RES, 6, 1930, 73.
        Meaning of "leve." See Bonnard in this section.
DEROCQUIGNY, J. Note sur Chaucer. C.T., B 1687,
    "an heep." Germ, 6, 1910, 203-6; RAA, 1927, 160-1.
DIECKMANN, EMMA POPE M. The Meaning of "Bur-
    doun" in Chaucer. MP, 26, 1929, 279-82.
DIVELEY, RUTH ANNA. The Meaning of "Gentilesse"
    in Chaucer. Master's Thesis, Univ of Washington,
    1929. Typewritten, 63 pp.
DONALDSON, E. TALBOT. Middle English Seint, Seinte.
    Stud Neophil, 21, 1949, 222-30.
        Rev: R. M. Wilson, YWES, 25.
DONOVAN, MORTIMER J. Three Notes on Chaucerian
    Marine Life. PQ, 31, 1952, 439-41.
        "Eles," HF, 2153-4; "oystre," Prol, 177-82;
    "pikerel"-"pike," MerchT, 1418-20.
DRAPER, JOHN W. Chaucer's "Wardrobe." ESt, 60,
    1926, 238-51.
DRENNAN, C. M. Chaucer's Prioress, CT, Prol., 136:
    "Ful semely after hir mete she raughte." NQ, ser. 11,
    9, 1914, 365.
        Meaning of "raughte."
DUSTOOR, P. E. Chaucer's Use of "Discreet." RES, 13,
    1937, 206-9.
        Rev: D. Everett, YWES, 68.

EHRENSPERGER, EDWARD G. Dream Words in Old and
Middle English. PMLA, 46, 1931, 80-9.
  Compares Chaucer and Gower, 84-5.
EINARSSON, STEFAN. Old and Middle English Notes.
JEGP, 36, 1937, 183-7.
EINENKEL, EUGEN. Bemerkung. Ang, 44, 1920, 385.
  On the meaning of "what."
EMERSON, OLIVER F. "Afterdiner," "Aftermete,"
  "Aftersoper." MLR, 11, 1916, 460-2.
  See also Henry Bradley, "At-after," MLR, 12,
  1917, 74-6.
----------. Some Notes on Chaucer and Some Conjec-
tures. PQ, 2, 1923, 81-96.
  On "gold ybete," T&C, II, 1228-9; KnT, A 979-80.
FAUST, GEORGE P. Two Notes on Chaucer. MLN, 47,
1932, 365-7.
  Meanings of "to-night" and "undern."
FISHER, JOHN H. Chaucer's Use of "Swete" and "Swote."
JEGP, 50, 1951, 326-31.
FLUGEL, EWALD. Benedicitee. 94-9, in Mätzke Memo-
rial Volume. Leland Stanford, Jr., Univ Publications,
no. 7, 1911.
  Rev: John Koch, ESt, 46, 1912, 109.
FORSTER, MAX. Chauceriana I. Arch, 132, 1914, 399-401.
  Meaning of "chapeleine."
GARRETT, MAX M. Chaucer in Minnesota. Dialect
Notes, 5, 1923, 245.
  Meaning of "piggesnye." See Manly, below in this
  section.
GEROULD, GORDON HALL. The Social Status of Chau-
cer's Franklin. PMLA, 41, 1926, 262-79.
  Meaning of "franklin," "sheriff," "countour,"
  "vavasour," "sergeant."
GIBBS, LINCOLN R. The Meaning of "Feeldes" in Chau-
cer's Knight's Tale, vv. 975-977. MLN, 24, 1909,
197-8.
GOFFIN, R. C. Chaucer and "Reason." MLR, 21, 1926,
13-18.
  CT, Prol, 27, E 25, and "hardily," C 457.
GREENLAW, EDWIN A. A Note on Chaucer's Prologue.
MLN, 23, 1908, 142-4.
  "Purchas" and "rente."

GRIFFITH, DUDLEY DAVID. On Word Studies in
Chaucer. 195-9, in Kirby and Woolf, Eds, Philologica.

For reviews, see section: General Criticism.

HALL, VESPER TREVOR. Oaths and Swearing in Chaucer's Writings. M.A. Thesis, Univ of Washington,
1934. 79 pp.

HENSHAW, MILLET. La Clameur de Haro. So Folklore
Quart, 14, 1950, 158-9.

Explains the custom and notes its survival in the
Channel Islands.

HERAUCOURT, W. What is Trouthe or Soothfastnesse.
In Englische Kultur in sprachwissenschaftlichen
Deutung. Max Deutschbein zum 60. Geburtstage.
Herausgegeben von W. Schmidt. Quelle und Meyer,
1936.

----------. Der sprachliche Feld der "goodes" und
seiner Gliedung bei Chaucer. Neuphil Monatschrift,
11, 1941, pts. 1-2.

HIBBARD, LAURA A. Chaucer's Shapen Was my Sherte.
PQ, 1, 1922, 222-5.

HILL, A. A. Ilium, the Palace of Priam. MP, 30, 1932,
94-6.

On the name in Chaucer and Shakespeare.

HINCKLEY, HENRY B. Chauceriana. MP, 14, 1916-7,
317-8; 15, 1917-8, 56; 16, 1918-9, 39-48.

Several word studies.

----------. Notes on Chaucer: A Commentary on the
Prologue and Six Canterbury Tales. Northampton:
Nonotuck Press, 1907. 324 pp.

Many word studies.

HOLMES, URBAN T. Chaucer's Tydif "A Small Bird."
PQ, 16, 1937, 65-7. See also F. P. Wilson, The Tidy.
PQ, 17, 1938, 216-8.

LGW, F154; SqT, 648.

Rev: D. Everett, YWES, 68.

HOLTHAUSEN, F. Zur Chaucers Hous of Fame. AB, 31,
1920, 137.

IMMACULATE, Sister MARY. "Sixty" as a Conventional
Number and Other Chauceriana. MLQ, 2, 1941, 59-
66.

Rev: D. Everett, YWES, 66.

JENKINS, T. ATKINSON. Vitremyte: Mot Latin-Fran-

çais Employé par Chaucer. 141-7, in Mélanges de
Linguistique et de Litterature, offerts à M. Alfred
Jeanroy. Droz, 1928.

JOHNSON, MARY LYNCH. [Letter on Chaucer's Use of
"dreadful."] Word Study, 13, Feb, 1938, 5.

JONES, CLAUDE. Chaucer's Taillynge Ynough. MLN,
52, 1937, 570.

KIRBY, THOMAS A. As Good Chepe. (TC, 3, 641.) MLN,
48, 1933, 527-8.

KITTREDGE, GEORGE L. [Prologue 256.] MLN, 23,
1908, 200.

　　"Purchas" and "rente." See Greenlaw and Bruce,
above in this section.

----------. On "Feeldes" in the Knight's Tale. MLN,
25, 1910, 28, 975-7.

　　See Gibbs, above in this section.

KUHL, ERNEST P. Notes on Chaucer's Prioress. PQ,
2, 1923, 302-9.

LAW, ROBERT A. In Principio. PMLA, 37, 1922, 208-
15.

LEVY, RAPHAEL. The Etymology of English "Bawd"
and Cognate Terms. PQ, 32, 1953, 83-9.

　　See concordance for examples in Chaucer not noticed in this article.

LINTHICUM, M. C. "Faldyng" and "medlee." JEGP, 34,
1935, 39-41.

　　Notes on 14th century cloth.

　　Rev: D. Everett, YWES, 106.

LIVINGSTON, CHARLES H. Middle English "Askances."
MLR, 20, 1925, 71-2.

LOTSPEICH, C. M. The Type OE "loca hwa," ME "looke
who." JEGP, 37, 1938, 1-2.

LOWES, JOHN L. Chaucer and Dante's Convivio. MP,
13, 1915, 19-33.

----------. The Loveres Maladye of Hereos. MP, 11,
1914, 491-546.

　　Rev: John Koch, AB, 25, 1914, 332-9. See also
Lowes, Hereos, Nation, 97, 1913, 233, and Hereos
Again, MLN, 31, 1916, 185-6.

LUMIANSKY, R. M. Chaucer's "For the Nones." Neophil, 35, 1951, 29-36.

MACAULAY, G. C. Notes on Chaucer. MLR, 4, 1908,
14-19.

MAGOUN, FRANCIS P. "Muchel broken harm," C. T.,
     E1425. Ang, 53, 1929, 223-4.
          Also "fern-asshen glas," F253-6, RR, 17, 1926,
     67-70.
MANLY, JOHN M. Piggesnye. C. T. A 3268. TLS, Oct
     6, 1927, 694. See also Agnes Arber, TLS, Nov 3,
     1927, 790.
          See Garrett, above in this section.
MAYHEW, A. L. "Dulcarnon" in Chaucer. NQ, ser. 11,
     1, 1910, 505-6.
MITCHELL, DWIGHT EMERSON. Chaucer's Use of Five
     Words of Emotion: Anger, Chere, Daunger, Lough,
     Smile. Master's Thesis, Univ of Washington, 1932.
     Typewritten, 73 pp.
MOORE, ARTHUR K. "Somer" and "Lenten" as Terms
     of Spring. NQ, 194, Feb 19, 1949, 82-3.
          Rev: G. D. Willcock, YWES, 76-7, and R. M.
     Wilson, 25.
MORGAN, MARGERY M. A Treatise in Cadence. MLR,
     47, 1952, 156-64.
          Footnote bibliography.
MOSSE, F. Chaucer et la Liturgie. Rev Germ, 14, 1923,
     283-9.
ONIONS, C. T. Middle English "Ord and Ende." MLR,
     24, 1929, 389-93.
          Etymology traced to Chaucer.
PACE, ELISHA BOYD. Word Studies in Chaucer's Works.
     M. A. Thesis, Univ of Washington, 1949.
PATCH, HOWARD. Chauceriana. ESt, 65, 1931, 351-9.
          Several word studies.
PATTERSON, R. F. Paindemaine. MLR, 7, 1912, 376.
          See Blau, above in this section.
PRINS, A. A. Further Notes on the Canterbury Tales.
     E Stud, 32, 1951, 250-1.
          On "in muwe."
PYLES, THOMAS. Dan Chaucer. MLN, 57, 1942, 437-9.
          Use of "Dan."
          Rev: D. Everett, YWES, 67-8.
ROBERTSON, D. W., Jr. Historical Criticism. Engl
     Inst Essays, 1950, 3-31. Columbia Univ Press, 1951.
          On the word "charity."
ROBERTSON, STUART. The Chaucerian-American "I
     guess." MLN, 48, 1933, 37-40.

ROPPOLO, JOSEPH, P. The Meaning of "at erst": Pro-
logue to Sir Thopas, B² 1884. MLN, 63, 1948, 365-71.
Suggests meaning of "then and not sooner."
Rev: D. Everett, YWES, 84.

SAGEN, LEDA. A Preliminary Study of Chaucer's Use
of "Gan." Master's Thesis, Univ of Washington, 1953.

SEDGWICK, W. B. Satalye. (C. T. Prologue, 58.) RES,
2, 1926, 346.

SKEAT, WALTER W. The Meaning of "save" in Chaucer.
Modern Language Quart, 1, 1898, 132.
See also Schöffler, AB, 29, 1918, 42-8.

SLAUGHTER, E. E. "Every Vertu at his Reste." MLN,
46, 1931, 448-53.
PF, 376.

STARR, HERBERT W. Oaths in Chaucer's Poems. West
Virginia Univ Bull: Philological Studies, 4, 1943, 44-
63.
Rev: D. Everett, YWES, 25, 1944, 53.

STEWART, GEORGE R. The Meaning of "Bacheler" in
Middle English. PQ, 13, 1934, 40-7.

TATLOCK, JOHN STRONG PERRY, and ARTHUR G.
KENNEDY. A Concordance to the Complete Works of
Geoffrey Chaucer and to the Romaunt of the Rose.
Carnegie Institute, 1927. 1110 pp.
For reviews, see section: Concordance and Indexes.

TATLOCK, JOHN STRONG PERRY. Bretherhed in Chaucer's Prologue. MLN, 31, 1916, 139-42.

----------. Notes on Chaucer. MLN, 29, 1914, 140-4.
In Principio, 141-2.

----------. Puns in Chaucer. Flügel Memorial Volume,
228-32. Stanford Univ, 1916.

----------. The Date of the Troilus: and Minor Chauceriana. MLN, 50, 1935, 277-96.
"Heeld the space," 293-4; "undermeles," 294.

----------. The Source of the Legend and Other Chauceriana. SP, 18, 1921, 419-28.
Meaning of "holynesse" and the domestic "our."

TUCKER, SUSIE J. "Sixty" as an Indefinite Number in
Middle English. RES, 25, 1949, 152-3.

UTLEY, FRANCIS L. "Mannyssh Wood" -- Merchant's
Tale (IV) 1530-1536. MLN, 53, 1938, 359-62.

WEBSTER, C. M. Chaucer's Turkish Bows. MLN, 47, 1932,
260.

WINTERSGILL, A. T. Chaucer: "Strothir" in "The
    Reeve's Tale." NQ, ser. 10, 12, 1909, 90.
        Replies by Walter W. Skeat and A. R. Bayley, 155.
    Rejoinder by Wintersgill, 235.
WYATT, A. J. Chaucer's "In Termes." RES, 4, 1928,
    439.
        See A. W. Reed, RES, 4, 1928, 220n.
YOUNG, KARL. Chaucer and the Liturgy. MLN, 30,
    1915, 97-9.
ZIA, YIN-CHIN LIU. The Meaning of "Virtue" in Chau-
    cer. M. A. Thesis, Univ of Washington, 1952. 54 pp.

CANTERBURY TALES
GENERAL

See Robinson, 1-17, 1001-5; Brusendorff, 53-136, 472-85; French, 192-201; Root, 151-60, 297-9; Kittredge, 146-218; Legouis, 136-99; Hammond, 150-264; Kaluza, 111-207; Wells, 1535-43, 1644-8, 1735-42, 1930-4, and CBEL, I, 232-49; Shelly, 194-283; Dempster, 27-58, 80-2.

For pilgrimages and shrines, see sections: General Backgrounds, and Religious Backgrounds.

Items on the "Marriage Group" are listed in the section: Wife of Bath's Tale.

For editions, see section: Editions with Notes; for inclusive contributions, see sections: General Criticism, Literary Relations and Sources, and Manuscripts.

ANDRAE, AUGUST. Zu Longfellows und Chaucers Tales. AB, 27, 1916, 56-62, 84-7. See also AB, 17, 1906, 70 ff.

ANON. Analysis of the Sources of the Accented Vowels in Chaucer's Canterbury Tales. Syllabus. Univ of California Press, 1909.

BALDWIN, RALPH F. The Unity of the Canterbury Tales. Doctoral Diss, Johns Hopkins, 1953. Anglistica, V. Copenhagen: Rosenkilde and Bagger, announced as forthcoming, 1953. About 145 pp.

BARR, JESSIE HELEN. The Exemplum in the Canterbury Tales. Master's Thesis, Columbia, 1916.

BASHE, E. J. The Prologue of the Tale of Beryn. PQ, 12, 1933, 1-16.

BAUGH, ALBERT C. The Original Teller of the Merchant's Tale. MP, 35, 1937, 16-26.
    Concerns revision and arrangement of the tales.

BENNETT, J. O. Chaucer's "Canterbury Tales." 182-9, in his Much Loved Books; Best Sellers of the Ages. Liveright, 1927.

BENSON, MARIAN E. Uses of Metaphor and Simile in

151

The Canterbury Tales. Master's Thesis, Columbia, 1931.

BLAKE, WILLIAM. Canterbury Pilgrims. 85-94, in E. D. Jones, Ed, English Critical Essays: Nineteenth Century. World's Classics. Oxford, 1916.

BRADDY, HALDEEN. Chaucerian Minutiae. MLN, 58, 1943, 18-23.

CookT, Prol (crowned A), SqT.

BROWN, BEATRICE DAW. A Thirteenth-Century Chaucerian Analogue. MLN, 52, 1937, 28-31

Influence of the Dialogus Miraculorum on the form of the Canterbury Tales.

Rev: YWES, 80.

BROWN, CARLETON. The Evolution of the Canterbury "Marriage Groups." PMLA, 48, 1933, 1041-59.

Rev: D. Everett, YWES, 108-10.

----------. Shul and Shal in Chaucer Manuscripts. PMLA, 26, 1911, 6-30.

Order of the tales.

----------. Three Notes on the Text of the Canterbury Tales. MLN, 56, 1941, 163-75.

MSS of the d* group present often original readings.

----------. Author's Revision in the Canterbury Tales. PMLA, 57, 1942, 29-50.

The Clerk's Tale; Order of the Tales in Blocks D and E; The Man of Law's Endlink; Placing Blocks D and E in the Canterbury Frame; The Clerk-Franklin and Merchant-Squire Links.

Rev: D. Everett, YWES, 50-1.

BRYAN, WILLIAM FRANK, and GERMAINE DEMPSTER, Eds. Sources and Analogues of Chaucer's Canterbury Tales. Univ of Chicago Press, 1941. 765 pp.

In this bibliography, the names of the contributors to this volume are entered under the separate tales.

Rev: W. E. Garrison, The Christian Century, 58, 1941, 721; Com, 34, 1941, 213; Geo. R. Coffman, SP, 38, 1941, 571-84 (review article under title: Chaucer's Library and Literary Heritage for the Canterbury Tales); D. Everett, YWES, 51; and MA, 12, 1943, 78-84; Germaine Dempster, MP, 38, 1940, 205-14; Earl Daniels, College English, 3, 1942, 603-4; Francis L. Utley, Spec, 17, 1942, 274-83; Margaret Galway, MLR, 37, 1942, 493-5; Boas, English, 4, 1942, 56;

W. G. Clawson, JEGP, 42, 1943, 118-20; Howard R.
Patch, MLN, 57, 1942, 383-5.

CAMPBELL, R. L. Extra-textual Data for a Classification of the Manuscripts of the Canterbury Tales. Doctoral Diss, Univ of Chicago, 1927. Abstract in Abstracts of Theses, Humanistic Series, 5, 1926-7,
453-6.

    For review, see section: Manuscripts.

CARTWRIGHT, JULIA. The Pilgrim's Way from Win-
chester to Canterbury. London: Murray, 1911.

CLAWSON, W. H. The Framework of the Canterbury
Tales. UTQ, 20, 1951, 137-54.

CLOYD, MANIE G. Chaucer's Romance Element. PQ,
11, 1932, 89-91.

    ". . . Varying percentages of words of Romance
origin in four selections from Chaucer's poetry, the
Prologue and the tales of the Second Nun, the Knight,
and the Man of Law."

COFFMAN, GEORGE R. Chaucer's Library and Literary
Heritage for the Canterbury Tales. SP, 38, 1941, 571-
84.

    Review of Sources and Analogues.

CORSON, HIRAM. Index of Proper Names and Subjects
to Chaucer's Canterbury Tales together with Compar-
isons and Similes, Metaphors and Proverbs, Maxims,
etc., in the Same. Oxford Univ Press, Chaucer Society, 1911. First series, no. 72. 121 pp.

    Rev: ESt, 46, 1912, 98-114.

CUMMINGS, HUBERTIS M. The Indebtedness of Chaucer's Works to the Italian Works of Boccaccio. Univ
of Cincinnati Studies, 10, pt. 2, 1916.

    Chaucer and the Decamerone, 176-80.

    For reviews, see section: Literary Relations and
Sources.

DARTON, F. J. HARVEY. A Chapter of Flattery. Mercury, 28, 1928, 623-32.

    On continuations of the Canterbury Tales.

DEMPSTER, GERMAINE. Manly's Conception of the
Early History of the Canterbury Tales. PMLA, 61,
1946, 379-415.

    Rev: D. Everett, YWES, 72-6.

----------. A Chapter in the Manuscript History of the
Canterbury Tales: The Ancestor of Group d; the

Origin of its Texts, Tale-Order, and Spurious Links.
PMLA, 63, 1948, 456-84.

Rejoinder by A. E. Hartung, PMLA, 67, 1952,
1173-81.

Rev: D. Everett, YWES, 72-4.

----------. The Fifteenth-Century Editors of the Canterbury Tales and the Problem of Tale Order. PMLA,
64, 1949, 1123-42.

Rev: D. Everett, YWES, 56-7.

----------. A Period in the Development of the Canterbury Tales Marriage Group and of Blocks B^2 and C.
PMLA, 68, 1953, 1142-59.

Concerns chronology and especially the time of
composition of a changed order for Melibeus, The
Clerk's Tale, and The Nun's Priest's Tale.

DUNN, THOMAS F. The Manuscript Sources of Caxton's
Second Edition of the Canterbury Tales. Diss, Univ
of Chicago, 1940.

Rev: D. Everett, YWES, 23, 1942, 52-3.

ENGEL, HILDEGARD. Structure and Plot in Chaucer's
Canterbury Tales. Diss, Bonn, 1931.

Brief discussion of the tales, classified according
to the type of source.

ERSKINE, JOHN. Canterbury Tales. 33-49, in his De-
light of Great Books. Bobbs, Merrill, 1928.

----------. Great Teller of Lively Stories: Chaucer and
the Canterbury Tales. Delineator, 111, 1927, 38.

EWALD, WILHELM. Der Humor in Chaucers Canterbury
Tales. Studien zur englischen Philologie, 45. Halle:
Niemeyer, 1911.

Rev: Robert K. Root, ESt, 45, 1912, 443-4; Fritz
Jung, LGRP, 33, 1912, 400-2.

FUETER, E. Die Rahmenerzählung bei Boccaccio und
Chaucer. Beilage zur allgemeinen Zeitung, no. 265-
6, 1906.

GRAULS, J., and J. F. VANDERHEIJDEN. Two Flemish Proverbs in Chaucer's Canterbury Tales. Rev
Belg, 13, 1934, 745-9.

GREEN, A. WIGFALL. Chaucer's Clerks and Medieval
Scholarly Tradition as Represented by Richard de
Bury's Philobiblon. ELH, 18, 1951, 1-6.

GREENFIELD, S. B. Sittingbourne and the Order of the
Canterbury Tales. MLR, 48, 1953, 51-2.

HART, WALTER M. A Note on the Interpretation of the
Canterbury Tales. Abstract of paper, TAPA, 39, 1908,
liii-iv.
HASELMAYER, LOUIS A. , Jr. The Portraits in Chau-
cer's Fabliaux. RES, 14, 1938, 310-4.
> Rev: YWES, 72-3.
HAVEN, Sister MARGARET A. Some Aspects of Chau-
cer's Age as Reflected in the Canterbury Tales.
Diss, Boston Coll, 1938.
HAWKINS, LAURENCE F. The Place of Group F in the
Canterbury Chronology. Doctoral Diss, New York
Univ, 1937. 57 pp.
> Rev: Dorothy Everett, MA, 7, 1938, 213-6; M. B.
> Ruud, MLN, 54, 1939, 140; Hermann Heuer, AB, 50,
> 1939, 296-8.
HEATH, SIDNEY. In the Steps of the Pilgrims. Tiptree,
Essex: The Anchor Press; New York: Putnam's, n. d.
73 ill, 296 pp. Rev and enl ed of Pilgrim's Life in the
Middle Ages, 1911.
> For references to Chaucer, see index.
HEIST, WILLIAM W. Folklore Study and Chaucer's Fa-
bliau-like Tales. Papers of the Michigan Academy
of Science, Arts, and Letters, 36, 1952, 251-8.
HELMING, VERNON P. Medieval Pilgrimages and Eng-
lish Literature to A. D. 1400. Doctoral Diss, Yale, 1937.
HERTWIG, DORIS. Der Einfluss von Chaucers Canter-
bury Tales auf die englische Literatur. Marburg
Diss, 1908.
HINCKLEY, HENRY B. Chauceriana. MP, 16, 1918, 39-
48.
> Canterbury Tales, 40-3.
----------. Notes on Chaucer: A Commentary on the
Prologue and Six Canterbury Tales. Northampton:
Nonotuck Press, 1907. 324 pp.
> The framing tale, 2-3; see next entry.
----------. The Framing-tale. MLN, 49, 1934, 69-80.
> Historical survey of frame-tale, to Chaucer.
HULBERT, J. R. The Canterbury Tales and their Narra-
tors. SP, 45, 1948, 565-77.
> Rev: D. Everett, YWES, 77.
JEFFERSON, BERNARD L. Chaucer and the Consolation
of Philosophy of Boethius. Princeton Univ Press, 1917.
> For reviews, see section: Literary Relations.

JOERDAN, OTTO. Das Verhältnis von Wort-, Satz-, und
    Vers-Akzent in Chaucers Canterbury Tales. Studien
    zur englischen Philologie, 55. Halle: Niemeyer, 1915.
        For reviews, see section: Style.
JONES, H. S. V. The Plan of the Canterbury Tales.
    MP, 13, 1915, 45-8.
KASE, CHARLES ROBERT. Observations on the Shift-
    ing Positions of Groups G and DE in the Manuscripts
    of the Canterbury Tales. Lancaster, Pa.: Lancaster
    Press, Inc, 1932. 89 pp. Also in Three Chaucer
    Studies, Oxford, 1932.
        For reviews, see section: Life, Brown, Carleton,
    Ed.
KERBY-MILLER, WILMA ANDERSON. Scribal Dialects
    in the C and D MSS of the Canterbury Tales. MS
    Diss, Univ of Chicago, 1939.
KILGOUR, MARGARET. The Manuscript Sources of
    Caxton's Second Edition of the Canterbury Tales.
    PMLA, 44, 1929, 186-201.
KIMPEL, BEN. The Narrator of the Canterbury Tales.
    ELH, 20, 1953, 77-86.
        Seeks to show that "There is no proof that the
    narrator in the Canterbury Tales is in any sense
    Chaucer."
KOCH, JOHN. Chaucers Boethiusübersetzung: Ein Bei-
    trag zur Bestimmung der Chronologie seiner Werke.
    Ang, 46, 1922, 1-51.
----------. Textkritische Bemerkungen zu Chaucers
    Canterbury Tales. ESt, 47, 1913, 338-414.
KORTEN, HERTHA. Chaucers literarische Beziehungen
    zu Boccaccio: Die künstlerische Konzeption der Can-
    terbury Tales und das Lolliusproblem. Rostock: Hin-
    storff, 1920.
        Rev: Walther Fischer, NS, 29, 1921, 172-3.
LAWRENCE, WILLIAM WITHERLE. Medieval Story,
    and the Beginnings of the Social Ideals of English-
    speaking People. Hewitt Lectures, 1911. Columbia
    Univ Press, 1911. 2nd ed, 1931. 236 pp.
        Canterbury Tales, 195-223.
        Rev: H. S. V. Jones, JEGP, 12, 1913, 340-1.
----------. Chaucer and the Canterbury Tales. Colum-
    bia Univ Press; Oxford (Toronto), 1950. 184 pp.
        Chapters: Realism and Artifice; The Fabliau Tales;

The Sequence of Tales; The Discussion of Marriage;
The Ending of the Tales; Bibliography.
    For reviews, see section: General Criticism.
LOOMIS, LAURA HIBBARD. Chaucer and the Breton
    Lays of the Auchinleck MS. SP, 38, 1941, 14-33.
        Argues for Chaucer's use of this MS in FrankT,
    WBT, MerT, and Sir Thopas.
        Rev: D. Everett, YWES, 60.
LOSSING, M. L. S. The Order of the Canterbury Tales;
    a Fresh Relation between A and B Types of MSS.
    JEGP, 37, 1938, 153-63.
LOWES, JOHN L. Chaucer and the Seven Deadly Sins.
    PMLA, 30, 1915, 237-371.
        Review of Tupper's article, below in this section
    (same title). See also Koch's articles listed in section:
    Bibliography, and AB, 25, 1914, 327-52, especially.
LYONS, CLIFFORD P. A Study on the Framework of the
    Canterbury Tales. Doctoral Diss, Johns Hopkins:
    The Framework of the Canterbury Tales. Listed as
    completed in Willard, 11, 1933, 53.
McKENNA, Sister MARY BONAVENTURE. Liturgy of
    the Canterbury Tales. Cath Educ Rev, 35, 1937, 474-
    80.
MANLY, JOHN MATTHEWS. Chaucer and the Rhetori-
    cians. Milford, 1926.
        For reviews, see section: Style.
----------. Some New Light on Chaucer. Holt, 1926.
    305 pp. Reprint, New York: P. Smith, 1952.
        Chapters: Chaucer's Education and Career; Some
    Family Matters; The Host, the Reeve, and the Miller;
    The Summoner, the Friar, and the Pardoner; The
    Man of Law and the Franklin; The Shipman and the
    Merchant; The Prioress, the Wife of Bath, the Second
    Nun, and the Nun's Priest; The Others; Chaucer as
    Artist.
        For reviews, see section: Life.
----------. Tales of the Homeward Journey. SP, 28,
    1931, 613-7.
        Rev: D. Everett, YWES, 87-8.
----------, and EDITH RICKERT. The Text of the Can-
    terbury Tales. 8 vols. Univ of Chicago Press, 1940.
        Vol. I: Origin and Development of Our Plan; De-
    scription of Manuscripts Containing for Each, Where

Applicable, Contents, Form, Collation, Date, Writ-
ing, Ink, Illumination, Binding, Present Condition,
Order of Tales, Affiliations and Textual Character,
Dialect and Spelling, and Provenance; Dialect and
Spelling; Illumination by Margaret Rickert; Recorded
Manuscripts; Reference Books for Volume I; Index of
Names; Mottoes Written in Manuscripts. Vol. II:
Collation; Critics of the Genealogical Method; List of
Manuscripts with Sigils and Dates; Chronological
Order of Manuscripts; Classification of Manuscripts;
Symbols Used in Chapters on Order of Tales; The Or-
der of Tales; Early and Revised Versions. Vol. III:
Text of the Canterbury Tales to the Merchant Endlink
and the Squire Headlink; Critical Notes; Glosses;
Headings and Endings; Divisions within the Tales. Vol.
IV: Text from Squire's Prologue to The Retraction;
Critical Notes. Vols. V-VIII: Corpus of Variants.
The frontispieces of the first four volumes are repro-
ductions of MS pages and Margaret Rickert's essay
on illumination contains nine MS reproductions.

    Rev: TLS, June 22, 1940, Heroism in Scholarship,
304; Carlton Brown, MLN, 55, 1940, 606-21, and 56,
1941, 163-75; Margaret Galway, MLR, 35, 1940, 534-
7; H. S. V. Jones, JEGP, 40, 1941, 142-5; Robert K.
Root, SP, 38, 1941, 1-13; Robert K. Root, SRL, 22,
1940, 20-1; Dorothy Everett, RES, 18, 1942, 93-109.
See also Germaine Dempster, PMLA, 61, 1946, 379-
415, Carleton Brown, PMLA, 57, 1942, 29-50, and
Stroud, below in this section.

MARBURG, CLARA. Notes on the Cardigan Chaucer
    Manuscript. PMLA, 41, 1926, 229-51.
        Includes Doctor-Pardoner link, 236-51.
MARKERT, EMIL. Chaucers Canterbury-pilger und ihr
    Tracht. Würzburg Diss, 1911.
MEAD, WILLIAM EDWARD. The English Medieval
    Feast. Houghton, 1931. 272 pp.
        Reference to three Chaucer pilgrims.
        For reviews, see section: Social Backgrounds.
MEYER, EMIL. Die Charakterzeichnung bei Chaucer.
    Studien zur englischen Philologie, 48. Halle:
    Niemeyer, 1913.
        For reviews, see under section: General Criticism.
MONTGOMERY, FRANZ. The Musical Instruments in

"The Canterbury Tales." Musical Quart, 17, 1931,
439-48.

MOORE, SAMUEL. The Position of Group C in the Canterbury Tales. PMLA, 30, 1915, 116-22.

MORSBACH, LORENZ. Chaucers Canterbury Tales und
das Decamerone. Weidmannsche Buchhandlung, Berlin, 1934, 49-70. Nachrichten von der Gesellschaft
der Wissenschaften zu Göttingen; Philol Hist Kl Fach-
gruppe 4, N. F. Bd. i.
See Root, below in this section.
Rev: W. Fischer, AB, 46, 1935, 68-70; D. Everett,
MA, 4, 1935, 54-6; D. Everett, YWES, 15, 1934, 94-
5.

----------. Chaucers Plan der Canterbury Tales und
Boccaccios Decamerone. ESt, 42, 1910, 43-52.
See Root, below in this section.

NATHAN, NORMAN. The Number of the Canterbury
Pilgrims. MLN, 67, 1952, 533-4.

OWEN, CHARLES A. , Jr. The Plan of the Canterbury
Pilgrimage. PMLA, 66, 1951, 820-6.
Suggests a round trip journey of five days and as-
signs the tales in this pattern.

PATCH, HOWARD R. Chaucer and Lady Fortuna. MLR,
22, 1927, 377-85.

PHONOGRAPHIC RECORDINGS.

AYRES, HARRY M. On Reading Chaucer: Prologue to
the Canterbury Tales; the Nonne Prestes Tale
read by H. M. Ayres. Garwick, nos. 21-2. Dis-
tributed by the National Council of Teachers of
English.

MALONE, KEMP. The Nun's Priest's Tale Recorded
for Authoritative Pronunciation in the Study of
Chaucer in Schools and Colleges. English Classics,
XTV, 17216-7. Johns Hopkins Univ.

PACKARD, FREDERICK C. Excerpts from the Pardoner's Tale Read by Frederick C. Packard. Harvard Film Service, 1942.

ROBINSON, FRED N. The Pardoner's Tale Read by
Fred N. Robinson. Harvard Vocarium Record.
Harvard College Library.

ROSS, ROBERT. Nonne Prestes Tale, Pardoner's
Prologue and Tale, Prologue to Canterbury Tales,
Read by Robert Ross. Caedmon Album, 1008.

SILVERA, FRANK. Prologue to Legend of Good Women and Selections Read by Frank Silvera. In Mark Van Doren, Chaucer through Milton, Caedmon Album, 1021.

WYLD, H. C. Pronunciation of Middle English: From the Prioress's Tale, from the Prologue of the Canterbury Tales. Linguaphone Institute, EWW 44, Chaucer 3-4.

For comment on recordings, South Carolina Speech Bull, 1, 29.

PIPER, EDWIN F. Canterbury Pilgrims. Sonnets. Iowa City: Clio Press, 1935. 59 pp.

POLLARD, A. W., and G. R. REDGRAVE. A Short Title Catalogue of Books Printed in England, Scotland and Ireland and of English Books Printed Abroad: 1475-1640. The Bibliographical Society, 1926. 609 pp.

Chaucerian printed editions are to be found reproduced on film in most university libraries. Univ Microfilms, Edwards Bros, Ann Arbor, Michigan.

For reviews, see section: Editions.

PRATT, ROBERT A., and KARL YOUNG. The Literary Framework of the Canterbury Tales. Sources and Analogues, 1-81.

PRATT, ROBERT A. Giovanni Sercambi Speziale. Ital, 25, 1948, 12-14.

----------. The Order of the Canterbury Tales. PMLA, 66, 1951, 1141-67.

PURDIE, A. B. Canterbury Pilgrims. CW, 94, 1912, 627-39.

READ, HERBERT. English Stained Glass. Putnam, 1926. 260 pp.

Many excellent illustrations of Canterbury windows.

ROOT, ROBERT K. Chaucer and the Decameron. ESt, 44, 1911, 1-7.

Refers to Morsbach, above in this section.

----------. The Text of the Canterbury Tales. SP, 38, 1941, 1-13.

Reviews Manly and Rickert, Text of the Canterbury Tales.

Rev: D. Everett, YWES, 54.

RUTTER, GEORGE McKELVY. Confessions in Mediaeval Literature. Summaries of Theses, Harvard Univ, 1930, 210-1.

RYE, WALTER. Some Historical Essays Chiefly Rela-
tive to Norfolk. Norwich: Hunt, 1929.
        Part 5, 327-37, on pilgrimages.
S. The Little Town of Bob-up-and-down. NQ, 162, 1932,
26.
SCHIRMER, W. F. Boccaccios Werke als Quelle G.
Chaucers. GRM, 12, 1924, 288-305.
SERCAMBI, GIOVANNI. [Proemio and Intermezzi from
the Novelle of Giovanni Sercambi; a Partial Reproduction of MS 193 in the Biblioteca Trivulziana, at
Milan, Italy.] 2 vols. MLA of America. Collection of
Photographic Facsimiles, no. 299. 1934. Deposited
in Library of Congress. Original a 15th century MS.
        ". . . Aims to include only those pages containing
introductory and connective material between the no-
velle proper. . . . The Novelle of Giovanni Sercambi,
of Lucca, which form an analogue of Chaucer's Can-
terbury Tales, are supposed to be told by a group of
pilgrims on an imaginary journey through Italy."
SHANNON, EDGAR F. Chaucer and the Roman Poets.
Harvard Studies in Comparative Literature, no. 7.
Harvard Univ Press, 1929. 401 pp.
        For reviews, see section: Literary Relations.
SKEAT, WALTER W. Chaucer: The Shipman's Prologue.
MLR, 5, 1910, 430-4.
        Order of the tales.
        Rev: AB, 22, 1911, 280-1.
----------. The Evolution of the Canterbury Tales.
Chaucer Society, 1907.
        Rev: John Koch, ESt, 41, 1910, 127-35.
SPEIRS, JOHN. Chaucer, the Maker. Farber and Far-
ber, 1951.
        Canterbury Tales, 97-194.
        For reviews, see section: General Criticism.
STOKOE, WILLIAM C., Jr. Structure and Intention in
the First Fragment of the Canterbury Tales. UTQ,
21, 1952, 120-7.
STROUD, THEODORE A. Scribal Errors in Manly and
Rickert's Text. MLN, 68, 1953, 234-7.
        Contains lists.
TATLOCK, JOHN STRONG PERRY. Boccaccio and the
Plan of the Canterbury Tales. Ang, 37, 1913, 69-
117.

----------. The Canterbury Tales in 1400. PMLA, 50,
1935, 100-39.

----------. A Comparative Study of All the Manuscripts
of the Canterbury Tales. Chaucer Society, Second
Series, 57. Projected but not published.

----------. The Date of the Troilus: and Minor Chauceriana. MLN, 50, 1935, 277-96.

Contains: The Friar's Order, "Heeld the space"
(Prol, 176); Undermeles (WBT, 875); The Bishop's
Hook (FriarT, 1317); The Merchant's Tale for the
Monk? ; The Horseman in the Hall (SqT, 80-1); The
Manciple's "My Sone."

----------. The Duration of the Canterbury Pilgrimage.
PMLA, 21, 1906, 478-85.

Rev: John Koch, AB, 25, 1914, 339-42.

----------. The Harleian MS 7334 and Revision of the
Canterbury Tales. Chaucer Society, Second Series,
41. 1907.

For reviews, see section: Manuscripts.

----------. The Mind and Art of Chaucer. Eds, Germaine Dempster and Sanford B. Meech. Syracuse
Univ Press, 1950. 114 pp.

Contains Canterbury Tales, Group A (I).

TRIGONA, F. PRESTIFILIPPO. Chaucer Imitatore del
Boccaccio. Studio Editoriale Moderno. Catania, 1923.

Rev: TLS, Aug 16, 1923.

TUPPER, FREDERICK. Chaucer and the Seven Deadly
Sins. PMLA, 29, 1914, 93-128.

Rev: John Koch, AB, 25, 1914, 327-32, and other
items bearing on this discussion listed in section:
Bibliography, under Koch. Also see Lowes, above
in this section (same title).

----------. Chaucer's Sinners and Sins. JEGP, 15, 1916,
56-106.

Rev: John Koch, AB, 28, 1917, 152-5.

----------. Wilful and Impatient Poverty. Nation, 99,
1914, 41.

----------. The Envy Theme in the Prologues and Epilogues. JEGP, 16, 1917, 551-72.

----------. The Quarrels of the Canterbury Pilgrims.
JEGP, 14, 1915, 256-70.

Parallels cited.

Rev: John Koch, AB, 28, 1917, 155.

----------. Saint Venus and the Canterbury Pilgrims.
  Nation, 97, 1913, 354-6.
VOCKRODT, G. Reimteknik bei Chaucer als Mittel zur
  chronologischen Bestimmung seiner im Reimpaar
  geschriebenen Werke. Halle, 1914.
WATT, FRANCIS. Canterbury Pilgrims and their Ways.
  Methuen, 1917; Dodd, 1918.
    Rev: Athen, 1918, 1, 35-6.
WILSON, S. C. Scottish Canterbury Pilgrims. SHR, 24,
  1927, 258-64.
WILSON, STANLEY GORDON FRANCIS. With the Pil-
  grims to Canterbury; and the History of the Hos-
  pital of St. Thomas. SPCK, Sheldon Press, 1934.
  90 pp.
WORK, JAMES A. The Position of the Tales of the Manciple and the Parson on Chaucer's Canterbury Pil-
  grimage. JEGP, 31, 1932, 62-5.
    See Manly, Tales of the Homeward Journey, above
  in this section.
YALE UNIVERSITY. Department of English. Notes on
  Chaucer's Canterbury Tales. Whitlock's Book Store,
  New Haven, 1931.
YOUNG, KARL. The Plan of the Canterbury Tales. 405-
  17, in Anniversary Papers . . . for George Lyman
  Kittredge. Ginn, 1913.
    Rev: Arch, 131, 1913, 494.

PROLOGUE
General and Lines 1-42, 714-858

    See Hammond, 150 ff. , 265-70, 323-4; Legouis,
162-80, 206-10; Manly SNL, 70-6; Hinckley, 1-5, 46-
9; Root, 160-3; Manly, 495-8; French, 202-9; Tatlock,
142; Malone, 144-235; Robinson, 751-3, 1005-6; Wells,
CBEL, I, 235-7, and supplements to the Manual after
1933; Shelly, 309-23; Speirs, 99-121.
    For editions, see section: Editions with Notes. For
phonetic transcription of 150 lines of the Prologue,
see also Moore, Historical Outlines, listed in section:
Languages. For phonographic recordings, see section: Canterbury Tales: General.
    Note that supplementary items on the persons of
the Prologue are to be found in the research on the

separate tales, especially when it concerns prologues,
links, and epilogues.

ANON. "Whan That Aprille --." Atlantic, 145, 1930, 568.
----------. Tabard Inn. London, Surrey Archaeological
    Society Collections, 13, 1897, 28.
----------. [Tabard Inn] Victoria County History of
    Surrey, 4, 1912, 127.
BAUM, PAULL F. Chaucer's Faste by the Belle, C. T.,
    A 719. MLN, 36, 1921, 307-9.
BORENIUS, TANCRED. The Iconography of St. Thomas
    of Canterbury. Archaeologia, 79, 1929, 29-54. Ad-
    denda, Archaeol, 81, 1931, 19-32. Still Further As-
    pects, Archaeol, 83, 1933, 171-86.
----------. St. Thomas Becket in Art. Methuen, 1932.
    122 pp., 44 plates.
        Rev: P. A. Brown, Spec, 9, 1934, 218-9; TLS,
    June 2, 1932, 409; J. Evans, Obs, July 17, 1932; W.
    L. Hildburgh, Folk-Lore, 43, 1932, 354-6; F. Wor-
    mald, Crit, 12, 1932, 142-4; J. D. Hobson, Sat Rev,
    153, 1932, 639; J. McN. Rushforth, Antiquaries Jour,
    12, 1932, 461-3.
BOWDEN, MURIEL. A Commentary on the Prologue to
    the Canterbury Tales. Macmillan, 1948. 316 pp.
        Rev: Joseph E. Houseman, English, 7, 1949, 240-
    1; Morton W. Bloomfield, MLQ, 11, 1950, 105-6; J. R.
    Hulbert, MP, 46, 1949, 204-5; M. Galway, RES, 1
    n. s., 1950, 357-8; R. H. Llewellyn, Spec, 25, 1950,
    124-6; H. R. Patch, MLN, 65, 1950, 64-6; Dorothy
    Everett, YWES, 77-8.
BROWN, CARLETON. The Man of Law's Head-link and
    the Prologue of the Canterbury Tales. SP, 34, 1937,
    8-35.
        Its relation to LGW.
----------. The Squire and the Number of the Canter-
    bury Pilgrims. MLN, 49, 1934, 216-22.
BROWN, PAUL ALONZO. The Development of the Leg-
    end of Thomas Becket. Doctoral Diss, Univ of Penn-
    sylvania, 1930. Publ at Philadelphia, 1930. 302 pp.
C., R. L. The Canterbury Road -- The Westminster
    Bridge Road. NQ, Oct 25, 1924, 301.
        Protests that the Westminster Bridge Road is not
    the Canterbury Road of Chaucer's time.

CONRAD, BERNARD R. The Date of Chaucer's Prologue.
    NQ, 152, 1927, 385.
COOK, ALBERT S. Chaucerian Papers. Trans Connec-
    ticut Academy of Arts and Sciences, 23, 1919, 1-63.
    Yale Univ Press.
        The "Sweet Breath" of Zephyr, 22-7.
        Rev: Arch, 141, 1921, 309.
----------. Chauceriana I. RR, 8, 1917, 210-26.
        Lines 1-8, pp. 224-6.
CUMMINGS, HUBERTIS. Chaucer's Prologue 1-7. MLN,
    37, 1922, 86-90.
CUNNINGHAM, J. V. The Literary Form of the Prologue
    to the Canterbury Tales. MP, 49, 1952, 172-81.
        Influence of the form of the dream vision prologue.
DEROCQUIGNY, J. Notes sur Chaucer. Rev Germ, 6,
    1910, 203-6.
EVERETT, DOROTHY. "If Even-song and Morwe-song
    Acorde." RES, 8, 1932, 446-7.
        Prol, 830.
GILES, E. Prologue to the Canterbury Tales. Journal
    of Education, 73, 1911, 349, 379, 411-2.
HANKINS, J. E. Chaucer and the Pervigilium Veneris.
    MLN, 49, 1934, 80-3.
        Source for opening lines of the Prologue.
        Rev: D. Everett, YWES, 87-8.
HINCKLEY, HENRY B. Chauceriana. MP, 14, 1916-7,
    317-8. See also Corrigenda, MP, 15, 1917-8, 56.
HOCKING, LORENA W. The Dress of the Canterbury
    Pilgrims. Master's Thesis, Columbia, 1917.
HORNSBY, ESTELLE MAY. A Project in High-School
    English. EJ (High School ed), 20, 1931, 668-9.
        Class set first lines of Prol to music and gave
    pageant.
HULBERT, JAMES R. Chaucer's Pilgrims. PMLA, 64,
    1949, 823-8.
        Rev: D. Everett, YWES, 57.
LOWES, JOHN LIVINGSTON. The Franklin's Tale, the
    Teseide, and the Filocolo. MP, 15, 1918, 689-728.
        CT, Prol, 1-7.
LUMIANSKY, R. M. Chaucer's Canterbury Tales, Pro-
    logue, 784-7. Explicator, 5, 1946, item 20.
McKEEHAN, IRENE PETTIT. Some Relationships be-
    tween the Legends of British Saints and Medieval Ro-

mance. Doctoral Diss, Univ of Chicago, 1924. Abstract in Abstracts of Theses, Humanistic Series, 2,
1923-4, 383-91.

St. Thomas of Canterbury among others.

MALONE, KEMP. Style and Structure in the Prologue of
the Canterbury Tales. ELH, 13, 1946, 38-45.

----------. Chapters on Chaucer. Johns Hopkins Press;
Oxford, 1951. 240 pp.

Chapters: Geoffrey Chaucer and the Fourteenth
Century; The Book of the Duchess; The House of
Fame; The Parliament of Fowls; The Legend of Good
Women; Troilus and Criseyde; The General Prolog;
The Canterbury Pilgrims. Index to proper names and
Pilgrims.

For reviews, see section: General Criticism.

MANLY, JOHN M. Lowell Lectures on Chaucer, reported in Boston Evening Transcript, Jan 22, 1924, p. 7;
Jan 24, p. 4; Jan 31, p. 20; Feb 5, p. 5; Feb 7, p. 3.

Most of the material in these lectures was incor-
porated in Some New Light, listed in section: Canterbury Tales: General.

MOORE, ARTHUR K. "Somer" and "Lenten" as Terms
for Spring. NQ, 194, Feb 19, 1949, 82-3.

Rev:G. D. Willcock, YWES, 76-7, and R. M. Wilson, 25.

NORRIS, HERBERT. Costume and Fashion. Vol. 2, Sen-
lac to Bosworth, 1066-1485. Dent, 1927. 485 pp.

Following Canterbury Pilgrims discussed or pic-
tured: Carpenter's Wife, Clerk, Doctor, Merchant,
Miller, Sergeant-at-Law, Shipmen, Squire, Squire's
Yeoman, Wife of Bath.

Rev: TLS, June 30, 1927, 451.

PATCH, HOWARD R. Characters in Medieval Literature.
MLN, 40, 1925, 1-14.

Deals in part with Canterbury Pilgrims.

PEARCE, T. M. Chaucer's Canterbury Tales, Prologue,
784-7. Explicator, 5, 1947, item 38.

See Lumiansky, above.

ROOT, ROBERT K. Chaucer and the Decameron. ESt,
44, 1911, 1-7.

On lines 725 ff. , the passage on decorum.

SEARS, CURT. The Ancient Borough of Southwark: A
Center of Literary and Historic Interest. Education,
58, 1938, 333-6.

SPEAIGHT, R. Thomas Becket. London: Longmans, 1940.
TUVE, ROSEMOND. Spring in Chaucer and before Him.
   MLN, 52, 1937, 9-16.
      Also see this author's Seasons and Months in sec-
   tion: General Criticism.
WILLARD, RUDOLPH. Chaucer's "Holt and Heeth."
   American Speech, 22, 1947, 196-8.
      Meaning of "holt."
WILSON, HERMAN OLAND. Blake's Criticism and
   Painting of the Canterbury Pilgrims. Master's Thesis,
   Univ of Washington, 1939.

                     Knight, Lines 43-78

      See Manly, 498-501; Robinson, 753-4; Hinckley,
   5-7; Manly SNL, 254-7.

ACKERMAN, ROBERT W. The Historical Knight in Mid-
   dle English Romances. Doctoral Diss, Michigan, 1938.
CAMDEN, CARROLL, Jr. Chauceriana. MLN, 47, 1932,
   360-2.
      "Worthy," line 43.
COOK, ALBERT S. Beginning the Board in Prussia.
   JEGP, 14, 1915, 375-8.
----------. The Historical Background of Chaucer's Knight.
   Trans Conn Acad of Arts and Sciences, 20, 1916, 161-240.
      For reviews, see section: General Criticism.
----------. Two Notes on Chaucer. MLN, 31, 1916, 441-2.
      On Lyeys, A58.
FINK, Z. S. Another Knight Ther Was. PQ, 17, 1938,
   321-30.
KING, GEORGIANA GODDARD. The Way of St. James:
   Architectural and Historical Study of the Pilgrimage
   Way from Santiago to Compostella. Peninsular Series,
   Hispanic Society. New York and London, 1920.
      See I, 95.
      Rev: George T. Northup, MP, 20, 1922, 109-10.
LIPPMANN, KURT. Das ritterliche Persönlichkeitsideal
   in der mittel-englischen Literatur des 13. und 14.
   Jahrhunderts. Diss, Leipzig, 1933. 130 pp.
      Rev: R. Hoops, AB, 46, 1935, 201-4.
MANLY, JOHN M. A Knight Ther Was. TAPA, 38, 1907, 89-
   107.

MELLER, WALTER CLIFFORD. A Knight's Life in the
    Days of Chivalry. T. Werner Laurie, 1924. 316 pp.
        For reviews, see section: Social Backgrounds.
SEDGWICK, W. B. Satalye. RES, 2, 1926, 346.
        Line 58.
STILLWELL, GARDINER, and HENRY J. WEBB. Chau-
    cer's Knight and the Hundred Years' War. MLN, 59,
    1944, 45-7.
        Rev: D. Everett, YWES, 52-3.
WAUGH, M. T. The Lollard Knights. SHR, 11, 1913, 58-
    63, 88-92.

Squire, Lines 79-100

    See Manly, 501-3; Robinson, 754; Hinckley, 7-9;
Manly SNL, 257.

BAUM, PAULL F. Notes on Chaucer. MLN, 32, 1917, 376-7.
        Lines 91, 95.
BROWN, CARLETON. The Squire and the Number of the
    Canterbury Pilgrims. MLN, 49, 1934, 216-22.
KUHL, ERNEST P., and HENRY J. WEBB. Chaucer's
    Squire. ELH, 6, 1939, 282-4.
PRINS, A. A. Two Notes on the Prologue of Chaucer's
    Canterbury Tales. E Stud, 30, 1949, 42-4 and 65-83.
        Line A85.
        Rev: YWES, 57-8.
STEWART, GEORGE R., Jr. The Meaning of Bacheler
    in Middle English. PQ, 13, 1934, 40-7.

Yeoman, Lines 101-17

    See Manly, 503-4; Robinson, 754; Hinckley, 9-10;
Manly SNL, 257.

KRAPPE, EDITH SMITH. A Note on Chaucer's Yeoman.
    MLN, 43, 1928, 176-7.

Prioress, Nun, and Three Priests, Lines 118-64

    See Manly, 504-8; Robinson, 754-6; Hinckley, 10-
14; Manly SNL, 202-25, and the section: Religious
Backgrounds.

ALEXANDER, Sister MARY (ELIZABETH GLOOR
   GROSS). Notes and Comments on the Prioresse.
   Master's Thesis, Univ of Washington, 1930. Type-
   written, 113 pp.
BOYD, BEVERLY. Chaucer's Prioress: Her Green
   Gauds. MLQ, 11, 1950, 404-16.
      Rev: D. Everett, YWES, 57-8.
BRADDY, HALDEEN. Chaucerian Minutiae. MLN, 58,
   1943, 18-23.
      Crowned A, line 161.
      Rev: D. Everett, YWES, 41, 42.
BRENNAN, MAYNARD J. Speaking of the Prioress.
   MLQ, 10, 1949, 451-7.
      Influence of the Benedictine Rule on the Prior-
   ess.
      Rev: D. Everett, YWES, 30, 1949, 58.
BYRNE, Sister MARY-OF-THE-INCARNATION. The
   Tradition of the Nun in Medieval England. Doctoral
   Diss, Catholic Univ of America, 1932. Catholic Univ,
   1932. 235 pp.
      For reviews, see section: Religious Backgrounds.
CAWLEY, A. C. A Note on Chaucer's Prioress and Cri-
   seyde. MLR, 43, 1948, 74-7.
      Rev: D. Everett, YWES, 78.
CLARK, THOMAS BLAKE. The Forehead of Chaucer's
   Prioress. PQ, 9, 1930, 312-4.
DAVIES, R. T. Chaucer's Madame Eglantine. MLN, 67,
   1952, 400-2.
DRENNAN, C. M. Chaucer's Prioress, CT, Prol. 136:
   "Ful semely after hir mete she raughte." NQ, ser. 11,
   9, 1914, 365.
EMERSON, OLIVER F. Some Notes on Chaucer and Some
   Conjectures. PQ, 2, 1923, 81-96.
      A164, on "prestes three."
FISCHER, WALTHER. Die französischen Sprachkennt-
   nisse von Chaucers Priorin. Probleme der englischen
   Sprache und Kultur. 149-51, in Festschrift für Jo-
   hannes Hoops. Heidelberg, 1925.
FORSTER, MAX. Chauceriana I. Arch, 132, 1914, 399-
   401.
      "Chapeleine," A164.
HAMILTON, MARIE PADGETT. The Convent of Chau-
   cer's Prioress and her Priests. 179-90, in Kirby and

Woolf, Eds, Philologica: The Malone Anniversary
Studies. Johns Hopkins Press, 1949.
    For reviews, see section: General Criticism.
HAMMOND, ELEANOR P. Two Chaucer Cruces. MLN,
22, 1907, 51.
    "St. Loy, " A120.
HARPER, GORDON H. Chaucer's Big Prioress. PQ, 12,
1933, 308-10.
HEINRICH, Sister MARY P. The Canonesses and Educa-
tion in the Early Middle Ages. Diss, Washington Univ.
Privately printed, 1924.
HEMINGWAY, SAMUEL B. Chaucer's Monk and Nun's
Priest. MLN, 31, 1915, 479-83.
HINCKLEY, HENRY B. Chaucer's Prioress. Paper read
by title at MLA meeting, New Haven, Dec 29, 1917.
Listed in PMLA, 33, 1918, xxvii-xxviii.
HOSTIA, Sister MARY. The Prioress and her Compan-
ion. CE, 14, 1953, 351-2.
KIRBY, THOMAS A. The French of Chaucer's Prioress.
29-34, in Studies for William A. Read, 1940.
    Portrait of Prioress not satirical.
KUHL, ERNEST P. Notes on Chaucer's Prioress. PQ, 2,
1923, 302-9.
----------. Chaucer's Madame Eglantine. MLN, 60,
1945, 325-6.
    Rev: D. Everett, YWES, 47.
LEHMANN, W. P. A Rare Use of Numerals in Chaucer.
MLN, 67, 1952, 317-21.
    A conjecture on "preestes three, " by which this
means the Prioress, the Priest, and her Nun. See
Leo Spitzer, MLN, 67, 1952, 502-4.
LIVINGSTON, CHARLES H. Le Fabliau "Des Deux Ang-
lais et de l'Anel. " PMLA, 40, 1925, 217-24.
    See Fischer, above in this section, on the Prior-
ess' French.
LOWES, JOHN L. The Prioress' Oath. RR, 5, 1914, 368-85.
----------. Simple and Coy: A Note on Fourteenth Cen-
tury Poetic Diction. Ang, 33, 1910, 440-51.
LUMIANSKY, R. M. The Nun's Priest in the Canterbury
Tales. PMLA, 68, 1953, 896-906.
    Reviews the Host's position in CT and suggests that
the Nun's Priest was visualized as "scrawny, humble,
and timid. "

LYNCH, JAMES J. The Prioress's Gems. MLN, 57,
    1942, 440-1.
    Symbolism of the ruby, the emerald, and the
    pearl.
    Rev: D. Everett, YWES, 55.
McCARTHY, Sister BRIGETTA. Chaucer's Pilgrim-
    Prioress. Benedictine Rev, 6, 1951, 38-40.
MADELEVA, Sister MARY (MARY EVALINE WOLFF).
    Chaucer's Nuns and Other Essays. Appleton, 1925.
    215 pp.
    Rev: D. Everett, YWES, 92.
----------. Chaucer's Nuns. 270-82, in Century of
    Catholic Essay, Raphael Henry Gross, Ed, Lippin-
    cott, 1946.
MANLY, JOHN M. The Prioress of Stratford. TLS, Nov
    10, 1927, 817.
MOORE, ARTHUR K. The "Eyen Greye" of Chaucer's
    Prioress. PQ, 26, 1947, 307-12.
    Questions the meaning of "greye" as "blue."
MORAN, EUGENE A. Dining in 1424. Commonweal, 12,
    1930, 363.
POWER, EILEEN. Medieval People. Houghton, 1929.
    Madame Eglentyne, Chaucer's Prioress in Real
    Life, 59-84, and The Menagier's Wife, a Paris
    Housewife of the Fourteenth Century, 85-110.
    For review, see section: Social Backgrounds.
SHERBO, ARTHUR. Chaucer's Nun's Priest Again.
    PMLA, 64, 1949, 236-46.
    See Hamilton, Philologica: The Malone Anniversa-
    ry Studies, 179-90.
    Rev: D. Everett, YWES, 58-9.
SMITH, FRED M. Chaucer's Prioress and Criseyde.
    West Virginia Univ Bull: Philological Papers, 6, 1949,
    1-11.
    Rev: YWES, 65-6.
SPITZER, LEO. "And Prestes Three." MLN, 67, 1952,
    502-4.
    Opposed the interpretation of Lehmann, see above
    in this section.
VAN HERK, A. Chauceriana. Neophil, 2, 1917, 292-4.
    On A164.
WAINWRIGHT, BENJAMIN B. Chaucer's Prioress A-
    gain: An Interpretive Note. MLN, 48, 1933, 34-7.

WENTWORTH, CLARENCE L. The Prioress' Oath. RR,
27, 1936, 268-9.
See Lowes's article, above in this section.

Monk, Lines 165-207

See Manly, 508-11; Robinson, 756-7; Hinckley, 14-
16; Manly SNL, 261-2; and the section: Religious
Backgrounds.

BENNETT, H. S. Medieval Literature and the Modern
Reader. Essays and Studies, 31, 1945, 7-18.
CT, Prol, 165-94.
BRESSIE, RAMONA. "A Governour Wily and Wys."
MLN, 54, 1939, 477-90.
Parallels similarities between William de Cloune,
Abbot of Leicester (1345-78), and Chaucer's Monk.
----------. Chaucer's Monk Again. MLN, 56, 1941, 161-
2.
Addendum to preceding article, in reply to Tat-
lock, below.
CRAWFORD, S. J. Chaucer and St. Augustine. TLS,
Nov 13, 1930, 942.
A177-8.
DONOVAN, MORTIMER J. Three Notes on Chaucer's
Marine Life. PQ, 31, 1952, 439-41.
"Oystre," lines 177-82.
EICHLER, ALBERT. Zu Chaucer, Canterbury Tales,
General Prologue, line 207. ESt, 70, 1935, 102-5.
"Broun as is a berye."
Rev: YWES, 106.
FRANK, GRACE. Chaucer's Monk. MLN, 55, 1940, 780-
1.
HEMINGWAY, SAMUEL B. Chaucer's Monk and Nun's
Priest. MLN, 31, 1916, 479-83.
KUHL, E. P. Chaucer's Monk. MLN, 55, 1940, 480.
Comment on Professor Tatlock's paper noted be-
low.
MACAULAY, G. C. Notes on Chaucer. MLR, 4, 1908,
14-19.
A177-81, 525 ff.
MAYNARD, THEODORE. Chaucer's Monk. Month, Feb,
1935, 165-8.

PRINS, A. A. Two Notes on the Prologue of Chaucer's
    Canterbury Tales. E Stud, 30, 1949, 42-4 and 65-83.
    A173-6.
        Rev: D. Everett, YWES, 57-8.
SCHNEIDER, RUDOLPH. Der Mönch in der englischen
    Dichtung bis auf Lewis's Monk, 1795. Palaestra.
    Leipzig: Mayer and Müller, 1928.
TATLOCK, JOHN STRONG PERRY. The Date of the
    Troilus: and Minor Chauceriana. MLN, 50, 1935, 277-
    96.
        On line 176, "Heeld the space," 293-4.
----------. Chaucer's Monk. MLN, 55, 1940, 350-4.
        An interpretation of the Monk's character stress-
    ing the unity of conception in his own prologue and
    the description of him in the General Prologue. See
    E. P. Kuhl and Grace Frank, above.
----------. Is Chaucer's Monk a Monk? MLN, 56, 1941,
    80.
        Reply to Kuhl's comment, above in this section.
VISSER, F. TH. "This ilke Monke leet olde thynges
    pace." E Stud, 30, 1949, 133.
        A175.
        Reply by A. A. Prins, E Stud, 30, 1949, 133-4.
WILLARD, RUDOLPH. Chaucer's "Text that seith that
    hunters been nat hooly men." Univ of Texas: Studies
    in English, 1947, 209-51.
        Rev: D. Everett, YWES, 29, 1948, 85.

Friar, Lines 208-69

    See Manly, 511-3; Robinson, 757-8; Hinckley, 16-
20; Manly SNL, 102-22; and the section: Religious
Backgrounds.

BOWERS, R. H. A Middle English Poem on Lovedays.
    MLR, 47, 1952, 374-5.
        Line 258.
BRUCE, J. DOUGLAS. Prologue to the Canterbury Tales.
    MLN, 34, 1919, 118-9.
        A256, "purchas" and "rente."
FRANK, ROBERT WORTH, Jr. Chaucer and the London
    Bell-Founders. MLN, 68, 1953, 524-8.
        A263.

GREENLAW, EDWIN A. A Note on Chaucer's Prologue.
    MLN, 23, 1908, 142-4.
        A256.
HORTON, OZE E. The Neck of Chaucer's Friar. MLN,
    48, 1933, 31-4.
KENNARD, JOSEPH SPENCER. The Friar in Fiction,
    and Other Essays. Brentano, 1923.
        Chaucer's friars, 11-16.
KITTREDGE, GEORGE L. [Prologue 256.] MLN, 23,
    1908, 200.
LAW, ROBERT A. In Principio. PMLA, 37, 1922, 208-
    15.
        A254.
LOWES, JOHN LIVINGSTON. Illustrations of Chaucer
    Drawn Chiefly from Deschamps. RR, 2, 1911, 113-
    28.
        Rev: John Koch, ESt, 46, 1912, 114.
MEAD, GILBERT W. Chaucer's Friar, a Typical XIV
    Century Friar. Master's Thesis, Columbia, 1917.
MOSSE, F. Chaucer et la Liturgie. Rev Germ, 14, 1923,
    283-9.
SPARGO, JOHN W. Chaucer's Love-Days. Spec, 15,
    1940, 36-56.
        The etymology and custom of love-days, A258.
TATLOCK, JOHN STRONG PERRY. Notes on Chaucer:
    The Canterbury Tales. MLN, 29, 1914, 140-4.
        In principio, A254, pp. 141-2.
----------. The Date of the Troilus: and Minor Chaucer-
    iana. MLN, 50, 1935, 277-96.
        The Friar's order, 289-92.
TILLOTSON, KATHLEEN. The Friar's Lisp. TLS, April
    25, 1936, 356.
VAN HERK, A. Chauceriana. Neophil, 2, 1917, 292-4.
        A254.
YOUNG, KARL. A Note on Chaucer's Friar. MLN, 50,
    1935, 83-5.
        Rev: D. Everett, YWES, 105.

Merchant, Lines 270-84

See Manly, 513-5; Robinson, 758-9; Hinckley, 20-
2; Manly SNL, 181-200; and section: Economic Backgrounds.

JOHNSON, OSCAR E. Was Chaucer's Merchant in Debt:
A Study in Chaucer's Syntax and Rhetoric. JEGP, 52,
1953, 50-7.
KNOTT, THOMAS A. Chaucer's Anonymous Merchant.
PQ, 1, 1922, 1-16.
Rev: John Koch, ESt, 57, 1923, 122-3.
RICKERT, EDITH. Extracts from a 14th Century Ac-
count Book. MP, 24, 1926, 111-9, 249-56.
Suggestion of model for Chaucer's Merchant.
STILLWELL, GARDINER. Chaucer's "Sad" Merchant.
RES, 20, 1944, 1-18.
Background of similar persons in O. F. fabliaux
and elsewhere.
Rev: D. Everett, YWES, 43-4.
WALKER, A. STANLEY. Note on Chaucer's Prologue.
MLN, 38, 1923, 314.
A276-7 and on chronology.

Clerk, Lines 285-308

See Manly, 515-17; Robinson, 759-60; Hinckley,
22-3; Manly SNL, 261. See also Krebs, in section:
Clerk's Tale.

CAMDEN, CARROLL, Jr. Chauceriana. MLN, 47, 1932,
360-2.
On "moral vertu," line 307.
HULTON, SAMUEL F. The Clerk of Oxford in Fiction.
Methuen, 1909.
JONES, H. S. V. The Clerk of Oxenford. PMLA, 27,
1912, 106-15.
LEA, CHARLES H. A Fourteenth Century Book-Lover.
(Richard de Bury.) Engl Rev, 44, 1927, 714-9.
Suggestion that among the Clerk's "twenty bokes"
would be Bury's Philobiblon.
LOWES, JOHN L. Illustrations of Chaucer Drawn Chief-
ly from Deschamps. RR, 2, 1911, 113-28.
Rev: John Koch, ESt, 46, 1912, 114.
RICHARDSON, M. E. The Clerk of Oxenford. TLS, May
5, 1932, 331.
See R. B. Turton, TLS, May 19, 1932, 368; M. E.
Richardson, TLS, May 26, 1932, 390; and DNB, under
Diss, Walter.

TURRELL, BLANCHE. The Clerk of Oxenford. Master's
Thesis, Columbia, 1918.

Man of Law, Lines 309-30

See Manly, 517-9; Robinson, 760-1; Hinckley, 23-4;
Manly SNL, 131-57.

COHEN, HERMAN. A History of the English Bar and
Attornatus to 1450. Sweet and Maxwell, 1929. 622 pp.
Rev: TLS, June 13, 1929, 465.
ELIASON, MARY. The Peasant and the Lawyer. SP, 48,
1951, 506-26.
FROST, GEORGE L. Chaucer's Man of Law at the Par-
vis. MLN, 44, 1929, 496-501.
GOFFIN, R. C. Notes on Chaucer. MLR, 18, 1923, 336-
7.
A323.
KNOWLTON, E. C. Chaucer's Man of Law. JEGP, 23,
1924, 83-93.
LINTHICUM, M. C. "Faldyng" and "Medlee." JEGP, 34,
1935, 35-41.
WYATT, A. J. Chaucer's "In Termes." RES, 4, 1928,
439.
See also A. W. Reed, RES, 4, 1928, 220 n.

Franklin, Lines 331-60

See Manly, 519-22; Robinson, 761; Hinckley, 24-7;
Manly SNL, 157-68.

BLENNER-HASSETT, ROLAND. Autobiographical As-
pects of Chaucer's Franklin. Spec, 28, 1953, 791-800.
BRYANT, JOSEPH A., Jr. The Diet of Chaucer's
Franklin. MLN, 63, 1948, 318-25.
A passage from Secreta Secretorum illuminates
Chaucer's comment on the Franklin's diet.
Rev: D. Everett, YWES, 79.
CAMDEN, CARROLL, Jr. Chauceriana. MLN, 47, 1932,
360-2.
On "sanguin complexion."
GEROULD, GORDON HALL. The Social Status of Chau-
cer's Franklin. PMLA, 41, 1926, 262-79.

LUMIANSKY, R. M. The Character and Performance of
Chaucer's Franklin. UTQ, 20, 1951, 344-56.
PRINS, A. A. Further Notes on the Canterbury Tales.
E Stud, 32, 1951, 250-1.
On "in muwe," A349.
SAVAGE, HENRY. "Seint Julian He Was." MLN, 58,
1943, 47-8.
Rev: D. Everett, YWES, 41.
WOOD-LEGH, K. L. The Franklin. RES, 4, 1928, 145-
51.

Tradesmen, Lines 361-78

See Manly, 522; Robinson, 761-2; Hinckley, 27-8;
Manly SNL, 258-9. See also the section: Economic
Backgrounds.

CAMDEN, CARROLL, Jr. A Query on Chaucer's Bur-
gesses. PQ, 7, 1928, 314-7.
FULLERTON, ANN B. The Five Craftsmen. MLN, 61,
1946, 515-23.
A careful analysis of the position of these crafts-
man.
Rev: D. Everett, YWES, 76-7.
HERNDON, SARAH. Chaucer's Five Gildsmen. Florida
State Univ Studies, 5, 1952, 33-44.
KIRBY, THOMAS A. The Haberdasher and his Com-
panions. MLN, 53, 1938, 504-5.
KUHL, ERNEST P. Chaucer's Burgesses. Trans Wis-
consin Academy of Sciences, Arts, and Letters, 18,
1916, 652-75.
Rev: G. G. Coulton, MLR, 12, 1917, 512.
NATHAN, NORMAN. The Number of the Canterbury
Pilgrims. MLN, 67, 1952, 533-4.

Cook, Lines 379-87

See Manly, 522-3; Robinson, 762; Hinckley, 28-9;
Manly SNL, 259-60; Curry, 37-53, 247-9.

BRADDY, HALDEEN. The Cook's Mormal and its Cure.
MLQ, 7, 1946, 265-7.
Rev: D. Everett, YWES, 77.

COOK, ALBERT S. Note on Mormal. MLN, 33, 1918,
   379.
----------. Chaucerian Papers. Connecticut Academy,
   23, 1919, 5-63.
     "Mormal, " 386.
CURRY, WALTER C. Two Notes on Chaucer. MLN, 36,
   1921, 272-6.
     A386.
LYON, EARL D. The Cook's Tale, its Social Background, and the Identity of the Cook. Diss, Univ of
   California, 1938.
----------. Roger de Ware, Cook. MLN, 52, 1937, 491-
   4.
     Rev: D. Everett, YWES, 80.

Shipman, Lines 388-410

     See Manly, 523-4; Robinson, 762; Hinckley, 29-31;
Manly SNL, 169-81.

CHALK, EDWIN S. Chaucer Allusions. NQ, 169, 1935,
   241.
     Mention of a visit to Dartmouth by Chaucer, and of
   the ship of the Shipman.
GALWAY, MARGARET. Chaucer's Shipman in Real
   Life. MLR, 34, 1939, 497-514.
LINTHICUM, M. C. "Faldyng" and "Medlee." JEGP, 34,
   1935, 39-41.
MABBOTT, T. O. Chaucer's Shipman and the Shipman's
   Gild. NQ, 192, 1947, 372.
     Supplementary to Stillwell, below in this section.
MALONE, KEMP. "From Hulle to Cartage." MLN, 45,
   1930, 229-30.
STILLWELL, GARDINER. Chaucer's Shipman and the
   "Shipman's Gild." NQ, 192, May 17, 1947, 203-5.
     Rev: D. Everett, YWES, 75.
STOBIE, MARGARET R. Chaucer's Shipman and the
   Wine. PMLA, 64, 1949, 565-9.
     Rev: D. Everett, YWES, 59.
WHITE, FLORENCE E. Chaucer's Shipman. MP, 26,
   1928, 249-55; 26, 1929, 279-84; 27, 1929, 123-8.
     Documents.

Physician, Lines 411-44

See Manly, 524-7; Robinson, 762-4; Hinckley, 31-6; Manly SNL, 260-1; Curry, 3-36, 241-6.

ANON. Memorabilia. NQ, 169, 1935, 397.
Brief account of Dr. J. D. Rolleston's paper on Chaucer and Mediaeval Medicine, in Comptes Rendus du IXe Congrès International d'Histoire de la Médecine, 14. IX, '32. Bukarest, 1935.

BASHFORD, H. H. Chaucer's Physician and his Forebears. Nineteenth Century, 104, 1928, 237-48.

CAMDEN, CARROLL, Jr. Chauceriana. MLN, 47, 1932, 360-2.
On lines 417-8, "Wel coude he fortunen."

CAMPBELL, DONALD. Arabian Medicine, and its Influence on the Middle Ages. Trübner's Oriental Series. Dutton, 1926.
Arabic influence in England, I, 175, 198-200.

CURRY, WALTER CLYDE. Chaucer's Doctor of Phisyk. PQ, 4, 1925, 1-24.

DOCK, GEORGE. Printed Editions of the Rosa Anglica of John of Gaddesden. Amsterdam (?), 1907. 11 pp.
Extrait du Janus, Archives Internationales pour l'Histoire de la Médecine et la Géographie Médicale. XIIe Année Livraisons, I, viii, 1907.

JOHN of GADDESDEN. Rosa Anglica; seu Rosa medicinae Johannis Anglici; an early modern Irish translation of a section of the mediaeval medical text-book; ed. with introduction, glossary, and English version by Winifred Wulff. Irish Texts Society. Publications, vol. 25. Simpkin, 1930. 434 pp.

LOWES, JOHN L. The Loveres Malady of Hereos. MP, 11, 1914, 491-546.
See also Hereos, Nation, 97, 1913, 233, and Hereos Again, MLN, 31, 1916, 185-6.
Rev: John Koch, AB, 25, 1914, 332-9.

NICHOLLS, ALBERT G. Medicine in Chaucer's Day. Dalhousie Rev, 12, 1932, 218-30.
Extensive treatment of Chaucer's Doctour of Phisyk and his relation to the medical knowledge of the time.

SULLIVAN, FRANK. Chaucer's Physician and Genesis
   XXXI:20. Los Angeles Tidings, Dec 31, 1948, p. 9.
TUPPER, FREDERICK. Chaucer's Doctour of Phisik.
   Nation, 96, 1913, 640-1.

Wife of Bath, Lines 445-76

See Wife of Bath's Tale, below. See also Manly,
527-8; Robinson, 764-5; Hinckley, 37-9; Manly SNL,
225-34; Curry, 91-118, 253-6.

BARNOUW, A. J. The Prente of Seinte Venus Seel. Na-
   tion, 103, 1916, 540.
   A468.
COOK, ALBERT S. Chaucer's Prologue 466. MLN, 22,
   1907, 126.
CURRY, WALTER C. More about Chaucer's Wife of
   Bath. PMLA, 37, 1922, 30-51.
KIRBY, THOMAS A. "Of remedies of love she knew per
   chaunce." North Central Bulletin, 11:14.
   Abstract of paper.
KITTREDGE, GEORGE LYMAN. Chauceriana. MP, 7,
   1910, 475-7.
   A449-52, 475-7.
LOWES, JOHN L. Illustrations of Chaucer Drawn Chief-
   ly from Deschamps. RR, 2, 1911, 113-28.
   Rev: John Koch, ESt, 46, 1912, 114.
SCHULTZE, K. Zu Chaucers Weib von Bath und Shake-
   speares Kaufmann von Venedig. GRM, 8, 1920,
   103-5.
   Lines 445 ff.
WRETLIND, DALE E. The Wife of Bath's Hat. MLN,
   63, 1948, 381-2.
   Rev: D. Everett, YWES, 79.

Parson, Lines 477-528

See Manly, 528-30; Robinson, 765-6; Hinckley, 39-
40; Manly SNL, 260.

COOK, ALBERT S. Chaucerian Papers. Connecticut
   Acad, 23, 1919, 5-63.
   A493-8, 527-8.

FANCHER, PAUL ADEE. Chaucer's Country Parson.
Master's Thesis, Columbia, 1916.
IVES, DORIS V. "A Man of Religion." MLR, 27, 1932,
144-8.
LOWES, JOHN L. Chaucer and Li Renclus de Moiliens.
Abstract of paper, PMLA, 29, 1914, xxix.
MACAULAY, G. C. Notes on Chaucer. MLR, 4, 1908,
14-19.
    A525 ff.
MAXFIELD, EZRA. Chaucer and Religious Reform.
PMLA, 39, 1924, 64-74.
PALMER, H. P. Excommunication in the Middle Ages.
QR, 251, 1928, 129-43.
SCHACHT, HEINRICH. Der gute Pfarrer in der englisch-
en Literatur bis zu Goldsmiths Vicar of Wakefield.
Diss, Berlin, 1904.
    Rev: Richard Ackermann, AB, 20, 1909, 42-4.
TATLOCK, JOHN STRONG PERRY. Bretherhed in Chau-
cer's Prologue. MLN, 31, 1916, 139-42.
----------. Chaucer and Wyclif. MP, 14, 1916, 257-68.

Plowman, Lines 529-41

See Manly, 530; Robinson, 766.

HORRELL, JOE. Chaucer's Symbolic Plowman. Spec,
14, 1939, 82-92.
STILLWELL, GARDINER. Chaucer's Plowman and the
Contemporary English Peasant. ELH, 6, 1939, 285-
90.
    Also in Programs Announcing Candidates for High-
er Degrees, Univ of Iowa, 1940.

Miller, Lines 542-66

See Manly, 530-1; Robinson, 766-7; Hinckley, 40-
2; Manly SNL, 94-101; Curry, 71-90, 251-2.

CURRY, WALTER C. Chaucer's Reeve and Miller.
PMLA, 35, 1920, 189-209.
GALWAY, MARGARET. The History of Chaucer's
Miller. NQ, 195, Nov 11, 1950, 486-8.
    Rev: D. Everett, YWES, 59-60.

HANFORD, JAMES H. The Progenitors of Golias. Spec,
   1, 1926, 38-58.
MANLY, JOHN M. Familia Goliae. MP, 5, 1907-8, 201-9.
PRATT, ROBERT A. The Beard of Chaucer's Miller.
   NQ, 195, 1950, 568.
THOMPSON, JAMES W. Origin of the Word, Goliardi.
   SP, 20, 1923, 83-98.
      References and suggested etymology.
UTLEY, FRANCIS L. The Last of the Miller's Head?
   MLN, 56, 1941, 534-6.
WHITING, B. J. The Miller's Head. MLN, 52, 1937, 417-9.
WILEY, AUTREY N. The Miller's Head Again. MLN,
   53, 1938, 505-7.
      Rev: YWES, 74.

Manciple, Lines 567-86

See Manly, 531-2; Robinson, 767; Hinckley, 42;
Manly SNL, 257-8.

Reeve, Lines 587-622

See Manly, 532-3; Robinson, 767-8; Hinckley, 42;
Manly SNL, 84-94; Curry, 71-90, 251-2.

CURRY, WALTER C. Chaucer's Reeve and Miller.
   PMLA, 35, 1920, 189-209.
MOFFETT, H. Y. Oswald the Reeve. PQ, 4, 1925, 208-
   23.
POWLEY, EDWARD B. Chaucer's Reeve. TLS, July 14,
   1932, 516.
      See Lilian J. Redstone, TLS, Oct 27, 1932, 789.

Summoner, Lines 623-68

See Manly, 533-5; Robinson, 768-9; Hinckley, 42-
4; Manly SNL, 102-22; Curry, 37-53, 247-9.

AIKEN, PAULINE. The Summoner's Malady. SP, 33,
   1936, 40-44.
BLOOMFIELD, MORTON W. Chaucer's Summoner and
   the Girls of the Diocese. PQ, 28, 1949, 503-7.
      Rev: YWES, 30, 1949, 59-60.

CURRY, WALTER C. The Malady of Chaucer's Summoner. MP, 19, 1922, 395-404.

HASELMAYER, LOUIS A. The Apparitor and Chaucer's Summoner. Spec, 12, 1937, 43-57.

KITTREDGE, GEORGE L. Chauceriana. MP, 7, 1910, 475-7. "A finch eek coude he pulle," A652.

LANGE, HUGO. Die Bedeutung der Heraldik für die Erklärung eines mittelalterlichen Dichters. Forschungen und Fortschritte, 13, 1937, 59-60.
> Rev: D. Everett, YWES, 81.

PALMER, H. P. The Troubles of a Mediaeval Bishop. LQR, 152, 1929, 172-84.
> Comparison of Grandisson's archdeacons with Chaucer's Summoner, 173-4.

PATCH, HOWARD R. Chauceriana. ES, 65, 1931, 351-9. A658.

SLEETH, CHARLES R. The Friendship of Chaucer's Summoner and Pardoner. MLN, 56, 1941, 138.
> Rev: D. Everett, YWES, 59.

SPARGO, JOHN W. "Questio Quid Iuris." MLN, 62, 1947, 119-22.
> Rev: D. Everett, YWES, 28, 1947, 75.

TATLOCK, JOHN STRONG PERRY. Chaucer and Wyclif. MP, 14, 1916, 257-68.
> A653-62.

WOOLF, HENRY B. The Summoner and his Concubine. MLN, 68, 1953, 118-21.

Pardoner, Lines 669-714

See Manly, 535-7; Robinson, 769-70; Hinckley, 44-6; Manly SNL, 122-30; Curry, 54-70, 249-51; Gerould, 55-71.

CURRY, WALTER C. The Secret of Chaucer's Pardoner. JEGP, 18, 1919, 593-606.

DIECKMANN, EMMA POPE M. The Meaning of "Burdoun" in Chaucer. MP, 26, 1929, 279-82.
> A673.

HENDRICKSON, D. W. The Pardoner's Hair -- Abundant or Sparse? MLN, 66, 1951, 328-9.

MOORE, SAMUEL. Chaucer's Pardoner of Rouncivall. MP, 25, 1927, 59-66.

MOSSE, F. Chaucer et la Liturgie. Rev Germ, 14, 1923,
283-9.
SLEETH, CHARLES R. The Friendship of Chaucer's
Summoner and Pardoner. MLN, 56, 1941, 138.
Connivance with Summoner would help Pardoner
make "the persoun and the peple his apes."
Rev: D. Everett, YWES, 59.
TUPPER, FREDERICK. The Pardoner's Tavern. JEGP,
13, 1914, 553-65.
YOUNG, KARL. Chaucer and the Liturgy. MLN, 30,
1915, 97-9.
A707-10.

Host

See Manly, 538; Robinson, 770; Manly SNL, 77-83.

LUMIANSKY, R. M. The Nun's Priest in the Canterbury
Tales. PMLA, 68, 1953, 896-906.
Reviews the Host's position.
RICKERT, EDITH. Godeleef, my Wyf. TLS, Dec 16,
1926, 935.
References to Harry Bailiff.

THE KNIGHT'S TALE

See Hammond, 270-4; Root, 163-73; Robinson, 770-
85, 1006; French, 210-5; Curry, 119-63, 256-60; Manly, 539-58; Shannon, 302-7; Hinckley, 50-120; Tatlock, 45, 226, 231.
For editions, all of which have introductions and
notes, see the section: Editions with Notes. Also see
Schlauch in section: Social Backgrounds, and Cummings in section: Literary Relations and Sources.
Cloyd, Romance Element, etc., in section: Language,
uses the Knight's Tale in computing his percentages
of romance words.

ACKERMAN, R. W. Tester: Knight's Tale, 2499. MLN,
49, 1934, 397-400.
AIKEN, PAULINE. Arcite's Illness and Vincent of
Beauvais. PMLA, 51, 1936, 316-9.
BAKER, COURTLAND D. A Note on Chaucer's

"Knight's Tale." MLN, 45, 1930, 460-2.
    See Hulbert, below in this section.
BATTAGLIA, S., Ed. Giovanni Boccaccio: Teseida. Fi-
    renze, 1938.
        Rev: Germaine Dempster, MP, 38, 1940, 205-14;
    R. A. Pratt, PMLA, 62, 1947, 598-9; G. Contini,
    Giorn Stor de la Litt Ital, 112, 1938, 86-96; C. S.
    Singleton, Spec, 14, 1939, 373-6.
BAUM, PAULL F. Characterization in the "Knight's
    Tale." MLN, 46, 1931, 302-4.
BENNETT, J. A. W. Chaucer, Dante, and Boccaccio.
    MA, 22, 1953, 114-5.
        Boccaccio's verses calling to mind Dante's for
    Chaucer.
BESCHORNER, FRANZ. Verbale Reime bei Chaucer.
    Studien zur englischen Philologie, 60. Niemeyer,
    1920.
        Rev: W. Preusler, Cbl, 72, 1921, 396-7; John
    Koch, LGRP, 43, 1922, 102-5.
BIVAR, A. D. H. The Death of Eucratides in Medieval
    Tradition. Jour Royal Asiatic Soc, pts. 1-2, 1950,
    7-13.
        "The grete Emetrius, the kyng of Inde," KnT, 2155.
BOCCACCIO, GIOVANNI. [Theseyda, in twelve books; a
    reproduction of Laurentian ms. 325 in the Biblioteca
    mediceo-laurenziana at Florence.] 2 vols. MLA of
    America. Collection of Photographic Facsimiles, no.
    311. 1935. Deposited in the Library of Congress.
BROOKS, CLEANTH. Chaucer: Saturn's Daughter. MLN,
    49, 1934, 459-61.
        Line 2453.
BROWNE, WILLIAM H. Notes on Chaucer's Astrology.
    MLN, 23, 1908, 53-4.
BUNGE, ELDO F. Chaucer's Knight's Tale. Master's
    Thesis, Univ of Iowa, 1932.
CAPONE, G. Marginalia a la Novella del Cavaliere di
    Goffredo Chaucer: La Concezione de la Storia nel
    Petrarca e nel Chaucer. Sassari, 1912.
----------. La Novella del Cavaliere di Geoffrey Chau-
    cer e la Teseide di Giovanni Boccaccio. 2 pts. Sas-
    sari, 1907, 1909.
CARDLE, MARGARET H. Chaucer's Knight's Tale.
    Master's Thesis, Univ of Iowa, 1934.

COOK, ALBERT S. Chaucer: Knight's Tale 2012-8. RR,
    9, 1918, 317.
----------. Chaucer's Fraknes. MLN, 31, 1916, 315.
----------. The Historical Background of Chaucer's
    Knight. Yale Univ Press, 1916.
        Also discusses "fracknes," see entry next above.
        For reviews, see section: General Criticism.
----------. The Last Months of Chaucer's Earliest
    Patron. Trans Connecticut Academy of Arts and Sci-
    ences, 21, 1916, 128.
        On lines A2148-52.
        Rev: F. Liebermann, Arch, 145, 1923, 258.
----------. Chaucerian Papers. Connecticut Acad, 23,
    1919, 1-63.
        Line 2148, "alauntz." Also see 21, 1916, 128-40,
    appendix B, for "alauntz" with illustrations.
----------. Miscellaneous Notes. MLN, 22, 1907, 207-
    9.
        Line 810.
CRIPPS-DAY, F. H. A History of the Tournament in
    England and France. London, 1918.
CURRY, WALTER CLYDE. Arcite's Intellect. JEGP,
    29, 1930, 83-99.
        Rev: D. Everett, YWES, 87-9.
----------. Astrologizing the Gods. Ang, 47, 1923, 213-
    43.
----------. Chaucer's Science and Art. Texas Rev, 8,
    1923, 307-22.
----------. Two Notes on Chaucer. MLN, 36, 1921, 272-
    4.
        On A884.
DAY, MABEL. A Note on "The Knightes Tale," A 2625.
    MLR, 23, 1928, 208.
DEROCQUIGNY, J. Notes sur Chaucer. Rev Germ, 6,
    1910, 203-6.
DODD, WILLIAM G. Courtly Love in Chaucer and Gower.
    Harvard Studies in English, 1. Ginn; Milford, 1913.
        For reviews see section: Literary Relations.
DUSTOOR, P. E. Chaucer's Astrology in "The Knightes
    Tale." TLS, May 5, 1927, 318.
        A1462, 2684.
----------. Notes on "The Knightes Tale." MLR, 22,
    1927, 438-41.

EGG, W. Chaucer: Knight's Tale: Eine literarische
Skizze. Jsb der Stattsrealschule in Marburg, 42.
Leipzig: Fock, 1912.
    Rev: A. Eichler, ZFOG, 66, 478.
EMERSON, OLIVER FARRAR. Chaucer's "Opie of
Thebes Fyn." MP, 17, 1919, 287-91.
----------. A New Note on the Date of Chaucer's
Knight's Tale. Studies in Language and Literature in
Celebration of the Seventieth Birthday of James M.
Hart. New York, 1910.
    Rev: Bernhard Fehr, AB, 23, 1911, 365-6; H. S. V.
Jones, JEGP, 10, 1911, 491-2.
----------. Some Notes on Chaucer and Some Conjec-
tures. PQ, 2, 1923, 81-96.
    On "y-bete," A979-80.
FAIRCHILD, HOXIE NEALE. Active Arcite, Contempla-
tive Palamon. JEGP, 26, 1927, 285-93.
    Rev: D. Everett, YWES, 108.
FRENCH, W. H. The Lovers in the Knight's Tale. JEGP,
48, 1949, 320-8.
    Character interpretation of Palamon and Arcite.
    Rev: D. Everett, YWES, 61.
FROST, WILLIAM. An Interpretation of Chaucer's
Knight's Tale. RES, 25, 1949, 289-304.
    See Webb, below.
    Rev: D. Everett, YWES, 60-1.
GARVIN, KATHARINE. Note on the Tournament in the
Knightes Tale. MLN, 46, 1931, 453-4.
GIBBS, LINCOLN R. The Meaning of "Feeldes" in
Chaucer's Knight's Tale, vv. 975-7. MLN, 24, 1909,
197-8.
    See Kittredge, below in this section.
GILDERSLEEVE, VIRGINIA C. Chaucer and Sir Aldin-
ger. MLN, 25, 1910, 30.
HAM, EDWARD B. Knight's Tale, 38. ELH, 17, 1950,
252-61.
    Rev: D. Everett, YWES, 61.
HAMMOND, ELEANOR P. Chaucer and Lydgate Notes.
MLN, 27, 1912, 91-2.
    "Shippes hoppesteres," A2017.
HARRIS, ELIZABETH L. The Mural as a Decorative De-
vice in Mediaeval Literature. Doctoral Diss, Vander-
bilt. Vanderbilt Univ Press, 1935. 89 pp.

HART, WALTER MORRIS. The Lady in the Garden.
    MLN, 22, 1907, 241-2.
HEMPL, GEORGE. Palamon and Arcite. MLN, 23, 1908,
    127-8.
        Discussion of opposition to Ten Brink's Palamon
    and Arcite theory, Tatlock and Mather cooperating.
HERBEN, STEPHEN J., Jr. Knight's Tale, A 1881 ff.
    MLN, 53, 1938, 595.
HIBBARD, LAURA A. Chaucer's Shapen Was my Sherte.
    PQ, 1, 1922, 222-5.
        A1566.
HINCKLEY, HENRY B. Chaucer and Ywaine and Gawin.
    Acad, 1906, II, 640-1.
        See also Skeat's reported opinion, Acad, 1906, II,
    647, and Hinckley's reply, Acad, 1907, I, 99.
----------. Chauceriana. MP, 14, 1916-7, 317-8; 15,
    1917-8, 56.
----------. The Grete Emetreus the King of Inde. MLN,
    48, 1933, 148-9.
HULBERT, J. R. What Was Chaucer's Aim in the
    Knight's Tale? SP, 26, 1929, 375-85.
        Rev: D. Everett, YWES, 114-5.
HUSTVEDT, S. B. Under the Sonne He Looketh. MLN,
    44, 1929, 182.
        A1697.
JEFFERSON, BERNARD L. Chaucer and the Consolation
    of Philosophy of Boethius. Princeton Univ Press, 1917.
    168 pp.
        Rev: Howard R. Patch, JEGP, 16, 1917, 620-4.
KAHANE, HENRY and RENEE. Akritas and Arcite: A
    Byzantine Source of Boccaccio's Teseida. Spec, 20,
    1945, 415-25.
KITTREDGE, GEORGE L. On "Feeldes" in the Knight's
    Tale. MLN, 25, 1910, 28.
KLAEBER, FR. Looking under the Sun. MLN, 37, 1922, 376.
        A1697.
KLEE, FR. Das Enjambement bei Chaucer. Diss, Halle,
    1913.
        Chronology.
KLEINECKE, WILHELM. Englische Fürstenspiegel vom
    Policraticus Johanns von Salisbury bis zum Basilikon
    Doron König Jakobs I. Stud. z. engl. Phil., 90. Nie-
    meyer, 1937. 223 pp.

Rev: G. Linke, Archiv, 174, 1938, 258-9; W.
Ebisch, AB, 49, 1938, 205-7; J. Huisinga, E Stud,
20, 1938, 34-5; K. Brunner, LGRP, 60, 1939, 284-6;
K. M., MLN, 55, 1940, 241; Hermann Heuer, ES, 75,
1942, 84-5.

KOCH, JOHN. Alte Chaucerprobleme und neue Lösungs-
versuche. ESt, 55, 1921, 161-225.
Palamon and Arcite, 196-209.

KUHL, E. P. Chaucer and the Red Rose. PQ, 24, 1945,
33-8.
KnT, 1038, 1053 ff. Associates the red rose with
Lancaster.
Rev: D. Everett, YWES, 52.

LANGE, HUGO. Review of Cummings, The Indebtedness.
AB, 29, 1918, 139.
KnT, 975 ff.

LIEBERMANN, FELIX. Theseus Herzogstitel bei Chaucer. Arch, 145, 1923, 101-2.

LOWES, JOHN LIVINGSTON. Chaucer and Dante. MP,
14, 1917, 705-35.
On A1329-31, p. 715.
----------. Chaucer's Friday. MLR, 9, 1914, 94.
A1534-9.
Rev: John Koch, AB, 25, 1914, 337.
----------. The Loveres Maladye of Hereos. MP, 11,
1914, 491-546.
See also Lowes, Hereos, Nation, 97, 1913, 233;
and Hereos Again, MLN, 31, 1916, 185-6.
Rev: John Koch, AB, 25, 1914, 332-9.
----------. The Franklin's Tale, the Teseide and the
Filocolo. MP, 15, 1918, 689-728.
KnT, A2431-3.

LUMIANSKY, R. M. Chaucer's Philosophical Knight.
Tulane Studies in English, 3, 1952, 47-68.

MACAULAY, G. C. Notes on Chaucer. MLR, 4, 1909,
14-19.
Lines A297, 309 ff.

MacCRACKEN, HENRY N. The Laborer, the Bochour,
and the Smyth. MLN, 28, 1913, 230.
Lines A2024-6.

MARCKWARDT, ALBERT H. Characterization in Chaucer's Knight's Tale. Univ of Michigan Contributions
in Modern Philology, No. 5; Oxford, 1947. 83 pp.

Rev: D. Everett, YWES, 76-7; A. W. Read, MLR,
43, 1948, 247-8.

MATHER, FRANK J. The Prologue, the Knight's Tale,
and the Nun's Priest's Tale. Houghton, 1908.
    Especially the comparison of the Knight's Tale
with the Teseide, lxi-lxxiii.

MEYER, EMIL. Die Charakterzeichnung bei Chaucer.
Studien zur englischen Philologie, 48. Niemeyer,
1913. 95 pp.
    For reviews, see section: General Criticism.

MUSCATINE, CHARLES. Form, Texture, and Meaning
in Chaucer's Knight's Tale. PMLA, 65, 1950, 911-29.
    Rev: D. Everett, YWES, 60-1.

OLLER, NARIE. The Knight's Tale: A Study of its Dramatic Quality. Master's Thesis, Columbia Univ, 1913.

PARR, JOHNSTONE. The Date and Revision of Chaucer's
Knight's Tale. PMLA, 60, 1945, 307-24.
    Evidence for dating the revision after the middle
of 1390. See Pratt and Weese, below in this section.

----------. "Life Is a Pilgrimage" in Chaucer's
Knight's Tale 2847-9. MLN, 67, 1952, 340-1.

PATCH, HOWARD R. Under the Sonne. MLN, 38, 1923,
60.
    A1697.

----------. Chauceriana. ES, 65, 1931, 351-9.
    A1096-7. Also see Chaucer and Medieval Romance
in section: General Criticism.

PATTISON, BRUCE. Music and Poetry in the English
Renaissance. London, 1948.
    Lines 1510-6.

PETERSEN, OTTOMAR. The Two Noble Kinsmen. Ang,
38, 1914, 213-26.

PRATT, ROBERT ARMSTRONG. The Knight's Tale.
Sources and Analogues, 82-105.

----------. Conjectures Regarding Chaucer's Manuscript of the Teseida. SP, 42, 1945, 745-63.
    Footnote bibliography on MSS.
    Suggests a rather poor MS without Boccaccio's
commentary.
    Rev: D. Everett, YWES, 54-5.

----------. Chaucer's Use of the Teseida. PMLA, 62,
1947, 598-621.
    Rev: D. Everett, YWES, 68-70. In PMLA, 63,

1948, 729 n, Pratt lists a few minor errata of this article.

----------. Was Chaucer's Knight's Tale Extensively
Revised after 1390? PMLA, 63, 1948, 726-36.
    See Parr, above in this section and following this
    article, pp. 736-9.
    Rev: D. Everett, YWES, 79-80.

PURVES, JOHN. The MS of Boccaccio's "Teseide."
TLS, Feb 21, 1929, 142.

ROBERTSON, STUART. Elements of Realism in the
Knight's Tale. JEGP, 14, 1915, 226-55.

----------. Old English Verse in Chaucer. MLN, 43,
1928, 234-6.

RONCAGLIA, A., Ed. Giovanni Boccaccio: Teseida
delle Nozze d'Emilia. Scrittori d'Italia. Bari, 1941.
    Rev: R. A. Pratt, PMLA, 62, 1947, 598-9.

ROOT, ROBERT K. Chaucer's Dares. MP, 15, 1917, 1-
22.
    Chaucer's catalogue of trees, 18-22, A2062-4.

SAVAGE, HENRY. "Under the sonne." Knight's Tale,
1697-8. TLS, June 14, 1934, 424.

----------. Arcite's Maying. MLN, 55, 1940, 207-9.
    Refers to a Book of the Hours to illustrate Arcite's
    actions.

SCHOFFLER, HERBERT. Chauceriana. AB, 29, 1918,
42-8.
    On "save," A2713, pp. 42-6.

SMITH, C. ALPHONSO. Under the Sonne He Loketh.
MLN, 37, 1922, 120-1.
    A1697.

SMITH, ROLAND M. Three Notes on the Knight's Tale.
MLN, 51, 1936, 315-22.
    Unlucky Days in the Chaucer Tradition, A1462 ff.;
    "Under the Sonne"; "The Thridde Nyght in May"; Al-
    literative Description of the Tournament, A2601-16.

----------. Five Notes on Chaucer and Froissart. MLN,
66, 1951, 27-32.
    KnT, 2062-8, Dane and Diane, and Acteon.

TATLOCK, JOHN STRONG PERRY. Palamon and Arcite.
MLN, 23, 1908, 127-8.
    On an earlier version of KnT.

----------. Notes on Chaucer: The Canterbury Tales.
MLN, 29, 1914, 140-4.
    Friday weather, A1539, p. 142.

----------. The Sources of the Legend and Other Chau-
ceriana. SP, 18, 1921, 419-28.
     Similarity between the Prol, LGW, and KnT, 1683-9.
----------. "Under the Sonne." MLN, 37, 1922, 377.
     A1697.
TORRACA, F. Knightes Tale e la Teseide. Società Re-
ale di Napoli. Accademia di Archeologia, Lettere e
Belle Arti. Atti, n. s. 10, 1928, 199-217.
VAN ROOSBROECK, GUSTAVE L. "Under the Sonne He
Loketh." MLN, 38, 1923, 59.
     A1697.
VOCKRODT, G. Reimteknik bei Chaucer als Mittel zur
chronologischen Bestimmung seiner im Reimpaar ge-
schriebenen Werke. Halle, 1914.
WAGER, WILLIS J. The So-called Prologue to the
Knight's Tale. MLN, 50, 1935, 296-307.
     KnT, 875-92, proposed as added for the CT.
WEBB, HENRY J. A Reinterpretation of Chaucer's The-
seus. RES, 23, 1947, 289-96.
     Rev: D. Everett, YWES, 78.
WEBSTER, C. M. Chaucer's Turkish Bows. MLN, 47,
1932, 260.
WEESE, WALTER E. "Vengeance and Pleyn Correcci-
oun," Knight's Tale 2461. MLN, 63, 1948, 331-3.
     See Parr, above.
     Rev: D. Everett, YWES, 79-80.
WILLIAMS, W. H. Palamon and Arcite and the Knight's
Tale. MLR, 9, 1914, 161-72, 309-23.
WILSON, H. S. The Knight's Tale and the Teseida A-
gain. UTQ, 18, 1949, 131-46.
     A story of submission to the divine plan which af-
ter grief makes its own justification.
     Rev: D. Everett, YWES, 61-2.

               THE MILLER'S PROLOGUE AND TALE

     See Hammond, 275; Root, 173-9; Robinson, 786-9,
1006-7; French, 215-7; Manly, 558-60, and SNL, 94-
101; Curry, 71 ff.

ALBRECHT, W. P. Chaucer's Miller's Tale. Expl, 9, 1951,
item 25.

ANDRAE, A. Zu Longfellows und Chaucers Tales. AB,
    27, 1916, 61.
BARNOUW, A. J. Chaucer's Miller's Tale. MLR, 7,
    1912, 145-8.
        See Koch, AB, 22, 1911, 271.
BEICHNER, PAUL E. Chaucer's Hende Nicholas. Med
    Stud, 14, 1952, 151-3.
----------. Absolom's Hair. Med Stud, 12, 1950, 222-
    33.
BROWN, DAVID. "Solas" in the Miller's Tale. MLN, 48,
    1933, 369-70.
        See Collins, below in this section (same title).
BRUSENDORFF, AAGE. "He Knew Nat Catoun for his
    Wit Was Rude." 320-39, in Studies in English Philol-
    ogy. A Miscellany in Honor of Frederick Klaeber, ed
    by Kemp Malone and Martin Ruud. Univ of Minnesota
    Press, 1929.
BUHLER, CURT F. "Wirk al thing by conseil." Spec,
    24, 1949, 410-2.
        Sources of the proverb in Chaucer.
        Rev: D. Everett, YWES, 62.
CLINE, RUTH H. Four Chaucer Saints. MLN, 60, 1945,
    480-2.
        The significance of swearing by St. Frideswide,
    St. Cuthbert, St. Yve, St. Thomas, the Apostle.
    MilT, 3449.
        Rev: D. Everett, YWES, 49-50.
COFFMAN, GEORGE R. A Note on the Miller's Pro-
    logue. MLN, 50, 1935, 311-2.
        "For I wol telle a legende."
----------. The Miller's Tale: 3187-3215: Chaucer and
    the Seven Liberal Arts in Burlesque Vein. MLN, 67,
    1952, 329-31.
COLLINS, FLETCHER. The Kinges Note, the Miller's
    Tale, line 31: Ave rex gentis Anglorum, a Suggestion.
    Spec, 8, 1933, 195-7.
----------. "Solas" in the Miller's Tale. MLN, 47,
    1932, 363-4.
        See Brown, above in this section.
COOTE, HENRY CHARLES. St. Peter's Sister. Acad,
    18, 1880, 64.
        Same, by T. F. Crane, Acad, 18, 1880, 156.
DONALDSON, E. T. Idiom of Popular Poetry in the

Miller's Tale. Eng Inst Essays, 1950, ed by Alan
S. Downes, 116-40.
ELLINWOOD, LEONARD. A Further Note on "Pilate's
Voys." Spec, 26, 1951, 482.
Pilate's voice defined as a musical term.
FARNHAM, WILLARD E. The Dayes of the Mone. SP,
20, 1923, 70-82.
A3514-8.
FROST, GEORGE L. Music of the Kinges Note; Reply to
F. Collins. Spec, 8, 1933, 526-8.
GARRETT, MAX M. Chaucer in Minnesota. Dialect
Notes, 5, 1923, 245.
On A3268. Also see Manly's and Robinson's notes.
GIBBON, JOHN MURRAY. Melody and the Lyric. From
Chaucer to the Cavaliers. Dent, 1930. 204 pp.
Kinges note, 7-8.
For review, see section: General Criticism.
HENSHAW, MILLETT. La Clameur de Haro. So Folk-
lore Quart, 14, 1950, 158-9.
MilT, 3286, 3825; Reeve'sT, 4072, 4307.
Explains the custom and notes its survival in the
Channel Islands.
KARPINSKY, L. C. "Augrim Stones." MLN, 27, 1912, 206-9.
KOELBING, EUGEN. Note on Source of the Miller's
Tale. Zeitschrift für vergleichende Litteratur-
geschichte, 13, 1899, 112.
See also Zu Chaucers Erzählung des Millers, 12,
1898, 448-50.
KUHL, E. P. "Daun Gerveys." MLN, 29, 1914, 156.
LINTHICUM, M. CHANNING. "Falding" and "Medlee."
JEGP, 34, 1935, 39-41.
Notes on 14th century English cloth. MilT, 3212.
Rev: D. Everett, YWES, 106.
LOWES, JOHN L. Chaucer and the Miroir de Mariage.
MP, 8, 1910-1, 305-34.
Influence on Miller's Prol, 325-6.
McPEEK, JAMES A. S. Chaucer and the Goliards. Spec,
26, 1951, 332-6.
MANLY, JOHN M. Piggesnye. CT, A, 3268. TLS, Oct
6, 1927, 694.
See also Agnes Arber, TLS, Nov 3, 1927, 790.
OWEN, CHARLES A., Jr. One Robin or Two? MLN, 67,
1952, 336-8.

PARKER, ROSCOE E. "Pilate's Voys." Spec, 25, 1950,
    237-44.
PRATT, ROBERT A. Was Robin the Miller's Youth Mis-
    spent? MLN, 59, 1944, 47-9.
        Rev: D. Everett, YWES, 43.
PYLE, FITZROY. A Metrical Point in Chaucer. NQ,
    170, 1936, 128.
ROOT, ROBERT K. Chaucer and the Decameron. ESt,
    44, 1911, 1-7.
        On A3171-86.
SPITZER, LEO. A Chaucerian Hapax Legomenon: "upon
    the viritoot." Lang, 26, 1950, 389-93.
        Line 3770.
        Rev: D. Everett, YWES, 61-2.
THOMPSON, STITH. The Miller's Tale. Sources and
    Analogues, 106-23.
VINE, GUTHRIE. The Miller's Tale. A Study of an Unre-
    corded Manuscript in the John Rylands Library in Rela-
    tion to the First Printed Text. Manchester Univ Press,
    1933. 17 pp. Reprinted from JRLB, 17, 1933, 333-47.
YOFFIE, LEAH R. Chaucer's "White Paternoster,"
    Milton's Angels, and a Hebrew Night Prayer. South-
    ern Folklore Quart, 15, 1951, 203-10.
        Line 3485.

THE REEVE'S PROLOGUE AND TALE

        See Hammond, 275-6; Root, 173-9; Robinson, 789-
    91, 1007; French, 217-9; Manly, 560-1, and SNL, 84-
    94; Curry, 71 ff.

BAUM, PAULL F. The Mare and the Wolf. MLN, 37,
    1922, 350-3.
        A4054-6.
BENNETT, H. S. Medieval Literature and the Modern
    Reader. Essays and Studies, 31, 1945, 7-18.
        Reeve'sT, A3943.
CLINE, RUTH H. Four Chaucer Saints. MLN, 60, 1945,
    480-2.
        The significance of swearing by St. Frideswide,
    St. Cuthbert, St. Yve, and St. Thomas, the Apostle.
        Reeve'sT, 4127.
        Rev: D. Everett, YWES, 49-50.

CROW, MARTIN M. The Reeve's Tale in the Hands of
    a North Midland Scribe. Univ of Texas Publications,
    3826, 1938, 14-24.
CURRY, WALTER CLYDE. Chaucer's Reeve and Miller.
    PMLA, 35, 1920, 189-209.
DEMPSTER, GERMAINE. On the Source of the Reeve's
    Tale. JEGP, 29, 1930, 473-88.
        Rev: D. Everett, YWES, 89.
DEROCQUIGNY, J. A Possible Source of Chaucer's Can-
    terbury Tales. MLR, 3, 1908, 72.
        See also Rev Germ, 6, 1910, 203-6.
DIECKMANN, EMMA POPE M. The Meaning of "Bur-
    doun" in Chaucer. MP, 26, 1929, 279-82.
        A4165.
HART, WALTER M. The Reeve's Tale: A Comparative
    Study of Chaucer's Narrative Art. PMLA, 23, 1908,
    1-44.
        See also his The Narrative Art of the Old French
    Fabliaux, Anniversary Papers (Kittredge), 209 ff.
----------. The Reeve's Tale. Sources and Analogues,
    124-47.
HOLTHAUSEN, FERDINAND. Zu Chaucers Reeve's
    Tale. AB, 33, 1922, 103-4.
KUHL, ERNEST P. Chaucer and the Church. MLN, 40,
    1925, 321-8.
        Chaucer's relations to the north country.
LANGE, MARIUS. Vom Fabliau zu Boccaccio und Chau-
    cer. Ein Vergleich zweier Fabliaux mit Boccaccios
    Decamerone ix, 6, und mit Chaucers Reeve's Tale.
    Britannica, viii. Friederischen, 1934. 155 pp.
        Rev: W. Keller, ZFEU, 33, 1934, 348-9; J. Raith,
    AB, 45, 1934, 269-70; J. P. O., MLR, 30, 1935, 268;
    D. Everett, YWES, 97; ESt, 70, 1936, 393-4; H. S. V.
    J(ones), JEGP, 36, 1937, 617; G. Dempster, MP, 35,
    1937, 102-3; H. Marcus, ESt, 70, 1936, 393-4.
MOFFETT, H. Y. Oswald, the Reeve. PQ, 4, 1925, 208-
    23.
MONTGOMERY, FRANZ. A Note on the Reeve's Pro-
    logue. PQ, 10, 1931, 404-5.
        On A3912. See next entry.
MYERS, LOUIS M. A Line in the Reeve's Prologue.
    MLN, 49, 1934, 222-6.
        Reply to Montgomery, above.

TATLOCK, JOHN STRONG PERRY. Notes on Chaucer:
The Canterbury Tales. MLN, 29, 1914, 140-4.
    Simkin's Ruse: The Reeve's Tale, 4057-4106, p.
142.
TOLKIEN, J. R. R. Chaucer as a Philologist: The
Reeve's Tale. Philological Soc Trans, 1934, 1-70.
WALKER, W. P. Did Chaucer Refer to Sheffield in Sus-
sex? Sussex Co Mag, 1947, 120-1.
    A3933, Reeve'sT.
WHITING, B. J. A Colt's Tooth. Mediaeval Studies in
Honor of Jeremiah Denis Matthias Ford, 319-31.
    A3888.
WINTERSGILL, A. T. Chaucer: "Strothir" in "The
Reeve's Tale." NQ, ser. 10, 12, 1909, 90.
    Replies by Walter W. Skeat and A. R. Bayley, 155.
Rejoinder by Wintersgill, 235.

THE COOK'S PROLOGUE AND TALE

    See Hammond, 276-7; Root, 179-80; Robinson,
791-2; French, 219-20; Manly, 562-3; Curry, 47 ff.
See also Tupper, Lowes, and Koch in section: Canterbury Tales: General.

BLENNER-HASSETT, R. "Whan He his 'Papir' Soughte,"
CT A4404. MLN, 57, 1942, 34-5.
    Rev: D. Everett, YWES, 54.
BRADDY, HALDEEN. Chaucerian Minutiae. MLN, 58,
1943, 18-23.
    CookT, indenture of apprenticeship.
CALL, REGINALD. "Whan He his Papir Soghte." MLQ,
4, 1943, 167-76.
DELANGE, J. The Relation and Development of English
and Icelandic Outlaw-Traditions. Univ of Utrecht
Diss, Haarlem, 1935.
GRAULS, J., and J. F. VANDERHEIJDEN. Two Flem-
ish Proverbs in Chaucer's Canterbury Tales. RBPH,
13, 1934, 745-9.
LYON, EARL D. Chaucer's Cook's Tale, its Social
Background, and the Identity of the Cook. Diss, Univ
of California, 1938.
----------. The Cook's Tale. Sources and Analogues,
148-54.

RICKERT, EDITH. Chaucer's Hodge of Ware. TLS, Oct
    20, 1932, 761.
        A4336, Cook's Prol.

INTRODUCTION, PROLOGUE,
AND THE MAN OF LAW'S TALE

For Epilogue (Robinson, 90), see section: Shipman's Tale.
    See Hammond, 277-83; Root, 181-7; Robinson, 792-
801, 1007; French, 220-31; Shannon, 307-12; Manly, 565-
74; Curry, 164-94, 260-3; Brusendorff, 127; Tatlock, 172.
    For Constance Saga, see Wells, 791, and supple-
ments. For discussion of sins and sinners, see Tupper,
Lowes, Koch in section: Canterbury Tales: General. For
Wreched Engendrynge and An Holy Meditation, see
section with that title.

AYRES, HARRY M. Chaucer and Seneca. RR, 10, 1919,
    1-15.
        B20-5.
BAIRD, ALBERT CRAIG. The Relation of Chaucer's and
    Gower's Versions of the Constance Story. Master's
    Thesis, Columbia Univ, 1912.
BAUM, PAULL F. The Man of Law's Tale. MLN, 64,
    1949, 12-14.
        Emphasizeş irony in MLT; examines conclusions
    of Duffey, below.
        Rev: D. Everett, YWES, 30, 1949, 62-3.
BEICHNER, PAUL E. Chaucer's Man of Law and Dis-
    paritas Cultus. Spec, 23, 1948, 70-5.
        Legal aspects of the marriage of Constance to the
    Sultan.
        Rev: D. Everett, YWES, 29, 1948, 81.
BLOCK, EDWARD A. Originality, Controlling Purpose,
    and Craftmanship of Chaucer's Man of Law's Tale.
    PMLA, 69, 1953, 572-616.
BRETT, CYRIL. Notes on Old and Middle English. MLR,
    22, 1927, 258-64.
        On B782 ff., p. 264.
BROWN, CARLETON. Chaucer and the Hours of the
    Blessed Virgin. MLN, 30, 1915, 231-2.
----------. The Man of Law's Head-link and the

Prologue of the Canterbury Tales. SP, 34, 1937, 8-35.
Its relation to LGW.

BROWNE, WILLIAM H. Notes on Chaucer's Astrology.
MLN, 23, 1908, 53-4.
MLT, 53.

CLOYD, MANIE G. Chaucer's Romance Element. PQ, 11,
1932, 89-91.
MLT used statistically.

COWLING, G. H. A Note on Chaucer's Stanza. RES, 2,
1926, 311-7.

CURRY, WALTER CLYDE. O Mars, O Atazir. JEGP,
22, 1923, 347-68.

----------. Chaucer's Science and Art. Texas Rev, 8,
1923, 307-22.

CURTISS, JOSEPH T. The Horoscope in Chaucer's Man
of Law's Tale. JEGP, 26, 1927, 24-32.
See Curry, O Mars, above in this section.

DUFFEY, BERNARD I. The Intention and the Art of the
Man of Law's Tale. ELH, 14, 1947, 181-93.
Rev: D. Everett, YWES, 28, 1947, 78-9.

EDWARDS, A. C. Knaresborough Castle and "The
Kynges Moodres Court." PQ, 19, 1940, 306-9.
Suggests the name of the castle was omitted out of
consideration for John of Gaunt.

FARNHAM, WILLARD E. The Dayes of the Mone. SP,
20, 1923, 70-82.

GALWAY, MARGARET. A Basque Word in Chaucer.
TLS, Oct 3, 1942, 492.
"Phislyas," B[2]1189; see J. Searle, TLS, 1942, 499;
Kenneth Sisam, TLS, Oct 24, 1942, 525; R. Gallop,
TLS, Nov 14, 1942, 564; R. K. Root, Chaucer's Sum-
moner, TLS, Jan 23, 1943, 43; Margaret Galway,
A Basque Word in Chaucer?, TLS, April 10, 1943,
180.

HORNSTEIN, LILLIAN HERLANDS. Trivet's Constance
and the King of Tars. MLN, 55, 1940, 354-7.
On the substitution for the incest motif deprecated
by Chaucer.

KNOWLTON, EDGAR C. Chaucer's Man of Law. JEGP,
23, 1924, 83-93.

KRAPPE, ALEXANDER HAGGERTY. The Offa-Con-
stance Legend. Ang, 61, 1937, 361-9.
Early history of the legend.

LANGHANS, VICTOR. Chaucers angebliche Ubersetzung
  des Traktates "De Contemptu Mundi" von Innocenz
  III. Ang, 52, 1928, 325-49.
    For review, see section: Literary Relations.
McNEAL, THOMAS H. Chaucer and the Decameron.
  MLN, 53, 1938, 257-8.
O'NEIL, MARGARET. Chaucer's Use of his Sources in
  the Man of Law's Tale. Master's Thesis, Univ of
  Washington, 1944.
ROOT, ROBERT K. Chaucer's Legend of Medea. PMLA,
  24, 1909, 124-54.
    See Kittredge, Chaucer's Medea and the Date of
  the Legend of Good Women. PMLA, 24, 1909, 343-63.
----------. The Date of Chaucer's Medea. PMLA, 25,
  1910, 228-40.
    Reply to Kittredge's article on Root's article, above.
----------. Chaucer's Summoner. TLS, Jan 23, 1943,
  43.
    Supports reading of "Sumnour" in Man of Law's
  Epilogue.
    Rev: D. Everett, YWES, 42-3.
ROSE, Sister MARIE. Chaucer and his Mayde Bright.
  Commonweal, 33, 1940, 225-7.
ROSENFELD, MARY-VIRGINIA. Chaucer and the Litur-
  gy. MLN, 55, 1940, 357-60.
    Influence of the liturgy on Constance's prayer.
SCHICK, ------. Die Urquelle der Offa-Konstanze-Saga.
  Britannica, Festschrift f. m. Foerster, Leipzig, 1929,
  p. 31. (Wells, 6th suppl, 1939.)
SCHLAUCH, MARGARET. Chaucer's Constance and Ac-
  cused Queens. Doctoral Diss, Columbia, 1927. New
  York State Library, 1927. 142 pp.
    Rev: NQ, 153, 1927, 161; Hugo Lange, AB, 39, 1928,
  334-8; C. H. Herford, MLR, 23, 1928, 65-6; G. H.
  Gerould, JEGP, 28, 1929, 285-6; H. R. Patch, ESt,
  67, 1932, 112-3.
----------. Studies in the Sources of the Man of Law's
  Tale. Thesis, Columbia Univ, 1925.
----------. The Man of Law's Tale. Sources and Ana-
  logues, 155-206.
----------. Historical Precursors of Chaucer's Con-
  stance. PQ, 29, 1950, 402-12.
    Rev: G. D. Willcock, YWES, 77.

SHANNON, EDGAR F. Chaucer and Lucan's Pharsalia.
   MP, 16, 1919, 609-14.
      B400-1.
----------. Chaucer's Metamorphoseos. MLN, 35, 1920,
   288-91.
      B93.
SMITH, ROLAND M. Chaucer's Man of Law's Tale and
   Constance of Castile. JEGP, 47, 1948, 343-51.
      Rev: D. Everett, YWES, 80-1.
SULLIVAN, W. L. Chaucer's Man of Law as a Literary
   Critic. MLN, 68, 1953, 1-8.
TATLOCK, JOHN STRONG PERRY. Notes on Chaucer:
   Earlier or Minor Poems. MLN, 29, 1914, 97-101.
TEUBERT, -----. Crescentia-Studien. Halle, 1916.
   (Wells, 6th Suppl, 1539.)
TRIVET, NICHOLAS. [Les cronicles qe Frere Nichol
   Tryuet escript a Dame Marie la Fille Mounseignour
   le Roi Edward le Fitz Henri; reproduced from Arun-
   del MS no. 56, fol. 2-77 (recto) in the British Mu-
   seum.] 76 sheets mounted on 38 l. MLA of America.
   Collection of Photographic Facsimiles, no. 111. 1930.
   Deposited in the Library of Congress.
      "The original is a 15th century vellum manu-
   script. Cf. Catalogue of manuscripts in the British
   Museum. Pt. 1, 1834. This work is also known as
   'Historia ab orbe condito usque ad suum tempus,'
   'Historia ad Christi Nativitatem' and 'De Gestis
   Imperatorum, Regum, et Apostolorum.' Cf. DNB.
   These chronicles are the annals from the creation
   to Edward III."
TUPPER, FREDERICK. Wilful and Impatient Poverty.
   Nation, 99, 1914, 41.
WHITING, B. J. "By My Fader Soule." II (B) 1178.
   JEGP, 44, 1945, 1-8.
      Rev: D. Everett, YWES, 50.
WICKERT, MARIA. Konstanze und die Legende der
   guten Frauen. Ang, 69, 1950, 89-104.
      Rev: D. Everett, YWES, 62-3.

   FOR THE EPILOGUE OF THE MAN OF LAW'S
TALE (Robinson, 90), see section: The Shipman's
Tale, and for the problems in the order of the tales,
see the section: Canterbury Tales: General.

THE WIFE OF BATH'S PROLOGUE AND TALE

See Hammond, 296-300; Root, 231-44; Robinson, 801-8,
1007-8; French, 272-84; Manly, 574-86; SNL, 227-41; Shannon, 318-9; Kittredge, 153, 185; Tatlock, 198; Curry, 91; Brusendorff, 475; Wells, Fragment D, CBEL, I, 244-5, and supplements to the Manual; Gerould, 72-80; Dempster, 59-61.

ALBRECHT, W. P. The Sermon on Gentilesse. CE, 12,
1951, 459.
See Roppolo, below in this section.
ANDERSON, CHARLES BURROUGHS. The Discussion of
Marriage in The Canterbury Tales. Master's Thesis,
Columbia, 1929.
ANDRAE, AUGUST. Zu Longfellows und Chaucers Tales.
AB, 27, 1916, 84.
AYRES, HARRY M. Chaucer and Seneca. RR, 10, 1919, 1-10.
On lines 1168-76, 1183-90.
BARNOUW, A. J. The Prente of Seinte Venus Seel. Na-
tion, 103, 1916, 540.
D604.
BROWN, CARLETON. The Evolution of the Canterbury
"Marriage Group." PMLA, 48, 1933, 1041-59.
Rev: D. Everett, YWES, 108-10.
BRUGGER, E. "Der schöne Feigling" in der arthurischen
Literatur. Zeitschrift f. rom. Phil. , 61, 1941, 1-44.
CHAPMAN, COOLIDGE OTIS. Chaucer on Preachers
and Preaching. PMLA, 44, 1929, 178-85.
D1207-10, 550, 555-8.
CODER, RALPH B. Chaucer's Wife of Bath. Univ of
Iowa: Doctoral Dissertations: Abstracts and Refer-
ences, 4, 1944, 189-93. Also Programs Announcing
Candidates for Higher Degrees, Univ of Iowa, 1941.
COFFMAN, GEORGE R. Another Analogue for the Vio-
lation of the Maiden in the Wife of Bath's Tale. MLN,
59, 1944, 271-4.
Rev: D. Everett, YWES, 46.
----------. Chaucer and Courtly Love Once More: The
Wife of Bath's Tale. Spec, 20, 1945, 43-50.
Rev: D. Everett, YWES, 50-1.
COOMARASWAMY, ANANDA K. On the Loathly Bride.
Spec, 20, 1945, 391-404.
On this theme in folklore.

CURRY, WALTER C. More about Chaucer's Wife of
   Bath. PMLA, 37, 1922, 30-51.
DELHAYE, PHILIPPE. Le Dossier Anti-Matrimonial
   de l'Adversus Jovinianum et son Influence sur Quel-
   ques Ecrits Latins du XIIe Siècle. Med Stud, 13, 1951,
   65-86.
DEMPSTER, GERMAINE. "Thy Gentilesse" in Wife of
   Bath's Tale, D1159-62. MLN, 57, 1942, 173-6.
      Rev: D. Everett, YWES, 56-7.
DEROCQUIGNY, J. A Possible Source of Chaucer's
   Canterbury Tales. MLR, 3, 1908, 72.
HEMINGWAY, SAMUEL B. Chaucer's Monk and Nun's
   Priest. MLN, 31, 1916, 479-83.
      Suggestions on the marriage group.
HINCKLEY, HENRY B. The Debate on Marriage in the
   Canterbury Tales. PMLA, 32, 1917, 292-305.
HUPPE, BERNARD F. Rape and Woman's Sovereignty
   in the Wife of Bath's Tale. MLN, 63, 1948, 378-81.
      Rev: D. Everett, YWES, 81-2.
JONES, RICHARD F. A Conjecture on the Wife of Bath's
   Prologue. JEGP, 24, 1925, 512-47.
      Rev: D. Everett, YWES, 88-9.
KENYON, JOHN S. Further Notes on the Marriage Group
   in the Canterbury Tales. JEGP, 15, 1916, 282-8.
---------. Wife of Bath's Tale: 1159-62. MLN, 54,
   1939, 133-7.
      Takes issue with Brusendorff's reading.
KERN, H. De Bronnen van "The Wife of Bath's Tale" en
   daarmed verwante Vertellingen. Verlagen en mede-
   deelingender kon. Akademie van Wetenschappen. Afd.
   Letterkunde, 4de reeks, 9.3.
KITTREDGE, GEORGE L. Chaucer and his Poetry.
   Harvard Univ Press, 1915.
      Presentation of the marriage theme, 185-210.
      For reviews, see section: General Criticism.
---------. Chaucer's Discussion of Marriage. MP, 9,
   1912, 435-67.
      Rev: John Koch, ESt, 46, 1912, 98-114.
KOKERITZ, HELGE. "The Wyf of Bathe" and "al hire
   secte." PQ, 26, 1947, 147-51.
      ClT, 1170-1: defines "secte" as "sex" and refutes
   Kittredge's interpretation as "sect."
      Rev: D. Everett, YWES, 75-6.

LAWRENCE, WILLIAM W. The Marriage Group in the
Canterbury Tales. MP, 11, 1913, 247-58.
    Also see this author's Chaucer and the Canterbury
Tales in the section: Canterbury Tales: General.
LOOMIS, LAURA HIBBARD. Chaucer and the Breton
Lays of the Auchinleck MS. SP, 38, 1941, 14-33.
    Rev: D. Everett, YWES, 60.
LOWES, JOHN LIVINGSTON. Illustrations of Chaucer
Drawn Chiefly from Deschamps. RR, 2, 1911, 121 ff.
    Rev: J. Koch, ES, 46, 1912, 114.
----------. Chaucer and the Miroir de Mariage. MP,
8, 1910-1, 305-34.
    Influence on WB Prol, 305-21.
----------. Chaucer and Dante's Convivio. MP, 13, 1915,
19-33.
----------. Second Nun's Prologue, Alanus and Macro-
bius. MP, 15, 1917, 193-202.
    On D1139-45, p. 199.
----------. Chaucer and Dante. MP, 14, 1917, 705-35.
    Boccaccio's verses calling to mind Dante's for
Chaucer. WB Prol, 604-20.
----------. Chaucer and the Seven Deadly Sins. PMLA,
30, 1915, 342 ff.
LYONS, CLIFFORD P. The Marriage Debate in the
Canterbury Tales. ELH, 2, 1935, 252-62.
    Rev: D. Everett, YWES, 104-5.
MARIELLA, Sister. The Parson's Tale and the Marriage
Group. MLN, 53, 1938, 251-6.
MOORE, ARTHUR K. Alysoun's Other Tonne. MLN, 59,
1944, 481-3.
    Structure of WB Prol and possible relation to
Deschamps' Miroir de Mariage.
    Lines 170-1.
    Rev: D. Everett, YWES, 46.
----------. Chaucer and Matheolus. NQ, 190, 1946,
245-8.
    Rev: D. Everett, YWES, 78-9.
----------. Studies in Mediaeval Prejudice: Antifemi-
nism. Bull of Vanderbilt Univ, 43, 1943, 11-12.
----------. The Pardoner's Interruption of the Wife of
Bath's Prologue. MLQ, 10, 1949, 49-57.
MOORE, SAMUEL. The Date of Chaucer's Marriage
Group. MLN, 26, 1911, 172-4.

OGLE, MARBURY BLADEN. Biblical Quotations in the
de Nugis Curialium of Walter Map. Abstract of
paper: TAPA, 66, 1935, xlii.
OWEN, CHARLES A. The Crucial Passages in Five of
the Canterbury Tales: A Study in Irony and Symbol.
JEGP, 52, 1953, 294-311.
    WBT, III (D) 925, 1066.
PRATT, ROBERT A. A Note on Chaucer and the Poli-
craticus of John of Salisbury. MLN, 65, 1950, 243-6.
    The reading of the Wife's fifth husband.
PYLE, FITZROY. A Metrical Point in Chaucer. NQ,
170, 1936, 128.
ROPPOLO, JOSEPH P. The Converted Knight in Chau-
cer's Wife of Bath's Tale. CE, 12, 1951, 263-9.
RUTTER, GEORGE M. The Wife of Bath. Western Re-
serve Univ Bull, 34, 1931, 60-4.
SCHLAUCH, MARGARET. The Marital Dilemma in the
Wife of Bath's Tale. PMLA, 61, 1946, 416-30.
    Rev: D. Everett, YWES, 79-80.
SCHULZE, K. Zu Chaucers Weib von Bath und Shake-
speares Kaufmann von Venedig. GRM, 8, 1920, 103-5.
SEATON, ETHEL. "Goode lief my wif." MLR, 41, 1946,
196-202.
    Chaucer's humor in use of St. Godeleva's name, D431.
    Rev: D. Everett, YWES, 77-8.
SHAVER, C. L. A Mediaeval French Analogue to the
Dunmow Flitch. MLN, 50, 1935, 322-5.
SLAUGHTER, EUGENE E. "Allas! allas! that ever love
was sinne!" MLN, 49, 1934, 83-6.
    Rev: D. Everett, YWES, 100.
----------. Clerk Jankyn's Motive. MLN, 65, 1950, 530-4.
    WB Prol, 628.
    By marrying a widow, he was excluded forever
from orders.
    Rev: D. Everett, YWES, 65.
SMITH, ALEX, Ed. Ballad "Wanton Wife of Bath." Pri-
vately printed, 30 copies. Glasgow, 1899. (Wells, 6th
suppl, 1541).
SMITH, ROLAND M. The Six Gifts. Jour of Celtic Stud-
ies, 1, 1949, 98-104.
    Suggests influence of Irish triads on WBT, 925-48;
ShT, 173-7; and NPT, 2914.
    Rev: D. Everett, YWES, 63.

STEELE, RICHARD. Chaucer and the "Almagest." Library, ser. 3, 10, 1919, 243-7.

TATLOCK, JOHN S. P. Notes on Chaucer: The Canterbury Tales. MLN, 29, 1914, 140-4.

The Wife of Bath's Revenge, III (B), 800-10.

TOYNBEE, PAGET. The Author of Chaucer's Book Cleped Valerie. Acad, 1891, II, 588-9.

TRAIN, LILLA. Chaucer's Ladyes Four and Twenty. MLN, 50, 1935, 85-7.

WBT, 992.

Rev: D. Everett, YWES, 114.

TUPPER, FREDERICK, and MARBURY B. OGLE. Master Walter Map's Book: De Nugis Curialium (Courtier's Trifles). Chatto and Windus, 1924.

Translation with introduction and notes. WB Prol, 671.

Rev: Wilfred P. Mustard, AJP, 45, 1924, 195-6.

TUPPER, FREDERICK. Saint Venus and the Canterbury Pilgrims. Nation, 97, 1913, 354-6.

UTLEY, FRANCIS L. Satire on Women in Greek, Latin, and Middle English. Doctoral Diss, Harvard, 1936.

See this author's The Crooked Rib, in section: Social Backgrounds.

VAN DE VOORT, DONNELL. Love and Marriage in Middle English Romance. Doctoral Diss, Vanderbilt Univ, 1938.

VOGT, G. M. Gleanings for the History of a Sentiment: Generositas Virtus, non Sanguis. JEGP, 24, 1925, 102-23.

----------. The Wife of Bath's Tale, Women Pleased, and La Fée Urgele; a Study in the Transformation of Folklore Themes in Drama. MLN, 37, 1922, 339-42.

WHITING, BARTLETT J. The Wife of Bath's Prologue and Tale. Sources and Analogues, 207-68.

----------. A Colt's Tooth. Mediaeval Studies in Honor of Jeremiah Denis Matthias Ford, 319-31.

D602.

THE FRIAR'S PROLOGUE AND TALE

See Hammond, 300-1; Root, 244-9; Robinson, 808-10, 1008; French, 284-7; Manly, 586-9; Shannon, 319; Kittredge, 190.

On the sins motif, see Kuhl, Lowes, Tupper, and Bloomfield in section: Religious Backgrounds.

AIKEN, PAULINE. Vincent of Beauvais and the Green Yeoman's Lecture on Demonology. SP, 35, 1938, 1-9.

ANDRAE, AUGUST. Zu Longfellows und Chaucers Tales. AB, 27, 1916, 85-6.

GREENLAW, EDWIN A. A Note on Chaucer's Prologue. MLN, 23, 1908, 142-4.
    On D1451.

HASELMAYER, LOUIS A., Jr. The Apparitor and Chaucer's Summoner. Spec, 12, 1937, 43-57.
    Rev: D. Everett, YWES, 80-1.

IMMACULATE, Sister MARY. Fiends as "Servant unto Man" in the Friar's Tale. PQ, 21, 1942, 240-4.
    D1501.
    St. Dunstan's power over fiends as shown by various incidents in the accounts of his biographers.
    Rev: D. Everett, YWES, 57.

KUHL, ERNEST P. Chaucer and the Church. MLN, 40, 1925, 335.

LANGE, HUGO. Chaucer and Mandeville's Travels. Archiv, 174, 1938, 79-81.
    FriarT, six notations.

LOWES, JOHN L. Illustrations of Chaucer Drawn Chiefly from Deschamps. Rom Rev, 2, 1911, 118.
    Rev: J. Koch, ES, 46, 1912, 114.

MALONE, KEMP. The Freres Contree. MLR, 26, 1931, 75-7.

SKEAT, WALTER W. Chaucer: A Curious Misplacement of Lines. NQ, ser. 11, 1, 1910, 201-2.
    D1294.

SUTHERLAND, R. C. Note on D 1645-62 of Chaucer's Friar's Tale. PQ, 31, 1952, 436-9.
    Relation of the text to Compline.

TAYLOR, ARCHER. The Devil and the Advocate. PMLA, 36, 1921, 35-59.
    Analogues of FriarT.

----------. Der Richter und der Teufel. 248-51, in Studies in Honor of Hermann Collitz. Johns Hopkins Press, 1930.
    Discusses newly collected versions of FriarT.

----------. The Friar's Tale. Sources and Analogues, 269-74.

TUPPER, FREDERICK. The Quarrels of the Canterbury
Pilgrims. JEGP, 14, 1915, 256-70.
Rev: J. Koch, AB, 28, 1917, 1-55.

THE SUMMONER'S PROLOGUE AND TALE

See Hammond, 301-2; Root, 249-52; Robinson, 810-
3, 1008; French, 288-90; Manly, 589-90.
On the sins motif, see Kuhl, Lowes, Tupper, and
Bloomfield in section: Religious Backgrounds.

CHAPMAN, COOLIDGE OTIS. Chaucer on Preachers
and Preaching. PMLA, 44, 1929, 178-85.
D2005-6, 2086-8, 1818-9, 2107-10, 1793-4, 1715-8,
1724-34, 1788-9.
CURRY, W. C. The Bottom of Hell. MLN, 38, 1923, 253.
Chaucer and Dante's Inferno. D1689 ff.
HAMILTON, MARIE PADGETT. The Summoner's "Psalm
of Davit." MLN, 57, 1942, 655-7.
D1933.
HART, WALTER MORRIS. The Summoner's Tale.
Sources and Analogues, 275-87.
KELLOGG, ALFRED L. The Fraternal Kiss in Chaucer's
Summoner's Tale. Scriptorium, 7, 1953, 115.
LANGE, HUGO. Chaucer and Mandeville's Travels. Ar-
chiv, 174, 1938, 79-81.
SumT, 2079-84.
----------. Die Bedeutung der Heraldik für die Erklär-
ung eines mittelalterlichen Dichters. Forschungen
und Fortschritte, 13, 1937, 59-60.
SOUTHWORTH, JAMES G. Chaucer's the Canterbury
Tales: D1746-53. Expl, 11, item 29.
On "blanket," line 1751.
STANFORD, MABEL. The Sumner's Tale and Saint Pat-
rick's Purgatory. JEGP, 19, 1920, 377-81.
TATLOCK, JOHN S. P. Notes on Chaucer: The Canter-
bury Tales. MLN, 29, 1914, 140-4.
Friars in hell, D1675-706; Friar's vision, D1854-
68, pp. 143-4.
TUPPER, FREDERICK. Anent Jerome and the Summon-
er's Friar. MLN, 30, 1915, 63.
----------. The Quarrels of the Canterbury Pilgrims.
JEGP, 14, 1915, 256-70.

----------. Chaucer's Bed's Head. MLN, 30, 1915, 5-
   12.
        Jerome and the Summoner's friar, 8-9.
WILLIAMS, ARNOLD. Chaucer and the Friars. Spec, 28,
   1953, 499-513.

THE CLERK'S PROLOGUE, TALE, ENVOY,
AND WORDS OF THE HOST

        See Hammond, 302-9; Root, 253-62; Robinson,
   813-7, 1008-9; French, 290-313; Manly, 590-6;
   Hinckley, 184-209; Brusendorff, 25; Kittredge, 193;
   Tatlock, 156; Wells, CBEL, I, 245-7, 151-2, and
   supplements to the Manual after 1933.
        For editions, see section: Editions with Notes.
   For discussion of the marriage group, see section:
   Wife of Bath's Tale. See also Schlauch, in section:
   General Criticism.

ADOLPHUS, A. E. Chauceriana. NQ, ser. 10, 8, 1907,
   202-3.
        ClT, 106-8, p. 203.
ANON. Forgotten Virtues. Harper's Weekly, 55, 1916, 6.
BALDWIN, CHARLES SEARS. Cicero on Parnassus.
   PMLA, 42, 1927, 106-12.
        E16, 31, 41.
CATE, WIRT A. The Problem of the Origin of the Gri-
   selda Story. SP, 29, 1932, 389-405.
        Rev: D. Everett, YWES, 13, 1932, 88-9.
COOK, A. S. Chauceriana I. RR, 8, 1917, 210-26.
        Chaucer's Clerk's Tale and a French Version of
   the Original, 210-22; "Nayled in his cheste," Clerk's
   Prol. 29, pp. 222-4.
----------. Chauceriana II. RR, 8, 1917, 353-82.
        Chaucer's Linian.
----------. Chaucer's Griselda and Homer's Arete.
   AJP, 39, 1918, 75-8.
----------. The First Two Readers of Petrarch's Tale
   of Griselda. MP, 15, 1918, 633-43.
COWLING, G. H. A Note on Chaucer's Stanza. RES, 2,
   1926, 311-7.
DEMPSTER, GERMAINE. The Clerk's Endlink. PMLA,
   67, 1952, 1177-81.

----------. Chaucer's Manuscript of Petrarch's Ver-
sion of the Griselda Story. MP, 41, 1943, 6-16.
   A criticism of Severs, listed in this section. See
also the writer's review of Severs.
FARNHAM, WILLARD E. Chaucer's Clerk's Tale. MLN,
33, 1918, 193-203.
   Possible influence of Boccaccio's Griselda story
on Chaucer's ClT.
----------. England's Discovery of the Decameron.
PMLA, 39, 1924, 123-39.
GLOMEAU, A. La Mystère de Griselidis. Paris, 1923.
GOLENISTCHEFF-KOUTOUZOFF, ELIE. L'Histoire de
Griseldis en France au XIVe et au XVe Siècle. E.
Droz, 1933. 291 pp.
   Rev: J. Raith, AB, 45, 1934, 235-7.
GRIFFITH, DUDLEY DAVID. The Origin of the Griselda
Story. University of Washington Publications in Lan-
guage and Literature, 8. Univ of Washington Press,
1931. 120 pp. Reprinted by Univ of Chicago Libraries,
1932. Part of Doctoral Diss, Univ of Chicago, 1916:
The Griselda Story and Chaucer's Clerk's Tale.
   Rev: H. J. Rose, Folk-Lore, 43, 1932, 111-2;
P. Meissner, AB, 44, 1933, 78-9; D. Everett,
YWES, 12, 1931, 90-1; J. W. Ashton, PQ, 13,
1934, 88-9.
GROENEVELD, HINDREK. Die älteste Bearbeitung der
Griseldissage in Frankreich. Marburg, 1886.
GUBERNATIS, ANGELO de. De Sacountala a Griselda.
Cronache della Civiltà Elleno-Latina, 3, 465 ff.
Abstract in Verhandlungen des XIII internationalen
Orientalischen-Congresses, 21 ff. Leyden, 1904.
HAMILTON, GEORGE L. Chauceriana I: The Date of the
Clerk's Tale and Chaucer's "Petrak." MLN, 23,
1908, 169-72.
HUBSCH, GOTTLIEB. The Pleasant Comodie of Patient
Grissill, an Edition, 1603. Doctoral Diss, Friedrich-
Alexanders-Universität, 1893. 63 pp.
HULTON, SAMUEL F. The Clerk of Oxford in Fiction.
London: Methuen, 1909.
   Rev: O. , EHR, 25, 1910, 413-4.
JUSSERAND, J. J. The School for Ambassadors and
Other Essays. Fischer Unwin, 1924.
   Includes The Tomb of Petrarch, 71-107; On the

Possible Meeting of Chaucer and Petrarch, 327-43.
    Rev: TLS, Nov 27, 1924.
KITTREDGE, GEORGE L. Arthur and Gorlagon. Harvard Studies and Notes, 8, 1903, 149-275.
    Relation to ClT, 241 n.
KOCH, JOHN. Berichtigungen. ESt, 69, 1934, 318-20.
    Readings of the Naples MS of ClT.
----------. Parallel Text Specimens, Part IX. Introduction to Specimen of Clerk's Tale. Chaucer Society,
   1st ser., 97.
KREBS, K. Der Bedeutungswandel von me. Clerk und
   damit zusammenhängende Probleme. Bonner Studien,
   21. Bonn: Harnstein, 1933. 162 pp.
    Rev: F. R. Schroeder, GRM, 22, 1934, 488; A.
   B(randl), Arch, 165, 1934, 301; L. Stettner, NJWJ,
   12, 1936, 375.
KUCHLER, WALTER. Griselda und Grishildur. NS, 33,
   1925, 354-7.
LASERSTEIN, KATHE. Der Griseldis-Stoff in der Welt-
   literatur. Forschungen zur neueren Literaturgeschich-
   te, 58. Duncker, 1928. 208 pp.
    Chaucer's part in development, 22-5.
    Rev: Eberhard Sauer, Euphorion, 29, 1928, 322-3;
   Wolfgang Wurzbach, LGRP, 50, 1929, 241-4.
LEVEQUE, EUGENE. Les Mythes et les Legendes de
   l'Inde, et la Perse. . . . Paris: E. Belin, 1880.
    See 524.
LOWES, JOHN L. Chaucer and the Miroir de Mariage.
   MP, 8, 1910-1, 305-34.
    See 333 n.
----------. Illustrations of Chaucer Drawn Chiefly from
   Deschamps. Rom Rev, 2, 1911, 125 ff.
    Rev: John Koch, ES, 46, 1912, 114.
McNEAL, THOMAS H. The Clerk's Tale as a Possible
   Source for "Pandosto." PMLA, 47, 1932, 453-60.
MALONE, KEMP. Patient Griseldus. RR, 20, 1929,
   340-5.
PATRUCCO, CARL E. La Storia nella Leggenda di
   Griselda. Piccolo Archivio Storico dell' Antico Mar-
   chesato di Saluzzo, 1, 3-6.
    Rev: Rassegna Bibliogr. della Letter. It., 9, 331;
   Giorn. Stor. della Letter. It., 40, 200; G. Widmann,
   LGRP, 26, 1905, 124-6.

PEARSALL, ROBERT B. Chaucer's "Panik." MLN, 67,
1952, 529-31.
   ClT, 590.
   Identifies "Panik" as "Panico," a castle and family
situated twenty miles south of Bologna.

PETRARCH. The Griselda Story. Reproductions of Manuscripts and Rare Printed Books. Now on deposit in
the Library of Congress.
   At least 27 MSS, all but one on film, from various
libraries.

PICHON, JEROME. Le Ménagier de Paris. La Societé
des Bibliophiles François, 1846.
   See 1, 99 ff.

POWER, EILEEN, Ed. Goodman of Paris (Le Ménagier
de Paris): A Treatise on Moral and Domestic Economy
by a Citizen of Paris (c. 1393) Now First Translated
into English with an Introduction and Notes. Broadway Medieval Library. Harcourt; Routledge, 1928.
348 pp.

----------. The Menagier's Wife, a Paris Housewife in
the Fourteenth Century. 85-110, in her Medieval
People. Houghton, 1924.
   For review, see section: Social Backgrounds.

SAVORINI, L. La Leggenda di Griselda. Rivista Abruz-
zese, 15, 1900, 21 ff., 123 ff., 399 ff., 460 ff., 515 ff.

SEVERS, JONATHAN BURKE. Chaucer's Source MSS for
the Clerkes Tale. PMLA, 47, 1932, 431-52.

----------. The Job Passage in the Clerkes Tale. MLN,
49, 1934, 461-2.
   Rev: D. Everett, YWES, 100.

----------. The Literary Relationships of Chaucer's
Clerkes Tale. Doctoral Diss, Yale Univ, 1935.

----------. The Clerk's Tale. Sources and Analogues,
288-331.

----------. The Literary Relationships of Chaucer's
Clerkes Tale. Yale Studies in English, 96. Yale U-
niv Press; London: Milford, 1942. 371 pp.
   Griselda story in the fourteenth century; Chaucer's
treatment of his Latin and French sources; textual
notes on the ClT.
   Rev: Robert A. Pratt, Spec, 17, 1942, 577-82; W.
F. Bryan, JEGP, 43, 1944, 250-1; G. Dempster, MP,
40, 1943, 285-8, and 41, 1943, 6-16; D. Everett, MA,

13, 1944, 47-51, and YWES, 57-9; B. R. , TLS, 1942, 444.
----------. Did Chaucer Revise the Clerk's Tale?
Spec, 21, 1946, 295-302.
        On internal revision in ClT, see Manly and Rick-
ert, The Text of the Canterbury Tales, II, under
Manuscripts, above.
        Rev: D. Everett, YWES, 27, 1946, 80.
SLEDD, JAMES. The Clerk's Tale: The Monsters and
the Critics. MP, 51, 1953, 73-82.
ULLMAN, B. L. Petrarch's Favorite Books. TAPA,
54, 1924, 21-38.
VALLESE, TARQUINIO, Ed. La Novella del Chierico di
Oxford da un Codice Inglese Inedito del XV Secolo.
Naples: Amodio, 1939. 77 pp.
        Rev: D. Everett, YWES, 28, 1947, 80.
WIDMANN, GUSTAVO. Griseldis in der deutschen Litera-
tur des 19 Jahrhunderts. Euphorion, 13, 1906, 535 ff.
ZEITLIN, JACOB. The Life of Solitude by Francis Pe-
trarch. Trans with introd and notes. Univ of Illinois
Press, 1924.

THE MERCHANT'S PROLOGUE, TALE,
AND EPILOGUE

        See Hammond, 309-10; Root, 262-6; Robinson,
817-21, 1009-10; French, 313-6; Manly, 596-7; Shannon, 319-20; Tatlock, 198; Kittredge, 201.
        For discussion of marriage as a theme, see sec-
tion: Wife of Bath's Tale.

ANDRAE, AUGUST. Zu Longfellows und Chaucers
Tales. AB, 27, 1916, 56-62.
BAUGH, ALBERT C. The Original Teller of the Merchant's Tale. MP, 35, 1937, 16-26.
BENNETT, J. A. W. Concerning Wade. . . . MLR, 31,
1936, 202-3.
        MerT, 1424, and T&C, III, 614.
        See Robinson's note, 818, and E. J. Bashe, PQ,
2, 1923, 282.
BOYS, RICHARD C. Some Modern Variations of "January and May." NQ, 172, 1937, 8.
BUHLER, CURT F. "Wirk al thing by conseil." Spec,
24, 1949, 410-2.

Sources of the proverb in Chaucer. MerT, 1485-6.
Rev: D. Everett, YWES, 62.

CASSIDY, FREDERIC G. Chaucer's "Broken Harm."
MLN, 58, 1943, 23-7.
Suggests "broken" as infinitive of "brook," to
make use of, MerT, 1425.

CLINE, RUTH H. Four Chaucer Saints. MLN, 60, 1945,
480-2.
The significance of swearing by St. Frideswide,
St. Cuthbert, St. Yve, and St. Thomas, the Apostle.
MerT, E1230.
Rev: D. Everett, YWES, 49-50.

DEMPSTER, GERMAINE. On the Source of the Decep-
tion Story in the Merchant's Tale. MP, 34, 1936, 133-
54.

----------. The Original Teller of The Merchant's Tale.
MP, 36, 1938, 1-8.
Rev: D. Everett, YWES, 76-7.

----------. The Merchant's Tale. Sources and Analogues, 333-56.

DONOVAN, MORTIMER J. Three Notes on Chaucer's
Marine Life. PQ, 31, 1952, 439-41.
MerT, 1418-20.

HINCKLEY, HENRY B. Chauceriana. PQ, 6, 1927, 313-
4.
Parallel between E1762-3 and Catullus.

HOLMAN, C. HUGH. Courtly Love in the Merchant's
and Franklin's Tales. ELH, 18, 1951, 241-52.

HOLTHAUSEN, F. Die Quelle von Chaucers Merchant's
Tale. ESt, 43, 1910, 168-76.

IMMACULATE, Sister MARY. "Sixty" as a Conventional Number and Other Chauceriana. MLQ, 2, 1941,
59-66.
The Hooly Sacrament, MerT, 1702.
Rev: D. Everett, YWES, 66.

KIRBY, THOMAS A. A Note on the Irony of the Merchant's Tale. PQ, 21, 1942, 433-5.
The meaning of "coughe," line 1957, and its
irony.
Rev: D. Everett, YWES, 59.

LOOMIS, LAURA HIBBARD. Chaucer and the Breton
Lays of the Auchinleck MS. SP, 38, 1941, 14-33.
Rev: D. Everett, YWES, 60.

LOWES, JOHN L. Chaucer and the Miroir de Mariage.
    MP, 8, 1910-1, 165-86.
        Influence on MerT, 167-86.
        Rev: John Koch, AB, 22, 1911, 272.
McGALLIARD, JOHN C. Chaucer's Merchant's Tale and
    Deschamps' Miroir de Mariage. PQ, 25, 1946, 193-220.
        Rev: D. Everett, YWES, 28, 1947, 80-1.
----------. Chaucerian Comedy: The Merchant's Tale,
    Jonson, and Molière. PQ, 25, 1946, 343-70.
        Rev: D. Everett, YWES, 28, 1947, 81-2.
MAGOUN, FRANCIS P. "Muchel broken harm," CT,
    E1425. Ang, 53, 1929, 223-4.
MILLER, MILTON. The Heir in the Merchant's Tale.
    PQ, 29, 1950, 437-40.
        A note adding irony to the situation.
OWEN, CHARLES A. The Crucial Passages in Five of
    the Canterbury Tales: A Study in Irony and Symbol.
    JEGP, 52, 1953, 294-311.
        MerT, IV (E), 1319-36.
PRATT, ROBERT A. Chaucer's Claudian. Spec, 22,
    1947, 419-29.
        MerT, 2038-41.
        Rev: D. Everett, YWES, 67-8.
ROBERTSON, D. W., Jr. The Doctrine of Charity in
    Medieval Gardens: A Topical Approach through Sym-
    bolism and Allegory. Spec, 26, 1951, 24-49.
SCHLAUCH, MARGARET. Chaucer's Merchant's Tale
    and a Russian Legend of King Solomon. MLN, 49,
    1934, 229-32.
        Rev: D. Everett, YWES, 101.
----------. Chaucer's Merchant's Tale and Courtly
    Love. ELH, 4, 1937, 201-12.
SEDGEWICK, G. G. The Structure of the Merchant's
    Tale. UTQ, 17, 1948, 337-45.
        Rev: D. Everett, YWES, 82-3.
TATLOCK, JOHN STRONG PERRY. Chaucer's Mer-
    chant's Tale. MP, 33, 1936, 367-81.
        Rev: D. Everett, YWES, 81-2.
----------. The Marriage Service in Chaucer's Mer-
    chant's Tale. MLN, 32, 1917, 373-4.
----------. The Date of the Troilus: and Minor Chau-
    ceriana. MLN, 50, 1935, 277-96.
        The Merchant's Tale for the Monk?, p. 295.

UTLEY, FRANCIS L. "Mannyssh Wood" -- Merchant's
Tale (IV) 1530-1536. MLN, 53, 1938, 359-62.

THE SQUIRE'S PROLOGUE AND TALE

See Hammond, 310-4; Root, 266-70; Robinson, 821-
6, 1010; French, 316-9; Manly, 597-605; Hinckley,
210-36; Cummings, 181 ff. ; Shannon, 321; Wells, CBEL,
I, 247, and supplements to the Manual after 1933.
For editions, see section: Editions with Notes.
For discussions of marriage as a theme, see section: Wife of Bath's Tale.

BAUM, PAULL F. Notes on Chaucer. MLN, 32, 1917, 376-7.
On F7-8.
BENNETT, JOSEPHINE WATERS. Chaucer and Mande-
ville's Travels. MLN, 68, 1953, 531-4.
Lines 69-72.
BRADDY, HALDEEN. Cambyuskan's Flying Horse and
Charles VI's "Cerf Volant." MLR, 33, 1938, 41-4.
----------. The Oriental Origin of Chaucer's Canacee-
Falcon Episode. MLR, 31, 1936, 11-19.
Rev: Dorothy Everett, YWES, 82-4.
----------. The Genre of Chaucer's Squire's Tale.
JEGP, 41, 1942, 279-90.
Rev: D. Everett, YWES, 59-61.
----------. Chaucerian Minutiae. MLN, 58, 1943, 18-
23.
SqT, source of the name "Elpheta."
----------. Three Chaucer Notes: Chaucer on Murder:
De Petro Rege de Cipro; Bretheren Two; Thilke Wik-
ke Ensample of Canacee. MLN, 62, 1947, 173-9.
Rev: D. Everett, YWES, 79-80.
BROWN, CALVIN S. , Jr. , and ROBERT H. WEST. "As
by the Whelp Chastised is the Leon." MLN, 55, 1940,
209-10.
SqT, 491. See Frank, below.
BUSHNELL, A. J. de H. Names and Sources of Chau-
cer's Squire's Tale. Blackwoods, 187, 1910, 654-7.
CHAPMAN, COOLIDGE OTIS. Chaucer and the Gawain-
Poet: A Conjecture. MLN, 68, 1953, 521-4.
Suggests relations between SqT and Sir Gawain
and the Green Knight.

COOK, ALBERT S. Chaucerian Papers. Trans Connec-
ticut Academy of Arts and Sciences, 23, 1919, 32.
Yale Univ Press, 1919.
    SqT, 57.
    Rev: Arch, 141, 1921, 309 ff.
FRANK, GRACE. Correspondence, "As by the Whelp
Chastised is the Leon." Squire's Tale, 491. MLN, 55,
1940, 481.
    Disagrees with Brown and West, above.
GETTY, AGNES K. Chaucer's Changing Conceptions of
the Humble Lover. PMLA, 44, 1929, 202-16.
HAWKINS, LAURENCE F. The Place of Group F in the
Canterbury Chronology. New York Univ Diss, 1937.
HINCKLEY, HENRY B. The Brazen Horse of Troy.
MLN, 23, 1908, 157-8.
----------. Chaucer and the Cleomedes. MLN, 24,
1909, 95.
    See Jones, below in this section.
----------. Chauceriana. MP, 16, 1918-9, 39-48.
    On F250, p. 43.
----------. Chauceriana. PQ, 6, 1927, 313-4.
    Parallel between F203 and Terence.
----------. Elfeta. Acad, 74, 1908, 866.
HOLMES, URBAN T. Chaucer's "tydif," a Small Bird.
PQ, 16, 1937, 65-7.
    SqT, 648.
    See Wilson, below in this section.
HOLTHAUSEN, F. Zu alt- und mittelenglischen Dich-
tungen: Zu Chaucers Squieres Tale. Ang, 14, 1892,
320.
    On F490-1.
JONES, H. S. V. Chaucer and Cleomedes. MLN, 24,
1909, 158.
    Reply to Hinckley, above. See also Jones, The Cle-
omedes and Related Folk Tales. PMLA, 23, 1908,
557-98.
----------. The Squire's Tale. Sources and Analogues,
357-76.
KITTREDGE, GEORGE LYMAN. Chauceriana. MP, 7,
1910, 481.
    Chaucer and Geoffrey de Vinsauf, F99-104.
LOOMIS, ROGER SHERMAN. Gawain in the Squire's
Tale. MLN, 52, 1937, 413-6.

LOWES, JOHN L. "As by the whelp chasted is the leoun."
Arch, 124, 1910, 132.
    F491.
----------. The Squire's Tale and the Land of Prester
John. Washington Univ Studies, 1, 1913, 3-18.
    Rev: John Koch, AB, 25, 1914, 332-3.
MacDONALD, CHARLOTTE. Drayton's "Tidy" and
Chaucer's "Tydif." RES, 21, 1945, 127-33.
    SqT, 649.
    Rev: D. Everett, YWES, 51.
MAGOUN, FRANCIS P., Jr. Chaucer's Sir Gawain and
the O. Fr. Roman de la Rose. MLN, 67, 1952, 183-5.
    Reference to Sir Gawain, SqT, 95.
----------. Chaucer and the Roman de la Rose. RR, 17,
1926, 69-70.
    F253-6, "fern-asshen glas."
NEVILLE, MARIE. The Function of the Squire's Tale in
the Canterbury Scheme. JEGP, 50, 1951, 167-79.
    Applies to the so-called marriage group.
SKEAT, WALTER W. Chaucer's Two Allusions to Per-
sius. NQ, ser. 10, 12, 1909, 6.
STILLWELL, GARDINER. Chaucer in Tartary. RES,
24, 1948, 177-88.
    Rev: D. Everett, YWES, 83.
TATLOCK, JOHN STRONG PERRY. Chaucer's Whelp
and Lion. MLN, 38, 1923, 506-7.
    F491.
----------. The Date of the Troilus: and Minor Chaucer-
iana. MLN, 50, 1935, 277-96.
    On the horseman in the hall, F80-1.
TOLLENAERE, F. de. "To maken of fern -- asshen
glas." E Stud, 31, 1950, 97-9.
    Rev: D. Everett, YWES, 65.
TUPPER, FREDERICK. Chaucer's Tale of Ireland.
PMLA, 36, 1921, 196-7.
    Rev: John Koch, ESt, 56, 1922, 30-2.
WHITING, B. J. "By My Fader Soule." (CT II(B), 1178).
JEGP, 46, 1947, 297.
    Not inappropriate to Squire; on assignment of group.
    Rev: D. Everett, YWES, 79.
----------. Gawain: His Reputation, his Courtesy, his
Appearance in Chaucer's Squire's Tale. Med Stud, 9,
1947, 189-234.

WILSON, F. P. The Tidy. PQ, 17, 1938, 216-8.
    Reply to U. T. Holmes, above in this section.

THE WORDS OF THE FRANKLIN,
THE FRANKLIN'S PROLOGUE AND TALE

See Hammond, 314; Root, 271-7; Robinson, 826-31,
1010; French, 319-24; Manly, 605-11; Hinckley, 237-
60; Shannon, 321-2; Kittredge, 204; Wells, CBEL, I,
247-8, and supplements to the Manual after 1933; Cummings, 181-97; Dempster, 62-7.
    For editions, see section: Editions with Notes.
    For discussion of marriage as a theme, see sec-
tion: Wife of Bath's Tale.

AMAN, A. Die Filiation der Frankeleynes Tale in Chau-
    cers Canterbury Tales. München Diss, 1912.
ARCHER, JEROME W. On Chaucer's Source for "Ar-
    veragus" in the Franklin's Tale. PMLA, 65, 1950,
    318-22.
    Rev: D. Everett, YWES, 65-6.
BALDWIN, CHARLES SEARS. Cicero on Parnassus.
    PMLA, 42, 1927, 106-12.
    Colors of rhetoric.
BAUM, PAULL F. Notes on Chaucer. MLN, 32, 1917,
    376-7.
    On F1538 ff.
BLENNER-HASSETT, ROLAND. Autobiographical As-
    pects of Chaucer's Franklyn. Spec, 28, 1953, 791-800.
BØGHOLM, N. A Rash Promise. Stud Neophil, 15, 1942,
    41-2.
    Versions of FrankT reflect culture of the tellers.
    Rev: D. Everett, YWES, 61.
DEMPSTER, GERMAINE. Chaucer at Work on the Com-
    plaint in the Franklin's Tale. MLN, 52, 1937, 16-23.
    Rev: YWES, 86.
----------. A Further Note on Dorigen's Exempla.
    MLN, 54, 1939, 137-8.
----------, and J. S. P. TATLOCK. The Franklin's
    Tale. Sources and Analogues, 377-97.
DONOVAN, MORTIMER J. The Form and Vogue of the
    Middle English Breton Lay. Doctoral Diss, Harvard,
    1951.

FARNHAM, WILLARD E. The Dayes of the Mone. SP,
    20, 1923, 70-82.
FRENCH, W. H. The Franklin's Tale, Line 942. MLN,
    60, 1945, 477-80.
        Rev: D. Everett, YWES, 51.
GEROULD, GORDON HALL. The Social Status of Chau-
    cer's Franklin. PMLA, 41, 1926, 262-79.
HAMMOND, ELEANOR P. Chaucer and Lydgate Notes.
    MLN, 27, 1912, 91-2.
        On F1017-8.
HARRISON, BENJAMIN S. The Rhetorical Inconsistency
    of Chaucer's Franklin. SP, 32, 1935, 55-61.
        Rev: D. Everett, YWES, 29.
HART, WALTER M. The Franklin's Tale. 185-234, in
    Haverford Essays, 1909.
        The narrative technique of FrankT compared with
    that of Breton lais.
HINCKLEY, HENRY B. Chauceriana. MP, 16, 1918, 39-
    48.
        On the interpretation of FrankT and on F734, F942,
    and F1325, pp. 43-8.
HOLMAN, C. HUGH. Courtly Love in the Merchant's
    and Franklin's Tales. ELH, 18, 1951, 241-52.
HUNTER, WILLIAM B., Jr. Canterbury Tales, V,
    1031 ff. MLN, 68, 1953, 174.
        Lines 1031-79, Aurelius' prayer to Apollo.
LOOMIS, LAURA HIBBARD. Chaucer and the Bre-
    ton Lays of the Auchinleck MS. SP, 38, 1941, 14-
    33.
        Did Chaucer make use of these stories? Finds
    borrowing in Franklin's Prol and Tale, WBT, MerT,
    and Sir Thopas.
        Rev: D. Everett, YWES, 60.
LOOMIS, ROGER S. A Parallel to the Franklin's Dis-
    cussion of Marriage. 191-4, in Philologica: The Ma-
    lone Anniversary Studies.
        Rev: D. Everett, YWES, 31, 1950, 66.
LOWES, JOHN L. Chaucer and the Miroir de Mariage.
    MP, 8, 1910-1, 305-34.
        Influence on FrankT, 324-5.
        Rev: John Koch, AB, 22, 1911, 272.
----------. The Franklin's Tale, Teseide, and the Fi-
    locolo. MP, 15, 1918, 689-728.

----------. Illustrations of Chaucer Drawn Chiefly from Deschamps. RR, 2, 1911, 125.
> On F1118-20.
> Rev: John Koch, ES, 46, 1912, 114.

----------. Chaucer and Dante. MP, 14, 1917, 721 ff.
> On F949-50, 1101.

LUMIANSKY, R. M. The Character and Performance of Chaucer's Franklin. UTQ, 20, 1951, 344-56.

OWEN, CHARLES A. The Crucial Passages in Five of the Canterbury Tales: A Study in Irony and Symbol. JEGP, 52, 1953, 294-311.
> FrankT, V (F) 988-98.

PATCH, HOWARD R. Chauceriana. ES, 65, 1931, 351-9.
> On F932.

RAJNA, PIO. Le Origini della Novella Narrata dal Frankeleyn nei Canterbury Tales del Chaucer. Romania, 32, 1903, 204-67.
> Rev: John L. Lowes, MP, 15, 1918, 689-728.

ROYSTER, JAMES F. Chaucer's "Colle Tregetour." SP, 23, 1926, 380-4.
> See 383.

SCHICK, J. Die ältesten Versionen von Chaucers Frankeleynes Tale. 89-107, in Studia Indo-Iranica, Ehrengabe für Wilhelm Geiger. Leipzig: Harrassowitz, 1931.

SLEDD, JAMES. Dorigen's Complaint. SP, 45, 1947, 36-45.

SKEAT, WALTER W. Chaucer's Two Allusions to Persius. NQ, ser. 10, 12, 1909, 6.
> On F721.

TATLOCK, J. S. P. Astrology and Magic in Chaucer's Franklin's Tale. 339-50, in Anniversary Papers . . . for George Lyman Kittredge. Ginn, 1913.
> Rev: John Koch, AB, 25, 1914, 339-41.

----------. Kayrrud in the Franklin's Tale. Paper read by title at meeting of MLA at Cambridge, Dec 31, 1913. Listed in PMLA, 29, 1914, xxvi.

----------. The Scene of the Franklin's Tale Visited. Chaucer Society, ser. 2, no. 51, 1914.
> Rev: John Koch, ESt, 49, 1915, 437; Arch, 134, 1916, 466; MLR, 12, 1917, 84.

TUPPER, FREDERICK. Saint Venus and the Canterbury Pilgrims. Nation, 97, 1913, 354-6.

WRENN, C. L. Chaucer's Knowledge of Horace. MLR, 18, 1925, 286-92.

THE PHYSICIAN'S TALE

See Hammond, 293-5; Root, 219-22; Robinson,
832-3, 1010-11; French, 266-8; Manly, 611-2; Shannon,
317-8; Tatlock, 152; Curry, 3; Wells, Group C,
CBEL, I, 243-4; 1647, 1740, 1933.

GREG, W. W. Facsimiles of Twelve Manuscripts in the
Library of Trinity College, Cambridge. Oxford, 1913.
Lines 1-20, 42-63, MS Trinity R. 3. 3.
MOORE, SAMUEL. The Position of Group C in the Can-
terbury Tales. PMLA, 30, 1915, 116-23.
Order of the tales.
SHANNON, EDGAR F. The Physician's Tale. Sources
and Analogues, 398-408.
TUPPER, FREDERICK. Chaucer's Bed's Head. MLN,
30, 1915, 5-12.
Source for C105 ff. , on maidenly virtues of Virginia.
YOUNG, KARL. The Maidenly Virtues of Chaucer's Vir-
ginia. Spec, 16, 1941, 340-9.
Vincent of Beauvais. See Tupper, above.
Rev: D. Everett, YWES, 60.

WORDS OF THE HOST
(OR INTRODUCTION TO THE PARDONER'S TALE),
THE PARDONER'S PROLOGUE AND TALE

See Hammond, 295-6; Root, 222-31; Robinson, 834-7,
1011; French, 268-72; Manly, 613-23; Hinckley, 157-83;
Kittredge, 211; Curry, 54; Gerould, 55-71; Dempster, 72-9.
For material on medieval sermons and preaching,
see section on Religious Backgrounds.
For editions, see section: Editions with Notes.
For phonographic recordings, see section: Canter-
bury Tales: General.

ANDERSON, G. K. Die Silberlinge des Judas and the
Accursed Treasure. SP, 48, 1951, 77-86.
ANDRAE, AUGUST. Zu Longfellows und Chaucers Tales.
AB, 27, 1916, 84-7.
AYRES, HARRY M. Chaucer and Seneca. Rom Rev, 10,
1919, 1-15.
C492 ff. , 513-6.

BUSHNELL, NELSON SHERWIN. The Wandering Jew
    and the Pardoner's Tale. SP, 28, 1931, 450-60.
        Rev: D. Everett, YWES, 89-90.
CANBY, HENRY S. The Short Story in English. Holt, 1909.
        See 72 ff. and A Study of the Short Story, 1913.
CHAPMAN, COOLIDGE OTIS. The Pardoner's Tale: A
    Mediaeval Sermon. MLN, 41, 1926, 506-9.
        See also PMLA, 44, 1929, 178-85.
CROSS, JAMES E. On the Meaning of A-blakeberyed.
    CT, C 406. RES, 2 n. s., 1951, 372-4.
DEMPSTER, GERMAINE. The Pardoner's Prologue.
    Sources and Analogues, 409-14.
GROSS, SEYMOUR L. Conscious Verbal Repetition in
    the Pardoner's Prologue. NQ, 198, 1953, 413-4.
HAMILTON, MARIE P. Death and Old Age in the Par-
    doner's Tale. SP, 36, 1939, 571-6.
        Rev: D. Everett, YWES, 22, 1941, 58.
----------. The Credentials of Chaucer's Pardoner.
    JEGP, 40, 1941, 48-72.
        Status of Pardoner. Evidence to support thesis
    that Pardoner was of the regular clergy -- an Austin
    canon from the Rounceval hospital at Charing Cross.
HART, WALTER M. The Pardoner's Tale and Der Dot
    im Stock. MP, 9, 1911, 17-22.
        Chaucer and Hans Sachs.
HEMINGWAY, SAMUEL B. The Two St. Pauls. MLN,
    32, 1917, 57-8.
        PardT, 521.
HENCH, ATCHESON L. On the Subtly Creeping Wine of
    Chaucer's Pardoner. MLN, 52, 1937, 27-8.
HENKIN, LEO J. Jacob and the Hooly Jew. MLN, 55,
    1940, 254-9.
        Disputes Skeat's interpretation of a passage (C361-5).
----------. The Pardoner's Sheep-Bone and Lapidary
    Lore. Bull of Hist of Medicine, 10, 1941, 504-12.
HINCKLEY, HENRY B. Chauceriana. MP, 16, 1918-9, 39-48.
        On C406 and C953, p. 43.
IMMACULATE, Sister MARY. "Sixty" as a Conventional
    Number and Other Chauceriana. MLQ, 2, 1941, 59-66.
        The first table, PardT, 639.
        Rev: D. Everett, YWES, 66.
KELLOGG, ALFRED L. An Augustinian Interpretation
    of Chaucer's Pardoner. Spec, 26, 1951, 465-81.

----------, and LOUIS A. HASELMAYER. Chaucer's
   Satire of the Pardoner. PMLA, 66, 1951, 251-77.
      The Pardoner's method of collecting alms.
KIRBY, THOMAS A. The Pardoner's Tale and the
   Treasure of Sierra Madre. MLN, 66, 1951, 269-70.
KRISHNAMURTI, S. Note on the Pardoner's Tale, Lines
   237-9. MLR, 39, 1944, 398.
LOWES, JOHN L. Illustrations of Chaucer Drawn
   Chiefly from Deschamps. Rom Rev, 2, 1911, 113-28.
      On lines 474, 651-3, 656.
      Rev: ES, 46, 1912, 114.
LUMIANSKY, R. M. A Conjecture Concerning Chaucer's
   Pardoner. Tulane Studies in English, 1, 1949, 1-29.
      Interprets the unity of the Pardoner's character.
      Rev: D. Everett, YWES, 59.
MOORE, ARTHUR K. The Pardoner's Interruption of the
   Wife of Bath's Prologue. MLQ, 10, 1949, 49-57.
      Proposed that the last part of the Prologue is di-
   rected against the Pardoner and the clergy.
      Rev: D. Everett, YWES, 64-5.
NORRIS, DOROTHY MacBRIDE. Chaucer's "Pardon-
   er's Tale" and Flanders. PMLA, 48, 1933, 636-41.
   Part of Doctoral Diss, Univ of Iowa, 1932.
OWEN, CHARLES A. The Crucial Passages in Five of
   the Canterbury Tales: A Study in Irony and Symbol.
   JEGP, 52, 1953, 294-311.
      PardT, VI(C), 772, 448.
OWEN, W. J. B. The Old Man in the Pardoner's Tale.
   RES, 2 n. s., 1951, 49-55.
RUTTER, G. M. An Holy Jewes Shepe. (CT, C350-1).
   MLN, 43, 1928, 536.
SEDGEWICK, G. G. The Progress of Chaucer's Pardon-
   er, 1880-1940. MLQ, 1, 1940, 431-58.
      Rev: D. Everett, YWES, 22, 1941, 57.
SEDGWICK, W. B. Chaucer's Pardoner's Prologue.
   MLR, 19, 1924, 336-7.
SLEDD, JAMES HINTON. Canterbury Tales: C 310, 320:
   "By Seint Ronyan." Med Stud, 13, 1951, 226-33.
SWART, J. Chaucer's Pardoner. Neophil, 36, 1952, 45-50.
THOMAS, RUSSELL. Ecclesiastical Satire in Chaucer
   and Erasmus; Parallel to the Pardoner's Description
   of his Preaching in Erasmus' Praise of Folly. MLN,
   45, 1930, 394-5.

TUPPER, FREDERICK. The Pardoner's Tavern. JEGP, 13, 1914, 553-65.

----------. The Pardoner's Tale. Sources and Analogues, 415-38.

WEATHERLY, EDWARD H. A Note on Chaucer's Pardoner's Prologue. MLN, 50, 1935, 310-1.

WELLS, WHITNEY. A New Analogue to the Pardoner's Tale. MLN, 40, 1925, 58-9.

> Jack London's use of the plot of PardT.

----------. An Unnoted Analogue to the Pardoner's Tale. MP, 25, 1927, 163-4.

WERNER, A. Chaucer's Pardoner's Tale: African Analogue. NQ, ser. 11, 4, 1911, 82-3.

> Mention of Swahili version of the story.

WHITING, B. J. More on Chaucer's Pardoner's Prologue. (VI (C), 377-390). MLN, 51, 1936, 322-7.

> Rev: D. Everett, YWES, 80.

WOOLF, HENRY B. The Pardoner's Tale: Another Analogue. MLN, 66, 1951, 267-9.

> In the New Yorker.

THE SHIPMAN'S PROLOGUE OR THE EPILOGUE OF THE MAN OF LAW'S TALE (Robinson, 90) AND THE SHIPMAN'S TALE

See Hammond, 283-5; Root, 187-90; Robinson, 837-9, 1011-2; French, 232-3; Manly, 624; Brusendorff, 70; Kittredge, 168; Tatlock, 205 ff.; Wells, CBEL, I, 240, and supplements to the Manual after 1933. See also Root, Chaucer's Summoner, in section: Man of Law's Tale.

CALDWELL, ROBERT A. Chaucer's "Taillynge Ynough" $B^2$1624 (ShT, 434). MLN, 55, 1940, 262-5.

> Reply to Jones, below.

CLINE, RUTH H. Four Chaucer Saints. MLN, 60, 1945, 480-2.

> The significance of swearing by St. Frideswide, St. Cuthbert, St. Yve, and St. Thomas, the Apostle. ShT, B1417 (VII, 227).

EKWALL, E. A Twelfth Century Lollard? E Stud, 28, 1947, 108-10.

> Discusses meaning of the word.

GOFFIN, R. C. Notes on Chaucer. MLR, 18, 1923, 335-6.

On B 1189 of Prol, "Ne phislyas ne termes queinte
of lawe" (Robinson, 90).
JONES, CLAUDE. Chaucer's Taillynge Ynough. MLN,
52, 1937, 570.
JONES, R. F. A Conjecture on the Wife of Bath's Pro-
logue. JEGP, 24, 1925, 512-47.
    Deals with Shipman's Prol.
PRATT, ROBERT A. Chaucer's Shipman's Tale and
Sercambi. MLN, 55, 1940, 142-5.
SILVERMAN, ALBERT H. Sex and Money in Chaucer's
Shipman's Tale. PQ, 32, 1953, 329-36.
    "Taillynge ynough," p. 330, and suggestion as
to the tale's theme.
SKEAT, WALTER W. Chaucer: The Shipman's Prologue.
MLR, 5, 1910, 430-4.
    Rev: John Koch, AB, 22, 1911, 280, and Ang, 49,
1925, 232.
SMITH, ROLAND M. The Six Gifts. Jour of Celtic Stud-
ies, 1, 1949, 98-104.
    Suggests Irish influence on the double triad of the
six gifts of women, WBT, 925-48, and ShT, 173-7,
and the single triad in NPT, 2914.
    Rev: D. Everett, YWES, 63.
SPARGO, JOHN WEBSTER. Chaucer's "Shipman's
Tale": The Lover's Gift Regained. Helsinki: Suoma-
lainen Tiedenkatemia, Societas Scientiarum Fennica,
1930. 72 pp. FF Communications, no. 91.
    Rev: M. B. Ruud, MLN, 50, 1935, 335-6.
----------. The Shipman's Tale. Sources and Analogues,
439-46.
TUPPER, FREDERICK. The Bearings of the Shipman's
Prologue. JEGP, 33, 1934, 352-72.
    Rev: D. Everett, YWES, 92-4.

THE PRIORESS' HEADLINK, PROLOGUE, AND TALE

    See Hammond, 285-7; Root, 190-8; Robinson, 839-
41, 1012; French, 233-42; Manly, 624-8; Legouis, 212;
Kittredge, 175-81.
    For editions, see section: Editions with Notes.
    For additional material on the Prioress, see sec-
tion: Religious Backgrounds.
    For religious lyrics, see section: A B C.

For phonographic recordings, see section: Canterbury Tales: General.

ADLER, MICHAEL. A "Ritual Murder." TLS, Sept 27,
1928, 687.
ANDRAE, AUGUST. Zu Longfellows und Chaucers Tales.
AB, 27, 1916, 84.
BLAND, C. C. SWINTON, Trans. Miracles of the
Blessed Virgin Mary. Routledge, 1928.
    Translation of Johannes Herolt's "Promptuarium
Discipuli de Miraculis Beate Marie Virginis," an
account of 99 miracles of the Virgin.
BROWN, CARLETON. On "Little Clergeon." MP, 3,
1905-6, 467-91.
    (In Hammond, 287.) See John Koch, ES, 37, 1907,
231.
----------. A Study of the Miracle of Our Lady Told by
Chaucer's Prioress. Chaucer Society, 2nd ser., 45,
1910.
    Rev: John Koch, AB, 22, 1911, 269.
----------. William Herebert and Chaucer's Prioresses
Tale. MLN, 38, 1923, 92-4.
----------. The Prioress's Tale. Sources and Ana-
logues, 447-85.
COWLING, G. H. A Note on Chaucer's Stanza. RES, 2,
1926, 311-7.
DEROCQUIGNY, J. Note sur Chaucer. C. T., B 1687,
"an heep." RAA, Dec, 1927, 160-1.
DRAPER, JOHN W. Chaucer's "Wardrobe." ESt, 60,
1926, 238-51.
    B2 1762 (VII, 572).
FRIEND, ALBERT C. Chaucer's Prioress' Tale: An
Early Analogue. PMLA, 51, 1936, 621-5.
    Rev: D. Everett, YWES, 78-9.
GEROULD, GORDON H. An Early Analogue of Chaucer's
Prioresses Tale. MLN, 24, 1909, 132-3.
HAMILTON, MARIE P. Echoes of Childermas in the
Tale of the Prioress. MLR, 34, 1939, 1-8.
HART, WALTER M. Some Old French Miracles of Our
Lady and Chaucer's Prioresses Tale. 29-53, in
Gayley Anniversary Papers. Univ of California Press,
1922.
MADELEVA, Sister MARY (MARY EVALINE WOLFF).

Chaucer's Nuns, and Other Essays. Appleton, 1925.
215 pp.

MICHELSON, H. The Jew in Early English Literature.
Diss. Amsterdam: H. J. Paris, 1926. 175 pp.
Rev: A. S. , Jewish Quart Rev, 19, 1929, 321-6.

PALMER, H. P. The Jews in England in Mediaeval
Times. LQR, 155, 1931, 226-38.

PRATT, ROBERT A. Chaucer Borrowing from Himself.
MLQ, 7, 1946, 259-64.
Rev: D. Everett, YWES, 69.

R. , J. H. Notes on Jews in XIII Century England. NQ,
167, 1934, 255-7, 273-4.
In second article is mention of analogue to
PriorT.

ROBERTSON, STUART. Chaucer and Wordsworth. MLN,
43, 1928, 104-5.
Verses 57-63.

ROSS, WOODBURN O. Another Analogue to the Prioresses Tale. MLN, 50, 1935, 307-10.

----------. A B Version of the Legend Told by Chaucer's Prioress. MLN, 52, 1937, 23-5.

ROTH, CECIL. Feast of Purim and the Origins of the
Blood Accusation. Spec, 8, 1933, 520-6.

----------. Mediaeval Lincoln Jewry and its Synagogue.
With a Foreword by Gustave Tuck. Jewish Hist Soc,
1934. 28 pp.
Rev: TLS, Dec 27, 1934, 923.

STATLER, MARGARET H. The Analogues of Chaucer's
Prioress' Tale: The Relation of Group C to Group A.
PMLA, 65, 1950, 896-910.
See Brown, above.
Rev: D. Everett, YWES, 63-4.

TRYON, RUTH W. Miracles of Our Lady in Middle English Poetry. PMLA, 38, 1923, 308-88.

TUPPER, FREDERICK. Chaucer's Bed's Head. MLN,
30, 1915, 5-12.
Chaucer and the Prymer, 9-11.

SIR THOPAS: PROLOGUE AND TALE

See Hammond, 287-9; Root, 199-203; Robinson,
841-6, 1012; French, 242-4; Manly, 628-34.
For editions, see section: Editions with Notes.

BLAU, ERNST. Zu Chaucer's Tale of Sir Thopas. AB,
    31, 1920, 237.
        On "payndemayne," B1915 (VII, 725). See Patterson
    in this section.
CAMDEN, CARROLL, Jr. The Physiognomy of Sir Tho-
    pas. RES, 11, 1935, 326-30.
        Rev: D. Everett, YWES, 108.
EVERETT, DOROTHY. A Note on "Ypotis." RES, 6,
    1930, 446-8.
FICKE, HERMANN S. Iewes Werk. PQ, 7, 1928, 82-5.
        See Loomis in this section. Lines 152-4.
FRIEDMAN, ALBERT B. Chaucer and Robin Hood. NQ,
    195, 1950, 210.
        Robin Hood's name in MS Py, Sir Thopas.
HERBEN, STEPHEN J., Jr. Arms and Armor in Chau-
    cer. Spec, 12, 1937, 475-87.
        Rev: D. Everett, YWES, 68.
KNOTT, THOMAS A. A Bit of Chaucer Mythology. MP,
    8, 1910, 135-9.
        On the characterization of Chaucer in the Prol of
    Sir Thopas.
KNOWLTON, E. C. Chaucer's Man of Law. JEGP, 23,
    1924, 90-2.
LANGE, HUGO. Chaucers Sir Thopas, Ritter Honiggold:
    Ein Beitrag zur Kenntnis Chaucers und Froissarts.
    Part I, DL, 37, 1916, 1299-303; part II (Zu Chaucers
    Sir Thopas), 1669-72; parts III, IV, 1827-32.
LAWRENCE, W. W. Satire in Sir Thopas. PMLA, 50,
    1935, 81-91.
        Rev: D. Everett, YWES, 107-8.
LINN, IRVING. The Arming of Sir Thopas. MLN, 51,
    1936, 300-11.
        Rev: D. Everett, YWES, 79-80.
LOCKE, EVALEEN, II. Satire of the Thirteenth and
    Fourteenth Centuries with Especial Reference to the
    Seven Deadly Sins. Master's Thesis, Univ of South-
    ern California, 1932, 148 pp.
        "A study of the extant satiric pieces in the English
    vernacular, between 1200 and 1399, to show the devel-
    opment in language, character, content, and tone."
LOOMIS, LAURA HIBBARD. Chaucer's Jewes Werk and
    Guy of Warwick. PQ, 14, 1935, 371-3.
        See Ficke in this section.

Rev: Dorothy Everett, YWES, 16, 1935, 108-9.

----------. Sir Thopas and David and Goliath. MLN, 51, 1936, 311-3.

Rev: Dorothy Everett, YWES, 79.

----------. Chaucer and the Auchinleck MS: Sir Thopas and Guy of Warwick. 111-28, in Essays and Studies in Honor of Carleton Brown. New York, 1940.

----------. Sir Thopas. Sources and Analogues, 486-559.

----------. Chaucer and the Breton Lays of the Auchinleck MS. SP, 38, 1941, 14-33.

Rev: D. Everett, YWES, 60.

LUMIANSKY, R. M. The Meaning of Chaucer's Prologue to Sir Thopas. PQ, 26, 1947, 313-20.

Rev: D. Everett, YWES, 29, 1948, 83-4.

MAGOUN, F. P., Jr. The Source of Chaucer's Rime of Sir Thopas. PMLA, 42, 1927, 833-44.

Rev: D. Everett, YWES, 107-8.

MANLY, JOHN M. Sir Thopas: A Satire. 52-73, in Essays and Studies, Vol. 13, collected by Caroline F. E. Spurgeon. Milford, 1928.

Rev: D. Everett, YWES, 89.

----------. The Stanza-Forms of Sir Thopas. MP, 8, 1910, 141-4.

NADAL, THOMAS W. Spenser's Muiopotmos in Relation to Chaucer's Sir Thopas and the Nun's Priest's Tale. PMLA, 25, 1910, 640-56.

PATTERSON, R. F. Paindemaine. MLR, 7, 1912, 376.

See Blau in this section.

REED, JESSICA. The Element of Satire in Sir Thopas. Master's Thesis, Univ of Washington, 1931. Typewritten, 51 pp.

ROCHLIN, S. A. Assegai. TLS, June 16, 1932, 447.

On "launcegay," B1938-43.

ROPPOLO, JOSEPH P. The Meaning of "at erst": Prologue to Sir Thopas, $B^2$1884. MLN, 63, 1948, 365-71.

Rev: D. Everett, YWES, 84.

ROSS, WOODBURN O. A Possible Significance of the Name Thopas. MLN, 45, 1930, 172-4.

Rev: D. Everett, YWES, 90.

SMITH, ROLAND M. Two Chaucer Notes. MLN, 51, 1936, 314-7.

The Name of Sir Thopas, 314-5.

SNYDER, FRANKLIN B. A Note on Sir Thopas. MP, 6,
1908, 133-5.

----------. Sir Thomas Norray and Sir Thopas. MLN,
25, 1910, 78-80.

STRONG, CAROLINE. Sir Thopas and Sir Guy. MLN,
23, 1908, 73-7, 102-6.

TROUNCE, A. McI. The English Tail Rhyme Romances.
MA, 1, 1932, 90-2.

MELIBEUS: HEADLINK AND TALE

See Hammond, 289-90; Root, 199-203; Robinson,
846-51, 1012; French, 244-7; Manly, 634; Tatlock,
188.

See Jefferson, Chaucer and the Consolation of
Philosophy, and Koch, Chaucers Boethiusübersetzung, on chronology.

AYRES, HARRY M. Chaucer and Seneca. Rom Rev, 10,
1919, 1-15.

BAUM, PAULL F. Chaucer's Metrical Prose. JEGP,
45, 1946, 38-42.

    Concerns the prose of Mel.

    Rev: D. Everett, YWES, 77.

BUHLER, CURT F. "Wirk al thing by conseil." Spec,
24, 1949, 410-2.

    Sources of the proverb in Chaucer. Line 1003.

COOK, ALBERT S. Chauceriana. RR, 8, 1917, 210-26.

    Source of Mel, 219-20.

GOLDSCHMIDT, E. PH. Medieval Texts and their First
Appearance in Print. Suppl Bibl Soc Trans, no. 16,
London, 1943.

    Rev: S. Gibson, YWES, 225-6, and 26, 1945,
73.

HOTSON, J. LESLIE. The Tale of Melibeus and John of
Gaunt. SP, 18, 1921, 429-52.

    Interpretation of Mel as political allegory.

    Rev: Arch, 145, 1923, 156.

KREUZER, JAMES R. A Note on Chaucer's Tale of
Melibee. MLN, 63, 1948, 53-4.

    Rev: D. Everett, YWES, 84.

LANDRUM, GRACE W. Chaucer's Use of the Vulgate.
PMLA, 39, 1924, 75-100.

LANGHANS, VICTOR. Die Datierung der Prosastücke
Chaucers. Ang, 53, 1929, 235-68.
> Mel, 236-43.
> Rev: M. B. Ruud, MLN, 45, 1930, 292; D. Ever-
> ett, YWES, 112-3.

LAWRENCE, WILLIAM W. The Tale of Melibeus. 100-
10, in Essays and Studies in Honor of Carleton
Brown. New York, 1940.

POWER, EILEEN, Ed. Goodman of Paris (Le Ménagier
de Paris); a Treatise on Moral and Domestic Economy by a Citizen of Paris (c. 1393). Now First Translated into English with an Introduction and Notes.
Broadway Medieval Library. Harcourt; Routledge,
1928. 348 pp.

SEIBERT, HARRIET. Chaucer and Horace. MLN, 31,
1916, 304-7.

SEVERS, J. BURKE. The Source of Chaucer's Melibeus.
PMLA, 50, 1935, 92-9.
> Rev: D. Everett, YWES, 109-10.

----------. The Tale of Melibeus. Sources and Analogues, 560-614.

STILLWELL, GARDINER. The Political Meaning of
Chaucer's Tale of Melibee. Spec, 19, 1944, 433-44.
> Also in Program announcing Candidates for High-
> er Degrees, Univ of Iowa, 1940.

THE MONK'S PROLOGUE AND TALE

> See Hammond, 291-2; Root, 203-7; Robinson, 851-
> 7, 1012-3; French, 247-57; Manly, 635-6; Shannon,
> 312-7; Brusendorff, 77, 492; Birney, 650-4.
>
> See Schlauch in section: General Criticism, and
> Jefferson, Chaucer and the Consolation of Philosophy,
> and Schirmer in section: Literary Relations.

AIKEN, PAULINE. Vincent of Beauvais and Chaucer's
Monk's Tale. Spec, 17, 1942, 56-68.
> Rev: D. Everett, YWES, 56.

BABCOCK, R. W. The Mediaeval Setting of Chaucer's
"Monk's Tale." PMLA, 46, 1931, 205-13.
> Rev: D. Everett, YWES, 88-9.

BEVINS, LLOYD EDWARD. Chaucer's Monk's Tale: A

Study of MSS Texts. Univ of Virginia, Abstracts of
Dissertations, 1951, 8-12.

BRADDY, HALDEEN. The Two Petros in the "Monkes
Tale." PMLA, 50, 1935, 69-80.
   Dating MonT.
   Rev: YWES, 110-1.

----------. Three Chaucer Notes: Chaucer on Murder:
De Petro Rege de Cipro; Bretheren Two; Thilke
Wikke Ensample of Canacee. MLN, 62, 1947, 173-9.
   Rev: D. Everett, YWES, 79-80.

----------. Chaucer's Don Pedro and the Purpose of
the Monk's Tale. MLQ, 13, 1952, 3-5.

CRAWFORD, S. J. Croesus's Dream. TLS, June 26,
1924, 404.
   B3937-48.

EMERSON, OLIVER F. Seith Trophee. MLN, 31, 1916,
142-6.

FARNHAM, WILLARD. The Medieval Heritage of Elizabethan Tragedy. Univ of California Press, 1936.
487 pp.
   Falls of Princes: Chaucer and Lydgate, 129-72.
   Rev: William W. Lawrence, MLN, 52, 1937, 435-
7; H. R. Patch, ESt, 71, 1937, 397-8; Percy Simpson,
MA, 7, 1938, 138-40.

FORSTER, MAX. Boccaccios De Casibus Virorum Il-
lustrium in englischen Bearbeitung. DL, 45, 1924,
1943-6.

FROST, GEORGE L. "That Precious Corpus Madrian."
MLN, 57, 1942, 177-9.
   Rev: D. Everett, YWES, 55.

GELBACH, MARIE. On Chaucer's Version of the Death
of Croesus. JEGP, 6, 1907, 657-60.

HART, J. M. Chaucer's "Vitramyte" Again. MLN, 21,
1906, 192.
   MonT, B3560-2.

HEMINGWAY, SAMUEL B. Chaucer's Monk and Nun's
Priest. MLN, 31, 1916, 479-83.

JENKINS, T. ATKINSON. Vitremyte: Mot Latin-Fran-
çais Employé par Chaucer. 141-7, in Mélanges de
Linguistique et de Litterature, offerts à M. Alfred
Jeanroy. Paris, 1928.

JOHNSON, DUDLEY R. The Biblical Characters of
Chaucer's Monk. PMLA, 66, 1951, 827-43.

Bible Historiale the prime source of the Biblical
portions of MonT.

JONES, CLAUDE. The Monk's Tale, a Mediaeval Sermon. MLN, 52, 1937, 570-2.

KITTREDGE, GEORGE LYMAN. The Date of Chaucer's
Troilus and Other Chaucer Matters. Chaucer Society,
2nd ser., 42, 1909.

See 41-52.

Rev: Arch, 124, 1910, 212.

----------. The Pillars of Hercules and Chaucer's Trophee. Putnam Anniversary Volume. Torch Press,
1909.

Rev: Arch, 124, 1910, 428; John Koch, AB, 22,
1911, 271.

LIEBERMANN, FELIX. Zu Chaucers Monk's Tale.
Arch, 148, 1925, 96-7.

LUKE, H. C. Visitors from the East to the Plantagenet
and Lancastrian Kings. Nineteenth Century, 108,
1930, 760-9.

King Peter of Cyprus, 764-7.

MacCRACKEN, HENRY N. A New Manuscript of Chaucer's Monk's Tale. MLN, 23, 1908, 93.

Cambridge Univ, Trinity MS, R. 3. 10.

MALONE, KEMP. Harry Bailly and Godelief. E Stud,
31, 1950, 209-15.

Prol, MonT, 1894. Considers the characters fic-
tional rather than historical.

Rev: D. Everett, YWES, 60.

NORRIS, DOROTHY MacBRIDE. Harry Bailey's "Corpus
Madrian." MLN, 48, 1933, 146-8. Part of Doctoral
Diss, Univ of Iowa, 1932.

RICHARDSON, H. G. "Godeleef my Wyf." TLS, Jan 20,
1927, 44.

RICKERT, EDITH. "Godeleef my Wyf." TLS, Dec 16,
1926, 935.

B3084 (VII, 1894).

----------. "Goode Lief, my Wyf." MP, 25, 1927, 79-
82.

ROOT, ROBERT K. The Monk's Tale. Sources and Analogues, 615-44.

SAVAGE, HENRY. Chaucer and the "Pitous Deeth" of
"Petro, Glorie of Spayne." Spec, 24, 1949, 357-75.

Rev: D. Everett, YWES, 63-4.

SEATON, ETHEL. "Goode lief my wyf." MLR, 41, 1946,
    196-202.
        Chaucer's humor in the use of St. Godeleva's
    name: B3084 (VII, 1894) and D431.
        Rev: D. Everett, YWES, 77-8.
SHANNON, EDGAR F. Notes on Chaucer. MP, 11, 1913,
    227-36.
        On "Busirus," B^2 3293 (VII, 2103), pp. 227-30.
----------. Chaucer and Lucan's Pharsalia. MP, 16,
    1919, 609-18.
        B^2 3909-10 (VII, 2719-20).
SILVERSTEIN, H. THEODORE. Chaucer's Brutus Cas-
    sius. MLN, 47, 1932, 148-50.
SOCOLA, EDWARD M. Chaucer's Development of For-
    tune in the Monk's Tale. JEGP, 49, 1950, 159-71.
        Rev: D. Everett, YWES, 64.
SPENCER, THEODORE. The Story of Ugolino in Dante
    and Chaucer. Spec, 9, 1934, 295-301.
        Rev: D. Everett, YWES, 101.
TATLOCK, JOHN STRONG PERRY. Chaucer's Vitre-
    myte. MLN, 21, 1906, 62.
        MonT, B3560-2 (VII, 2370-2).
----------. The Date of the Troilus: and Minor Chaucer-
    iana. MLN, 50, 1935, 277-96.
        MerT for MonT?
TUPPER, FREDERICK. Chaucer and Trophee. MLN,
    31, 1916, 11-14.
YOUNG, KARL. Chaucer's "Vitremyte." SP, 40, 1943,
    494-501.
        On the origin and meaning (a hood of glass delud-
    ing the wearer) of a word in MonT, B3562.
        Rev: D. Everett, YWES, 43-4.

                THE NUN'S PRIEST'S PROLOGUE, TALE,
                        AND EPILOGUE

        See Hammond, 292-3; Root, 207-18; Robinson, 857-
    62, 1013; French, 257-65; Manly, 636-46; Curry, 219-40,
    266-7; Hinckley, 121-56; Shannon, 317; Dempster, 68-71.
        On the Nun's Priest, see also the section: Canter-
    bury Tales: Prologue, under Prioress.
        For editions, see section: Editions with Notes.
    For references on dreams, see section: Works

Other than the Canterbury Tales: General. For phonographic recordings, see section: Canterbury Tales:
General.

ADOLPHUS, A. E., and WALTER W. SKEAT. Chaucer-
iana: The Nonne Preestes Tale, 367-71. NQ, ser. 10,
8, 1907, 202-3, 252, 514.
     B^2 4323-7 (VII, 3133-7).
AIKEN, PAULINE. Vincent of Beauvais and Dame Per-
telote's Knowledge of Medicine. Spec, 10, 1935, 281-7.
BOONE, LALIA P. Chauntecleer and Partlet Identified.
MLN, 64, 1949, 78-81.
     Golden Spangled Hamburgs.
BROWN, CARLETON. Mulier est Hominis Confusio.
MLN, 35, 1920, 479-82.
BRUSENDORFF, AAGE. "He knew nat Catoun for his
wit was rude." 320-39, in Miscellany in Honor of
Frederick Klaeber. Univ of Minnesota Press, 1929.
     B4130, 4161, 4165 (VII, 2940, 2971-5).
CHANTILLY. Musée Condé. MSS (472). [Nine Romances
of the Round Table in French verse . . . , and se-
lections from the Romans de Renart . . . , a repro-
duction of MS 472 (formerly 626) in the library of the
Musée Condé, Chantilly, France.] 2 vols. MLA of
America. Collections of Photographic Facsimiles,
no. 292. 1934. Deposited in Library of Congress.
     Contains Renart's cock and fox story.
COOK, ALBERT S. Chaucer and Venantius Fortunatus.
MLN, 39, 1924, 376-8.
     B3090-2 (VII, 2800-2).
CURRY, WALTER C. Chauntecleer and Pertolote on
Dreams. ESt, 58, 1924, 24-60.
     Also see Texas Rev, 8, 1923, 307.
D(ICKINS), B(RUCE). Seynd bacoun. (CT. B4035). 76-7,
in Leeds Studies in English and Kindred Languages,
no. 4, 1935.
     Rev: D. Everett, YWES, 112.
DIECKMANN, EMMA M. ". . . Moore Feelynge Than
Had Boece, . . ." MLN, 53, 1938, 177-80.
DONOVAN, MORTIMER J. The Moralite of the Nun's
Priest's Sermon. JEGP, 52, 1953, 498-508.
GRANGENT, C. H. Chanticleer. 67 ff., in Anniversary
Papers (Kittredge). Ginn, 1913.

GREINER, F. J. Form and Sources of the Nun's
    Priest's Tale. Cath Educ Rev, 36, 1938, 213-8.
HAUER, L. Flattery as a Theme in Middle English Lit-
    erature (with Special Reference to Chaucer's Nun's
    Priest's Tale). Diss, Univ of Iowa, 1937.
HEMINGWAY, SAMUEL B. Chaucer's Monk and Nun's
    Priest. MLN, 31, 1916, 479-83.
HENSHAW, MILLETT. La Clameur de Haro. Southern
    Folklore Quart, 14, 1950, 158-9.
        NPT, 3380; B4570, and 3045; B4235.
        Explains the custom and notes its survival in the
    Channel Islands.
HINCKLEY, HENRY B. Chauceriana. MP, 16, 1918-9,
    39-48.
        Especially 40-42.
HOTSON, J. LESLIE. Colfax versus Chantecler. PMLA,
    39, 1924, 762-81.
        Rev: J. Koch, Arch, 157, 1930, 104-10; E. V. Gor-
    don, YWES, 5, 1924, 85.
HULBERT, JAMES R. The Nun's Priest's Tale.
    Sources and Analogues, 645-53.
KENYON, JOHN S. Further Notes on the Marriage
    Group in the Canterbury Tales. JEGP, 15, 1916, 282-
    8.
KITTREDGE, GEORGE L. Chauceriana. MP, 7, 1910,
    481-2.
        Chaucer and Geoffrey de Vinsauf.
KLINEFELTER, RALPH A. Chaucer's Nun's Priest's
    Tale, 2843. Expl, 10, 1952, item 32.
LAW, ROBERT ALGER. In Principio. PMLA, 37, 1922,
    208-15.
        Reply to MacCracken's note in his College Chau-
    cer, 206 n.
LECOMPTE, I. C. Chaucer's Nun's Priest's Tale and
    the Roman de Renard. MP, 14, 1917, 737-49.
LUMIANSKY, R. M. The Nun's Priest in the Canterbury
    Tales. PMLA, 68, 1953, 896-906.
        Proposes the interpretation that the Nun's Priest
    is "scrawny, humble and timid."
McKENZIE, KENNETH. Unpublished Manuscripts of
    Italian Bestiaries. PMLA, 20, 1905, 380-433.
McKNIGHT, G. H. Medieval Vox and Wolf. PMLA, 23,
    1908, 497-509.

See also his Middle English Humorous Tales in
Verse, and its bibliography. Heath Belles Lettres
Series, 1913.

NADAL, THOMAS W. Spenser's Muiopotmos in Relation
to Chaucer's Sir Thopas and the Nun's Priest's Tale.
PMLA, 25, 1910, 640-56.

OWEN, CHARLES A. The Crucial Passages in Five of
the Canterbury Tales: A Study in Irony and Symbol.
JEGP, 52, 1953, 294-311.
NPT, VII, 3157-71; B²4347-61.

PATCH, HOWARD R. Chauceriana. ES, 65, 1931, 351-9.
On B²4584 (VII, 3394).

PETERS, EMIL. Der griechische Physiologus und seine
orientalischen Quellen. Berlin, 1898.

PRATT, ROBERT A. The Classical Lamentations in the
Nun's Priest's Tale. MLN, 64, 1949, 76-8.
Influence of Geoffrey de Vinsauf's Nova Poetria.
Rev: D. Everett, YWES, 64.

SAKANISHI, SHIO. A Note on the Nonne Preestes Tale.
MLN, 47, 1932, 150-1.

SEVERS, J. BURKE. Chaucer's Originality in the Nun's
Priest's Tale. SP, 43, 1946, 22-41.
Rev: D. Everett, YWES, 78.

SHAVER, CHESTER L. Chaucer's "Owles and Apes."
MLN, 58, 1943, 105-7.
Parallels, NPT, 3092.
Rev: D. Everett, YWES, 44.

SMITH, ROLAND M. The Six Gifts. Jour of Celtic Studies, 1, 1949, 98-104.
Suggests influence of Irish triads on NPT, VII,
2914 (B²4104).

TATLOCK, JOHN STRONG PERRY. Notes on Chaucer:
The Canterbury Tales. MLN, 29, 1914, 140-4.
Chantecleer's chivalry, B²4372-3; pursuit of the
fox, B²4565-91; Ha, Ha, the fox, B²4571, pp. 142-3.

TUPPER, FREDERICK. Saint Venus and the Canterbury
Pilgrims. Nation, 97, 1913, 354-6.

VAN HERK, A. Chauceriana. Neophil, 2, 1917, 292-4.
On B²4010 (VII, 2820).

WELLS, JOHN EDWIN. A Manual of Writings on Middle
English.
On bestiaries and animal tales, see 182-5, 791,
and the supplements.

THE SECOND NUN'S PROLOGUE AND TALE

See Hammond, 315-6; Root, 277-80; Robinson,
862-6, 1013; French, 324-7, 369-70; Manly, 647;
Wells, Group G, CBEL, I, 248-9, and supplements
to the Manual after 1933; Brusendorff, 131; Birney,
648.

For religious lyrics, see sections: A B C, and The
Prioress' Tale.

BROWN, CARLETON. Chaucer and the Hours of the
Blessed Virgin. MLN, 30, 1915, 231-2.
----------. Prologue of Chaucer's Lyf of Seint Cecile.
MP, 9, 1911, 1-16.
CAMPBELL, J. M. Patristic Studies and the Literature
of Mediaeval England. Spec, 8, 1933, 465-78.
"Corones two" explained by patristic study, 471-2.
CORNELIUS, ROBERTA D. Corones Two. PMLA, 42,
1927, 1055-7.
COWLING, G. H. A Note on Chaucer's Stanza. RES, 2,
1926, 311-7.
ELIASON, NORMAN E. Chaucer's Second Nun? MLQ,
3, 1942, 9-16.
Rev: D. Everett, YWES, 53-4.
EMERSON, OLIVER FARRAR. Saint Ambrose and Chau-
cer's Life of St. Cecilia. PMLA, 41, 1926, 252-61.
On "corones two" and the "palm of martirdom"
passages.
GARDNER, WILLIAM B. Chaucer's "Unworthy Sone of
Eve." University of Texas: Studies in English, 1947,
77-83.
Appropriateness of the word "sone" to the Second
Nun.
Rev: D. Everett, YWES, 29, 1948, 85.
GEROULD, GORDON HALL. Saints' Legends. Houghton,
1916.
Especially 239-44.
For reviews, see section: Literary Relations and
Sources.
----------. A Note on St. Caecilia. MLN, 68, 1953, 173.
----------. The Second Nun's Prologue and Tale.
Sources and Analogues, 664-84.
HAMMOND, ELEANOR PRESCOTT. The Nine-Syllable

Pentameter Line in Some Post-Chaucerian MSS. MP, 23, 1924-5, 129-52.

HENSHAW, MILLETT. The Preface of St. Ambrose and Chaucer's Second Nun's Tale. MP, 26, 1928, 15-16.
    Rev: D. Everett, YWES, 90.

HOLTHAUSEN, F. Zu Chaucers Cecilien-Legends. Arch, 87, 1891, 265-72.

JONES, CLAUDE. The "Second Nun's Tale," a Mediaeval Sermon. MLR, 32, 1937, 283.

KITTREDGE, GEORGE L. The Date of Chaucer's Troilus and Other Chaucer Matters. Chaucer Society, ser. 2, 42, 1909.
    See 41 ff.
    Rev: Arch, 124, 1910, 212.

LOWES, JOHN LIVINGSTON. The Corones Two of the Second Nun's Tale. PMLA, 26, 1911, 315-23.
    Rev: John Koch, ESt, 46, 1912, 114.

----------. The Corones Two of the Second Nun's Tale: A Supplementary Note. PMLA, 29, 1914, 129-33.
    Rev: John Koch, AB, 25, 1914, 332-9.

----------. Second Nun's Prologue, Alanus, and Macrobius. MP, 15, 1917, 193-202.

MacCRACKEN, HENRY N. A Further Parallel to the Corones Two of the Second Nun's Tale. MLN, 27, 1912, 63.

McMANUS, JOHN PAUL. The Little Office of the Blessed Virgin Mary and Invocatio ad Mariam of the Second Nun's Prologue. Unpubl Diss, Univ of Washington Libraries, 1953.
    Discussion of the Prymer. Shows the phrase, "sone of Eve," was regularly sung by the nuns; so it does not refer to a Canterbury pilgrim other than the Second Nun.

McMASTER, HELEN N. The Legend of St. Cecilia in Middle English Literature. Doctoral Diss, Yale, 1936.

MADALEVA, Sister MARY (MARY EVALINE WOLFF). Chaucer's Nuns, and Other Essays. Appleton, 1925. 215 pp.
    For review, see section: Canterbury Tales: Prologue, under Prioress.

MARIE, Sister ROSE. Chaucer and his Mayde Bright. Commonweal, 33, 1940, 225-7.

PARKER, ROSCOE E. A Note on "Corones Two." MLN,
41, 1926, 317-8.
PRATT, ROBERT A. Chaucer Borrowing from Himself.
MLQ, 7, 1946, 259-64.
Concerns Prol.
Rev: D. Everett, YWES, 69.
ROSENFELD, MARY-VIRGINIA. Chaucer and the Litur-
gy. MLN, 55, 1940, 357-60.
TATLOCK, JOHN STRONG PERRY. St. Cecilia's Gar-
lands and their Roman Origin. PMLA, 45, 1930, 169-
79.
TUPPER, FREDERICK. Chaucer's Bed's Head. MLN,
30, 1915, 5-12.
Chaucer and the Prymer, 9-11.

THE CANON'S YEOMAN'S PROLOGUE AND TALE

See Hammond, 316-7; Root, 280-3; Robinson, 866-
9, 1013-4; French, 327-33; Manly, 647-53; Manly
SNL, 235-52.
For editions, see section: Editions with Notes. Also see section: Scientific Backgrounds.

AIKEN, PAULINE. Vincent of Beauvais and Chaucer's
Knowledge of Alchemy. SP, 41, 1944, 371-89.
CYT and Speculum Naturale.
Rev: D. Everett, YWES, 47-8.
ANDRAE, AUGUST. Zu Chaucers und Longfellows
Tales. AB, 27, 1926, 84-5.
BAUM, PAULL F. The Canon's Yeoman's Tale. MLN,
40, 1925, 152-4.
COFFMAN, GEORGE R. Canon's Yeoman's Prologue G,
Lines 563-66: Horse or Man. MLN, 59, 1944, 269-71.
Rev: D. Everett, YWES, 46-7.
DAMON, S. FOSTER. Chaucer and Alchemy. PMLA, 39,
1924, 782-8.
DE GIVRY, GRILLOT. Witchcraft, Magic and Alchemy.
Trans by J. Courtenay Locke. Harrap, 1932. 395 pp.
For review, see section: Scientific Backgrounds.
DE VOCHT, H. Chaucer and Erasmus. ES, 41, 1910, 385-92.
DUNCAN, EDGAR HILL. Alchemy in the Writings of
Chaucer, Jonson, and Donne. Bull of Vanderbilt
Univ, 41, 1940, 16-17. Abstract of Thesis.

----------. The Yeoman's Canon's "Silver Citrinaci-
oun." MP, 37, 1940, 241-62.
----------. Chaucer and "Arnold of the Newe Toun."
MLN, 57, 1942, 31-3.
       Indebtedness of CYT to Arnold of Villa Nova.
       Rev: D. Everett, YWES, 61.
EDWARDS, H. L. R. Hermoniake. TLS, Oct 24, 1936, 863.
       Concerns "ermony," lines 790, 798, 824.
HAMILTON, MARIE P. The Clerical Status of Chaucer's
Alchemist. Spec, 16, 1941, 103-8.
       "Chaucer's Alchemist was a Black Canon, a Can-
on Regular of St. Augustine."
       Rev: D. Everett, YWES, 59.
KITTREDGE, GEORGE L. The Canon's Yeoman's Pro-
logue and Tale. Trans Royal Society of Literature
(London), 30, 1910, 87.
KRAPPE, EDITH SMITH. A Note on Chaucer's Yeoman.
MLN, 43, 1928, 176-7.
LOWES, JOHN L. The Dragon and his Brother. MLN,
28, 1913, 229.
       On G1428-40.
NOWAK, L. Die Alchemie und die Alchemisten in der
englischen Literatur. Breslau Diss, 1934. 83 pp.
READ, JOHN. Alchemy and Alchemists. Folk-Lore, 44,
1933, 251-78.
RICHARDSON, H. G. Year Books and Plea Rolls as
Sources of Historical Information. Trans of Royal
Historical Society, ser. 4, 5, 1922, 28-51.
       Suggestion on Canon's Yeoman, 38-9.
RUSKA, JULIUS. Chaucer und das Buch Senior. Ang,
61, 1937, 136-7.
       Alchemical knowledge.
SINGER, DOROTHY WALEY, assisted by ANNIE AN-
DERSON. Catalogue of Latin and Vernacular Alchem-
ical Manuscripts in Great Britain and Ireland. Brus-
sels: Lamertin, 1928, 1930. 2 vols.
SPARGO, JOHN W. The Canon's Yeoman's Tale.
Sources and Analogues, 685-98.
WAITE, ARTHUR EDWARD. The Secret Tradition in Alche-
my: Its Development and Records. Knopf, 1927. 415 pp.
YOUNG, KARL. The "Secree of Secrees" of Chaucer's
Canon's Yeoman. MLN, 58, 1943, 98-105.
       Rev: D. Everett, YWES, 46.

THE MANCIPLE'S PROLOGUE AND TALE

See Hammond, 317-8; Root, 283-4; Robinson, 870-
2, 1014; French, 333-4; Manly, 654-5; Shannon, 322-
5; Wells, Fragment H, CBEL, I, 249, and the Manual, 742, 981, and the supplements after 1933.
    For editions, see section: Editions with Notes.

ANDRAE, AUGUST. Zu Chaucers und Longfellows
    Tales. ES, 45, 1912, 347.
DICKSON, ARTHUR. Canterbury Tales, I, 355 ff. MLN,
    62, 1947, 562.
        Parallel from the Vulgate, Exodus 15.
        Rev: D. Everett, YWES, 82.
GRAULS, J., and J. F. VANDERHEIJDEN. Two Flem-
    ish Proverbs in Chaucer's Canterbury Tales. RBPH,
    13, 1934, 745-9.
LUMIANSKY, R. M. Chaucer and the Idea of the Un-
    faithful Man. MLN, 62, 1947, 560-2.
        On lines 187-95 of ManT as a brief statement of
    unfaithful men which occupies a central position in
    LGW.
        Rev: D. Everett, YWES, 83.
READ, JOHN. Prelude to Chemistry; an Outline of Al-
    chemy, its Literature and Relationships. Macmillan,
    1937. 329 pp.
        For reviews, see section: Scientific Backgrounds.
ROOT, ROBERT K. The Manciple's Prologue. MLN, 44,
    1929, 493-6.
        See Work, The Position of the Tales, below in this
    section.
        Rev: D. Everett, YWES, 115.
SEIBERT, HARRIET. Chaucer and Horace. MLN, 31,
    1916, 304-7.
SEVERS, J. BURKE. Is the Manciple's Tale a Success?
    JEGP, 51, 1952, 1-16.
SHUMAKER, WAYNE. Chaucer's Manciple's Tale as
    Part of the Canterbury Group. UTQ, 22, 1953, 147-
    56.
TATLOCK, JOHN STRONG PERRY. The Date of the
    Troilus: and Minor Chauceriana. MLN, 50, 1935, 277-
    96.
        The Manciple's "my sonne," 296.

STILLWELL, GARDINER. Analogues to Chaucer's Manciple's Tale in the Ovide Moralisé and Machaut's
Voir-Dit. PQ, 19, 1940, 133-8.

WORK, JAMES A. The Manciple's Prologue. SP, 29,
1932, 11-14.

----------. The Position of the Tales of the Manciple
and the Parson on Chaucer's Canterbury Pilgrimage.
JEGP, 31, 1932, 62-5.

----------. The Manciple's Tale. Sources and Analogues, 699-722.

THE PARSON'S PROLOGUE AND TALE

See Hammond, 318-20; Root, 284-8; Robinson, 872-
80, 1014; French, 334-8; Manly, 655-6; Brusendorff,
132, 147; Wells, CBEL, I, 249, and the supplements
to the Manual after 1933; Birney, 648-50.

For material on medieval sermons and preaching
see section on Religious Backgrounds, although it
should be kept in mind that the Parson's Tale was
probably not a single sermon for public preaching
but that it might be classed as a treatise for devotional reading.

ALLINGTON, C. A. Christianity in England. London,
1942, p. 69.
      Rev: TLS, 1942, 448.

AYRES, HARRY M. Chaucer and Seneca. RR, 10, 1919,
3 ff.

BLOOMFIELD, MORTON W. The Seven Deadly Sins: An
Introduction to the History of a Religious Concept,
with Special Reference to Medieval English Literature.
Michigan State College Press, 1952. 482 pp. Also
Abstract, Univ of Wisconsin, Summaries of Doctoral
Dissertations, 3, 1938, 286-8.
      See index for references to Chaucer.

----------. The Origin of the Conception of the Seven
Deadly Sins. Harvard Theological Rev, 34, 1941, 121-
8.

CHAPMAN, COOLIDGE OTIS. The Parson's Tale: A
Mediaeval Sermon. MLN, 43, 1928, 229-34.

DEMPSTER, GERMAINE. The Parson's Tale. Sources
and Analogues, 722-60.

FRIEND, ALBERT C. Sampson, David, and Solomon in
the Parson's Tale. MP, 46, 1948, 117-21.
   Rev: D. Everett, YWES, 85.
GUINAGH, KEVIN. Source of the Quotation from Augus-
tine in the Parson's Tale, 985. MLN, 55, 1940, 211-2.
   Augustine's Liber de Vera et Falsa Poenitentia.
10. 25 (Migne, P. L. XL. 1122).
HOMANS, GEORGE C. Free Bull. RES, 14, 1938, 447-9.
IMMACULATE, Sister MARY. "Sixty" as a Conventional
Number and Other Chauceriana. MLQ, 2, 1941, 59-66.
   "She is the lyf of angeles," ParsT, 948.
   Rev: D. Everett, YWES, 66.
JOHNSON, DUDLEY R. "Homicide" in the Parson's
Tale. PMLA, 57, 1942, 51-6.
   A source study.
   Rev: D. Everett, YWES, 61-2.
KELLOGG, ALFRED L. St. Augustine and the Parson's
Tale. Traditio, 8, 1952, 424-30.
LANDRUM, GRACE W. Chaucer and the Vulgate. PMLA,
39, 1924, 75-100.
LANGHANS, VICTOR. Die Datierung der Prosastücke
Chaucers. Ang, 53, 1929, 235-68.
   ParsT, 243-68.
   For reviews, see section: Melibeus.
LIDDELL, MARK. The Source of Chaucer's Person's
Tale. Acad, 49, 1896, 447-8 and 509.
LOWES, JOHN LIVINGSTON. Chaucer and the Miroir de
Mariage. MP, 8, 1910-1, 165-86.
   Especially 171-2.
MARIELLA, Sister. The Head, the Foot, and the Rib of
Adam. NQ, 171, 1936, 119.
   Answer, O. F. Babler, NQ, 171, 1936, 229.
----------. The Parson's Tale and the Marriage Group.
MLN, 53, 1938, 251-6.
MAXFIELD, EZRA K. Chaucer and Religious Reform.
PMLA, 39, 1924, 64-74.
   Discusses Chaucer's Parson.
PFANDER, H. G. Some Medieval Manuals of Religious
Instruction in England and Observations on Chaucer's
Parson's Tale. JEGP, 35, 1936, 243-58.
   Rev: Dorothy Everett, YWES, 17, 1936, 84-5.
SANDERLIN, GEORGE. Quotations from St. Bernard
in the Parson's Tale. MLN, 54, 1939, 447-8.

SLAUGHTER, EUGENE E. Love and the Virtues and
Vices in Chaucer. Nashville, Tennessee, 1946.

SPIES, HEINRICH. Chaucers religiose Grundstimmung
und die Echtheit der Parson's Tale: Eine textkritische
Untersuchung. 626-721, in Festschrift für Lorenz
Morsbach. Studien zur englischen Philologie, 50.
Niemeyer, 1913.

Rev: John Koch, AB, 25, 1914, 84-6.

TUPPER, FREDERICK. Chaucer's Bed's Head. MLN,
30, 1915, 5-12.

A parallel to the Parson's sermon, 11-12.

WORK, JAMES A. Chaucer's Sermon and Retractions.
MLN, 47, 1932, 257-9.

----------. The Position of the Tales of the Manciple
and Parson in Chaucer's Canterbury Pilgrimage.
JEGP, 31, 1932, 62-5.

RETRACTIONS

See Hammond, 320-2; Root, 288; Robinson, 880-1,
1015; Manly, 656-8; Brusendorff, 429.

DEAR, F. M. Chaucer's Book of the Lion. MA, 7, 1918,
121-35.

HAMMOND, ELEANOR. Chaucer's "Book of the Twenty-
five Ladies." MLN, 48, 1933, 514-6.

JAMES, STANLEY B. The Repentance of Chaucer.
Month, 1934, 41-6.

LANGHANS, VICTOR. Chaucer's Book of the Leoun: De
Contemptu Mundi. Ang, 52, 1928, 113-22.

Rev: D. Everett, YWES, 90. See also Ang, 52, 1929,
325-48, and listings in section: Wretched Engendering.

McNABB, VINCENT JOSEPH. Geoffrey Chaucer: A Study
in Genius and Ethics. Stones from the Brook, vol. 1.
Limited ed. St. Dominic's Press, 1934.

For review, see section: General Criticism.

RUTTER, GEORGE McKELVY. Confessions in Mediaeval Literature. Summaries of Theses, Harvard Univ,
1930, 210-1.

SPIES, HEINRICH. Chaucers Retractio. 383-94, in
Festschrift für Adolf Tobler. Braunschweig: Wester-
mann, 1905.

Rev: John Koch, ESt, 37, 1907, 227.

TATLOCK, JOHN STRONG PERRY. Chaucer's Retractions. PMLA, 28, 1913, 521-9.
    Rev: John Koch, AB, 25, 1914, 339-42.
THURSTON, HERBERT. The Conversion of Boccaccio
and Chaucer. Studies (Educ Co of Dublin), 25, 1936,
215-25.
WORK, JAMES A. Chaucer's Sermon and Retractions.
MLN, 47, 1932, 257-9.

WORKS OTHER THAN
THE CANTERBURY TALES: GENERAL
INCLUDING APOCRYPHA

See Hammond, 325-53, 406-63; Legouis, 61-70;
Root, 158-9; Curry, 195-218 and on Dream Lore and
Dream Poems, 233-40, 263-5; Brusendorff, 43-52,
278-84, 426-49; Manly, 81-6; Wells, CBEL, I, 220-
32 and the Manual, supplements, 1531-4, 1641-4, 1733-
5, 1927-30; Clemen, 211 ff.

For editions, see section: Editions with Notes.
Also see section: General Criticism.

ARNOLD, MAX. Die Verwendung der Traummotivs in
    der englischen Dichtung von Chaucer bis auf Shake-
    speare. Kiel Diss, 1912.
BIRNEY, EARLE. The Beginnings of Chaucer's Irony.
    PMLA, 54, 1939, 637-55.
    Discussion of the dreamer, 645.
BONNER, FRANCIS W. A History of Chaucer Apoc-
    rypha. Doctoral Diss, Univ of North Carolina,
    1949.
----------. The Genesis of Chaucer Apocrypha. SP,
    48, 1951, 461-81.
CHAUCER, GEOFFREY. [Chaucer's Troilus and a few
    short poems; reproduced from Ms Gg. 4. 27, fol. 5-
    132^r, in the library of Cambridge University.] 115
    negatives mounted on 59 leaves. MLA of America.
    Collection of Photographic Facsimiles, no. 307. 1935.
    Deposited in the Library of Congress.
    For contents, see section: Manuscripts.
COHEN, HELEN L. The Ballade. Columbia Univ Press,
    1915. 397 pp.
    Especially 233-52.
    Rev: L. E. Kastner, MLR, 11, 1916, 240-3; Arch,
    134, 1916, 466.
COWLING, G. H. A Note on Chaucer's Stanza. RES, 2,
    1926, 311-7.

CURRY, WALTER CLYDE. Chauntecleer and Pertelote
on Dreams. ES, 58, 1924, 24-60.

HAMILTON, MARIE P. A Latin and English Passage on
Dreams. SP, 33, 1936, 1-9.

HAMMERLE, KARL. Das Fortunamotiv von Chaucer bis
Bacon. Ang, 65, 1941, 87-100.

HAMMOND, ELEANOR PRESCOTT. On the Editing of
Chaucer's Minor Poems. MLN, 23, 1908, 20-1.

----------. Chaucer and Lydgate Notes. MLN, 27, 1912,
91-2.

    Attribution of Leonor et Eugenie to Chaucer in
Bibliothèque Universelle des Romans.

JACK, ADOLPHUS A. A Commentary on the Poetry of
Chaucer and Spenser. Glasgow: Maclehose and Jackson; Macmillan, 1920. 369 pp.

    Apocrypha and Imitations, 117-40.

    For reviews, see section: General Criticism.

KELCHNER, GEORGIA DUNHAM. Dreams in Old Norse
Literature and their Affinities in Folklore. Cambridge Univ Press, 1935. 154 pp.

    Rev: Edward C. Ehrensperger, MLN, 52, 1937,
133-4.

KOCH, JOHN. Ausgewählte kleinere Dichtungen Chaucers. Leipzig, 1880.

    See Miss Hammond's Manual for description, 352.
See Berichtigungen. Ang, 4, Anzeiger 49, for Koch's
corrections of this edition, and Kleinere Dichtungen,
Heidelberg, 1928.

----------. Chaucerproben. ES, 53, 1919, 161-7.

    Translation into German of Newfangelness, To
Rosamounde, and Merciles Beautee and announcement
of new edition of the minor poems.

LANGHANS, VICTOR. Untersuchungen zu Chaucer.
Halle: Niemeyer, 1918.

    A B C, BD, Mars, Venus, Fortune, PF, Romance
of the Rose, HF, LGW, T&C. See under The Legend
of Good Women for controversial views.

----------. Zu Chaucers Traumgedichten und deren
Auffassung durch A. Brusendorff. Ang, 39, 1927, 323-53.

LAWSON, RUTH MARGARET. Chaucer's Personal Envoy Poems: A Study in Historical Background. Master's Thesis, Univ of Washington, 1929. Typewritten,
71 pp.

LOWES, JOHN L. Chaucer and Dante. MP, 14, 1917,
    705-35.
McCARTHY, Sister MARY B. The English Lyrics of the
    Fourteenth Century. Diss, Minnesota, 1938.
MALONE, KEMP. Chapters on Chaucer. Johns Hopkins
    Press; Oxford, 1951. 240 pp.
        Chapters: Geoffrey Chaucer and the Fourteenth
    Century; The Book of the Duchess; The House of
    Fame; The Parlement of Fowls; The Legend of Good
    Women; Troilus and Criseyde.
        For reviews, see section: General Criticism.
MOORE, SAMUEL. The Date of Chaucer's Marriage
    Group. MLN, 26, 1911, 172-4.
        On the Envoy poems.
STEARNS, JOHN BARKER. Studies of the Dream as a
    Technical Device in Latin Epic and Drama. Doctoral
    Diss, Princeton, 1924. Lancaster Press, Inc, 1927.
    73 pp.
        Study of the dream (1) as inspiration to writing;
    (2) as motivation; (3) as atmosphere; (4) as the true
    dream, the dream post mediam noctem.
STEARNS, MARSHALL W. A Note on Chaucer's Use of
    Aristotelian Philosophy. SP, 43, 1946, 15-21.
        Chaucer uses Aristotle's theory of cognition to ex-
    plain the working of love, the cause of dreams, and
    the origin of various illusions and delusions.
        Rev: D. Everett, YWES, 67.
----------. Chaucer Mentions a Book. MLN, 57, 1942,
    28-31.
        Contends that Chaucer's use of a book in the love
    visions is not a convention.
SYPHERD, W. OWEN. Le Songe Vert and Chaucer's
    Dream-Poems. MLN, 24, 1909, 46-7.
        See Romania, 33 (Le Songe Vert), and Sypherd's
    Studies in the Hous of Fame, Chaucer Society, ser.
    2, 39, 1907.
        Rev: John Koch, ESt, 41, 1910, 113-21.
TATLOCK, JOHN STRONG PERRY. Notes on Chaucer:
    Earlier or Minor Poems. MLN, 29, 1914, 97-101.
        Contains: Bells Ringing without Hands: T. and C.
    III, 188-9; The Folly of Second Marriage: Bukton, 13-
    16; Cleopatra's Serpent-Pit: L. G. W. 678-80, 696-
    702; Ariadne's Crown: L. G. W. 2223-4.

----------. The Mind and Art of Chaucer. Syracuse
Univ Press, 1950. 114 pp.
     Concerns T&C, A&A, HF, PF, LGW, Less Con-
Conspicuous Works. For reviews and list of chapters,
see section: General Criticism.
TILLOTSON, G. Dreams in English Literature. Mer-
cury, 27, 1933, 516-23.
TUPPER, FREDERICK. The Envy Theme in the Pro-
logue and Epilogues. JEGP, 16, 1917, 551-72.
VOCKRODT, G. Reimteknik bei Chaucer als Mittel zur
chronologischen Bestimmung seiner im Reimpaar ge-
schriebenen Werke. Halle, 1914.
WIGBERT, HOLLE. Chaucer Balladendichtung. Thesis,
Bonn, 1951.
     Selections to be printed.

A B C

     See Hammond, 354-5; Legouis, 63-5; Root, 57-8;
Kaluza, 13-15; Robinson, 969-70, 1034; French, 82-4;
Brusendorff, 238-41; Koch, 9-10; Wells, CBEL, I,
221-2 and supplements to the Manual after 1933. Also
see Landrum, Chaucer's Use of the Vulgate, PMLA,
39, 1924, 75-100.
     For editions, see section: Editions with Notes.

ANDERSON, MARJORIE. Blanche, Duchess of Lancas-
ter. MP, 45, 1948, 152-9.
     Rev: D. Everett, YWES, 87-8.
BRITT, MATTHEW. The Hymns of the Breviary and the
Missal. Benziger Bros, 1922. Rev ed, 1924.
BROWN, CARLETON. Chaucer and the Hours of the
Blessed Virgin. MLN, 30, 1915, 231-2.
----------. Prologue of Chaucer's Lyf of Seint Cecile.
MP, 9, 1911, 1-16.
     Date of the A B C.
----------. A Register of English Didactic and Religious
Verse. Oxford, vol. 1, 1916; vol. 2, 1920.
     See index.
     Rev: Seymour de Ricci, Journal des Savants, 15, 1917,
284-6; Fr. Klaeber, ESt, 55, 1921, 411-3; Frank A. Patter-
son, JEGP, 20, 1921, 270-5; John M. Manly, MP, 18, 1920-
1, 287-8; Hermann M. Flasdieck, AB, 35, 1924, 167-8.

----------. Religious Lyrics of the Fourteenth Century.
Oxford, 1924.

Rev: S. B. Liljegren, AB, 35, 1924, 353-4; Bea-
trice D. Brown, MLN, 40, 1925, 52-4; Karl Young,
MLN, 39, 1924, 419-24; John W. Buckham, Univ of
Calif Chron, 26, 1924, 379-80; NQ, 146, 1924, 163-4;
TLS, Feb 21, 1924.

CHAMBERS, E. K., and E. SIDGWICK. Early English
Lyrics: Amorous, Divine, Moral and Trivial. Sidgwick and Jackson, 1921.

See the essay by Chambers, Some Aspects of the
Medieval Lyrics, 257-96.

Rev: W. Fischer, AB, 33, 1922, 9; TLS, Oct 5,
1922.

CHAUCER, GEOFFREY. A Chaucer A. B. C. Being a
Hymn to the Holy Virgin in an English Version. From
the French of Guillaume de Deguilleville. Initial letters designed and illuminated by Lucia Joyce. Pref
by Louis Gillet. Obelisk Press, 1936.

COOK, ALBERT S., Ed. A Literary Middle English
Reader. Ginn, 1915. 554 pp.

Religious lyrics, 436-75.

COULTER, CORNELIA C. Latin Hymns in the Middle
Ages. SP, 21, 1924, 571-85.

GRIPKEY, Sister M. VINCENTINE. The Blessed Virgin
Mary as Mediatrix in the Latin and Old French Leg-
end Prior to the Fourteenth Century. Doctoral Diss,
Catholic Univ of America, 1938. Catholic Univ of
America, 1938. 238 pp.

LANGHANS, VICTOR. Untersuchungen zu Chaucer.
Halle: Niemeyer, 1914.

For the A B C, see 302 ff. and for reviews, see
section: The Legend of Good Women.

McNABB, VINCENT JOSEPH. Geoffrey Chaucer; a
Study in Genius and Ethics. Stones from the
Brook, vol. 1. Limited edition. St. Dominic's
Press, 1934.

Rev: TLS, Nov 15, 1934, 798.

O'BRIEN, J. "Ave-Marie or Tweye": Chaucer's Poem
ABC. Columbia, 26, 1947, 2.

PATTERSON, FRANK A. Middle English Penitential
Lyrics: A Study and Collection of Early Religious
Verse. Columbia Univ Press, 1911.

SEVERS, J. BURKE. Two Irregular Chaucerian Stanzas.
  MLN, 64, 1949, 306-9.
    Questions irregularity of line 39, A B C, and For-
  mer Age, 47.
    Rev: D. Everett, YWES, 69.
TUPPER, FREDERICK. Chaucer's Bed's Head. MLN,
  30, 1915, 9.
    Chaucer and the Prymer.
YOUNG, KARL. Chaucer and the Liturgy. MLN, 30,
  1915, 97-9.

AN AMOROUS COMPLEINT
OR
COMPLEINT D'AMOURS

  Hammond, 416-7; Root, 79; Brusendorff, 273-437;
Robinson, 982, 1039; French, 115-6; Wells, CBEL, I,
222; Birney, 640-1.

ANELIDA AND ARCITE

  See Hammond, 355-8; Legouis, 52; Root, 68-9;
Kaluza, 16-18; Robinson, 897-900, 1018-9; French,
98-101; Brusendorff, 258-61; Koch, 56-61; Clemen,
226; Shannon, 15-44; Tatlock, 83; Wells, CBEL, I,
222, and supplements to the Manual after 1933. Also see
Lowes, MP, 14, 1917, 725, and PMLA, 33, 1918, 319.
  For editions, see section: Editions with Notes.

ANON. A Facsimile of Anelida and Arcite from Unique
  Copy of Westminster Edition of William Caxton in Cam-
  bridge University Library. Cambridge Univ Press, 1905.
BRIGHT, JAMES W. Minor Notes on Chaucer. MLN, 17,
  1902, 278-80.
    Lines 71-3.
BUSH, DOUGLAS. Chaucer's "Corinne." Spec, 4, 1929,
  106-7.
COOK, ALBERT S. Two Notes on Chaucer. MLN, 31,
  1916, 441-2.
    On "ermony," line 72.
FABIN, MADELEINE. On Chaucer's Anelida and Arcite.
  MLN, 34, 1919, 266-72.
    Influence of Machaut's lays.

HULBERT, JAMES R. Chaucer and the Earl of Oxford.
MP, 10, 1912-3, 433-7.
KER, W. P. Essays on Medieval Literature. Macmillan,
1906. Pp. 83 ff.
KOCH, JOHN. Alte Chaucerprobleme und neue Lösungs-
versuche. ESt, 55, 1921, 161-225.
A&A, 209-15.
----------. Ein neues Datum für Chaucers Quene Aneli-
da and Fals Arcite. ESt, 56, 1922, 28-35.
LANGHANS, VICTOR. Chaucers Anelida and Arcite.
Ang, 44, 1919, 226-45.
On chronology.
PRATT, ROBERT A. Chaucer's Use of the Teseida.
PMLA, 62, 1947, 598-621.
SHANNON, EDGAR F. The Source of Chaucer's Anelida
and Arcite. PMLA, 27, 1912, 461-85.
TUPPER, FREDERICK. Chaucer's Tale of Ireland.
PMLA, 36, 1921, 186-222.
On "Corinne," 216. Some discussion of chronology,
but mainly proposing identification of persons in the poem.
Rev: John Koch, ESt, 56, 1922, 30-2.

ASTROLABE

See Hammond, 359-60; Kaluza, 207-8; Root, 85-6;
Robinson, 983-8, 1040-2; French, 133-4; Brusendorff,
175-7; Wells, CBEL, I, 232, and the supplements to
the Manual after 1933.
For editions, see section: Editions with Notes.

ANON. The Astrolabe. Bodleian Quart Rev, 2, 1919, 238.
ELMQUIST, KARL E. An Observation on Chaucer's As-
trolabe. MLN, 56, 1941, 530-4.
Not written only for "Lowys my sone," but for
general circulation.
GOLDSCHMIDT, E. PH. Medieval Texts and their First
Appearance in Print. Supplement to the Bibliograph-
ical Society's Transactions, no. 16. London, 1943.
Rev: S. Gibson, YWES, 24, 1943, 225-6, and 26,
1945, 73.
GUNTHER, R. T. Chaucer and Messahalla on the Astro-
labe. Oxford, 1930, 1932. 234 pp.
For review, see section: Editions with Notes.

HARVEY, S. W. Chaucer's Debt to Sacrobosco. JEGP, 34, 1935, 34-8.

KITTREDGE, GEORGE L. Lewis Chaucer or Lewis Clifford? MP, 14, 1917, 513-8.

LANGHANS, VICTOR. Die Datierung der Prosastücke Chaucers. Ang, 53, 1929, 235-68.

> Astrolabe, 235.

> For reviews, see section: Melibeus.

MANLY, JOHN M. "Litel Lowis my Sone." TLS, June 7, 1928, 430.

> See also Walter Rye, TLS, June 28, 1928, 486, and H. W. Garrod, Oct 11, 1928, 736.

MOORE, SAMUEL. On the Date of Chaucer's Astrolabe. MP, 10, 1912, 203-5.

PINTELON, P. Chaucer's Treatise on the Astrolabe, MS 4862-4869, of the Royal Library in Brussels. Rijksuniversitet te Gent, Werken uitgegeven door de Facultiet van de Wijsbegeerte en Letteren, 89. Antwerp: De Sikkel; The Hague: Nijhoff, 1941. 127 pp.

> Rev: S. d'Ardenne, E Stud, 24, 1942, 125, and Moyen Age, 51, 1941, 206-9; F. Krog, AB, 54-5, 1944, 160-2.

VEAZIE, WALTER B. Chaucer's Text-book of Astronomy: Johannes de Sacrobosco. Univ of Colorado Studies. Series B, Studies in the Humanities, 1, 1940, 169-82.

WAUGH, M. T. The Lollard Knights. SHR, 11, 1913, 55-92.

> Lewis Clifford, 58-63.

WILLOUGHBY, E. F. Chaucer's Treatise on the Astrolabe: MS 4862-4869 of the Royal Library in Brussels. Antwerp: De Sikkel, 1940.

WILSON, B. D. The Astrolabe and Medieval English Life. Popular Astronomy, 57, 1949, 155-70.

WILSON, WINIFRED G. Chaucer's Astrolabe. Life and Letters Today, 37, 1943, 75-81.

BALADE OF COMPLEYNT

Hammond, 410; Root, 79; Brusendorff, 437; Robinson, 983, 1040; French, 116; Wells, CBEL, I, 222 and supplements to the Manual after 1933.

BERYN

BASHE, E. J. The Prologue of the Tale of Beryn. PQ,
12, 1933, 1-16.

DEAR, F. M. Chaucer's Book of the Lion. MA, 7, 1938,
105-12.

McINTOSH, HELEN MARIE. The Literary Background
of The Tale of Beryn. Doctoral Diss, Chicago, 1932.
Abstract in Abstracts of Theses, Humanistic Series,
9, 1930-2, 461-4.

REPRODUCTIONS OF MANUSCRIPTS AND RARE
PRINTED BOOKS. Now on deposit in the Library of
Congress. Roman de Berinus. Paris: Bibl Nat, MS.
15097. 250 sheets. Also MS. fr. 777, 302 sheets, and
Paris: Bibl de l'Arsenal, MS. 3343, 507 sheets.

BOETHIUS

See Hammond, 86-7, 360-2; Kaluza, 36-43; Root,
80-5; Robinson, 906-22, 1021-3; French, 117-22; Brusendorff, 174-5.

See also Schlauch in section: General Criticism.

For editions, see section: Editions with Notes.

BARK, WILLIAM. The Legend of Boethius' Martyrdom.
Spec, 21, 1946, 312-7.

Important bibliography.

BARRETT, H. M. Boethius: Some Aspects of his Time
and Work. Cambridge Univ Press; New York: Macmillan, 1940.

Rev: E. K. Rand, Spec, 16, 1941, 350-1; NQ, Aug
17, 1940, 126; MA, 10, 1924, 29.

BOETHIUS. [Boecii De Consolatione Philosophie, with
commentary by Guillaume de Conches; a reproduction
of MS Latin 14380 in the Bibliothèque Nationale,
Paris] 197 sheets on 197 l. MLA of America. Collection of Photographic Facsimiles, no. 99. 1929. Deposited in Library of Congress.

----------. [Boetii De Consolatione Philosophie, with
the English version ascribed to Chaucer, in five
books, and Exposicio preclara quam Johannes Theutonicus prescripsit et finivit A. D. 1306. 8 Idus Junii;
a reproduction of MS Ii, III 21. in the Cambridge U-

niversity Library.] 2 vols. 299 sheets on 150 l.
MLA of America. Collection of Photographic Facsimiles, no. 73. 1928. Deposited in the Library
of Congress.

"The translation attributed to Chaucer alternates
with the Latin text of Boethius. . . . The original is
a 14th century manuscript. . . . Cf. A catalogue of
manuscripts preserved in the Library of the University of Cambridge. V. III, 1858, MS, Ii III. 21."

----------. [De Consolatione Philosophiae, a Latin
text, a Translation into Old French by Jean de Meun
and a Commentary by Nicholas Trivet. Reproduced
from MS Latin 18424, fol. 1-184 (recto) in the Bibliothèque Nationale, Paris.] 2 vols. 367 sheets on 367 l.
MLA of America. Collection of Photographic Facsimiles, no. 100. 1930. Deposited in the Library of Congress.

----------. [La Consolation de Philosophie de Boece
Traduyete en Français par Maistre Jean de Meun: a
Reproduction of MS Français 1097, fol. 1-44 (recto)
in the Bibliothèque Nationale, Paris.] 88 sheets on
44 l. MLA of America. Collection of Photographic
Facsimiles, no. 15. 1925. Deposited in the Library of
Congress.

CLINE, JAMES M. Chaucer and Jean de Meun: De Consolatione Philosophiae. ELH, 3, 1936, 170-81.

    Rev: D. Everett, YWES, 74-6.

----------. A Study in the Prose of Chaucer's Boethius.
Doctoral Diss, Princeton. Listed as completed in
Willard, 6, 1928, 69.

COOPER, LANE. A Concordance of Boethius: The Five
Theological Tractates and the Consolation of Philoso-
phy. Publications no. 1, The Mediaeval Academy of
America, 1928.

    Rev: E. K. Rand, Spec, 4, 1929, 223-7; J. G.
Robertson, MLR, 24, 1929, 243.

DEDECK-HERY, V. L. Jean de Meun et Chaucer, Tra-
ducteurs de la Consolation de Boece. PMLA, 52,
1937, 967-91.

----------. The Manuscripts of the Translation of Boethius Consolatio by Jean de Meung. Spec, 15, 1940,
432-43.

----------. Le Boece de Chaucer et les Manuscrits

Français de la Consolatio de J. de Meun. PMLA, 59, 1944, 18-25.

    Rev: D. Everett, YWES, 51-2.

----------. Boethius' De Consolatione by Jean de Meun. Med Stud, 14, 1952, 165-275.

    An edition of Jean de Meun's translation.

DOLSON, GUY BAYLEY. The Consolation of Philosophy of Boethius in English Literature. Doctoral Diss, Cornell, 1926. Published in abstract at Ithaca, N.Y., 1926. 3 pp.

DUNN, WILLIAM P. The De Musica of Boethius, with Particular Reference to the Music of the Fourteenth Century as Reflected in Chaucer. Master's Thesis, Columbia Univ, 1917.

FEHLAUER, FRIEDRICH. Die englischen Ubersetzungen von Boethius "De Consolatione Philosophiae." In Normannia, Germanisch-Romanische Bücherei, 1909. Published by Emil Felber, Berlin, 1909.

    Chaucer, 31-48.

FONTAINE, WILLIAM T. V. Concept and Remedies of Fortune in Boethius and Bruno. Doctoral Diss, Univ of Pennsylvania, 1936.

HAMMOND, ELEANOR PRESCOTT. Boethius: Chaucer: Walton: Lydgate. MLN, 41, 1926, 534-5.

JEFFERSON, BERNARD L. Chaucer and the Consolation of Philosophy of Boethius. Princeton Univ Press, 1917; Milford, 1920. 168 pp.

    Rev: Howard Patch, JEGP, 16, 1917, 620-4.

KOCH, JOHN. Chaucers Boethiusübersetzung: Ein Beitrag zur Bestimmung der Chronologie seiner Werke. Ang, 46, 1922; 1-51.

KOTTLER, BARNET. Chaucer's Boece and the Late Medieval Textual Tradition of the Consolatio Philosophiae. Doctoral Diss, Yale, 1953.

KRAPPE, ALEXANDER HAGGERTY. Two Mediaeval Derivatives of Boethius, De Consolatione Philosophiae. Leuvensche Bijdragen, 18, 1926, 1-6.

    Wace's Roman de Ron and the Chronicle of Richard of London.

LANGHANS, VICTOR. Die Datierung der Prosastücke Chaucers. Ang, 53, 1929, 235-68.

    Boethius, 235-6.

    For reviews, see section: Melibeus.

LOWES, JOHN L. Chaucer's Boethius and Jean de Meun.
RR, 8, 1917, 383-400.

LUTEY, WILLIAM GLEN. The Philosophy of Boethius.
Master's Thesis, Univ of Washington, 1931. Typewritten, 60 pp.

PATCH, HOWARD R. Consolatio Philosophiae, 4, m. 6,
23-24. Spec, 8, 1933, 41-51.
Speculations on source of Boethius' formula of
earth and fire.

----------. Fate in Boethius and the Neoplatonists.
Spec, 4, 1929, 62-72.

----------. Necessity in Boethius and the Neoplatonists.
Spec, 10, 1935, 393-404.

----------. The Tradition of Boethius: A Study of his
Importance in Medieval Culture. Oxford, 1935. 200 pp.
Rev: Richard McKeon, MP, 34, 1936, 197-8; H. F.
Stewart, EHR, 52, 1937, 298-9; E. T. Silk, Spec, 11,
1936, 425-7; TLS, April 18, 1936, 337; NQ, 171, 1936,
287; A. Brandl, Arch, 170, 1936, 146-7; Lane Cooper,
MLN, 53, 1938, 222-4; reply, Howard R. Patch,
MLN, 53, 1938, 398; C. J. F., Oxford Mag, 50,
1937, 171-2.

----------. The Beginnings of the Legend of Boethius.
Spec, 22, 1947, 443-5.

SCIENCE, MARK, Ed. Boethius: De Consolatione Philo-
sophiae, translated by John Walton. With Introduction,
Notes, and Glossary. Milford for EETS, 1927. 379 pp.
Rev: NQ, 154, 1928, 467-8; H. Buckhurst, RES, 5,
1928, 341; TLS, Oct 10, 1929, 780; H. Flasdieck,
LGRP, 1929, 18-19; E. Ekwall, AB, 40, 1929, 228-31;
A. Kirkman, MLR, 25, 1930, 197-8; J. R. Hulbert,
MLN, 45, 1930, 334-5.

----------. A Suggested Correction of the Text of Chaucer's Boethius. TLS, Mar 29, 1923, 199-200.

SILK, EDMUND T. An Edition of Chaucer's Boethius in
the Cambridge MS Ii. 3. 21. Doctoral Diss, Yale.
Listed as completed in Willard, 9, 1931, 102.

----------. Saeculi Noni Auctoris in Boetii Consolatio-
nem Philosophiae Commentarius. American Academy
in Rome. Printed in Italy, 1935.
Rev: E. K. Rand, AJP, 57, 1936, 338-41; Jacob
Hammer, AHR, 42, 1937, 722-3; Pierre Courcelles,
Moyen Age, 46, 1937, 74-5.

----------. The Study of Boethius' "Consolatio Philoso-
phiae" in the Middle Ages. Abstract in TAPA, 62,
1931, xxxvii-xxxviii.
STEWART, H. F., and E. K. RAND. Boethius: De Con-
solatione Philosophiae. Loeb Classical Library.
Heinemann; Putnam, 1918.
Latin text and 17th century translation.
WHEAT, MARY AGNES. The Influence of Boethius on
Chaucer and the English Renaissance. Master's
Thesis, Iowa, 1933.
WITCUTT, W. P. Chaucer's Boethius. Amer Rev, 8,
1936, 61-70.

BOOK OF THE DUCHESS

See Hammond, 362-6; Kaluza, 23-7; Kittredge, 37-
72; Legouis, 71-82; Root, 59-63; Robinson, 881-6,
1015-6; French, 86-90; Brusendorff, 294-5; Curry,
195-218, 263-5; Koch, 10-19; Shannon, 3-12, 330-1;
Wells, CBEL, I, 222-3; Malone, 19-41; Birney, Irony,
643; Clemen, 29; Patch, 35; Shelly, 45; Speirs, 40.
For discussion of dream poems see section: Works
Other than the Canterbury Tales: General and for
editions see section: Editions with Notes.

BRADDY, HALDEEN. Chaucer's Book of the Duchess
and Two of Granson's Complaintes. MLN, 52, 1937,
487-91.
----------. Three Chaucer Notes. 81-99, in Essays and
Studies in Honor of Carleton Brown, New York, 1940.
Symbolic Colors; Ceyes and Alcione; Sir Guichard
d'Angle, a Poitevine Friend.
BRONSON, BERTRAND H. The Book of the Duchess Re-
opened. PMLA, 67, 1952, 863-81.
Argues against deprecation of the poem.
----------. Concerning Houres Twelve. MLN, 68, 1953,
515-21.
Line 1322.
COOK, ALBERT S. Chaucerian Papers. Trans Connecti-
cut Academy of Arts and Sciences, 23, 31 ff. Yale
Univ Press, 1919.
Rev: Arch, 141, 1921, 309 ff.
COOLEY, FRANKLIN D. Two Notes on the Chess Terms

in The Book of the Duchess. MLN, 63, 1948, 30-5.
    Rev: D. Everett, YWES, 87.
CUSHMAN, L. W. Chaucer's Book of the Duchess. Univ
of Calif Chron, 11, 1909, 252-66.
DONOVAN, MORTIMER J. The Book of the Duchess: vv.
16-21. NQ, 195, 1950, 333-4.
    Rev: D. Everett, YWES, 69.
FRENCH, W. H. Medieval Chess and the Book of the
Duchess. MLN, 64, 1949, 261-4.
    Rev: D. Everett, YWES, 68.
HAMMERLE, KARL. The Book of the Duchesse, 599-
616. Ang, 66, 1942, 70-2.
HARRISON, BENJAMIN S. Medieval Rhetoric in the
Book of the Duchesse. PMLA, 49, 1934, 428-42.
    Rev: D. Everett, YWES, 88-9.
KITCHEL, ANNA THERESA. Chaucer and Machaut's Dit
de la Fontaine Amoureuse. Vassar Medieval Studies,
1923, 219-31.
KITTREDGE, GEORGE L. Guillaume de Machaut and
the Book of the Duchess. PMLA, 30, 1915, 1-24.
    See also MP, 7, 1910, 465.
KREUZER, JAMES R. The Dreamer in the Book of the
Duchess. PMLA, 66, 1951, 543-7.
LEWIS, N. B. The Anniversary Service for Blanche,
Duchess of Lancaster, 12th September, 1374. JRLB,
21, 1937, 176-92.
LOOMIS, ROGER S. Chaucer's Eight Years Sickness.
MLN, 59, 1944, 178-80.
LOWES, JOHN L. Chaucer and Ovide Moralisé. PMLA,
33, 1918, 319.
----------. Illustrations of Chaucer Drawn Chiefly from
Deschamps. RR, 2, 1911, 113-28.
    Especially 121-3.
    Rev: John Koch, ESt, 46, 1912, 114.
NADAL, THOMAS W. Spenser's Daphnaida and Chaucer's
Book of the Duchess. PMLA, 23, 1908, 646-61.
PRESTON, RAYMOND. Chaucer and the Ballades Notées
of Guillaume de Machaut. Spec, 26, 1951, 615-23.
    BD, 848-54.
ROSENTHAL, CONSTANCE L. A Possible Source of
Chaucer's Booke of the Duchesse -- Li Regret de
Guillaume by Jehan de la Mote. MLN, 48, 1933, 511-
4.

SAVAGE, HOWARD W. Chaucer's "Long Castel." MLN,
    31, 1916, 442-3.
SCHOENBAUM, SAMUEL. Chaucer's Black Knight.
    MLN, 68, 1953, 121-2.
        Questions identification of the Black Knight as
    John of Gaunt.
SHANNON, EDGAR F. Chaucer's Use of Octosyllabic
    Verse in the Book of the Duchess and the Hous of
    Fame. JEGP, 12, 1913, 277-94.
----------. Notes on Chaucer. MP, 11, 1913, 227-36.
        A cave under a rock ygrave, 163-4.
STEARNS, MARSHALL W. A Note on Chaucer's Attitude
    toward Love. Spec, 17, 1942, 570-4.
        Suggests Chaucer's eight years' lovesickness as a
    compliment to Duchess Blanche.
STEVENSON, S. W. Chaucer's Ferses Twelve. ELH, 7,
    1940, 215-22.
        On chess terms.
SYPHERD, W. OWEN. Le Songe Vert and Chaucer's
    Dream-Poems. MLN, 24, 1909, 46-7.
TORRACA, FRANCESCO. Un Passo Oscuro di G. Chau-
    cer. Jour of Comparative Literature, 1, 1903, 82-4.
        Not in Hammond.
TUPPER, FREDERICK. Chaucer and Lancaster. MLN,
    32, 1917, 54.
----------. Chaucer and Richmond. MLN, 31, 1916, 250-
    2.

BUKTON

See Hammond, 366-7; Kaluza, 21; Root, 76-7;
Robinson, 979-80, 1038; French, 110-1; Brusendorff,
292-3; Koch, 101; Wells, CBEL, I, 225-6 and the
supplements to the Manual after 1933; and Kuhl, Chaucer and the Church, in section: Religious Backgrounds.
For editions, see section: Editions with Notes.

BRADDY, HALDEEN. Sir Peter and the Envoy to Bukton.
    PQ, 14, 1935, 368-70.
        Rev: D. Everett, YWES, 94.
KITTREDGE, GEORGE L. Chaucer's Envoy to Bukton.
    MLN, 24, 1909, 14-15.
        Compared with Deschamps.

KUHL, ERNEST P. Chaucer's My Maistre Bukton. PMLA,
   38, 1923, 115-32.
LOWES, JOHN L. The Date of the Envoy to Bukton. MLN,
   27, 1912, 45-8.
   Rev: John Koch, ESt, 46, 1912, 114.
MOORE, SAMUEL. The Date of Chaucer's Marriage
   Group. MLN, 26, 1911, 172-4.
TATLOCK, JOHN STRONG PERRY. Notes on Chaucer:
   Earlier or Minor Poems. MLN, 29, 1914, 47-101.
   The folly of second marriage with a parallel from
   John of Salisbury. Verses 13-16.
   Rev: John Koch, AB, 25, 1914, 339-42.

COMPLAINT TO HIS LADY
OR
BALADE OF PITY

Hammond, 411-2; Root, 68; Robinson, 971, 1035;
Brusendorff, 45, 225; Wells, CBEL, I, 223; Birney,
640; Clemen, 223.

LOWES, JOHN LIVINGSTON. Chaucer and Dante. MP,
   14, 1917, 724.
TIMMER, B. J. La Belle Dame sans Merci. E Stud, 11,
   1929, 20-2.
   On "faire rewtheleęs."

COMPLAINT UNTO PITY

See Hammond, 390-1; Robinson, 970-1, 1034-5;
French, 85-6; Brusendorff, 268-73; Shannon, 330;
Root, 58; Wells, CBEL, I, 224, and supplements to
the Manual after 1933; Birney, 639-40; Clemen, 215.

BRIGHT, JAMES W. Minor Notes on Chaucer. MLN, 17,
   1902, 278-9.
   Deals with lines 29-35.
LOWES, JOHN LIVINGSTON. Chaucer and Dante. MP,
   14, 1917, 722.
   Lines 29-35.

COURT OF LOVE

KITTREDGE, GEORGE L. Henry Scogan. Harvard Studies and Notes, 1, 1892, 109-17.
LANGE, HUGO. Zu Scogan und The Court of Love. Arch,
110, 1903, 104.
> See Hammond, 418-9; Brandl, in Social Backgrounds.

FORMER AGE

> See Hammond, 367-8; Root, 70-1; Kaluza, 18; Rob-
inson, 974-5, 1036; French, 102; Brusendorff, 293-4;
Koch, 95-6; Shannon, 45-7; Wells, CBEL, I, 224, and
supplements to the Manual after 1933. See also
Schlauch, in section: General Criticism, and Koch,
in section: Boethius, p. 44.

PRESTON, RAYMOND. "Poyson, Man-slaughtre, and
Mordre in Sondry Wise." NQ, 195, Mar 4, 1950, 95.
> Rev: D. Everett, YWES, 69.
SEVERS, J. BURKE. Two Irregular Chaucerian Stanzas.
MLN, 64, 1949, 306-9.
> Questions irregularity of ABC, 39; Former Age, 47.
> Rev: D. Everett, YWES, 69.

FORTUNE

> See Hammond, 369-71; Root, 71-2; Kaluza, 18-19;
Robinson, 975-6, 1036; French, 103-4; Brusendorff,
241-5; Koch, 96, and in section: Boethius, p. 44;
Wells, CBEL, I, 224, and supplements to the Manual
after 1933. Also see Jefferson in section: Boethius.

GALWAY, MARGARET. Chaucer among Thieves. TLS,
April 20, 1946, 187.
> Rev: D. Everett, YWES, 81-2.
HAMMERLE, KARL. Das Fortunamotiv von Chaucer bis
Bacon. Ang, 65, 1940, 87-100.
PATCH, HOWARD R. Chaucer and Lady Fortune. MLR,
22, 1927, 377-88.
----------. The Goddess Fortune in Medieval Literature.
Harvard Univ Press, 1927. 215 pp.
> For reviews, see section: Literary Relations.

----------. The Tradition of the Goddess Fortuna: In
Roman Literature and in the Transitional Period.
Smith College Studies in Modern Language, 3, 1922,
no. 3. The Tradition of the Goddess Fortuna: In Medieval Philosophy and Literature. Smith College Studies
in Modern Language, 3, 1922, no. 4.

GAMELYN

See Wells, 766, [15].

EBBUTT, MAUDE I. Hero-myths and Legends of the
British Race; with 51 Full-page Illustrations by J. H.
F. Bacon and Others. Myths Series. Farrar, 1931.
375 pp.
HIBBARD, LAURA. Mediaeval Romance in England. A
Study of the Sources and Analogues of the Non-cyclic
Metrical Romances. Oxford Univ Press, 1924. 342 pp.
Gamelyn, 156-63.
For reviews, see section: Literary Relations.
SHANNON, EDGAR F. , Jr. Medieval Law in the Tale of
Gamelyn. Spec, 26, 1951, 458-64.
SNELL, F. J. The Age of Chaucer. Bell, 1901. 242 pp.
Gamelyn, 1-6.
Rev: ESt, 32, 1903, 117-24.

GENTILESSE

See Hammond, 371-2; Root, 74; Kaluza, 20; Robinson, 977, 1037; French, 107-8; Brusendorff, 254-8;
Koch, 97-9; Wells, CBEL, I, 224, and supplements
to the Manual after 1933.
For editions, see sections: Editions with Notes
and Manuscripts.

ALBRECHT, W. P. The Sermon on Gentilesse. CE, 12,
1951, 459.
BRANDL, ALOIS. Review of William A. Neilson. The
Origins and Sources of the Court of Love, Studies and
Notes (Harvard), 6. Arch, 106, 1901, 390-401.
BRITTAIN, ROBERT E. A Textual Note on Chaucer:
Gentilesse, 20. MLN, 51, 1936, 433-5.
DIVELEY, RUTH ANNA. The Meaning of Gentilesse

in Chaucer. Master's Thesis, Univ of Washington,
1929. Typewritten, 63 pp.

KITTREDGE, GEORGE L. Henry Scogan. Harvard Studies and Notes, 1, 1892, 109-17.

LOWES, JOHN L. Chaucer and Dante's Convivio. MP,
13, 1915, 19-33.
Source material.

TUPPER, FREDERICK. Chaucer and the Woman Question. Paper read by title at meeting of MLA at New
York, Dec 31, 1914. Listed in PMLA, 30, 1915, xxix.

VOGT, G. M. Gleanings for the History of a Sentiment:
Generositas Virtus, non Sanguis. JEGP, 24, 1925,
102-23.

HOUSE OF FAME

See Hammond, 372-7; Kaluza, 44-55; Kittredge,
73-107; Legouis, 86-97; Root, 128-34; Robinson, 886-
97, 1016-8; French, 122-6; Shannon, 48-119; Brusendorff, 148-66; Koch, 40-56, and ES, 57, 1923, 44;
Curry, 195-218, 263-5, and Texas Rev, 8, 1923, 307;
Tatlock, 34; Wells, CBEL, I, 224-5; Malone, 42-60;
Speirs, 42-7; index to Patch, The Other World; Clemens, 72 ff.; Patch, 42 ff.

For editions, see section: Editions with Notes.
On Lollius, see section: Literary Relations.

ALLEN, HOPE E. The Mystical Lyrics of the Manuel des
Pechiez. RR, 9, 1918, 187 n.
Meaning of Cadence.

BAUM, PAULL F. Chaucer's "The House of Fame."
ELH, 8, 1941, 248-56.

BESSER, INGEBORG. Chaucers The House of Fame:
Eine Interpretation. Brittania, 20. Hamburg: Fried-
erichsen, de Gruyter, 1941. 122 pp.
Rev: Will Héraucourt, AB, 53, 1942, 55-6; Walter
F. Schirmer, Arch, 182, 1943, 129-30.

BRANDL, ALOIS. Anfange der Autobiographie in England.
Sitzungber. d. Kgl. Preuss. Akad., 35, 1908, 724-33.
Rev: R. Imelmann, ESt, 45, 1912, 398-402.

BRIGHT, JAMES W. Minor Notes on Chaucer. MLN, 17,
1902, 278-9.
HF, I, 183-4.

BRONSON, BERTRAND H. Chaucer's Hous of Fame:
   Another Hypothesis. University of California Publi-
   cations in English, 3, 1934, 171-92. Separately re-
   printed, Univ of Calif Press, 1934.
      Rev: Hugo Lange, AB, 1936, 132-3; D. Everett,
   YWES, 16, 1935, 95-6.
BROWN, MARGERY L. The House of Fame and the Cor-
   baccio. MLN, 32, 1917, 411-5.
BUCK, KATHARINE M. Chaucer and the "Mabinogion."
   TLS, Jan 29, 1931, 79.
      Identification of Colle Tregetour.
BUHLER, CURT F. Chaucer's House of Fame: Another
   Caxton Variant. Papers of the Bibliographical Society
   of America, 42, 1948, 140-3.
      Rev: D. Everett, YWES, 88.
COOK, ALBERT S. Skelton's Garland of Laurel and
   Chaucer's House of Fame. MLR, 11, 1916, 9-14.
CORNOG, WILLIAM HAFNER. The Anticlaudian of
   Alain de Lille; Prologue, Argument and Nine Books
   Translated, with an Introduction and Notes. Doctoral
   Diss, Univ of Pennsylvania, 1935. Printed in Phila-
   delphia, 1935. 192 pp.
      Influence on HF, 43.
      Rev: H. R. Patch, MLN, 52, 1937, 233-4.
DILTS, DOROTHY ARLENE. Observations on Dante and
   the "Hous of Fame." MLN, 57, 1942, 26-8.
      Rev: D. Everett, YWES, 64.
DONOVAN, MORTIMER J. Three Notes on Chaucer's
   Marine Life. PQ, 31, 1952, 439-41.
      "Eles," HF, 2153-4.
EPSTEIN, HANS J. The Identity of Chaucer's Lollius.
   MLQ, 3, 1942, 391-400.
      Suggests Lollius Bassus.
      Rev: D. Everett, YWES, 63-4.
ESTRICH, ROBERT M. A Possible Provençal Source for
   Chaucer's Hous of Fame, 300-310. MLN, 55, 1940, 342-9.
      Rev: YWES, 75-6.
FORD, H. C. Observations on the Language of Chaucer's
   House of Fame. Revision of 1899 ed. Lexington, Va, 1908.
FRANCIS, W. NELSON. Chaucer's "Airish Beasts."
   MLN, 64, 1949, 339-41.
      HF, 932 and 965.
      Rev: D. Everett, YWES, 67-8.

FRIEND, ALBERT C. Chaucer's Version of the Aeneid.
Spec, 28, 1953, 317-23.

GOFFIN, R. C. Quiting by Tidinges in the House of
Fame. MA, 12, 1943, 40-4.
Equates "tyding" with story.

HAMILTON, GEORGE L. On a Note to Hous of Fame,
358. MLN, 23, 1908, 63.
On source.

HENKIN, LEO J. The Apocrypha and Chaucer's House of
Fame. MLN, 56, 1941, 583-8.

HOLTHAUSEN, F. Zu Chaucers Hous of Fame. AB, 31,
1920, 137.

HUTCHINS, CHESLEY M. L'Anticlaudianus: Etude de
Chronologie. Romania, 50, 1924, 1-13, 986.

IMELMANN, RUDOLF. Chaucers Haus der Fama. ESt,
45, 1912, 397-431.
Rev: John Koch, AB, 25, 1914, 82-4.

JACK, ADOLPHUS A. A Commentary on the Poetry of
Chaucer and Spenser. Glasgow: Maclehose and Jack-
son; Macmillan, 1920.
On date of HF, p. 37.
For reviews, see section: General Criticism.

JONES, H. LLOYD, Jr. The Date of Chaucer's House of
Fame. Delaware Notes, 19th ser., 1946, 47-55.

KITTREDGE, GEORGE L. The Date of Chaucer's Troilus and Other Chaucer Matters. Chaucer Society, 2nd
ser. 42, 1909.
See 53-60.

KOCH, JOHN. Nochmals: Die Bedeutung von Chaucers
Hous of Fame. ESt, 50, 1916, 359-82.

----------. Textkritische Bemerkungen zu Chaucers
Hous of Fame. AB, 27, 1916, 139-53.

----------. Der gegenwärtige Stand der Chaucerforschung. Ang, 49, 1925, 193-243.
See 214.

KUHL, E. P. Chaucer and the Red Rose. PQ, 24, 1945,
33-8.
HF, 134 ff.
Rev: D. Everett, YWES, 52.

LANGE, HUGO. Chaucers "Myn Auctour called Lollius"
und die Datierung des Hous of Fame. Ang, 42, 1918,
345-51.

----------. Der heliakische Aufgang der Fixsterne

bei Dante und Chaucer. Deutsches Dante-Jahrbuch,
21, 1939, 19-41.
    Rev: W. H., Archiv, 178, 1940, 46-7.
----------. Die Adler in Liebesvisionen Chaucers. Sitz-
ungsberichte der Berliner Gesellschaft, Feb 9, 1937.
Arch, 175, 1939, 209.
LANGHANS, VICTOR. Untersuchungen zu Chaucer.
Halle: Niemeyer, 1918.
    See 71 ff., and for reviews, see section: Legend of
    Good Women.
LOWES, JOHN L. Chaucer and Ovide Moralisé. PMLA,
33, 1918, 302-25.
    See 324.
----------. Chaucer and the Roman d'Eneas. PMLA, 32,
1917, liv-lv.
----------. Chaucer and Dante. MP, 14, 1917, 705-35.
    HF, 1800-3, 1229-32.
MACAULAY, G. C. Notes on Chaucer. MLR, 4, 1908,
14-19.
    See p. 18 on line 528, "Dant in English."
MacCRACKEN, HENRY N. Dant in English: A Solution.
Nation, 89, 1909, 276-7.
    See Macaulay, above in this section.
MANLY, JOHN M. What Is Chaucer's House of Fame?
73-81, in Anniversary Papers of G. L. Kittredge.
Ginn, 1913.
MEECH, SANFORD BROWN. Chaucer and an Italian
Translation of the Heroides. PMLA, 45, 1930, 110-
28.
MILLER, AMANDA H. Chaucer's "Secte Saturnyn."
MLN, 47, 1932, 99-102.
NORWOOD, ANNE. Chaucer's House of Fame, in 1924.
Master's Thesis, Univ of Washington, 1924. Type-
written, 123 pp.
PATCH, HOWARD R. Chaucer's Desert. MLN, 34, 1919,
321-8.
----------. Chauceriana. ES, 65, 1931, 351-9.
    Lines 742-6.
----------. Notes on Spenser and Chaucer. MLN, 33,
1918, 177-80.
----------. Precious Stones in the House of Fame. MLN,
50, 1935, 312-7.
    Rev: D. Everett, YWES, 94-5.

PRATT, ROBERT ARMSTRONG. Chaucer Borrowing
    from Himself. MLQ, 7, 1946, 259-64.
        Concerns Invocation to Venus.
        Rev: D. Everett, YWES, 69.
----------. Chaucer's Claudian. Spec, 22, 1947, 419-29.
    HF, 71-2, 445-50, 1507-12.
        Rev: D. Everett, YWES, 67-8.
----------. Chaucer's Use of the Teseida. PMLA, 62,
    1947, 598-621.
RAND, EDWARD KENNARD. Chaucer in Error. Spec, 1,
    1926, 222-5.
        Criticism of Nitchie (see section: Literary Rela-
    tions and Sources). Explains seeming errors of Chau-
    cer in regard to Iulo-Ascanius, I, 177-8, and Titus,
    III, 1467.
RHYS, ERNEST, Ed. The Prelude to Poetry. Dent, 1927.
        Invocation to the House of Fame. Also see intro-
    duction.
RIEDEL, FREDERICK CARL. The Meaning of Chaucer's
    "House of Fame." JEGP, 27, 1928, 441-69. Master's
    Thesis, Columbia, 1927.
        Rev: M. B. Ruud, PQ, 8, 1929, 296; D. Everett,
    YWES, 86-7.
ROOT, ROBERT KILBURN. Chaucer's Dares. MP, 15,
    1917, 1-22.
        Joseph of Exeter as source, 1464 ff.
ROYSTER, JAMES F. Chaucer's "Colle Tregetour." SP,
    23, 1926, 380-4.
RUGGIERS, P. G. Unity of Chaucer's House of Fame.
    SP, 50, 1953, 16-29.
SHACKFORD, MARTHA H. The Date of Chaucer's House
    of Fame. MLN, 31, 1916, 507-8.
SHANNON, EDGAR F. Chaucer and Lucan's Pharsalia.
    MP, 16, 1919, 609-18.
----------. Chaucer's Use of Octosyllabic Verse in the
    Book of the Duchess and the Hous of Fame. JEGP, 12,
    1913, 277-94.
----------. Notes on Chaucer. MP, 11, 1913, 230-6.
        Aeolus in the Hous of Fame, 1571-605.
SMITH, ROLAND M. "Mynstralcie and Noyse" in the
    House of Fame. MLN, 65, 1950, 521-30.
        Lines 1233-50, 1927-34, 1941-4.
        Rev: D. Everett, YWES, 69.

----------. Chaucer's "Castle in Spain," HF 1117. MLN,
   60, 1945, 39-40.
      Rev: D. Everett, YWES, 58-9.
SMYSER, H. M. Chaucer's Two-Mile Pilgrimage. MLN,
   56, 1941, 205-7.
      Suggestions as to meaning of HF, 111-8.
SYPHERD, WILBUR O. The Completeness of Chaucer's
   Hous of Fame. MLN, 30, 1915, 65-8.
----------. Studies in Chaucer's Hous of Fame. Chau-
   cer Society, 2nd ser., 39, 1908.
      Rev: John Koch, ESt, 41, 1910, 113-21; Mabel A.
   Stanford, JEGP, 19, 1920, 381 n.; see Hammond,
   541.
TATLOCK, JOHN STRONG PERRY. Chaucer's Elcanor.
   MLN, 36, 1921, 95-7.
TEAGER, FLORENCE E. Chaucer's Eagle and the Rhe-
   torical Colors. PMLA, 47, 1932, 410-8. Part of Doc-
   toral Diss, Univ of Iowa, 1931.
THOMPSON, E. N. S. The Octosyllabic Couplet. PQ,
   18, 1939, 257-68.
      See 258.
TUVE, ROSEMOND. Guillaume's Pilgrim and the Hous
   of Fame. MLN, 45, 1930, 518-22.
      Rev: D. Everett, YWES, 83-4.
WHITFORD, H. C. An Uncollected Sixteenth-Century
   Allusion to The House of Fame. MLN, 52, 1937, 31-2.
WHITING, B. J. "The Hous of Fame" and Renaud de
   Beaufeu's "Le Biaus Descouveus." MP, 31, 1933,
   196-8.
WILLIAMS, JERRY TURNER. Words into Images in
   Chaucer's House of Fame. MLN, 62, 1947, 488-90.
      Finds in the Hebrew Zohar an analogue to the ac-
   count of how words are received into the House of
   Fame.
      Rev: D. Everett, YWES, 83-4.
WILLIAMSON, GEORGE. Notes by W. P. Ker. TLS,
   Jan 8, 1931, 28.
      Ker's suggestion of identification for Colle Tre-
   getour.
ZIEGLER, JULIAN. Two Notes on J. T. Williams'
   "Words into Images in Chaucer's House of Fame."
   MLN, 64, 1949, 73-6.
      Rev: D. Everett, YWES, 68.

LA BELLE DAME SANS MERCY

See Robinson, 971, 1035; French, 97-8.

TIMMER, B. J. La Belle Dame Sans Merci. ESt, 11,
  1929, 20-2.
  On the source of "Faire Rewthelees."

LACK OF STEADFASTNESS

See Hammond, 394; Kaluza, 20; Root, 74-5; Robinson, 977-8, 1037-8; French, 108-9; Brusendorff,
273-6; Koch, 99-100; Wells, CBEL, I, 225, and supplements to the Manual after 1933. See Schlauch, in
section: General Criticism, and on verse, see Cowling, in section: Style Including Versification.

BRADDY, HALDEEN. The Date of Chaucer's Lak of
  Steadfastnesse. JEGP, 36, 1937, 481-90.
HOLT, L. H. Chaucer's Lac of Stedfastnesse. JEGP,
  6, 1907, 419-31.
MacCRACKEN, HENRY N. Notes Suggested by a Chau-
  cer Codex. MLN, 23, 1908, 212-4.
PACE, GEORGE BLOCKER. The Texts of Truth, Lak
  of Stedfastnesse, and the Purse. Univ of Virginia Ab-
  stracts of Dissertations, 1942, 12-14.
----------. Chaucer's Lak of Stedfastnesse. SB, 4,
  1951, 105-22.
  Text edition of the poem.

LEGEND OF GOOD WOMEN

See Robinson, 952-69, 1030-3; French, 126-32;
Brusendorff, 137-48; Koch, 61-95; Shannon, 169-301;
Curry, 195-218, 263-5; Hammond, 378-83; Kaluza, 98-
111; Legouis, 97-108; Root, 135-50; Shelly, 155-76;
Speirs, 82-94; Malone, 80-99; Patch, 123; Wells, CBEL,
I, 230-2, and supplements to the Manual after 1933.
  For references to Wreched Engendrynge (G414),
see section having that title.
  For editions, see section: Editions with Notes.
  For phonographic recordings, see section: Canter-
bury Tales: General.

For discussions of dream poems, see section:
Works Other than the Canterbury Tales: General. For
discussions of courtly love, see section: Social Backgrounds. For studies of literary influence, see section: Literary Relations and Sources.

AIKEN, PAULINE. Chaucer's Legend of Cleopatra and
the Speculum Historiale. Spec, 13, 1938, 232-6.
   Rev: D. Everett, YWES, 68.
AMY, ERNEST F. The Manuscripts of the Legend of
Good Women. JEGP, 21, 1922, 107-18.
----------. The Text of Chaucer's Legend of Good
Women. Princeton Univ Press, 1918.
ATWOOD, E. BAGBY. Two Alterations of Virgil in
Chaucer's Dido. Spec, 13, 1938, 454-7.
   LGW, 924 ff.
BAUM, PAULL F. Chaucer's "Glorious Legende." MLN,
60, 1945, 377-81.
   LGW, F483.
BRESSIE, RAMONA. The Date of Thomas Usk's Testa-
ment of Love. MP, 26, 1928, 17-29.
   Borrowings by Usk.
BROWN, CARLETON. Chaucer's Serpent-Pit. MLN, 29,
1914, 198-9.
   Supplementary to Tatlock, Notes on Chaucer, be-
low in this section.
----------. Lydgate and the Legend of Good Women.
ESt, 47, 1913, 59-62.
----------. The Man of Law's Head-link and the Pro-
logue of the Canterbury Tales. SP, 34, 1937, 8-
35.
   Relation to LGW.
----------. The Date of Prologue F to the Legend of
Good Women. MLN, 58, 1943, 274-8.
   Rev: D. Everett, YWES, 46-7.
BRYANT, JOSEPH A. Another Appetite for Form. MLN,
58, 1943, 194-6.
   LGW, 1582-3, 2228-30.
   Rev: D. Everett, YWES, 47-8.
CHAPMAN, COOLIDGE OTIS. Chaucer and Dante. TLS,
Aug 29, 1952, 565.
   Suggests LGW, 924-7, echoes words of Statius in
Purgatorio, 22, 64-9.

CHRISTY, J. Z. Queen Philippa in Chaucer. NQ, Dec 8,
    1923, 451.
        A(G)145, B(F)213. A request for information.
CONNELLY, WILLARD. Imprints of the Heroides of
    Ovid on Chaucer's The Legend of Good Women. Class-
    ical Weekly, 17, 1924, 9-13.
COOK, ALBERT S. Chaucer, L. G. W., Prol 334 (358).
    MP, 6, 1909, 475-6.
----------. Chaucerian Papers. Trans Conn Acad of Arts
    and Sciences, 23, 32. Yale Univ Press, 1919.
        On LGW, 125-7.
CURRY, W. C. O Mars, O Atazir. JEGP, 22, 1923, 347-68.
    Hypermnestra.
DODD, WILLIAM G. Courtly Love in Chaucer and Gower.
    Harvard Studies in English, 1. Ginn; Milford, 1913.
        For reviews, see section: Literary Relations.
EINENKEL, E. Bemerkung zu dem Streit über Chaucers
    Legendprolog. Ang, 50, 1926, 106.
EMERSON, OLIVER F. Chaucer's "Opie of Thebes Fyn."
    MP, 17, 1919, 287-91.
        LGW, 2668-70.
ESTRICH, ROBERT M. Chaucer's Maturing Art in the
    Prologues to the Legend of Good Women. JEGP, 36,
    1937, 326-37.
        Rev: D. Everett, YWES, 75.
----------. A Study of the Sources and Interpretation of
    Chaucer's Legend of Good Women. Doctoral Diss,
    Ohio State Univ, 1935. Abstract in Abstracts of Doc-
    tors' Dissertations, 18, 1936, 145-53.
----------. Chaucer's Prologue to the Legend of Good
    Women and Machaut's Le Jugement dou Roy de Na-
    varre. SP, 36, 1939, 20-39.
FRENCH, JOHN C. The Problem of the Two Prologues
    of Chaucer's Legend of Good Women. Johns Hopkins
    Diss, 1905.
        Rev: John Koch, ESt, 37, 1907, 233; J. S. P. Tat-
    lock, MLN, 21, 1906, 58-62.
GALWAY, MARGARET. Chaucer's Sovereign Lady; a
    Study of the Prologue to the Legend and Related
    Poems. MLR, 33, 1938, 145-99.
        See TLS, Oct 10, 1942, and Brown, The Date of
    Prol F, above.
        Rev: D. Everett, YWES, 66-8.

----------. Chaucer's Hopeless Love. MLN, 60, 1945, 431-9.
    Suggests, as Alceste, Joan of Kent.
    Rev: D. Everett, YWES, 52-3.
----------. Cancelled Tributes to Chaucer's Sovereign
    Lady. NQ, 193, Jan 10, 1948, 2-3.
    Rev: D. Everett, YWES, 91-2.
----------. Chaucer, Graunson, and Isabel of France.
    RES, 24, 1948, 273-80.
    Rev: D. Everett, YWES, 91-2.
GARRETT, ROBERT M. Cleopatra the Martyr and her
    Sisters. JEGP, 22, 1923, 64-74.
GHOSH, P. C. Cleopatra's Death in Chaucer's "Legende
    of Gode Wommen." MLR, 26, 1931, 332-6.
    Rev: D. Everett, YWES, 86.
GODDARD, HAROLD C. Chaucer's Legend of Good Wom-
    en. JEGP, 7, 1908, 87-129; 8, 1909, 47-112.
        Rev: G. C. Macaulay, MLR, 6, 1911, 136-7; Robert
    K. Root, ESt, 41, 1910, 411-4; Wilhelm Dibelius, DL,
    31, 1910, 614; Arch, 123, 1909, 473-4; Ch. Bastide,
    Rev Crit, 68, 1909, 407-8; John Koch, AB, 22, 1911,
    276. See also Lowes, Is Chaucer's Legend . . . , below.
GRIFFITH, DUDLEY DAVID. An Interpretation of Chau-
    cer's Legend of Good Women. 32-41, in Manly Anni-
    versary Studies. Univ of Chicago Press, 1923.
    Rev: E. P. Hammond, ESt, 60, 1926, 310-4.
HAMILTON, MARIE P. Chaucer's "Marcia Catoun."
    MP, 30, 1933, 361-4.
----------. Bernard, the Monk: Postscript. MLN, 62,
    1947, 190-1.
    LGW, 16. See Roland M. Smith, below.
    Rev: D. Everett, YWES, 83.
HAMMOND, ELEANOR PRESCOTT. Chaucer's "Book of
    the Twenty-five Ladies." MLN, 48, 1933, 514-6.
HIBBARD, LAURA A. Chaucer's "Shapen Was my
    Sherte." PQ, 1, 1922, 222-5.
    LGW, 2629.
HINCKLEY, HENRY B. Chaucer and Ywaine and Gawin.
    Acad, 1906, II, 640-1.
    Skeat's reported criticism, Acad, 1906, II, 647;
    Hinckley's reply, Acad, 1907, I, 99.
HOLMES, URBAN T. Chaucer's "tydif," a Small Bird.
    PQ, 16, 1937, 65-7.
    LGW, F164.

HOLTHAUSEN, FERDINAND. Die Ballade in Chaucers
    Legendenprolog. Arch, 147, 1924, 251.
HULBERT, JAMES R. Chaucer and the Earl of Oxford.
    MP, 10, 1912-3, 433-7.
        On date of LGW.
----------. A Note on the Prologues to the Legend of
    Good Women. MLN, 65, 1950, 534-6.
        Rev: D. Everett, YWES, 68-9.
HUPPE, BERNARD F. Chaucer: A Criticism and a
    Reply. MLR, 43, 1948, 393-9.
        Opposes Galway, above, with reply by Margaret
    Galway, MLR, 43, 1948, 399-400.
        Rev: D. Everett, YWES, 90-1.
----------. Historical Allegory in the Prologue to the
    Legend of Good Women. MLR, 43, 1948, 393-9.
        See Galway, above, and following this article.
        Rev: D. Everett, YWES, 90-1.
IMMACULATE, Sister MARY. "Sixty" as a Conventional
    Number and Other Chauceriana. MLQ, 2, 1941, 59-66.
        Rev: D. Everett, YWES, 66.
JACK, ADOLPHUS A. A Commentary on the Poetry of
    Chaucer and Spenser. Glasgow: Maclehose and Jack-
    son; Macmillan, 1920.
        See 74, 340.
        For reviews, see section: General Criticism.
JEFFERSON, BERNARD L. Queen Anne and Queen Al-
    ceste. JEGP, 13, 1914, 434-43.
KAUT, THELMA. Chaucer's Age and the Prologues to
    the Legend. MLN, 49, 1934, 87.
        Rev: D. Everett, YWES, 91.
KITTREDGE, GEORGE LYMAN. Chaucer's Alceste. MP,
    6, 1909, 435-9.
----------. Chaucer's Medea and the Date of the Legend
    of Good Women. PMLA, 24, 1909, 343-63.
        Rev: John Koch, AB, 22, 1911, 275.
----------. Chauceriana. MP, 7, 1910, 471-4, 482-3.
        On "Make the metres of hem as thee liste, " B(F)
    562, and Marçia Catoun, B(F) 252.
KOCH, JOHN. Alte Chaucerprobleme und neue Lösungs-
    versuche. ESt, 55, 1921, 161-225.
----------. Chaucerschriften. ES, 37, 1907, 131 ff.
        Reviews Smith, Bilderbeck, Tatlock, Lowes.
----------. Das Handschriftenverhältnis in Chaucers

Legend of Good Women. Ang, 43, 1919, 197-244; 44, 1920, 23-71.

----------. Chaucers Boethiusübersetzung. Ang, 46, 1922, 37 ff.

Chronology.

----------. Nachtrag zu meinem letzten Aufsatz über Chaucers Legendprolog. Ang, 50, 1926, 104-5.

----------. Nochmals zur Frage des Prologs in Chaucers "Legend of Good Women." Ang, 50, 1926, 62-9, 104-5.

----------. Chaucers Belesenheit in den römischen Classikern. ES, 57, 1923, 8-84.

KUHL, E. P. Chaucer and the Red Rose. PQ, 24, 1945, 33-8.

LGW, F226, G160. Associates the red rose in Chaucer with Lancaster.

Rev: D. Everett, YWES, 52.

LANGE, HUGO. Die Ahnlichkeitstheorie in Chaucers Legendenprolog. ESt, 69, 1934, 32-4.

Rev: D. Everett, YWES, 91.

----------. Chaucer und die Prologe zur Legend of Gode Women. Ang, 41, 1917, 393-400.

----------. Die Legendenprologfrage: Zur Steur der Wahrheit. Ang, 44, 1920, 72-8.

See Langhans' reply, AB, 31, 1920, 207-8.

----------. Neue Beiträge zu einer endgültigen Lösung der Legendenprologfrage bei Chaucer. Ang, 49, 1925, 173-80. Fortsetzung, 267-78. Rejoinder, Ang, 51, 1927, 128-35.

Rev: D. Everett, YWES, 89-90.

----------. Neue Wege zur Lösung der Legendenprologfrage bei Chaucer. Ang, 52, 1928, 123-35.

Rev: D. Everett, YWES, 87.

----------. Nochmals die Legendenprologfrage: Eine Entgegnung an V. Langhans. Ang, 55, 1931, 106-13.

----------. Die Sonnen- und die Lilienstelle in Chaucers Legendenprolog: Ein neuer Beweis für die Priorität der F-Redaktion. Ang, 44, 1920, 373-85.

See also Eugen Einenkel, Bemerkungen, Ang, 44, 1920, 385.

Rev: John Koch, ESt, 55, 1921, 196.

----------. Die Paradiesvorstellung in Mandevilles Travels im Lichte mittelalterlicher Dichtung; zur

Lösung der Legendenprologfrage bei Chaucer. ESt,
72, 1938, 312-4.

----------. Uber die Farben König Richards II von England in Beziehung zur Chaucerdichtung: Eine heraldische Studie zugleich ein weiterer Beitrag zur
Legendenprologfrage. Ang, 42, 1918, 142-4, 352-6.

----------. Victor Langhans, und die Unechtheit des
F-Prologs in Chaucers Legende von guten Frauen.
Ang, 51, 1927, 128-35.

----------. Zur Datierung des GG-Prologs zu Chaucers
Legende von den guten Frauen. Eine heraldische Stu-
die. DL, 37, 1916, 891-7.
  Also in Ang, 39, 1915, 347-55.
  Rev: J. Koch, ES, 56, 1921, 175 ff.

----------. Zur Priorität des F-Textes in Chaucers
Legendenprolog und zur Interpretation von F 531/2 =
Gg. 519/20. Ang, 44, 1920, 213-6.
  See Langhans, below in this section.

----------. Chaucer and Mandeville's Travels. Archiv,
174, 1938, 79-81.
  LGW, 1114-22.

LANGHANS, VICTOR. Hugo Lange und die Lösung der Legendenprologfrage bei Chaucer. Ang, 50, 1926, 70-103.

----------. Hugo Langes Artikel in Anglia, N. F. XXXII,
s. 213. Ang, 44, 1920, 337-45.

----------. Nochmals Chaucers Legendenprolog und
kein Ende? Ang, 54, 1930, 99-106.

----------. Der Prolog zu Chaucers Legende von guten
Frauen. Ang, 41, 1917, 162-81.

----------. Untersuchungen zu Chaucer. Niemeyer, 1918.
  Rev: Hugo Lange, AB, 29, 1918, 355-68; 30, 1919,
  5-20; DL, 39, 1918, 1024-6; John Koch, LGRP, 40,
  1919, 90-6; W. Heldt, Neophil, 4, 1919, 183-6. See
  also Lange, Neue Beiträge, above in this section.

----------. Zu Chaucers Legendenprolog. Ang, 43, 1919,
69-90.

----------. Zur F-Fassung von Chaucers Legendprolog.
ESt, 56, 1922, 36-58.

LOOMIS, ROGER S. Chaucer's Eight Years' Sickness.
MLN, 59, 1944, 178-80.
  Opposes Galway, see above.

LOSSING, MARIAN. The Prologue of the Legend of Good
Women and the Lai de Franchise. SP, 39, 1942, 15-35.

Denies Lowes's contention that the Lai is an un-
doubted source of LGW. Also see Brown, The Date of
Prol F, etc. , above.

Rev: D. Everett, YWES, 65-6.

LOWES, JOHN LIVINGSTON. Chaucer and Ovid Moralisé. PMLA, 33, 1918, 302-25.

---------. Chaucer and the Miroir de Mariage. MP, 8,
1910±1, 305-34.

Influence on Prol, 322-6.

---------. The Franklin's Tale, Teseide, and Filocolo.
MP, 15, 1918, 689-728.

Lines 1894-9, 1038-43.

---------. Chaucer's Etik. MLN, 25, 1910, 87-9.

---------. Is Chaucer's Legend of Good Women a
Travesty? JEGP, 8, 1909, 513-69.

Reply to Goddard, above in this section.

---------. The Prologue to the Legend of Good Women
as Related to the French Marguerite Poems and to
the Filostrato. PMLA, 19, 1904, 593-683. Considered
in its Chronological Relations, PMLA, 20, 1905, 794-
864.

Rev: John Koch, ESt, 37, 1907, 232-40; A. W.
Pollard, Acad, 1906, I, 61-2, 99, 227-9.

---------. The Two Prologues of the Legend of Good
Women: A New Test. 95-104, in Anniversary Papers
. . . for George Lyman Kittredge. Ginn, 1913.

Rev: John Koch, AB, 25, 1914, 332-3.

---------. Chaucer and Dante's Convivio. MP, 13, 1915,
19-33.

---------. Chaucer and Dante. MP, 14, 1917, 714.

MACAULAY, G. C. Notes on Chaucer. MLR, 4, 1909,
14-19.

Lines 285 ff. and 298 ff.

MacDONALD, CHARLOTTE. Drayton's "Tidy" and
Chaucer's "Tydif." RES, 21, 1945, 127-33.

LGW, F154.

Rev: D. Everett, YWES, 51.

MALONE, KEMP. A Poet at Work: Chaucer Revising
his Verses. In English Studies Today, C. L. Wrenn
and G. Bullogh, Eds, Oxford Univ Press, 1951, 98-
103. A reprint from the Proc Amer Phil Soc, 94,
1950, 317-21.

Lines 27-39, LGW, compared in both versions.

MANLY, JOHN M. Chaucer's Lady of the Daisies? MP,
    24, 1927, 257-9.
        Rev: D. Everett, YWES, 106.
MATHER, FRANK J. Pesen at Actium: A Chaucer Crux.
    JEGP, 43, 1944, 375-9.
        Rev: D. Everett, YWES, 50-1.
MEECH, SANFORD BROWN. Chaucer and an Italian
    Translation of the Heroides. PMLA, 45, 1930, 110-
    28.
        Rev: D. Everett, YWES, 78-9.
----------. Chaucer and the Ovide Moralisé -- a Fur-
    ther Study. PMLA, 46, 1931, 182-204.
        See this author's Chaucer and Medieval Ovidiana.
    Doctoral Diss, Yale, 1930.
        Rev: D. Everett, YWES, 85.
MOORE, SAMUEL. The Prologue to Chaucer's Legend
    of Good Women in Relation to Queen Anne and Richard.
    MLR, 7, 1912, 488-93.
MOSES, W. R. An Appetite for Form. MLN, 49, 1934,
    226-9.
OGLE, MARBURY BLADEN. Biblical Quotations in the
    De Nugis Curialium of Walter Map. Abstract of
    paper, TAPA, 66, 1935, xlii.
PRATT, ROBERT A. Chaucer's Claudian. Spec, 22,
    1947, 419-29.
        LGW, G267-80.
        Rev: D. Everett, YWES, 67-8.
RAND, EDWARD KENNARD. Ovid and his Influence.
    Marshall-Jones, 1925.
        For reviews, see section: Literary Relations.
ROBERTSON, D. W., Jr. Historical Criticism. Engl
    Inst Essays, 1950, 3-31. Columbia Univ Press, 1951.
        On the word "charity"; on LGW the daisy; on Truth
    and other Chaucerian references passim.
ROOT, ROBERT K. Chaucer's Legend of Medea. PMLA,
    24, 1909, 124-54.
----------. The Date of Chaucer's Medea. PMLA, 25,
    1910, 228-40.
RUGGIERS, PAUL G. Tyrants of Lombardy in Dante
    and Chaucer. PQ, 29, 1950, 445-8.
        LGW, 373-90, compared with a passage in the
    Convivio.
SAMUEL, L. Semiramis in the Middle Ages: The His-

tory of a Legend. Medievalia et Humanistica (Boulder,
Colorado), 2, 1944, 32.
    PF, 288; LGW, 706 ff.
SCHIRMER, W. F. Boccaccios Werke als Quelle G.
Chaucers. GRM, 12, 1924, 288-304.
SCHOFIELD, WILLIAM H. The Sea-Battle in Chaucer's
Legend of Cleopatra. 139-52, in Anniversary Papers
. . . for George Lyman Kittredge. Ginn, 1913.
SEIBERT, HARRIET. Chaucer and Horace. MLN, 31,
1916, 304-7.
SKEAT, WALTER W. The Legend of Good Women Done
into Modern English. King's Classics. Chatto, 1907.
    See xiii-xiv, where Skeat accepts the A Prologue
as the revised version.
SMITH, ROLAND M. Action at Actium: An Alliterative
Crux in Chaucer. JEGP, 44, 1945, 56-61.
    "He poureth pesen on the haches slidere," LGW,
648. Reply to Mather, above.
    Rev: D. Everett, YWES, 58-9.
----------. The Limited Vision of Saint Bernard. MLN,
61, 1946, 38-44.
    LGW, 16.
    Rev: D. Everett, YWES, 80-1.
----------. Bernard, the Monk: Nota Amplificata. MLN,
62, 1947, 432.
    Supplementary to Hamilton, above.
----------. Five Notes on Chaucer and Froissart. MLN,
66, 1951, 27-32.
    The Absolon Balade, LGW, F249-69.
TATLOCK, JOHN STRONG PERRY. Chaucer and the
Legenda Aurea. MLN, 45, 1930, 296-8.
----------. Chaucer's "Bernard the Monk." MLN, 46,
1931, 21-3.
----------. The Source of the Legend and Other Chau-
ceriana. SP, 18, 1921, 419-28.
----------. Notes on Chaucer: Earlier or Minor Poems.
MLN, 29, 1914, 97-101.
    On Cleopatra's serpent pit, 678-90, and Ariadne's
crown, 2223-4.
TOYNBEE, PAGET. The Author of Chaucer's Book
Cleped Valerie. Acad, 1891, II, 588-9.
TUCKER, SUSIE J. "Sixty" as an Indefinite Number in
Middle English. RES, 25, 1949, 152-3.

TUPPER, FREDERICK. Chaucer's Lady of the Daisies.
JEGP, 21, 1922, 293-317.
     See Manly, above in this section.
----------, and MARBURY B. OGLE. Courtier's Tri-
fles. Chatto and Windus, 1924.
     Translation of Walter Map's De Nugis Curialium,
with introduction and notes.
     For review, see section: Wife of Bath's Tale.
WEBSTER, K. G. T. Two Notes on Chaucer's Sea-
Fight. MP, 25, 1928, 291-2.
     Rev: D. Everett, YWES, 87.
WEESE, WALTER E. Alceste and Joan of Kent. MLN,
63, 1948, 474-7.
     See Galway, above; an examination of her evidence.
     Rev: D. Everett, YWES, 90-1.
WHITNEY, M. P. The Queen of Mediaeval Virtues:
Largesse. Vassar Mediaeval Studies, 1923, 180-215.
WIEN, CLEMENTINE E. The Source of the Subtitle to
Chaucer's Tale of Philomela. MLN, 58, 1943, 605-7.
     LGW, 2228-30. Finds source of Deus Dator Forma-
rum in writings of Arab Avicenna. See Bryant, above.
     Rev: D. Everett, YWES, 47-8.
WILSON, F. P. The Tidy. PQ, 17, 1938, 216-8.
     Reply to U. T. Holmes, above in this section.
WIMSATT, W. K., Jr. Vincent of Beauvais and Chau-
cer's Cleopatra and Croesus. Spec, 12, 1937, 375-81.
YOUNG, KARL. Chaucer's Appeal to the Platonic Deity.
Spec, 19, 1944, 1-13.
     Prints five accessus on Ovid's Metamorphoses
containing the concept of primal forms or ideas al-
luded to in the opening lines of Philomela. See Bryant and Wien, above in this section.
     Rev: D. Everett, YWES, 49-50.

MARS

     See Robinson, 971-4, 1035; French, 90-2; Brusen-
dorff, 261-8; Koch, 25-7; Shannon, 12-13; Hammond,
384-6; Kaluza, 15-16; Root, 63; Legouis, 66; Wells,
CBEL, I, 225, and supplements to the Manual after 1933.

BASKERVILL, CHARLES R. English Songs on the Night
Visit. PMLA, 36, 1921, 594.

BROWNE, WILLIAM H. Notes on Chaucer's Astrology.
   MLN, 23, 1908, 53-4.
      Compleynt of Mars, 54.
COWLING, G. H. Chaucer's "Complaintes of Mars and
   Venus." RES, 2, 1926, 405-10.
EMERSON, OLIVER F. Some Notes on Chaucer and
   Some Conjectures. PQ, 2, 1923, 82-3.
      Lines 113-4.

                     MERCILES BEAUTE

      See Hammond, 436-7; Root, 72; Kaluza, 19; Robin-
   son, 982, 1039-40; French, 104-5; Koch, 40, and
   Chaucerproben, in section: Works Other than the
   Canterbury Tales: General; Legouis, 62; Brusendorff,
   440,489; Wells, 766 [15], CBEL, I, 226, and supplements to the Manual after 1933; Birney, 642.

LOWES, JOHN LIVINGSTON. The Chaucerian Merciles
   Beaute and Three Poems of Deschamps. MLR, 5,
   1910, 33-9.
MERCILES BEAUTE: A TRIPLE ROUNDEL. Percy Fo-
   lios, I, i. Berkeley, Calif: Archetype Press, 1936.
RENWICK, W. L. Chaucer's Triple Roundel, Merciles
   Beaute. MLR, 16, 1921, 322-3.
SALOMON, LOUIS B. The Devil Take Her. A Study of
   the Rebellious Lover in English Poetry. Univ of
   Pennsylvania Press, 1931. 366 pp.
      Discusses Chaucer's Merciles Beaute, 67-9.
      Rev: TLS, April 7, 1932, 253; G. T., MLR, 27,
   1932, 497; G. C. M. S., RES, 9, 1933, 119; P. Meiss-
   ner, AB, 44, 1933, 347-8.
SKEAT, WALTER W. The Chaucerian Merciles Beaute.
   MLR, 5, 1910, 194.

                   NEWFANGELNESSE
                        OR
              AGAINST WOMEN UNCONSTANT

      See Hammond, 440; Root, 78; Robinson, 981-2,
   1039; French, 115; Koch, 39; Brusendorff, 203, 225,
   441; Birney, 641; Wells, CBEL, I, 227, and supplements to the Manual after 1933.

SALOMON, LOUIS B. The Devil Take Her. A Study of
the Rebellious Lover in English Poetry. Univ of
Pennsylvania Press, 1931. 366 pp.
>Discusses Balade Against Women Unconstant, 117.
For reviews, see section: Merciles Beaute.

PARLEMENT OF FOULES

>See Hammond, 387-90; Kaluza, 55-70; Legouis,
82-6, 233-40; Root, 63-8; Robinson, 900-6, 1019-20;
French, 92-7; Brusendorff, 286-9; Koch, 27-39;
Shannon, 13-15; Curry, 195-218, and Texas Rev, 8,
1923, 307; Tatlock, 41; Cummings, 14-18, 132; Wells,
CBEL, I, 226-7; Malone, 61-79; Speirs, 47-8; Clemens, 161 ff. ; Patch, 45.

>For editions and modernizations, see sections so
entitled. Also see Schlauch, in section: General Criticism.

>For discussions of dream poems, see section:
Works Other than the Canterbury Tales: General.

ADOLPHUS, A. E. Chauceriana. NQ, ser. 10, 8, 1907,
202-3.
>On lines 309-13, p. 203.
BOMBARDIER. Chaucer: Ornithologist. Blackwoods,
256, 1944, 120-5.
BRADDY, HALDEEN. Chaucer's Parlement of Foules
in its Relation to Contemporary Events. Doctoral
Diss, New York Univ, 1934. Lancaster Press, Inc,
1932. 101 pp. Also in Three Chaucer Studies, Oxford,
1932.
>For reviews, see section: Life, under Brown,
Carleton, Ed.
----------. The Historical Background of the Parlement
of Foules. RES, 11, 1935, 204-9.
>Reply to Manly's review, RES, 10, 1934, 257-73.
Rejoinder, J. M. Manly, RES, 11, 1935, 209-13.
----------. The Parlement of Foules: A New Proposal.
PMLA, 46, 1931, 1007-19.
>Rev: D. Everett, YWES, 83.
BRIGHT, JAMES W. Minor Notes on Chaucer. MLN, 17,
1902, 278-80.
>Verses 298-301.

BRONSON, BERTRAND H. In Appreciation of Chaucer's
   Parlement of Foules. University of California Publi-
   cations in English, 3, 1935, 193-224. Separately re-
   printed, Univ of California, 1935.
        Rev: Hugo Lange, AB, 47, 1936, 132-3.
----------. The Parlement of Foules Revisited. ELH,
   15, 1948, 247-60.
        Rev: D. Everett, YWES, 89-90.
COOK, ALBERT S. Parlement of Foules, 353. MLN, 21,
   1906, 111-2; 22, 1907, 146.
        On the medieval classification of bees as birds.
DAMON, PHILLIP W. The Parlement of Foules and the
   Pavo. MLN, 67, 1952, 520-4.
DOUGLAS, THEODORE WAYLAND. What Is the Parle-
   ment of Foules? MLN, 43, 1928, 378-84.
        Rev: D. Everett, YWES, 85-6.
EMERSON, OLIVER FARRAR. The Suitors in the Parle-
   ment of Foules. MP, 8, 1910, 45-62.
        Rev: John Koch, AB, 22, 1911, 274-5.
----------. Some Notes on Chaucer and Some Conjec-
   tures. PQ, 2, 1923, 81-95.
        Lines 204-10.
----------. The Suitors in the Parlement of Foules
   Again. MLN, 26, 1911, 109-11.
----------. What Is the Parlement of Foules? JEGP,
   13, 1914, 566-82.
        Reply to Manly, below in this section. See also
   Lange (same title).
FARNHAM, WILLARD EDWARD. The Contending Lov-
   ers. PMLA, 35, 1920, 247-323.
        See 321-3.
----------. The Fowls in Chaucer's Parlement. Univer-
   sity of Wisconsin Studies in Language and Literature,
   2, 1918, 340-66.
----------. The Sources of Chaucer's Parlement of
   Foules. PMLA, 32, 1917, 492-518. Part of Diss, Har-
   vard Univ.
GOFFIN, R. C. Heaven and Earth in the Parlement of
   Foules. MLR, 31, 1936, 493-9.
HAMMOND, ELEANOR P. Chaucer and Dante and their
   Scribes. MLN, 31, 1916, 121.
        PF, 211. See also Miss Hammond's review of Koch,
   A Detailed Comparison, etc., in section: Manuscripts,

and her article, The Nine Syllabled Pentameter Line,
in section: Style.

JONES, H. S. V. Parliament of Fowls, 693 f. MLN, 27,
1912, 95.

KNOWLTON, EDGAR C. The Goddess Nature in Early
Periods. JEGP, 19, 1920, 224-53.

----------. Nature in Middle English. JEGP, 20, 1921,
186-207.

On the allegorical figure, Nature.

----------. Spenser and Nature. JEGP, 34, 1935, 366-
76.

KOCH, JOHN. Alte Chaucerprobleme und neue Lösungs-
versuche. ESt, 55, 1921, 161-225.

PF, 215-25.

----------. Chaucers Boethiusübersetzung. Ang, 46,
1922, 36 ff.

Chronology.

LANGE, HUGO. Hat Chaucer den Kompass Gekannt und
Benutzt? Ang, 58, 1934, 333-44.

Rev: D. Everett, YWES, 89.

----------. Ein neuer Chaucerfund; zu John Kochs
Richard-Anna-theorie (Vogelparlament). ESt, 68,
1933, 174-87.

Rev: D. Everett, YWES, 113-4.

----------. What Is the Parlement of Foules: A Chau-
cernotiz. Ang, 40, 1916, 394-6.

Review and summary of Emerson and Manly, in
this section.

----------. Die Kenntnis der Missweisung oder mag-
netischen Deklination bei dem Londoner Geoffrey
Chaucer (1380). Zugleich ein Beitrag zur Lösung
einiger Chaucerprobleme. Forschungen und Fortschritte, 11, 1935, 156-7.

Rev: D. Everett, YWES, 17, 1936, 72-3.

----------. Zu Chaucers Vogelparlament. Ang, 60,
1936, 397-400.

----------, and A. NIPPOLDT. Die Deklination am 20.
Mai 1380 in London. Quellen und Studien zur Geschichte der Naturwissenschaften, 5, 1936, 38-56.

On PF, verses 113-9 and 148 ff.

LANGE, HUGO. Die Nordnordwest-Stellung der Venus
und der Nordwestwind in Chaucers Vögelparlament.
Ang, 64, 1940, 196-204.

LANGHANS, VICTOR. Altes und neues zu Chaucers
    Parlement of Foules. Ang, 54, 1930, 25-66.
        Rev: D. Everett, YWES, 81-3.
----------. Untersuchungen zu Chaucer. Halle: Niemey-
    er, 1918.
        See 19 ff.
        For reviews, see section: Legend of Good Women.
LOWES, JOHN LIVINGSTON. Chaucer and Dante. MP,
    14, 1917, 706.
        PF, 288-94, 139-56.
LUMIANSKY, R. M. Chaucer's Parlement of Foules: A
    Philosophical Interpretation. RES, 24, 1948, 81-9.
        Rev: D. Everett, YWES, 88-9.
McKEEHAN, IRENE PETTIT. Guillaume de Palerne: A
    Medieval "Best Seller." PMLA, 41, 1926, 785-809.
        Suggestion on meaning of the Parlement, 809.
McLAY, W. S. Imagery and Slang. TLS, Jan 8, 1938,
    28.
        On line 556. A humorous comment.
MALONE, KEMP. Chaucer's Daughter of Cupid. MLR,
    45, 1950, 63.
        PF, 211-6. On "Wille"; corrects Robinson. See
    Pratt, SP, 42, 1945, 745-83.
MANLY, JOHN M. What Is the Parliament of Foules?
    Studien zur englischen Philologie, 50. 279-90, in
    Festschrift für L. Morsbach. Niemeyer, 1913.
        See Emerson and Lange, above.
----------. Three Recent Chaucer Studies. RES, 10,
    1934, 257-73.
        Review of Carleton Brown, Ed. See section: Life.
----------. A Defense of his Criticism of Three Chau-
    cer Studies. RES, 11, 1935, 209-13.
MOFFATT, DOUGLAS M. The Complaint of Nature by
    Alain de Lille Translated from the Latin. Yale Stud-
    ies, 36. Holt, 1908. 95 pp.
        Rev: J. Koch, AB, 20, 1909, 164-6.
MOORE, SAMUEL. A Further Note on the Suitors in the
    Parlement of Foules. MLN, 26, 1911, 8-12.
NELSON, N. E. Cicero's De Officiis in Christian
    Thought: 300-1300. Univ of Michigan Essays and Stud-
    ies in English and Comparative Literature, 10, 1933,
    59-160.
OWEN, CHARLES A., Jr. The Role of the Narrator in

the Parlement of Foules. CE, 14, 1953, 264-9.
PATRICK, DAVID. The Satire in Chaucer's "Parliament
of Birds." PQ, 9, 1930, 61-5.
Rev: D. Everett, YWES, 81-2.
PIEPER, WILLY. The Parlement in Middle English Lit-
erature. Arch, 146, 1923, 187-212.
See note, p. 487, in Stillwell, below in this section.
PRATT, ROBERT ARMSTRONG. Chaucer Borrowing
from Himself. MLQ, 7, 1946, 259-64.
Concerns Invocation to Venus.
Rev: D. Everett, YWES, 69.
----------. Chaucer's Claudian. Spec, 22, 1947, 419-29.
PF, 99-105.
Rev: D. Everett, YWES, 67-8.
----------. Chaucer's Use of the Teseida. PMLA, 62,
1947, 598-621.
REID, MARY E. The Historical Interpretations of the
Parlement of Foules. Univ of Wisconsin Studies, 18,
1923, 60-70.
RICKERT, EDITH. Geoffrey Chaucer: A New Interpre-
tation of the Parlement of Foules. MP, 18, 1920, 1-
29.
ROOT, ROBERT K. Chaucer's Dares. MP, 15, 1917, 1-22.
Chaucer's catalogue of trees, 18-22.
SHACKFORD, MARTHA H. The Date of Chaucer's Hous
of Fame. MLN, 31, 1916, 507-8.
Influence on date of PF.
SLAUGHTER, E. E. "Every Vertu at his Reste." MLN,
46, 1931, 448-53.
PF, 376.
SMITH, ROLAND M. Five Notes on Chaucer and Frois-
sart. MLN, 66, 1951, 27-32.
Candace, PF, 288.
STAHL, WILLIAM H., Ed and Tr. Macrobius' Com-
mentary on the Dream of Scipio. Records of Civiliza-
tion, 48. Columbia Univ Press, 1952. 278 pp.
STILLWELL, GARDINER. Unity and Comedy in Chau-
cer's Parlement of Foules. JEGP, 49, 1950, 470-95.
THACKABERRY, ROBERT E. Chaucer's Parlement of
Foules: A Reinterpretation. Doctoral Diss, Abstract,
Univ of Iowa Studies, n.s., 342, 1937.
TUPPER, FREDERICK. Chaucer's Tale of Ireland.
PMLA, 36, 1921, 197 ff.

PROPHECY

See Hammond, 447-8.

CAMPBELL, GERTRUDE H. Chaucer's Prophecy in
1586. MLN, 29, 1914, 195-6.

PROVERBS OF CHAUCER

See Hammond, 449-50; Robinson, 983, 1040;
French, 114-5; Brusendorff, 284-6, 439; Root, 78;
Wells, CBEL, I, 227, and supplements to the Manual
after 1933.

KITTREDGE, GEORGE L. Chauceriana. MP, 7, 1910,
465-83.
"No man caste his pilche away," 478-9.

PURSE

See Hammond, 392-3; Root, 78; Kaluza, 22-3;
Robinson, 980-1, 1039; French, 113-4; Brusendorff,
253-4; Koch, 101; Wells, CBEL, I, 223-4, and supplements to the Manual after 1933.
For editions, see section: Editions with Notes.

BUHLER, CURT F. A New Lydgate-Chaucer Manuscript.
MLN, 52, 1937, 1-9.
COOK, ALBERT S. Chaucerian Papers. Trans Connec-
ticut Acad. Yale Univ Press, 1919. Pp. 33-8.
HAMMOND, ELEANOR P. Lament of a Prisoner against
Fortune. Ang, 32, 1909, 481-91.
LEGGE, M. DOMINICA. Gracious Conqueror. MLN, 68,
1953, 18-21.
MacCRACKEN, HENRY N. An Odd Text of Chaucer's
Purse. MLN, 27, 1912, 228-9.
PACE, GEORGE BLOCKER. The Texts of Truth, Lak of
Stedfastnesse, and the Purse. Univ of Virginia: Ab-
stracts of Dissertations, 1942, 12-14.
Photostat of Magdalene College, Cambridge MS
2066, now in the Univ of Virginia Library.
Rev: D. Everett, YWES, 24, 1943, 49.
----------. The Text of Chaucer's Purse. Papers of

the Bibl Soc of the Univ of Virginia, 1, 1948, 105-21.
    Rev: D. Everett, YWES, 92-3.
SMITH, ROLAND M. Five Notes on Chaucer and Frois-
    sart. MLN, 66, 1951, 27-32.
        Conquerour of Brutes Albyon, Purse, 22.

THE BALADE OF A REEVE

UTLEY, FRANCIS L. The Crooked Rib. Ohio State Univ
    Press, 1944.
        Accepted by Brusendorff with reservations. See
    the above, 170, where the piece is rejected.
        For reviews, see section: Social Backgrounds.

THE ROMAUNT OF THE ROSE

    See Hammond, 450-4; Kaluza, 27-36; Root, 45-56;
    Robinson, 988-1000, 1043-8; French, 75-82; Brusen-
    dorff, 296, 425; Curry, 195-218, 263-5; Wells, CBEL,
    I, 227-8, and supplements to the Manual after 1933;
    Speirs, 35-40.

BASKERVILL, CHARLES R. English Songs on the Night
    Visit. PMLA, 36, 1921, 569.
        On lines 2646-80.
CHAUCER, GEOFFREY. The Romaunt of the Rose Ren-
    dered out of French into Anglise by Geoffrey Chaucer
    Illustrated by Keith Henderson and Norman Wilkinson.
    Chatto and Windus (Florentine Press), 1918.
COOK, ALBERT S. Chaucer and Venantius Fortunatus.
    MLN, 39, 1924, 376-8.
----------. Two Notes on Chaucer. MLN, 31, 1916, 441-
    2.
        On Fryse, 1093.
FANSLER, DEAN S. Chaucer and the Roman de la Rose.
    Columbia Univ Press, 1914. 269 pp.
        Important bibliography.
        Rev: E. Koeppel, AB, 25, 1914, 203-5; John Koch,
    ESt, 49, 1915, 431-7; Grace E. Hadow, MLR, 11, 1916,
    90-2; Arch, 134, 1916, 466.
FURNIVALL, FRED J., Ed. The Romaunt of the Rose.
    Chaucer Society, 1st ser., 1911, 82.
        Rev: ESt, 46, 1912, 98-114.

GUNN, ALAN M. F. A Reinterpretation of the Roman de
la Rose: A Study in Chaucerian Background. Micro-
film Abstracts, 4, 1943, 109-11. Princeton Univ Diss.
   Rev: D. Everett, YWES, 25, 1944, 56-7.
----------. The Mirror of Love: A Reinterpretation of
the Romance of the Rose. Texas Technological College
Research Publication. Lubbock, Tex: Texas Tech
Press, 1951. Reprint, 1952. 608 pp.
   Bibliography, 524-44; Appendixes: Figures of Am-
plification, Epigraphs and Quotations, Names and
Titles, Subjects and Figures. For references to Chau-
cer, see Names and Titles; Bibliography of Courtly
Love, 327 n.
   Rev: Urban T. Holmes, Jr., PQ, 14, 1953, 465-7;
C. S. L., MA, 22, 1953, 27-31.
HINCKLEY, HENRY B. Chaucer and Ywaine and Gawin.
Acad, 1906, II, 640-1.
   Skeat's reported criticism, Acad, 1906, II, 647;
Hinckley's reply, Acad, 1907, I, 99.
JACK, ADOLPHUS A. A Commentary on the Poetry of
Chaucer and Spenser. Maclehose and Jackson; Macmil-
lan, 1920.
   See 117 ff.
KALUZA, MAX. Erwiderung. Continued reply to Luick.
   See Hammond, 453.
KOCH, JOHN. Alte Chaucerprobleme und neue Lösungs-
versuche. ESt, 55, 1921, 161-225.
   See 161-74.
KUHL, E. P. Chaucer and the Red Rose. PQ, 24, 1945, 33-8.
   Romaunt of the Rose, 1680, 907. Associates the
red rose in Chaucer with Lancaster.
   Rev: D. Everett, YWES, 52.
KUNSTMANN, JOHN G. Chaucer's "Archangel." MLN,
55, 1940, 259-62.
   Line 915.
LANGE, HUGO. Rettungen Chaucers: Neue Beiträge zur
Echtheitsfrage von Fragment A des mittelenglischen
Rosenroman. Ang, 35, 1911, 338-46; 36, 1912, 479-
91; 37, 1913, 146-62; 38, 1914, 477-90.
LANGHANS, VICTOR. Untersuchungen zu Chaucer.
Halle: Niemeyer, 1918.
   See 223 ff.
   For reviews, see section: Legend of Good Women.

LANGLOIS, ERNEST. Les Manuscrits du Roman de la
    Rose par Guillaume de Lorris et Jean de Meun:
    Description et Classement. Lille et Paris, 1910. In-
    troduction, 1914. Text and Notes, 1920.
        See also this author's Origines et Sources du Ro-
    man de la Rose. Paris, 1890. On courtly love.
        Rev: T. A. Jenkins, MP, 19, 1921-2, 424-6.
LOWES, JOHN LIVINGSTON. Chaucer's Boethius and
    Jean de Meun. RR, 8, 1917, 383-400.
MAGOUN, F. P., Jr. Chaucer and the Roman de la
    Rose, vv. 16096-105. RR, 17, 1926, 69-70.
MARY, ANDRE. Roman de la Rose. Pagot, 1928.
        Modern French version.
        Rev: Jacques Laurent, Moyen Age, 39, 1929, 115-7.
PARE, GERARD M. Le Roman de la Rose et la Scolas-
    tique Courtoise. Publ de l'Inst d'Etudes Méd d'Otta-
    wa, 10, 1941.
        Refers to T&C, IV, 960 ff. Philosophic discussion
    of divine knowledge.
        Rev: Bastin, Rev Belge, 23, 354.
RAND, E. K. The Metamorphoses of Ovid in Le Roman
    de la Rose. In Studies in the History of Culture: The
    Discipline of the Humanities, 103. Menasha, Wiscon-
    sin: Banta, 1942. Festschrift for W. G. Leland, pub-
    lished for the Conference of Secretaries of the A. C.
    L. S.
        Rev: S. H. Cross, Spec, 17, 1942, 311-3.
REEVES, W. P. Romance of the Rose, 1705. MLN, 38,
    1923, 124.
SCHOFFLER, HERBERT. Chauceriana. AB, 29, 1918,
    46-8.
        Graynes de Paris, 1369.
SNYDER, EDWARD D. The Wild Irish. MP, 17, 1919-20,
    687-725.
        On lines 3807-11, pp. 712-3.
THOMPSON, D'ARCY, W. "Archangel" as a Bird-Name
    in Chaucer. NQ, 175, 1938, 332.
        Line 915.
        Rev: D. Everett, YWES, 62.
THOMPSON, NESTA M. A Further Study of Chaucer and
    the Romance of the Rose. Doctoral Diss, Stanford,
    1926. Stanford Univ Abstracts of Dissertations, 1,
    1927, 95-101.

"My purpose in this paper is to justify my belief
that the present English version of the Romance of
the Rose is not the work of Chaucer."
WALTER, J. H. Astrophel and Stella and The Romaunt
of the Rose. RES, 15, 1939, 265-73.
WARREN, F. M. On the Date and Composition of
Guillaume de Lorris' Roman de la Rose. PMLA, 23,
1908, 269-84.
WEBSTER, C. M. Chaucer's Turkish Bows. MLN, 47,
1932, 260.
WHITTERIDGE, G. The Word "Archangel" in Chaucer's
Romaunt of the Rose. E and G Studies, 1950.
    Rev: R. M. Wilson, YWES, 30.

TO ROSEMOUNDE

See Hammond, 460-1; Robinson, 974, 1036; French,
105-6; Koch, 39-40; Kaluza, 19; Brusendorff, 437;
Root, 72-3; Wells, CBEL, I, 227; Birney, 641-2.

KOCH, JOHN. Chaucerproben. ES, 53, 1919, 161-7.
    Text and translation into German.
KOKERITZ, HELGE. Chaucer's Rosemounde. MLN, 63,
1948, 310-8.
    Textual editing of the poem from MS.
LOWES, JOHN LIVINGSTON. Illustrations of Chaucer
Drawn Chiefly from Deschamps. Rom Rev, 2, 1911,
128.
    Rev: J. Koch, ES, 46, 1912, 114.
RICKERT, EDITH. A Leaf from a Fourteenth-Century
Letter Book. MP, 25, 1927, 249-55.
    On p. 255 is the suggestion that this poem was
written for the child-wife of Richard II.

SCOGAN

See Hammond, 393; Root, 75-6; Kaluza, 21; Robinson, 978-9, 1038; French, 109-10; Brusendorff, 289-
91; Koch, 100-1; Wells, CBEL, I, 226, and supplements to the Manual after 1933.

BRANDL, ALOIS. Review of William A. Neilson, The
Origins and Sources of the Court of Love, Studies

and Notes (Harvard), 6. Arch, 106, 1901, 390-401.
FARNHAM, WILLARD E. John (Henry) Scogan. MLR,
16, 1921, 120-8.

See also Neil C. Brooks, Scogan's Quem Quaeritis
and Till Eulenspiegel, MLN, 38, 1923, 57; and Willard E. Farnham, Scogan's Quem Quaeritis, MLN,
37, 1922, 289-92.

Suggests John and Henry Scogan were the same
person. On identity of the author of Scogan's Jests.
FRENCH, WALTER C. The Meaning of Chaucer's "En-
voy to Scogan." PMLA, 48, 1933, 289-92.
GOFFIN, R. C. "Lenvoy de Chaucer a Scogan." MLR,
20, 1925, 318-21.
KITTREDGE, GEORGE LYMAN. Henry Scogan. Harvard
Studies and Notes, 1, 1892, 109-17.
----------. Chauceriana. MP, 7, 1910, 465-83.

On lines 38-40, the "rusting" muse and its source.
MOORE, SAMUEL. The Date of Chaucer's Marriage
Group. MLN, 26, 1911, 172-4.

Influence of lines 36-42.
PHIPPS, THOMAS M. Chaucer's Tullius. MLN, 58, 1943,
108-9.

Suggests identification of Scogan, 28, and traces
"Tullius kyndenesse" to Tullius Hostilius.

Rev: D. Everett, YWES, 49.

TROILUS AND CRISEYDE

See Robinson, 922-52, 1023-30; French, 135-91;
Brusendorff, 166-74; Shannon, 120-68, 331-2; Hammond, 395-401; Kaluza, 70-98; Kittredge, 108-45;
Legouis, 121-35; Root, 87-127; Wells, CBEL, I, 228-
30, and supplements to the Manual since 1933; Patch,
56, 104; Shelly, 110-5; Speirs, 48-82; Malone, 100-43;
Dempster, 10-26.

On Lollius, see also section: Literary Relations.

For editions, see section: Editions with Notes.

See also sections: General Criticism, and Modernizations and Translations. On legends of Troy, see
Wells, 106-11.

For other references on courtly love, see section:
Social Backgrounds.

AP ROBERTS, ROBERT P. Criseyde and the Moral of
    Chaucer's Troilus. Univ of California: Summary of
    Thesis in Program of Final Examination, 1950.
----------. Notes on Troilus and Criseyde, IV 1397-
    1414. MLN, 57, 1942, 92-7.
        Rev: D. Everett, YWES, 62-3.
ATWOOD, E. BAGBY. The Rawlinson Excidium Troie,
    a Study of Source Problems in Mediaeval Troy Litera-
    ture. Spec, 9, 1934, 379-404.
        Deals with Dares and Dictys.
----------. The Excidium Troiae and Medieval Troy
    Literature. MP, 35, 1937, 115-28.
----------, and WHITTAKER, VIRGIL K., Eds. Ex-
    cidium Troiae. Medieval Academy of America, 1944.
        Slightly related to Chaucer.
        Rev: H. E. Butler, MA, 13, 1944, 73-6.
AYRES, HARRY M. Chaucer and Seneca. RR, 10, 1919,
    1-15.
        Lines I, 687, 704, 791, 845, 881, 960; II, 22; IV,
    653.
BAKER, MARY CATHARINE. Andre le Chapelain and his
    Relation to Courtly Love. Master's Thesis, Univ of
    Washington, 1935. Typewritten, 262 pp.
        Contains Concerning Love, by Andreas, royal
    chaplain of the French: a partial translation and sum-
    mary of the Latin text of E. Trojel, reprinted in De
    Amore, Libri Tres.
BARNES, NATHANIEL WARING. The Troilus and Cressi-
    da Story since Chaucer, with Special Reference to
    Henryson's Testament of Cresseid. Master's Thesis,
    Columbia Univ, 1905.
BARROW, SARAH F. The Medieval Society Romances.
    Columbia Univ Press, 1924. 141 pp.
        On courtly love, 6-67; on the Troilus, 123-4.
BASKERVILL, CHARLES R. English Songs on the Night
    Visit. PMLA, 36, 1921, 593-4.
        On the use of the "aube."
BAUM, PAULL F. Chaucer's Nautical Metaphors. SAQ,
    49, 1950, 67-73.
        Rev: D. Everett, YWES, 67.
BEATTY, JOSEPH M., Jr. Mr. Graydon's "Defense of
    Criseyde." SP, 26, 1929, 470-81.
        See Graydon and French, in this section.

BENNETT, J. A. W. "Concerning Wade . . ." MLR, 31,
   1936, 202-3.
BENOIT de SAINTE-MAURE. Le Roman de Troie, Pub-
   lié d'après Tous les Manuscrits Connus par Léopold
   Constans. 4 vols. Didot, 1907-12.
BLOOMFIELD, MORTON W. The Source of Boccaccio's
   Filostrato, III, 74-79, and its Bearing on the MS
   Tradition of Lucretius, De Rerum Natura. Class
   Philol, 47, 1952, 162-5.
      Concerns T&C, III, 1-38.
BONNARD, G. A Note on Chaucer's "Troilus and Cri-
   seyde," V, 1637. RES, 5, 1929, 323-4.
      See Day, below in this section.
BOUGHNER, DANIEL C. Elements of Epic Grandeur in
   the Troilus. ELH, 6, 1939, 200-10.
BOYS, RICHARD C. An Unusual Meaning of "Make" in
   Chaucer. MLN, 52, 1937, 351-3.
BRENNAN, MARY MADELINE. The Development of the
   Chief Characters of the Troilus and Cressida Theme.
   Master's Thesis, Univ of Southern California, 1928.
   122 pp. Listed with annotation in Trends in Scholar-
   ship, Univ of Southern California, 1936, 50.
      "A comparative and chronological study . . . em-
   phasizing the Homeric, Vergilian, Chaucerian,
   Shakespearian, and Dryden versions."
BRESSIE, RAMONA. The Date of Thomas Usk's Testa-
   ment of Love. MP, 26, 1928, 17-29.
      Borrowings by Usk.
BROATCH, J. W. The Indebtedness of Chaucer's Troilus
   to Benoît's Roman. JEGP, 2, 1898, 14-29.
      On Lollius. See Hammond, 399.
BROWN, CARLETON. Another Contemporary Allusion
   in Chaucer's Troilus. MLN, 26, 1911, 208-11.
----------. The Author of The Pearl, Considered in the
   Light of his Theological Opinions. PMLA, 19, 1904,
   115-53.
      Contains material on Strode.
BUHLER, CURT F. Notes on the Campsall Manuscript
   of Chaucer's Troilus and Criseyde. Now in the Pier-
   pont Morgan Library. Spec, 20, 1945, 457-60.
      Rev: D. Everett, YWES, 55-6.
BULLETT, GERALD. The Fortunes of Cressida. New
   Statesman, 21, 1923, 361-3.

CAWLEY, A. C. A Note on Chaucer's Prioress and Criseyde. MLR, 43, 1948, 74-7.
    Rev: D. Everett, YWES, 78.
CHAUCER, GEOFFREY. [Chaucer's Troilus and a few
  short poems; reproduced from MS Gg. 4. 27. fol. 5-
  132^r, in the library of Cambridge University.] 115 neg-
  atives mounted on 59 leaves. MLA of America. Collection of Photographic Facsimiles, no. 307. 1935.
  Deposited in the Library of Congress.
    Contains A B C, Scogan, Truth, T&C, and three
  other poems.
---------. The Noble and Amerous Ancyent Hystor-/ry
  of Troylus and Cresyde/ in the Tyme of/ the Syege of
  Troye. Cõpyled by Geffraye/ Chaucer. [London, 1517]
  [San Marino, Calif, 1925.] Facsimile of 141 sheets.
  MLA of America. Collection of Photographic Facsimi-
  les, no. 31. Reproduced from a copy of the second
  edition in the Henry E. Huntington Library. Negative
  deposited in the Library of Congress.
---------. Troilus and Criseyde. n. p. , n. pr. , n. d.
  [Westminster, William Caxton, 1484? London, 1923.]
  Facsimile, 234 mounted leaves. MLA of America.
  Collection of Photographic Facsimiles, no. 14. Re-
  produced from copy C. 11 c. 10 in the British Museum.
  Duplicates may be obtained through the Library of
  Congress.
CLARK, JOHN W. Dante and the Epilogue of the Troilus.
  JEGP, 50, 1951, 1-10.
    Influence of Paradiso, 14 and 22.
COFER, BERNICE GRACE. Chaucer's Religious Con-
  sciousness in Troilus and Criseyde. Univ of Wash-
  ington, Seattle: Abstracts of Theses, 4, 1939, 119-
  20.
COHEN, GUSTAVE. Chretien de Troyes et son Oeuvre.
  Un Grand Romancier d'Amour et d'Aventure au XIIe
  Siècle. Boivin, 1931. 516 pp.
    Rev: Reto R. Bezzola, Zur künstlerischen Persön-
  lichkeit Chretiens. Anlässlich einen neuen Mono-
  graphie, Arch, 167, 1935, 42-54.
COOK, ALBERT S. Chaucer: Troilus and Criseyde 3: 1-
  28. Arch, 119, 1907, 40-54.
---------. Chauceriana. RR, 8, 1917, 210-26.
    See 226, T&C, V, 817.

COPE, JACKSON I. Chaucer, Venus and the "Seventhe
    Spere." MLN, 67, 1952, 245-6.
        T&C, V, 1809.
CUMMINGS, HUBERTIS M. Il Filostrato: The Story of the
    Love of Troilo as It Was Sung in Italian and Is Now Trans-
    lated into English Verse. Princeton Univ Press, 1924.
        See also this author's Chaucer's Indebtedness to
    the Italian Works of Boccaccio.
        Rev: Nathaniel E. Griffin, MLN, 40, 1925, 292-7;
    MLR, 20, 1925, 233.
CURRY, WALTER CLYDE. Destiny in Chaucer's Troi-
    lus. PMLA, 45, 1930, 129-68.
        Rev: D. Everett, YWES, 84-5.
----------. Fortuna Maior. MLN, 38, 1923, 94-6.
DAY, MABEL. Chaucer's "Troilus and Criseyde," v.
    1637. RES, 6, 1930, 73.
        Answer to Bonnard, above in this section.
DEL RE, ARUNDELL. Chaucer's Troilus and Criseide.
    In The Secret of the Renaissance and Other Essays
    and Studies. With a Foreword by L. Binyon. Tokio:
    Kaitakusha, The Japanese Y.M.C.A. Press, 1930.
DENOMY, ALEXANDER. The Two Moralities of Chau-
    cer's Troilus and Criseyde. Trans Royal Soc of Cana-
    da, sec. 2, vol. 44, 1950, 35-46.
        Courtly love. See also this author's articles in
    section: Social Backgrounds.
DE SELINCOURT, ERNEST. Troilus and Criseyde. 50-
    77, in Oxford Lectures on Poetry. Oxford Univ Press,
    1934.
        For review, see section: General Criticism.
DICKINS, BRUCE, Ed. The Testament of Cresseid, by
    Robert Henryson. Limited ed. Porpoise Press, 1925;
    Faber and Faber, 1943. 46 pp.
        Rev: D. Everett, YWES, 103.
DODD, WILLIAM GEORGE. Courtly Love in Chaucer and
    Gower. Harvard Studies in English, 1. Ginn; Milford,
    1913.
        Rev: Karl Young, JEGP, 15, 1916, 154-61; George
    L. Hamilton, AJP, 35, 1914, 87-90.
ELLSWORTH, G. MASON. Troilus II, 1298. MLR, 42,
    1947, 358-9.
        Comment on "yeres two" of widowhood; opposes
    Kirby, below in this section.

EMERSON, OLIVER FARRAR. Chaucer's "Opie of Thebes Fyn." MP, 17, 1919-20, 287-8.

---------. Some Notes on Chaucer and Some Conjectures. PQ, 2, 1925, 81-96.
> See 85 ff.

FARNHAM, WILLARD. The Medieval Heritage of Elizabethan Tragedy. Univ of California Press, 1936. 487 pp.
> Fall of Princes: Chaucer and Lydgate, 129-72.

FLESCHENBERG, O. SCHISSEL von. Daresstudien. Halle: Niemeyer, 1908.

FRENCH, J. MILTON. Defense of Troilus. PMLA, 44, 1929, 1246-51.
> Answer to Graydon. See also Beatty, above in this section.

GALWAY, MARGARET. The Troilus Frontispiece. MLR, 44, 1949, 161-77.
> On Joan of Kent, an addendum with color reproduction from MS 61, Corpus Christi College, Cambridge.
> Rev: D. Everett, YWES, 67.

GOFFIN, R. C. "Here and Howne" in Troilus and Criseyde. IV, 210. MLR, 40, 1945, 208-10.
> Rev: D. Everett, YWES, 56-7.

GOLLANCZ, Sir ISRAEL. The Pearl. Chatto, 1921.
> See xlvi-xlix for material on Strode. See also DNB.

GORDON, R. K., Ed and Trans. The Story of Troilus, as Told by Benoît de Sainte-Maure, Giovanni Boccaccio, Geoffrey Chaucer, Robert Henryson. Dent, 1934. 383 pp.
> Rev: TLS, Oct 11, 1934, 691; K. John, NSt, 8, 1934, 402; G. Tillotson, Fortnightly Rev, 142, 1934, 508-9.

GRAYDON, JOSEPH S. Defense of Criseyde. PMLA, 44, 1929, 141-77.
> See Beatty and French, above in this section.
> Rev: D. Everett, YWES, 113-4.

GRIFFIN, NATHANIEL EDWARD. Chaucer's Portrait of Criseyde. JEGP, 20, 1921, 39-46.

---------. Dares and Dictys. Johns Hopkins Diss. Furst, 1907. 121 pp.
> For reviews, see section: Literary Relations and Sources.

---------, and ARTHUR BECKWITH MYRICK, Trans. The Filostrato of Giovanni Boccaccio. A Translation

with Parallel Text and Introduction. Univ of Pennsylvania, 1930. 505 pp.
   Rev: TLS, Mar 13, 1930, 204; M. B. Ruud, MLN,
   45, 1930, 289.
GRIFFIN, NATHANIEL EDWARD, Ed. Guido de Colum-
nis. Historia Destructionis Troiae. Mediaeval Acad
of America, 1936. 295 pp.
   Edition in Latin with introduction.
   Rev: Robert K. Root, Spec, 12, 1937, 523-4; J. H.
   M., MA, 7, 1938, 56-9; E. Bagby Atwood, MP, 35,
   1938, 448-50; F. M. Powicke, Hist, 23, 1938, 70; S. Harrison Thomson, AHR, 43, 1938, 594-5; A. Vernet, Rev
   Hist, 180, 1937, 151-2; K. M., MLN, 55, 1940, 78.
GUIDO DELLE COLONNE. Historia Trojana. Reproductions of Manuscripts and Rare Printed Books. Now
on deposit in the Library of Congress. Paris: Bibl
Nat, MS. latin 5694. 263 sheets.
----------. Historia Trojana. Brit Mus, Addit. 36671.
148 sheets. Also Paris: Bibl Nat, MS. latin 5695. 145
sheets. Now on deposit in the Library of Congress.
----------. Historia Trojana. Reproductions of Manu-
scripts and Rare Printed Books. Now on deposit in
the Library of Congress. (Scripsit Albertus filius
Jonis Alberti Presbiter, A. D. 1300.) 76 sheets. Also
Brussels: Bibl Royale, MS. 9240. French 13th centu-
ry translation. 197 sheets.
HAGOPIAN, JOHN V. Chaucer's Troilus and Criseyde,
III, 1744-71. Expl, 10, 1951, item 2.
HALL, VESPER TREVOR. Oaths and Swearing in Chau-
cer's Writings. Master's Thesis, Univ of Washington,
1934. Typewritten, 79 pp.
HAMILTON, GEORGE L. The Indebtedness of Chaucer
to Guido delle Colonne's Historia Trojana. Columbia
Univ Press, 1903.
   On Lollius, 1-50.
----------. Troilus and Criseyde V, Argumentum in
Thebaidem. MLN, 23, 1908, 127.
   On the Latin hexameters and on the source of the
   lines following V, 1498.
HAMMERLE, KARL. Das Fortunamotiv von Chaucer
bis Bacon. Ang, 65, 1941, 87-100.
HAMMOND, ELEANOR P. A Burgundian Copy of Chau-
cer's Troilus. MLN, 26, 1911, 32.

HASELMAYER, LOUIS A. The Portraits in Troilus and
    Criseyde. PQ, 17, 1938, 220-3.
HIBBARD, LAURA A. Chaucer's "Shapen was my Sherte."
    PQ, 1, 1922, 222-5.
HILL, ARCHIBALD A. Diomede: The Traditional Devel-
    opment of a Character. 1-25, in Essays and Studies
    in English and Comparative Literature. Univ of
    Michigan Publ Language and Literature, vol. 8. Univ
    of Michigan Press, 1932.
----------. Ilium, the Palace of Priam (with Reference
    to Chaucer and Shakespeare). MP, 30, 1932, 94-6.
HINCKLEY, HENRY B. Chauceriana. MP, 16, 1918-9,
    39-48.
        Lines I, 39-40, 687, 740, 963, 1065; II, 188.
----------. Chauceriana. PQ, 6, 1927, 313-4.
        Parallel with Horace.
HUGHES, HOMER H. Chaucer's Criseyde and her An-
    cestry. Diss, Texas, 1948.
JACK, ADOLPHUS A. A Commentary on the Poetry of
    Chaucer and Spenser. Glasgow: Maclehose and Jack-
    son; Macmillan, 1920.
        See 47 ff.
        For reviews, see section: General Criticism.
JOHNSON, I. Index Criticus Verborum Daretis Phrygii.
    Vanderbilt Univ Diss, privately printed, 1938.
        Rev: Romania, 66, 138 (a notice).
JONES, H. S. V. The Clerk of Oxenford. PMLA, 27,
    1912, 106-15.
        Material on Strode, 112-5.
KELLY, AMY. Eleanor of Aquitaine and her Courts of
    Love. Spec, 12, 1937, 3-19.
KIRBY, THOMAS A. As Good Chepe. (TC, 3, 641.)
    MLN, 48, 1933, 527-8.
----------. A Note on Troilus, II, 1298. MLR, 29, 1934,
    67-8.
----------. "Troilus," II, 1298, Again. MLR, 33, 1938, 402.
----------. Chaucer's Troilus: A Study in Courtly Love.
    Louisiana State Univ Press, 1940. 337 pp.
        Courtly love history illustrated from literature in
    original and translation; selected bibliography, 6 pp.
        Rev: Haldeen Braddy, RES, 16, 1940, 463-5; D. D.
    Griffith, MLQ, 2, 1941, 140; Robert K. Root, MLN,
    56, 1941, 300-1.

KITTREDGE, GEORGE LYMAN. Chaucer's Troilus and
    Guillaume de Machaut. MLN, 30, 1915, 69.
----------. Chauceriana. MP, 7, 1910, 465-83.
        T&C, II, 19-21, 614-6; IV, 1408.
----------. The Date of Chaucer's Troilus and Other
    Chaucer Matters. Chaucer Society, 2nd ser. , 42,
    1909, 82 pp.
        Rev: Arch, 124, 1910, 212-3; John Koch, AB, 22,
    1911, 273-4.
KOON, MAXINE. Analysis and Classification of Diver-
    gences in Troilus and Criseyde from the Filostrato.
    Master's Thesis, Univ of Washington, 1932. Type-
    written, 78 pp.
KORTEN, HERTHA. Chaucers literarische Beziehungen
    zu Boccaccio: Die künstlerische Konzeption der Can-
    terbury Tales und das Lolliusproblem. Hinstorff,
    1920.
        Rev: Walther Fischer, NS, 29, 1921, 172-3.
LANGE, HUGO. Chaucers "Myn Auctour Called Lollius"
    und die Datierung des Hous of Fame. Ang, 42, 1918,
    345-51.
----------. Chaucer and Mandeville's Travels. Archiv,
    174, 1938, 79-81.
        T&C, V, 379-85.
LANGHANS, VICTOR. Untersuchungen zu Chaucer.
    Halle: Niemeyer, 1918.
        See 223 ff.
        For reviews, see section: Legend of Good Women.
LARSEN, SWEN A. The Boat of Chaucer's "connyng":
    Troilus and Criseyde, II, 3-4. NQ, 194, 1949, 332.
        Meaning of "connyng."
        Rev: D. Everett, YWES, 66-7.
LEWIS, CLIVE S. The Allegory of Love: A Study in Med-
    ieval Tradition. Oxford Univ Press, 1936; reprint,
    1948. 378 pp.
        Contains chapters on courtly love, RR, and Chaucer.
        For reviews, see section: General Criticism.
----------. What Chaucer Really Did to "Il Filostrato."
    56-75, in Essays and Studies, vol. 17. Collected by
    W. H. Hadow. Clarendon Press, 1932 for 1931.
        Rev: TLS, May 26, 1932, 385; C. J. Sisson, MLR,
    27, 1932, 495-6; NQ, 163, 1932, 36; D. Everett,
    YWES, 13, 1932, 82-3.

LONG, PERCY WALDRON. From Troilus to Euphues.
    367-76, in Anniversary Papers . . . for George Ly-
    man Kittredge. Ginn, 1913.
LOWES, JOHN LIVINGSTON. The Date of Chaucer's
    Troilus and Criseyde. PMLA, 23, 1908, 285-306.
        Rev: John Koch, ESt, 41, 1909, 126.
----------. The Franklin's Tale, Teseide, and the Fi-
    locolo. MP, 15, 1918, 689-728.
        T&C, III, 1427-9, 1437-40.
----------. The Loveres Maladye of Hereos. MP, 11,
    1914, 491-546.
        T&C, I, 484-7.
        Rev: John Koch, AB, 25, 1914, 332-9. See also
    Lowes, Hereos, Nation, 97, 1913, 233; and Hereos
    Again, MLN, 31, 1916, 185-6.
----------. Simple and Coy: A Note on Fourteenth Cen-
    tury Poetic Diction. Ang, 33, 1910, 440-51.
----------. Chaucer and Dante. MP, 14, 1917, 705-35.
        T&C, III, 1387-93; IV, 22-4, 25-6, 785-91, 1534-40.
LUMIANSKY, R. M. The Function of the Proverbial
    Monitory Elements in Chaucer's Troilus and Criseyde.
    Tulane Studies in English, 2, 1950, 5-48.
        Rev: D. Everett, YWES, 66-7.
MACAULAY, G. C. Review of Hammond on Lollius.
    MLR, 4, 1909, 527.
McCORMICK, Sir WILLIAM S. , and ROBERT K. ROOT.
    Specimen Extracts from Nine Known Unprinted MSS
    of Chaucer's Troilus and from Caxton's and Thynne's
    First Editions. Chaucer Society, 1st ser. , 89. 1914.
        Rev: John Koch, ESt, 48, 1914, 251.
MacCRACKEN, HENRY N. More Odd Texts of Chaucer's
    Troilus. MLN, 25, 1910, 126-7.
McCULLY, BRUCE. Chivalry in Chaucer. Abstract of
    paper, TAPA, 44, 1913, lxv-lxvi.
MAGOUN, FRANCIS P. "Himselven Lik a Pilgrym to
    Desguise": Troilus, V, 1577. MLN, 59, 1944, 176-8.
        Rev: D. Everett, YWES, 49.
MASON, ELLSWORTH G. Troilus, II, 1298. MLR, 42,
    1947, 358-9.
        Opposes Kirby, above.
        Rev: D. Everett, YWES, 82-3.
MAYHEW, A. L. "Dulcarnon" in Chaucer. NQ, ser. 11,
    1, 1910, 505-6.

MAYO, ROBERT D. The Trojan Background of the Troilus. ELH, 9, 1942, 245-56.
  Questions that the impending doom of Troy is a genuine esthetic factor in the poem.
  Rev: D. Everett, YWES, 62.
MEECH, SANFORD BROWN. Chaucer and an Italian Translation of the Heroides. PMLA, 45, 1930, 110-28.
  For review, see section: Literary Relations.
----------. Figurative Contrasts in Chaucer's Troilus and Criseyde. Eng Inst Essays, 1950, ed by Alan S. Downer, 57-88.
MENNER, ROBERT J. The Man in the Moon and Hedging. T&C, I, 1024. JEGP, 48, 1949, 1-14.
MEYER, EMIL. Die Charakterzeichnung bei Chaucer. Studien zur englischen Philologie, 48. Halle: Niemeyer, 1913.
  For reviews, see section: General Criticism.
MIZENER, ARTHUR. Character and Action in the Case of Criseyde. PMLA, 54, 1939, 65-81.
  Crisyede's character fixed, not changing.
MOORE, ARTHUR K. Middle English Verse Epistles. MLR, 44, 1949, 86-7.
  On "Go, litel bok," T&C, V, 1786.
  Rev: G. D. Willcock, YWES, 85.
MURRY, JOHN MIDDLETON. Troilus and Cressida. Adelphi, 1, 1923, 151-4.
MUSCATINE, CHARLES. The Feigned Illness in Chaucer's Troilus and Criseyde. MLN, 63, 1948, 372-7.
  Rev: D. Everett, YWES, 85.
NEFF, SHERMAN B. Chaucer's Pandarus. Western Humanities Rev, 4, 1950, 343-8.
  Rev: D. Everett, YWES, 67.
----------. Chaucer's Cressida, "lufsom lady dere." 45-51, in Elizabethan Studies in Honor of George F. Reynolds. Colorado Univ Stud in Lang and Lit: Series B, Studies in Humanities, 1945.
  Rev: D. Everett, YWES, 56.
OLSON, GRACE ANDERSON. The Peculiar Features in the Fifth Book of Chaucer's Troilus and Criseyde. Unpubl Master's Thesis, Univ of Chicago Library, 1940.
OWEN, CHARLES A., Jr. Chaucer's Troilus and Criseyde, II, 925-31. Expl, 9, 1951, item 26.

PADELFORD, FREDERICK M. Transition English Song
    Collections. Cambridge History of English Literature,
    2, 444. Putnam, 1908.
        On the "aube."
PARDEE, CHARLOTTE CAROLINE. A Comparison of
    Boccaccio's Filostrato with Chaucer's Troilus and
    Criseyde. Master's Thesis, Columbia Univ, 1925.
PARIS, GASTON. Le Conte de la Charrette (II, of Lan-
    celot du Lac). Romania, 12, 1883, 459-534.
        L'Esprit du Poème de Chrétien, 516-34, on court-
    ly love.
----------. [Les Cours d'Amour du Moyen Age.] Jour-
    nal des Savants, ser. 3, 53, 1888, 664-75, 727-36.
        Review of above title by E. Trojel, covering
    "whole subject of the authenticity of the courts of love. "
PARSONS, A. E. The Trojan Legend in England. MLR,
    24, 1929, 253-64, 394-408.
        The legend's treatment by Geoffrey of Monmouth,
    and its political applications.
PATCH, HOWARD R. Chauceriana. ES, 65, 1931, 351-9.
        See 357-9.
----------. Troilus on Determinism. Spec, 6, 1931,
    225-43.
        Rev: D. Everett, YWES, 84.
----------. Troilus on Predestination. JEGP, 17, 1918,
    399-422.
PERNICONE, V. I Manoscritti del Filostrato di G.
    Boccaccio. Studi di Filologia Italiana. Boll della R.
    Accademia della Crusca, 5, Firenze, 1938, 41 ff.
PIEPER, WILLY. The Parlement in Middle English
    Literature. Arch, 146, 1923, 187-212.
PRATT, ROBERT ARMSTRONG. A Geographical Prob-
    lem in Troilus and Criseyde. MLN, 61, 1946, 541-3.
        Rev: D. Everett, YWES, 81.
----------. Chaucer's Claudian. Spec, 22, 1947, 419-29.
        T&C, V, 1020.
        Rev: D. Everett, YWES, 67-8.
----------. Chaucer's Use of the Teseida. PMLA, 62,
    1947, 598-621.
PRESTAGE, EDGAR, Ed. Chivalry: A Series of Studies
    to Illustrate its Historical Significance and Civilizing
    Influence, by members of King's College, London.
    Knapp, 1928. 231 pp.

For reviews and note, see section: Literary Re-
lations.
PRESTON, RAYMOND. Chaucer and the Ballades Notées
of Guillaume de Machaut. Spec, 26, 1951, 615-23.
    T&C, V, 561-81; III, 463-4, 1456-63.
PURCELL, J. M. The Troilus Verse. PQ, 12, 1933, 90-1.
READ, WILLIAM A. On Chaucer's Troilus and Criseyde
    I, 228. JEGP, 20, 1921, 397-8.
ROBERTSON, D. W., Jr. Chaucerian Tragedy. ELH,
    19, 1952, 1-37.
    T&C as a tragedy.
ROLLINS, C. P. A Leaf from the Kelmscott Chaucer.
Limited ed. Duschnes, 1941.
ROLLINS, HYDER E. The Troilus-Criseyde Story from
Chaucer to Shakespeare. PMLA, 32, 1917, 383-429.
ROOT, ROBERT KILBURN, Ed. The Book of Troilus
and Criseyde. Edited from all the known MSS. Prince-
ton Univ Press, 1926. 573 pp.
    Rev: D. Everett, YWES, 77-8; TLS, Aug 19, 1926,
    547; F. N. Robinson, Spec, 1, 1926, 461-7; John S. P.
    Tatlock, SRL, 3, 1926, 362; Karl Young, MLN, 41,
    1926, 537-45; E. Einenkel, AB, 37, 1926, 265-8;
    John M. Manly, NR, 50, 1927, 26; George N. Shuster,
    Commonweal, 5, 1926, 220-1; A. J. Wyatt, RES, 3,
    1927, 240-1; E. P. Hammond, AB, 38, 1927, 315-8;
    J. Koch, ESt, 64, 1929, 84-100; W. F. Schirmer, NS,
    36, 1928, 33-5; J. R. Hulbert, MP, 24, 1926, 243-4.
----------. Chaucer's Dares. MP, 15, 1917, 1-22.
    Chaucer's Trojan Portraits, 6-18, and Joseph of
    Exeter as source.
----------. The MSS of Chaucer's Troilus and Criseyde
    with 23 Collotype Facsimiles of the MSS. Chaucer So-
    ciety, 1st ser., 98, 1915.
----------, and HENRY N. RUSSELL. A Planetary
    Date for Chaucer's Troilus. PMLA, 39, 1924, 48-63.
ROOT, ROBERT K. Shakespeare Misreads Chaucer.
    MLN, 38, 1923, 346-8.
----------. The Textual Tradition of Chaucer's Troilus.
    Chaucer Society, 1st ser., 99, 1916.
    Rev: J. Douglas Bruce, MLN, 34, 1919, 37-40.
SACKETT, SAMUEL. Correspondence. English, 8, 1951,
    264-5.
    Inquiry about "haselwoode," T&C, V, 505, 1174; III, 890.

ST MARIE, LOUIS HAROLD. The Humility Element in
    Chaucer's Troilus and Criseyde in Relation to the
    Courtly Love Tradition. MS Thesis, Univ of Washing-
    ton Libraries, 1946.
SAMS, HENRY W. The Dual Time-Scheme in Chaucer's
    Troilus. MLN, 56, 1941, 94-100.
        Showing (1) the actual basic time-scheme of three
    years and (2) the practical, artistic scheme of one
    year shown by nature images.
SCHAAR, CLAES. Troilus' Elegy and Criseyde's. Stud
    Neophil, 24, 1952, 185-91.
SCHLAUCH, MARGARET. Medieval Narrative. A Book
    of Translations. Prentice-Hall, 1929. 456 pp.
        Dares' Fall of Troy, 243-79.
SCHOFIELD, WILLIAM H. Chivalry in English Litera-
    ture: Chaucer, Malory, Spenser, Shakespeare. Har-
    vard Studies in Comparative Literature, vol. 2. Har-
    vard Univ Press, 1912. 294 pp.
        Chaucer, 11-72.
        Rev: Thomas Mühe, AB, 30, 1919, 158-61; R. Ack-
    ermann, LGRP, 35, 1914, 283-4.
SEIBERT, HARRIET. Chaucer and Horace. MLN, 31,
    1916, 304-7.
SHANLEY, JAMES L. The Troilus and Christian Love.
    ELH, 6, 1939, 271-81.
        On the ending of the poem.
SHANNON, EDGAR F. Chaucer and Lucan's Pharsalia.
    MP, 16, 1919, 609-14.
SLAUGHTER, EUGENE A. Chaucer's Pandarus: Virtu-
    ous Uncle and Friend. JEGP, 48, 1949, 186-95.
        Rev: YWES, 65.
SMITH, FRED M. Chaucer's Prioress and Criseyde.
    West Virginia Univ Bull: Philological Papers, 6, 1949,
    1-11.
        T&C, V, 806 ff. and especially "slydynge of co-
    rage," line 835.
        Rev: D. Everett, YWES, 65-6.
SMITHERS, G. V. A Middle English Idiom and its An-
    tecedents. E and G Stud, 1948.
        "I bidde wisshe yow no more sorwe," T&C, II,
    406.
SPARGO, JOHN W. Chaucer's "Kankedort." T&C, II,
    1752. MLN, 64, 1949, 264-6.

Suggests derivation from "kankered ort," a place of crablike and irregular movements.
Rev: R. M. Wilson, YWES, 25-6.

SPEIRS, JOHN. Chaucer: (1) Troilus and Criseyde. Scrutiny, 9, 1942, 84-108.

SPITZER, LEO. "Kanke(r)dort," a State of Suspense, a Difficult Position. MLN, 64, 1949, 502-4.
Suggests "quandary" as a related word in reply to and doubt of Spargo's derivation, "kankered ort."
Rev: R. M. Wilson, YWES, 25-6.

STEARNS, M. W. Robert Henryson and the Leper Cresseid. MLN, 59, 1944, 265-9.

STEVENS, JAMES W. A Classification of Amplification and Addition in Troilus and Criseyde. Master's Thesis, Univ of Washington, 1936. Typewritten, 107 pp.

STROUD, THEODORE A. Boethius' Influence on Chaucer's Troilus. MP, 49, 1951, 1-9.

TATLOCK, JOHN STRONG PERRY. Dante and Guinicelli in Chaucer's Troilus. MLN, 35, 1920, 443.

----------. Notes on Chaucer: Earlier or Minor Poems. MLN, 29, 1914, 97-101.
Bells ringing without hands, T&C, III, 188-9; IV, 788; V, 1791-2; Chaucer and Dante.

----------. The Date of the Troilus: and Minor Chauceriana. MLN, 50, 1935, 277-96.
Rev: D. Everett, YWES, 98-9, 105.

----------. The Epilog of Chaucer's Troilus. MP, 18, 1920-1, 625-59.

----------. The Welsh Troilus and Cressida and its Relation to Elizabethan Drama. MLR, 10, 1915, 265-82.

----------. The People in Chaucer's Troilus. PMLA, 56, 1941, 85-104.

TUCKER, SAMUEL MARION. Chaucer's Troilus and Criseyde as an Epos. Master's Thesis, Columbia Univ, 1901.

TUPPER, FREDERICK. The Envy Theme in Prologue and Epilogues. JEGP, 16, 1917, 551-72.

VAN DOREN, MARK. The Noble Voice: A Study of Ten Great Poems. New York: Holt, 1946.
Essay on T&C, 257-82.

WAGER, WILLIS J. "Fleshly Love" in Chaucer's Troilus. MLR, 34, 1939, 62-6.

WALCUTT, CHARLES CHILD. The Pronoun of Address in Troilus and Criseyde. PQ, 14, 1935, 282-7.

Rev: D. Everett, YWES, 99.

WALKER, HAZEL PEARL. Chaucer's Use of Proverbs in Troilus and Criseyde. Master's Thesis, Univ of Iowa, 1932.

WELLS, JOHN E. A Manual of the Writings in Middle English. Yale Univ Press, 1916.

On Legends of Troy, 106-11, 779-80. On Lollius, 664-5, 872-3. Also see CBEL, I, 228-30, and supplements to this Manual after 1933.

WENNER, FLORENCE WILLIAMS. Troilus and Crisyde (sic). Three Versions. Master's Thesis, Univ of Arizona, 1933.

WHITING, B. J. Troilus and Pilgrims in War Time. MLN, 60, 1945, 47-9.

Additional examples to Magoun, above in this section, from Giraldus and Froissart. T&C, V, 1577.

WILCOX, JOHN. French Courtly Love in English Composite Romances. Papers of Michigan Academy of Science, Arts, and Letters, 18, 1933, 575-90.

WILKINS, ERNEST H. Criseida. MLN, 24, 1909, 65-7.

MS reading of this name in the Filostrato.

----------. Cantus Troili. ELH, 16, 1949, 167-73.

Relation to no. 132 of Petrarch's Canzoniere.

Rev: D. Everett, YWES, 66.

WRENN, C. L. Chaucer's Knowledge of Horace. MLR, 18, 1923, 286-92.

WRIGHT, PHINEAS PERSONS. A Comparison of Chaucer's Troilus and Criseyde with Boccaccio's Il Filostrato. Master's Thesis, Univ of Virginia, 1931.

WYCLIFFE, JOHN. [Responsis ad XVIII Argumenta Strode; a Reproduction of MS 3929, folios 218a-223a in the National Library, Vienna.] 11 sheets on 11 l. MLA of America. Collection of Photographic Facsimiles, no. 62. 1927. Deposited in the Library of Congress.

"The original is a 15th century manuscript."

YOUNG, KARL. Aspects of the Story of Troilus and Criseyde. Univ of Wisconsin Studies in Language and Literature, 2, 1918, 367-94.

For bibliography of courtly love material,
367 n.
----------. Chaucer's Renunciation of Love in Troilus.
MLN, 40, 1925, 270-6.
On the Epilogue.
----------. The Origin and Development of the Story of
Troilus and Criseyde. Chaucer Society, 2nd ser., 40,
1908.
On Lollius, 189-95, and Koch's review, 125-6.
Rev: John Koch, ESt, 41, 1910, 121-6.
----------. Chaucer's Troilus and Criseyde as Romance.
PMLA, 53, 1938, 38-63.
Rev: D. Everett, YWES, 69-70.

TRUTH

See Robinson, 976-7, 1036-7; French, 106-7; Bru-
sendorff, 245-52; Koch, 96-7; Hammond, 401-3;
Root, 73-4; Kaluza, 19; Legouis, 68; Wells, CBEL,
I, 227, and supplements to the Manual after 1933.

HERAUCOURT, W. What Is Trouthe or Soothfastnesse.
In Englische Kultur in sprachwissenschaftlicher
Deutung. Max Deutschbein zum 60. Geburtstage, 75-
84. Leipzig: Quelle und Meyer, 1936.
JONES, CLAUDE. Chaucer's "Truth" Modernized, 1756.
NQ, 171, 1936, 455.
KITTREDGE, GEORGE L. Lewis Chaucer or Lewis
Clifford? MP, 14, 1917, 513-8.
MacCRACKEN, HENRY N. Notes Suggested by a Chau-
cer Codex. MLN, 23, 1908, 213.
MANLY, JOHN M. Note on the Envoy of Truth. MP, 11,
1913, 226.
PACE, GEORGE B. The Text of Chaucer's Truth, Lak
of Stedfastnesse, and the Purse. Univ of Virginia:
Abstracts of Dissertations, 1942, 12-14.
Photostat of Magdalene College, Cambridge MS
2066, secured through Pace for the Univ of Virginia
Library. See Utley, Crooked Rib, 276.
Rev: D. Everett, YWES, 24, 1943, 49.
RAGAN, JAMES F. The "Hevenlich Mede" in Chaucer's
Truth. MLN, 68, 1953, 534-5.
Suggests that "mede" means "meadow" here.

RICKERT, EDITH. Thou Vache. MP, 11, 1913, 209-25.
    Identification of Vache, a friend of Chaucer.
ROBERTSON, D. W., Jr. Historical Criticism. Engl
    Inst Essays, 1950, 3-31. Columbia Univ Press, 1951.
    On Truth.

VENUS

    See Robinson, 978, 1038; French, 112-3; Brusen-
dorff, 261-8; Koch, 100; Hammond, 404; Kaluza, 22;
Root, 77; Wells, CBEL, I, 223, and supplements to
the Manual after 1933.

BRADDY, HALDEEN. Sir Oton de Graunson -- 'Flour of
    Hem that Make in Fraunce.' SP, 35, 1938, 10-24.
        Venus, line 82.
----------. Chaucer and the French Poet Graunson.
    Louisiana State Univ Press, 1947. 100 pp.
        For reviews, see section: Literary Relations.
COHEN, HELEN L. The Ballade. Columbia Univ Press,
    1915.
        For reviews, see section: General Criticism.
COWLING, G. H. Chaucer's "Complaintes of Mars and
    Venus." RES, 2, 1926, 405-10.
GRANSON, OTON de. Complainte amoureuse de Sainct
    Valentin [by] Gransson [reproduced from MS français.
    1131, fol. 69-71 (recto) in the Bibliothèque nationale,
    Paris.] 5 sheets on 3 l. MLA of America. Collection
    of Photographic Facsimiles, no. 67. 1927. Deposited
    in Library of Congress.
        "The original is a 15th century manuscript."
PIAGET, ARTHUR. Oton de Granson et ses Poesies.
    Romania, 19, 1890, 237-59, 403-48.

WOMANLY NOBLESSE

    See Hammond, 463; Robinson, 974, 1036; French,
117; Brusendorff, 276-8; Wells, CBEL, I, 227; Root,
79.

WORDS UNTO ADAM
OR
CHAUCER'S WORDS UNTO ADAM,
HIS OWNE SCRIVEYN

See Robinson, 1036; French, 102; Brusendorff, 276-
8; Koch, 40; Hammond, 405; Kaluza, 18; Root, 69-70;
Legouis, 71; Wells, CBEL, I, 223, and supplements
to the Manual since 1933.

BRESSIE, RAMONA. Chaucer's Scrivener. TLS, May 9,
1929, 383; John M. Manly, TLS, May 16, 1929, 403;
Bernard M. Wagner, TLS, June 13, 1929, 474.
HAMMOND, ELEANOR P. Chaucer and Dante and their
Scribes. MLN, 31, 1916, 121.
KUHL, ERNEST P. A Note on Chaucer's Adam. MLN,
29, 1914, 263-4.
   Scriveners of Chaucer's day.
ROOT, ROBERT K. Publication before Printing. PMLA,
28, 1913, 417-31.
   "It is the purpose of this paper to set forth on the
basis of contemporary evidence the conditions of pub-
lication which prevailed in Western Europe during the
14th and early 15th centuries."

WRETCHED ENGENDERING

For other references on Pope Innocent, see section: Man of Law's Tale.

BROWN, BEATRICE DAW. Chaucer's Wreched Engen-
drynge. MP, 35, 1938, 325-33.
   A reply to Germaine Dempster's An Holy Medyta-
cion.
BROWN, CARLETON. An Affirmative Reply [to Tatlock
and Dempster on authorship of An Holy Medytacion].
MLN, 51, 1936, 296-300.
----------. Chaucer's Wreched engendring. PMLA, 50,
1935, 997-1011.
DEMPSTER, GERMAINE. Chaucer's Wretched Engender-
ing and An Holy Medytacion. MP, 35, 1937, 27-9.
----------. Did Chaucer Write "An Holy Medytacion"?
MLN, 51, 1936, 284-95.

FISCHER, W. [Review of Brown, Dempster, and Tatlock on the Wretched Engendering.] AB, 47, 1936,
291-2.
    See also Dorothy Everett, YWES, 70-2.
GASCOIGNE, GEORGE. The Droome of Doomes Day.
Imprinted at London for Gabriell Cawood: dwelling in
Paules Churchyard, at the Signe of the holy Ghost,
1576. In George Gascoigne, The Glasse of Governe-
ment/ The princely Pleasures at Kenelworth Castle/
The Steele Glass, and Other Poems and Prose Works,
edited by John W. Cunliffe, Cambridge at the University Press, 1910.
    See The first Booke of the Vewe of Worldly Vani-
ties, 217-74, which is reported by Cunliffe as a translation of De Contemptu Mundi. Felix E. Schelling
(The Life and Writings of George Gascoigne, 96-7)
states that the first part of the Droome of Doomes
Day is a translation of Pope Innocent III, De Contemptu Mundi, and that Gascoigne is "both careful and ac-
curate in his work."
    Contributed by David C. Fowler.
INNOCENT III. De Contemptu Mundi. Reproductions of
Manuscripts and Rare Printed Books. Now on deposit
in the Library of Congress. Brit Mus, MS. Royal 7
D xvii, fols. 184-212. 29 sheets.
KOEPPEL, E. Chaucer und Innocenz der Dritten Trak-
tat De Contemptu Mundi. Arch, 84, 1890, 405-18
(Hammond, 92). Nachtrag, Arch, 85, 1890, 48.
TATLOCK, JOHN STRONG PERRY. Has Chaucer's
"Wretched Engendering" Been Found? MLN, 51, 1936,
275-84.
WEBSTER, MILDRED. The Vocabulary of An Holy Medy-
tacion. PQ, 17, 1938, 359-64.
    Shows the vocabulary of An Holy Medytacion to be
similar to Chaucer's.

GENERAL BACKGROUNDS
INCLUDING HISTORICAL
AND PHILOSOPHIC BACKGROUNDS

See French, 1-43; Manly, 44-67; Root, 1-13; Malone, 1-18. See also CBEL, I, 115-9, The Political
Backgrounds (M. McKisack); 119-24, The Social Backgrounds (D. C. Douglas); and 124-7, Education (T. A.
Walker; rev: G. R. Potter and J. W. Adamson).

ACKERMAN, ROBERT W. Armor and Weapons in the
Middle English Romances. Research Studies, State
College of Washington, 7, 1939, 104-18.
ANON. Chaucer's England Revived. Review of Reviews,
48, 1913, 205-7.
    Illustrated description of pageant reproducing the
Canterbury pilgrimage.
BEARD, CHARLES A. The Office of Justice of the Peace
in England. Columbia Univ Press, 1904.
BELL, H. E. The Price of Books in Mediaeval England.
Library, 17, 1936, 312-32.
BENHAM, ALLEN R. English Literature from Widsith
to Chaucer -- A Source Book. Yale Univ Press, 1916.
634 pp.
    Sections on political, social, and industrial back-
grounds, gilds and trade, religious orders, city life,
cultural and linguistic backgrounds, and literary
characteristics. Chaucer, 605-13.
    For reviews, see section: General Criticism.
BENHAM, WILLIAM, and CHARLES WELCH. Mediae-
val London. Seeley, 1901.
    Profusely illustrated.
BENNETT, H. S. England from Chaucer to Caxton. Methuen, 1928. 246 pp.
    Collection of passages illustrating English life.
Chaucer, 73-4 and 179-83.
BESANT, Sir WALTER. Mediaeval London. London: A
& C Black, 1906. 2 vols.

BLAND, D. S. Chaucer and the Inns of Court: A Reexamination. E Stud, 33, 1952, 145-55.

BOEHNER, PHILOTHEUS. Medieval Logic: An Outline of its Development from 1250 to c1400. Univ of Chicago Press; Manchester Univ Press, 1952. 130 pp.

BOYNTON, PERCY H. Chaucer's London. Chautauquan, 60, 1910, 41-64.

----------. London in English Literature. Univ of Chicago Press, 1913. 346 pp.

    Chaucer's London, 1-33.

    Rev: Athenaeum, 1913, II, 307; C. E. Rhodes, Chautauquan, 71, 1913, 270; Nation, 97, 1913, 238.

BRENDON, J. A. The Age of Chaucer. Blackie, 1924. 80 pp.

    A book for elementary students.

BRESSIE, RAMONA. A Medieval Library of the Fifteenth Century: MS Sloane 35. 48 fol. 158. MLN, 54, 1939, 246-56.

BUHLER, J. Die Kultur des Mittelalters. A. Kroner, 1931. 360 pp.

C., H. H. E. English Monastic Scriptoria. Bodleian Quarterly Record, 4, July, 1924.

CALENDAR of the Close Rolls. Richard II. Vol. 5, 1392-1396. H. M. Stationery Office, 1925. Vol. 6, 1396-1399. 1927. 753 pp. Henry IV, Vol. 1, 1399-1402. 1927. 597 pp. Vol. 2, 1402-1405. 1929. 529 pp. Vol. 3, 1405-1409. 1931. 530 pp.

    Rev: NQ, 149, 1925, 161; Charles Clay, Antiquaries Jour, 6, 1926, 212-3; 8, 1928, 120-2.

CALENDAR of the Fine Rolls, Preserved in the Public Record Office. Richard II, Vol. 9, 1377-1383. H. M. Stationery Office, 1927. 542 pp. Vol. 10, Richard II, 1388-1391. 1929. 513 pp. Vol. 11, Richard II, 1391-1399. 1929. 433 pp. Vol. 12, Henry IV, 1379-1405. 1931. 460 pp.

    Rev: James F. Willard, Spec, 3, 1928, 408-10; A. S., Hist, 16, 1932, 374.

CAMBRIDGE MEDIEVAL HISTORY. Vols. 1-8, 1924-1936. Planned by the late J. B. Bury and edited by J. R. Tanner, C. W. Previte-Orton, and Z. N. Brooke. Macmillan and Cambridge Univ Press, 1924-36. 8 vols.

    Relevant material in Vols. 5, 6, 7, and 8; chapters on The Monastic Orders; Commerce and Industry;

The Medieval Universities; Chivalry; England: Edward
III and Richard II; The Jews in the Middle Ages; Peas-
ant Life and Rural Conditions; Political Theory in the
Later Middle Ages; Magic; Witchcraft, Astrology, and
Alchemy; Education in the Fourteenth and Fifteenth
Centuries; and Painting, Sculpture, and the Arts.
Volume of maps published 1936.
    Rev: Vol. 5: Am Pol Sci Rev, 20, 1926, 919; G. G.
Coulton, Nation and Athen, 39, 1926, 505; R. S., Sat
Rev, 141, 1926, 654; C. H. Haskins, SRL, 3, 1926,
51; TLS, May 27, 1936, 351. Vol. 6: D. C. Munro,
AHR, 36, 1930, 105; Am Pol Sci Rev, 24, 1930, 797;
G. G. Coulton, Nation and Athen, 46, 1930, 543; New
Statesman, 34, 1930, 504; Sat Rev, 149, 1930, 330; C.
H. Haskins, SRL, 6, 1931, 1087; Spect, 144, 1930, 63;
TLS, Feb 20, 1930, 129. Vol. 7: Sat Rev, 154, 1932,
134; Spect, 149, 1932, 134; Spect, 149, 1932, 318; TLS,
Sept 15, 1932, 635. Vol. 8: G. G. Coulton, N St, 11,
1936, 767; A. L. Rowse, Spect, 156, 1936, 889; F. M.
Powicke, EHR, 52, 1937, 690-2; V. H. Galbraith,
Hist, 22, 1937, 267-9; TLS, Nov 21, 1936, 944; J. W.
Thompson, SRL, 14, Sept 5, 1936, 16-17; K. Feiling,
Obs, April 26, 1936; L. W. Eshelman, New York
Times Book Rev, June 14, 1936, 18; J. McS., CW,
144, 1936, 246-7; G. N. Schuster, Commonweal, 24,
1936, 489-90; O. Evennett, Dublin Rev, 199, 1936,
283-99; Carl Stephenson, AHR, 43, 1938, 351-5; MA,
7, 1938, 134-7.
CHAYTOR, H. J. The Troubadours and England. Cam-
bridge Univ Press, 1923.
    For reviews, see section: Literary Relations.
CHEYNEY, EDWARD P. Dawn of a New Era: 1250-1453.
Harpers, 1936.
CLARKE, MAUDE V. Forfeitures and Treason in 1388.
Royal Historical Society Transactions, ser. 4, 14,
1931, 65-94.
    Reference to Chaucer.
----------. Fourteenth Century Studies. Ed by L. S.
Sutherland and M. McKisack. Oxford, 1937. 317 pp.
    Rev: Charles Johnson, Hist, 22, 1938, 354-5; G.
L. Haskins, AHR, 43, 1938, 597-8.
CLAY, RICHARD. A Book of Printing Types and Orna-
ments Used by Richard Clay and Sons at the Chaucer

Press, Bungay. Bungay, Suffolk, Chaucer Press, 1930.

CLINE, RUTH HUFF. Tournaments of English and French Literature Compared with Those of History: 1100-1500. Unpubl Diss, Univ of Chicago Library, 1940.

COOK, ALBERT S. A Literary Middle English Reader. Ginn, 1915.

Selections of special interest: Tales, 117-98; A Pilgrimage of Compostella, 261; Illustrations of Life and Manners, 361-87; Lyrics, 406-75; Plays, 476-524.

COULTON, GEORGE GORDON. Chaucer and his England. Methuen; Putnam, 1908. 3rd ed, Dutton, 1921; 4th ed, Methuen, 1927; 5th ed, Methuen; Dutton, 1937; 8th ed, Dutton, 1950, ill.

Rev: G. C. Macaulay, MLR, 4, 1909, 525; H. B. Fuller, The Freeman, 6, 1922, 93-4; Nation, 87, 1909, 443-4; Dial, 46, 1909, 185-6.

----------. The Chronicler of European Chivalry (Froissart). The Studio, 1930. 133 pp.

Notable for its illustrations and plates, of medieval origin, reprinted from MSS. Several references to Chaucer.

Rev: T. S. R. Boase, Hist, 16, 1931, 161-2.

----------. Life in the Middle Ages. Selected, Translated and Annotated. Cambridge Univ Press. Vol. 1, Religion, Folk-Lore, and Superstition, 1928. 246 pp. Vol. 2, Chronicles, Science and Art, 1929. 183 pp. Vol. 3, Men and Manners, 1929. 170 pp. Vol. 4, Monks, Friars and Nuns, 1929. 380 pp. Also published 4 vols. in 1, Macmillan, 1930, ill.

Rev: P. J. Heather, Folk-Lore, 39, 1928, 190-5; T. Hampe, DL, 1929, 681-3; P. J. Heather, Folk-Lore, 40, 1929, 103-6; W. F. Schirmer, AB, 42, 1931, 7-8; M. Rösler, ESt, 65, 446-7; R. F. Trehearne, Hist, 16, 1931, 247.

----------. The Medieval Scene. An Informal Introduction to the Middle Ages. Cambridge Univ Press, 1930. 163 pp.

Rev: C. Wright, Commonweal, 14, 1931, 22-4; E. C. Lodge, Hist, 16, 1931, 154-5.

----------. The Medieval Village. Cambridge Studies in

Medieval Life and Thought. Cambridge Univ Press, 1925. 635 pp.

Rev: NQ, 150, 1926, 53-4; Margarete Rösler, ESt, 63, 1928, 163-6; P. J. Heather, Folk-Lore, 39, 1928, 190-5.

----------. Studies in Medieval Thought. London and New York: Nelson, 1940.

Rev: TLS, July 12, 1940, 342; NQ, 178, 1940, 216; History, 25, 1940, 95.

----------. Medieval Panorama. Cambridge Univ Press; Macmillan, 1938. 801 pp.

Rev: W. R. Trask, New York Times Book Rev, Dec 19, 1938, 5; A. Van Gennep, Mercure de France, June 1, 1939, 404-6; Lloyd Thomas, HJ, 37, 1939, 499-504; M. L. Zisovitz, SRL, April 8, 1939, 18; J. T. McNeill, Church History, 8, 1939, 175-6; H. H. Coulton, Cath Hist World, 25, 1939, 189-92; NQ, 176, 1939, 16-7; J. McSorley, CW, 149, 1939, 116; C. V. Wedgwood, Spect, Jan 6, 1939, 26-7; B. Wilkinson, Canadian Forum, 18, 1939, 351; G. Post, Spec, 15, 1940, 349-53; Hilda Johnstone, Hist, 25, 1940, 172-3; J. Jacobs, Nineteenth Century, 125, 1940, 722-7. Many other laudatory reviews in newspapers.

CRANZ, FERDINAND E. Aristotelianism in Medieval Political Theory: A Study of the Reception of the Politics. Doctoral Diss, Harvard, 1938.

CRUMP, C. G., and E. F. JACOB. The Legacy of the Middle Ages. Clarendon Press, 1926. 549 pp.

Rev: TLS, Dec 30, 1926, 956; Charles H. Haskins, SRL, 3, 1927, 663; L. J. Paetow, Spec, 2, 1927, 225-7; N. Neilson, AHR, 32, 1927, 846-8; Henry B. Van Hoesen, Libr Jour, 52, 1927, 1169-70.

CUNNINGHAM, GEORGE H. London: Being a Comprehensive Survey of the History, Tradition, and Historical Associations of Buildings and Monuments Arranged under Streets in Alphabetical Order. Dent, 1928. 887 pp.

Several references to Chaucer's relation to parts of the city.

Rev: TLS, Feb 16, 1928, 111.

CUTTS, EDWARD LEWES. Scenes and Characters of the Middle Ages. 7th ed, Simpkin, 1930. 552 pp.

DAICHES, DAVID. Literature and Society. Gollancz, 1938. Chaucer, 53-64 and other references.

DARBY, H. C., Ed. An Historical Geography of England
   before A. D. 1800. Cambridge Univ Press, 1936. 566 pp.
      Fourteenth Century England, by R. A. Pelham,
   230-65; Medieval Foreign Trade: Western Ports, by
   D. T. Williams, 266-97; Medieval Foreign Trade:
   Eastern Ports, by R. A. Pelham, 298-329.
      Rev: G. N. Clark, EHR, 52, 1937, 138-40; M. M.
   Postan, Econ Hist Rev, 7, 1937, 231-2; F. Mossé,
   Rev Germ, 28, 1937, 187; TLS, July 25, 1936, 614;
   A. P. Newton, Hist, 23, 1938, 57.
DAVIES, R. TREVOR, Ed. Documents Illustrating the
   History of Civilization in Medieval England (1066-1500).
   Methuen, 1926. 413 pp.
----------. A Sketch of the History of Civilization in
   Medieval England, 1066-1500. Macmillan, 1924.
      Rev: TLS, July 31, 1924.
DAVIS, H. W. C. Medieval England. Clarendon Press,
   1924.
      Rev: TLS, Feb 14, 1924; TLS, May 13, 1924; E. F.
   Jacob, RES, 1, 1925, 111-4; NQ, Nov 22, 1924, 147,
   381-2.
DAWSON, CHRISTOPHER. The Classical Tradition and
   the Origins of Medieval Culture. Studies, 20, 1931,
   209-24.
DE WULF, MAURICE. History of Medieval Philosophy.
   Trans by E. C. Messenger. Longmans, 1926; 3rd ed,
   rev, 1938. Reissue Dover Publications, 1952 (Vol. 1).
      Vol. 2, From Aquinas to End of 16th Century.
      Rev: J. M. S., CW, 144, 1926, 253-4; E. A. Moody,
   Com, 28, 1936, 390-1; G. B. Phelan, Philosophical
   Rev, 46, 1937, 436-7; W. O'Meara, Com, 29, 1939,
   446.
----------. Philosophy and Civilization in the Middle
   Ages. Princeton Univ Press, 1922.
DUCKETT, ELEANOR S. The Gateway to the Middle
   Ages. Macmillan, 1938.
      Rev: E. K. Rand, AHR, 43, 1938, 85-6; J. J. O'-
   Connor, Com, 28, 1938, 14; B. Memecke, Classical
   Weekly, 32, 1938, 29-30; T. C. P., CW, 147, 1938,
   502-3; M. H. Shepherd, Jour of Religion, 18, 1938,
   313-4; M. B. Ogle, Spec, 14, 1939, 115-7; J. T. Mc-
   Neil, Church History, 8, 1939, 187-8; M. Gerner, MP,
   36, 1939, 314-8; Hilda Johnstone, Hist, 25, 1940, 172-3.

ELIASON, MARY H. A Study of Some Relations between
    Literature and History in the Third Estate of the
    Fourteenth Century: Chaucer, Piers the Plowman,
    and English Mystery Cycles. Unpubl Diss, Univ of
    North Carolina, 1938.
FUNK-BRENTANO, FR. The Middle Ages. Trans from
    the French by Elizabeth O'Neill. Putnam, 1923.
GILSON, ETIENNE. The Spirit of Mediaeval Philosophy.
    Trans by A. H. C. Downes. London: Sheed and Ward;
    Scribners, 1936. 490 pp. L'Esprit de la Philosophie
    Médiévale. Etudes des Philosophies Médiévales, 33.
    2nd ed, Vrin, 1944. 446 pp.
        Rev: TLS, May 30, 1936, 448; N. Micklem, QQ,
    43, 1936, 223-5; B. Drury, NYTBR, Nov 8, 1936, 9;
    R. McKeon, Yale Rev, 26, 1937, 396-7; L. M. Ham-
    mond, VQR, 13, 1937, 470-4; G. B. Phelan, Com, 25,
    1937, 366-7; More Books (Bull Boston Publ Lib), 12,
    1937, 21-2; V. Michel, UTQ, 6, 1937, 278-81; J. R.
    Cresswell, Philosophical Rev, 47, 1938, 310-3.
----------. Reason and Revelation in the Middle Ages.
    Scribners, 1938.
        Rev: J. Buckler, VQR, 5, 1939, 311-4; D. E. Rob-
    erts, Jour of Religion, 19, 1939, 389-90; J. H. R., Jr.,
    Jour of Philosophy, 36, 1939, 495-6; P. Colum, JEGP,
    38, 1939, 143-7; J. M. E. S., CW, 150, 1940, 626-7;
    F. W. Beare, UTQ, 9, 1940, 244-6.
----------. La Philosophie au Moyen Age des Origines
    Patristiques à la Fin du XIVe Siècle. 2nd ed, rev and
    aug. Bibliothèque Historique. Payot, 1944. 782 pp.
GROSS, CHARLES. Sources and Literature of English
    History from the Earliest Times to About 1485. 2nd ed,
    Longmans, 1915.
GUILFORD, E. L. Travellers and Travelling in the Mid-
    dle Ages. Sheldon Press, 1924.
HADOW, GRACE E. Chaucer and his Times. Holt; Wil-
    liams and Norgate, 1914.
HARTLEY, DOROTHY, and MARGARET M. ELLIOTT.
    Life and Work of the People of England. A Pictorial
    Record from Contemporary Sources. Putnam, 1929.
    81 pp.
        Vol. 2, The Fourteenth Century.
        Rev: J. G. N., Antiquaries Jour, 12, 1932, 91-
    2.

HARTLEY, DOROTHY, Ed. The Old Book, a Medieval
    Anthology. Knopf, 1930. 318 pp.
        Includes some Chaucer selections.
        Rev: Cornelia Coulter, Spec, 7, 1932, 131-2.
HASKINS, CHARLES H. The Spread of Ideas in the Middle
    Ages. Spec, 1, 1926, 19-30.
----------. Studies in Mediaeval Culture. Clarendon
    Press, 1929. 306 pp.
        Illustrations of medieval civilization through Latin
    literature of the times.
        Rev: C. Gauss, NR, 63, 1930, 50-1; W. Farnham,
    Univ Calif Chron, 32, 1930, 397-8; E. E. Merton,
    Spec, 5, 1930, 225-6; F. M. Powicke, EHR, 45, 1930,
    478-9; L. C. MacKinney, AHR, 36, 1931, 362-3.
HEARNSHAW, F. J. C., Ed. Medieval Contributions to
    Modern Civilization. Lectures delivered at King's
    College, Univ of London. Harrap, 1921.
        Rev: F. M. P(owicke), EHR, 37, 1922, 398-400.
----------. Select Extracts from Chronicles and Records
    Relating to English Towns of the Middle Ages. SPCK:
    Macmillan, 1919.
----------, Ed. The Social and Political Ideas of Some
    Great Medieval Thinkers. Lectures delivered at
    King's College, Univ of London. Harrap, 1923.
        Rev: TLS, Aug 23, 1923; CR, 124, 1923, 539-40.
HEIDRICH, KATE. Das geographische Weltbild des spät-
    eren englischen Mittelalters. Freiberg, 1915.
        Rev: John Koch, AB, 27, 1916, 18-22; O. Glöde,
    LGRP, 37, 1916, 358-9; Rudolf Imelmann, NS, 24,
    1916, 180-1; Arch, 134, 1916, 465.
HERBEN, STEPHEN J., Jr. Arms and Armor in Chau-
    cer. Spec, 12, 1937, 475-87.
        Includes general discussion of the accuracy of
    Chaucer's references to arms and has particular ap-
    plication to the arming of Sir Thopas.
        Rev: D. Everett, YWES, 68.
HIBBARD, LAURA A. The Books of Simon de Burley,
    1387. MLN, 30, 1915, 169-71.
        The library of a possible friend of Chaucer.
HOME, GORDON. Medieval London. Benn, 1927. 382 pp.
        Includes plan of medieval London, and some Chau-
    cer references.
        Rev: TLS, Aug 4, 1927, 529.

HOPPER, VINCENT FOSTER. Medieval Number Sym-
    bolism: Its Sources, Meaning, and Influences in
    Thought and Expression. Columbia Univ Press, 1938.
    Columbia Univ Stud in Eng and Comp Lit.
        Rev: T. M. Pearce, D. F. Smith, and D. Wynn,
    New Mexico Quart, 8, 1938, 280; J. T. McNeill, Jour
    of Religion, 19, 1939, 303; E. A. M., Jour of Philos-
    ophy, 36, 1939, 386; D. E. Smith, AHR, 44, 1939,
    428; K. Malone, MLN, 55, 1940, 78.
HUFF, LLOYD D. Place Names in Chaucer. Doctoral
    Diss, Indiana, 1950.
HUGHES, DOROTHY. Illustrations of Chaucer's England.
    Preface by A. W. Pollard. Longmans, 1918.
        Rev: William E. Mead, JEGP, 18, 1919, 150-3.
JOHNSTON, L. Four Centuries of Medieval Criticism.
    CW, 139, 1934, 417-25.
        Causes of erroneous popular view of Middle Ages
    traced.
JUSSERAND, J. J. English Wayfaring Life in the Middle
    Ages (Fourteenth Century). Trans from the French
    by Lucy Toulmin-Smith. New ed rev and enl by the
    author. Unwin, 1920.
        Rev: F. B., The Boston Transcript, Feb 19, 1921,
    6; P. K. F., Discovery, 2, 1921, 51; Outlook, 127,
    1921, 432; NQ, 8, 1921, 79.
KER, NEIL R. Medieval Libraries in Great Britain: A
    List of Surviving Books. London: Royal Historical So-
    ciety, 1941. 169 pp.
        Rev: Rev. Beryl Smalley, Library, 23, 1942, 48-9;
    F. M. Powicke, Hist, 26, 1942, 297-9; W. Levison,
    MA, 11, 1942, 111-5.
KIBRE, PEARL. Intellectual Interests Reflected in Li-
    braries of the Fourteenth and Fifteenth Centuries.
    JHI, 7, 1946, 257-97.
KIMBLE, GEORGE H. Geography of the Middle Ages.
    London: Methuen, 1938.
        Rev: Lynn Thorndike, AHR, 44, 1939, 868-70; H.
    C. O., EHR, 54, 1939, 181-2; D. B. Durand, Isis, 30,
    1939, 540-2; Edwin Raisz, Spec, 15, 1940, 356-8.
KNOLL, KURT. London im Mittelalter, seine wirtschaft-
    liche, politische und kulturelle Bedeutung für das brit-
    ische Volk. Wiener Beit. zur englischen Philologie,
    56. Braumüller, 1932. 219 pp.

Rev: L. M. Larson, JEGP, 31, 1932, 574; M. Rös-
ler, ESt, 68, 1933, 295-7; L. von Hibler, AB, 44,
1933, 146-8; F. Bock, DL, 54, 1933, 230-1.
KUHL, ERNEST P. Illustrations of Chaucer in the Life
of the Fourteenth Century. Manuscript Diss in the
Harvard Univ Library, 1913.
LEACH, ARTHUR F. Schools of Mediaeval England.
Macmillan, 1915.
LEVETT, ADA ELIZABETH. Studies in Manorial Histo-
ry. Oxford: Clarendon Press, 1938.
On manorial organization of St. Alban's Abbey.
MacCULLOCH, J. A. Medieval Faith and Fable. With a
Foreword by Sir J. G. Frazer. M. Jones, 1932. 345
pp.
Rev: TLS, April 7, 1932, 236; Spect, 148, 1932,
710; E. A. Moody, Commonweal, 17, 1932, 111; W. A.
Wigram, CQR, 114, 1932, 313-4; K. M. , MLN, 49,
1934, 556-7.
McFARLANE, K. B. John Wyclif and the Beginnings of
English Non-conformity. Macmillan, 1953.
MARCUS, JACOB R. The Jew in the Medieval World: A
Source Book: 315-1791. Cincinnati, Ohio: Sinai Press,
1938. 504 pp.
Rev: C. G. Woodson, Jour of Negro Hist, 23, 1938,
494-5; D. M. Quinn, SAQ, 38, 1939, 238-9; H. Hail-
perin, Class Weekly, 32, April 7, 1939, 248-9; S. W.
Bacon, AHR, 44, 1939, 873-4; MA, 8, 1939, 82-3.
MOHL, RUTH. The Three Estates in Medieval and Re-
naissance Literature. Doctoral Diss, Columbia, 1933.
Columbia Univ Press, 1933. 425 pp.
Chaucer's relation to the estates, 102-3.
Rev: C. S. L. , MA, 3, 1934, 68-70; NR, 77, 1934,
318; M. M. Knappen, Int Jour of Ethics, 44, 1934,
282; A. Szogs, AB, 46, 1935, 235-7; H. S. V. Jones,
JEGP, 35, 1936, 308.
MORGAN, R. B. Readings in English Social History.
Vol. II, 1272-1485. Cambridge Univ Press, 1921.
Rev: E. Kruisinga, E Stud, 3, 1921, 114-5.
MUNRO, DANA C. The Middle Ages. Century, 1921.
See chapters on nobles, monasticisms, the peas-
ants, towns and trade, heresy and friars, the univer-
sities. Also see bibliographies.
NEWHALL, RICHARD A. The English Conquest of Nor-

mandy: A Study of Fifteenth Century Warfare. Yale
Univ Press, 1924.

OLSON, CLAIR C. , and MARTIN M. CROW. Chaucer's
World. Compiled by Edith Rickert. Illustrations se-
lected by Margaret Rickert. Columbia Univ Press;
Oxford (Title: Chaucer's England), 1948.

   Chapters: London Life, The Home, Training and
Education, Careers, Entertainment, Travel, War,
The Rich and the Poor, Religion, Death and Burial.
Bibliography. Index.

   Rev: D. Everett, YWES, 70-1; Geo. R. Coffman,
AHR, 54, 1948, 114-6; James Howard, MLQ, 10, 1949,
407-8; John E. Housman, English, 7, 1949, 293-4; H.
S. Bennett, MLR, 44, 97-9; Geo. R. Coffman, RES,
1 n. s., 1950, 156-8; Henry L. Savage, JEGP, 49,
1950, 107-11; H. B. Woolf, New Mexico Quart Rev, 18,
1948, 475.

PAETOW, LOUIS J. A Guide to the Study of Medieval
History. Rev ed. Kegan Paul; Crofts, 1931. 643 pp.
1st ed, 1917.

   Extensive bibliographies for study of Middle Ages.
   Rev: TLS, Oct 1, 1931, 757; G. N. Shuster, Commonweal, 14, 1931, 134-6; H. B. Van Hoesen, AHR,
37, 1932, 296-8; M. R. P. McGuire, CHR, 17, 1932,
471-5; F. M. Powicke, Hist, 17, 1932, 52-4.

PATCH, HOWARD ROLLIN. Chaucer and the Common
People. JEGP, 29, 1930, 376-84.

----------. The Other World According to Descriptions
in Medieval Literature. Harvard Univ Press, 1950.

   See index for Chaucer references.

PENDRILL, CHARLES. London Life in the Fourteenth Century. Allen & Unwin; New York, Adelphi Co, 1925. 287 pp.

PLUCKNETT, THEODORE F. T. , Ed. Year Books of
Richard II: 1389-1390. Edited for the Ames Foundation.
Spottiswoode, 1930. 205 pp.

   Rev: TLS, April 10, 1930, 309; J. F. Willard, Spec,
6, 1931, 161-2; W. S. Holdsworth, Econ Hist Rev, 3,
1931, 148-51.

POOLE, REGINALD L. Illustrations of the History of
Medieval Thought and Learning. 2nd ed, rev. SPCK,
1921.

POWICKE, F. M. Medieval England, 1066-1485. Home
Univ Library. Butterworth, 1931. 256 pp.

Rev: TLS, Dec 24, 1931, 1034; C. H. W. , Hist, 17, 1933, 374-5.

PUTNAM, B. H. Transformation of the Keepers of the Peace into the Justices of the Peace, 1327-1380. Royal Historical Society Transactions, ser. 4, 12, 1929, 19-48.

Discussion of crime during the period, and its control.

QUILLER-COUCH, ARTHUR T. The Age of Chaucer. J. M. Dent, 1926.

An introductory study.

Rev: Dorothy Everett, YWES, 98-9.

REINHARD, JOHN REVELL. Medieval Pageant. London: Dent; New York: Harcourt, Brace, 1939.

Rev: TLS, July 1, 1939, 394; W. R. Trask, NYTBR, May 14, 1939, 14; R. T. F. , Personalist, 21, 1940, 90-1.

RICKERT, EDITH. King Richard II's Books. Library, ser. 4, 13, 1932, 144-7.

ROOT, ROBERT K. Publication before Printing. PMLA, 28, 1913, 417-31.

"It is the purpose of this paper to set forth on the basis of contemporary evidence the conditions of publication which prevailed in Western Europe during the 14th and early 15th centuries. "

SALZMAN, L. F. English Life in the Middle Ages. Oxford Univ Press, 1926. 287 pp.

Main section on Chaucer, 158-62.

Rev: TLS, Oct 28, 1926, 733; NQ, 151, 1926, 323; K. G. T. Webster, Spec, 2, 1927, 485; R. Imelmann, DL, 48, 1927, 1612-3.

SAMUEL, IRENE. Semiramis in the Middle Ages: The History of a Legend. Medievalia et Humanistica, 2, 1944, 32-44.

MLT, PF, LGW.

SCHRAMM, WILBUR LANG. The Cost of Books in Chaucer's Time. MLN, 48, 1933, 139-45.

SCHRODER, EDWARD. Einiges vom Buchtitel in der englischen Literatur des Mittelalters. Ang, 62, 1938, 234-57.

SCOTT, JONATHAN FRENCH, ALBERT HYMA, and A. H. NOYES, Compilers. Readings in Medieval History. Crofts, 1933. 642 pp.

Source book.

Rev: F. J. Tschan, CHR, 20, 1934, 339; E. Joran-
son, AHR, 40, 1934, 160-1.

STEARNS, MARSHALL W. A Note on Chaucer's Use of
Aristotelian Philosophy. SP, 43, 1946, 15-21.

Consecutive steps of the process of knowing: sensa-
tion, imagination, rational thought, with examples
from MerT, 1977-81 and elsewhere; SqT, 371-2; HF,
36-40; MilT, 3611-7; T&C, I, 295-8, 365-6; III, 1541-
4, 1499-502; V, 372-8.

STEEL, ANTHONY. Richard II. With a Foreword by G.
M. Trevelyan. Cambridge Univ Press, 1941.

Rev: TLS, Nov 8, 1941, 556; NQ, 181, 1941, 321-2;
DUJ, 3, 1942, 133; review article, V. H. Galbraith,
Hist, 26, 1942, 223-39.

STILLWELL, GARDINER. John Gower and the Last
Years of Edward III. SP, 45, 1948, 454-71.

Mostly on Miroir de l'Omme but adds to the research on the politics of the period.

STRETTON, GRACE. Some Aspects of Medieval Travel;
Notably Transport and Accommodation, with Special
Reference to the Wardrobe Accounts of Henry, Earl of
Derby, 1390-1393. Royal Hist Soc Trans, ser. 4, 7,
1924, 77-96. Master's Thesis, Univ of London, 1924?
Also, Medieval Travel as Illustrated by the Wardrobe
Accounts of the Earl of Derby, 1390-1393. Abstract in
Bull of the Inst of Hist Research, 2, 1924, 53-4.

STUART, DOROTHY MARGARET. Men and Women of
Plantagenet England. Harcourt, 1932. 286 pp.

Many references to Chaucer, especially 61-3, 239-
44.

Rev: TLS, April 21, 1932, 294.

TATLOCK, JOHN STRONG PERRY. The Middle Ages --
Romantic or Rationalistic? Spec, 8, 1933, 295-304.

Common conception of Middle Ages as altogether
romantic is in error. Considerable reference to Chaucer, and illustration from him.

TAYLOR, HENRY OSBORNE. Mediaeval Mind; a History
of the Development of Thought and Emotion in the Middle Ages. 4th ed. Macmillan, 1925. 2 vols.

See references on courtly love.

THOMAS, A. H. , Ed. Calendar of Pleas and Memoranda
Rolls, A. D. 1323-1364, Preserved among the Archives
of the Corporations of the City of London at the Guild-

hall. Cambridge Univ Press, 1926. 334 pp. Same, 1364-81, 1929. 359 pp. Same, 1382-1412, 1932. 369 pp.
    Rev: TLS, Sept 2, 1926, 579; TLS, Nov 7, 1929, 897; J. Tait, EHR, 45, 1930, 482-3; C. Jenkins, Hist, 15, 1931, 359-60; F. M. Powicke, Econ Hist Rev, 3, 1931, 147-8; TLS, Sept 8, 1932, 619; NQ, 163, 1932, 341; J. Tait, EHR, 48, 1933, 691-2.

THOMAS, A. H. Life in Medieval London. Brit Archaeol Assoc Jour, 2nd ser., 35, 1929, 122-48.

THOMAS, MARY EDITH. Medieval Skepticism and Chaucer: An Evaluation of the Skepticism of the 13th and 14th Centuries, of Geoffrey Chaucer and his Immediate Predecessors -- An Era that Looked Back on an Age of Faith and Forward to an Age of Reason. New York: The William-Frederick Press, 1950. 184 pp. Notes and bibliography.
    Rev: G. R. Owst, RES, 4 n. s., 1953, 68-9; H. R. P., MLN, 67, 1952, 269-71; D. Everett, MLR, 48, 1953, 64-5; Haldeen Braddy, MLQ, 15, 1954, 74-5; A. L. Kellogg, Spec, 27, 1952, 258-60.

THOMPSON, JAMES WESTFALL. Economic and Social History of Europe in the Later Middle Ages (1300-1530). The Century Historical Series. Century, 1931.
---------. The Middle Ages, 300-1500. Knopf, 1931. 2 vols. Cheaper ed, Routledge, 1935.
    Rev: TLS, Oct 8, 1932, 768; B. N. Shuster, Commonweal, 14, 1932, 134-6; G. Mattingly, SRL, 7, 1932, 911; L. Thorndike, AHR, 36, 1932, 793-5; R. McKeon, Nation, 134, 1932, 347-8; G. La Piana, Spec, 7, 1932, 302-16; C. R. Cheney, Hist, 17, 1932, 162-4; Z. N. Brooke, EHR, 48, 1933, 107-9.
---------. Reference Studies in Medieval History. Univ of Chicago Press, 1923.
    Part 3, The End of the Middle Ages, 1291-1498. See especially black death, 245-6; church, 252-8; gilds and gild life, 282-5; town life and trade, 290; the rise of capitalism, 291-4.
---------. The Medieval Library. The Univ of Chicago Studies in Library Science. Univ of Chicago Press, 1939.
    Rev: TLS, Nov 18, 1939, 676; E. A. S., LAR, 6, 1939, 527-8; T. C. P., CW, 150, 1939, 112-4; B. Knollenberg, SRL, Dec 23, 1939, 16; O. E. Schroeder, Cath Hist Rev, 25, 1940, 496-8; S. H. Thomson,

Church Hist, 9, 1940, 266-7; F. M. Corey, Classical
Weekly, 34, 1940, 4-6; J. S. Beddie, Spec, 15, 1940,
243-5; P. Kibre, AHR, 45, 1940, 615-6; R. T. F.,
Personalist, 21, 1940, 91.
----------. The Literacy of the Laity in the Middle
Ages. Univ of California Publications, 9. Univ of
California Press, 1939.
    Rev: M. W. Baldwin, Cath Hist Rev, 25, 1939,
348-9; H. W. Miller, Classical Weekly, 33, 1940,
259-60; G. C. Boyce, AHR, 45, 1940, 373-4; L.
Thorndike, Spec, 15, 1940, 125-6.
THOMPSON, STITH. Motif-Index of Folk Literature. 6
vols. Indiana Univ Studies, nos. 96, 97, 100-1, 105-
6, 108-10, 111-2; FF Communications, Helsingfors,
106-9, 116-7. 647 pp.
    Rev: H. M. Smyser, Spec, 13, 1938, 368.
THOMPSON, W. H. Chaucer and his Times. A. Brown,
1936. 136 pp.
THORNDIKE, LYNN. Anonymous Treatise in Six Books
on Metaphysics and Natural Philosophy. Philosophical
Rev, 40, 1931, 317-40.
    Treatise is 14th century, preserved in Latin MS at
Paris. Appendix to article lists contents of the 6 books.
----------. Elementary and Secondary Education in the
Middle Ages. Spec, 15, 1940, 400-8.
----------. Dates in Intellectual History: Fourteenth
Century. JHI, Suppl. No. 1, 1945.
    A year-by-year record.
----------. University Records and Life in the Middle
Ages. Columbia Univ Press, 1944.
    Texts on university life.
    Rev: C. H. W., Hist, 30, 1945, 107.
TOUT, THOMAS F. Chapters in the Administrative
History of Mediaeval England: The Wardrobe, the
Chamber, and Small Seals. 6 vols. Longmans, 1920-
33.
    Rev: F. Liebermann, Arch, 140, 1920, 261; J. F.
Willard, Spec, 5, 1930, 127-9; TLS, Jan 15, 1931, 36;
C. G. Crump, EHR, 47, 1932, 109-15; J. F. Willard,
Spec, 7, 1932, 161-2; TLS, Mar 30, 1933, 234.
----------. The Collected Papers . . . with a Memoir and
Bibliography. 3 vols. Manchester Univ Press, 1932-4.
    Several relevant studies.

Rev: AHR, 40, 1935, 546-7; EHR, 50, 1935, 357,
359; Hist, 20, 1935, 365; TLS, May 24, 1934, 370,
and Jan 24, 1935, 42.
----------. Literature and Learning in the English Civ-
il Service in the Fourteenth Century. Spec, 4, 1929,
365-89.
Chaucer, 381-8.
See also R. L. Schuyler and Hermann Ausubel,
Eds. The Making of English History, pp. 133-48. New
York: Dryden, 1952.
----------. The English Civil Service in the Fourteenth
Century. Bull of the John Rylands Library, 3, 1916-7,
185-214.
VANCE, W. R. Law in Action in Medieval England. Vir-
ginia Law Rev, 17, 1930, 1-22.
Given over to detailed account of litigation over the
Berkeley lands in the late 14th century and the 15th
century.
WARD, A. W. Chaucer. English Men of Letters Series,
9. Macmillan, 1909. 199 pp.
Chaucer's times, 1-46.
WILLARD, JAMES F., and WILLIAM MORRIS, Eds.
The English Government at Work: 1327-1336. Vol. I.
Mediaeval Academy of America, 1940.

SOCIAL BACKGROUNDS

See CBEL, I, 119-24; Gerould, 33-54.

For discussions of marriage, see section: Wife of Bath's Tale.

ABRAM, A. English Life and Manners in the Later Middle Ages. Routledge, 1913. 352 pp.

ATKINSON, DOROTHY F. Some Notes on Heraldry and Chaucer. MLN, 51, 1936, 328-31.

AUDIAU, JEAN. Les Troubadours et l'Angleterre. Contribution à l'Etude des Poètes Anglais de l'Amour au Moyen-Age (13e et 14e Siècles). Paris: Vrin, 1927. 136 pp.

> Rev: L. E. K., MLR, 24, 1929, 109-10.

BAKER, MARY CATHARINE. Andre le Chapelain and his Relation to Courtly Love. Master's Thesis, Univ of Washington, 1935. Typewritten, 262 pp.

> Contains Concerning Love, by Andreas, royal chaplain of the French: a partial translation and summary of the Latin text of E. Trojel, reprinted in De Amore, Libri Tres, 71-262.

BARROW, SARAH F. The Medieval Society Romances. Columbia Univ Press, 1924.

> For courtly love.

BENNETT, H. S. Life on the English Manor; a Study of Peasant Conditions, 1150-1400. Macmillan, 1937. 364 pp.

> Rev: C. D. A., SRL, 17, Jan 15, 1938, 20-1; B. H. Putnam, Spec, 13, 1938, 351-2; Reginald Lennard, EHR, 53, 1938, 289-92; N. Neilson, AHR, 43, 1938, 838-40; T. A. M. Bishop, Econ Hist Rev, 8, 1938, 193-4.

BOAS, RALPH PHILIP, and BARBARA M. HAHN. Social Backgrounds of English Literature. Atlantic Monthly Press, 1923. Rev ed, Little, Brown, 1934.

> The Age of Chaucer, 44-67.

BORN, LESTER KRUGER. The Perfect Prince: A Study in Thirteenth and Fourteenth-Century Ideals. Spec, 3, 1928, 470-504.

BOSTWICK, JOSEPHINE OSBORNE. Feudalism and
Chivalry in the Time of Chaucer. Master's Thesis,
Columbia, 1911.

BRANDL, ALOIS. Review of William A. Neilson, The
Origins and Sources of the Court of Love, Studies and
Notes (Harvard), 6. Arch, 106, 1901, 390-401.

BROOKE, IRIS. English Costume of the Later Middle
Ages. The Fourteenth and Fifteenth Centuries. Macmillan, 1935. 88 pp.
    Rev: TLS, Nov 16, 1935, 742; Nation, 142, 1936,
    720.

CARLYLE, R. W. and A. J. A History of Mediaeval Political Theory in the West. Vol. 6, Political Theory
from 1300 to 1600. Blackwood, 1936. 551 pp.
    Fourteenth century, 1-132.
    Rev: Francis W. Coker, AHR, 42, 1937, 734-7;
    F. M. Powicke, EHR, 53, 1938, 126-8; L. Halphen,
    Rev Hist, 180, 1937, 362.

CHADWICK, DOROTHY. Social Life in the Days of Piers
Plowman. Cambridge Univ Press, 1922. 138 pp.

CHAMBERS, FRANK McMINN. Some Legends Concerning Eleanor of Aquitaine. Spec, 16, 1941, 459-68.

COFFMAN, GEORGE RALEIGH. Old Age in Chaucer's
Day. MLN, 52, 1937, 25-6.

----------. Chaucer and Courtly Love Once More: The
Wife of Bath's Tale. Spec, 20, 1945, 43-50.
    Footnote bibliography of courtly love.
    Rev: D. Everett, YWES, 50-1.

COHEN, HERMAN. A History of the English Bar and
Attornatus to 1450. Sweet and Maxwell, 1929. 622 pp.
    Rev: TLS, June 13, 1929, 465.

COOK, ALBERT STANBURROUGH. Chaucer's Griselda
and Homer's Arete. AJP, 39, 1918, 75-8.
    Position of women.

----------. The Historical Background of Chaucer's
Knight. Yale Univ Press, 1916.
    For reviews, see section: General Criticism.

COULTON, GEORGE G. The Middle Ages: The Peasant's
Revolt. 199-273, in Great Events in History, ed by G.
R. S. Taylor. Cassell, 1934.

----------. Social Life in England from the Conquest to
the Reformation. Cambridge Univ Press, 1919; Macmillan, 1939.

CROSLAND, JESSIE. The Conception of "Mesure" in
    Some Medieval Poets. MLR, 21, 1926, 380-4.
        "Mesure" -- temperance, moderation -- as social
    ideal in Middle Ages. Chaucer mentioned and quoted,
    381-2.
CROSS, TOM PEETE, and W. A. NITZE. Lancelot and
    Guinevere: A Study in the Origins of Courtly Love.
    Chicago, 1930.
DENHOLM-YOUNG, N. MS Bodley 751; The Library
    Catalogue. EHR, 48, 1933, 437-43.
        List of books, 1310-28.
DENOMY, ALEXANDER J. An Inquiry into the Origins
    of Courtly Love. Med Stud, 6, 1944, 175-260.
----------. Fin' Amors: The Pure Love of the Trouba-
    dours, its Amorality and Possible Source. Med Stud,
    7, 1945, 139-207.
        Rev: H. I. Marrow, Rev du Moyen-Age Latin, 3,
    1947, 81-9.
----------. Andreas Capellanus Discovered and Redis-
    covered. Med Stud 8, 1946, 300-1.
----------. The Heresy of Courtly Love. Boston College
    Candlemas Lectures in Christian Literature. New
    York: The Declan X. McMullen Co, 1947. 92 pp.
        Rev: Geo. Kane, RES, 43, 1948, 524-5; Sidney
    Painter, MLN, 63, 1948, 363-4; John J. Parry, MLQ,
    10, 1949, 107-9. See Silverstein, below in this section.
----------. The De Amore of Andreas Capellanus and
    the Condemnation of 1277. Med Stud, 8, 1946, 107-49.
----------. Courtly Love and Courtliness. Spec, 28,
    1953, 44-63.
DE ROUGEMENT, DENIS. Love in the Western World.
    Trans by M. Belgion. Harcourt, 1940.
        Chapter on courtly love.
DICKINSON, JOHN. The Mediaeval Conception of Kingship
    and Some of its Limitations, as Developed in the "Poli-
    craticus" of John of Salisbury. Spec, 1, 1926, 308-37.
        Rev: Josef Balogh, Spec, 3, 1928, 580-2.
DODD, WILLIAM G. Courtly Love in Chaucer and Gow-
    er. Harvard Studies in English, 1. Ginn; Milford, 1913.
        For reviews, see section: Literary Relations.
DOLL, HELENE. Mittelenglische Kleidernamen in
    Spiegel literarischer Denkmäler des 14. Jahrhunderts.
    Giessen Diss.

Rev: Erika von Erhardt-Siebold, AB, 44, 1933, 337-40.
EMERSON, OLIVER F. Chaucer and Medieval Hunting.
RR, 13, 1922, 115-50.
See Savage, below in this section.
FISHER, JOHN HURT. The Treatise of Love. EETS, 1951.
GETTY, AGNES. Chaucer's Changing Conceptions of the
Humble Lover. PMLA, 44, 1929, 202-16.
GRAHAM, HUGH. Chaucer's Educational Background.
Thought, 9, 1934, 222-35.
GREEN, OTIS H. Courtly Love in the Spanish Cancione-
ros. PMLA, 64, 1949, 247-301.
HARTLEY, DOROTHY. Mediaeval Costume and Life.
A Review of their Social Aspects Arranged under Var-
ious Classes and Workers with Instructions for Mak-
ing Numerous Types of Dress, with an Introduction
and Notes on Mediaeval Costume Features by Francis
M. Kelly. Scribner, 1932. 142 pp.
Many illustrations.
Rev: TLS, Mar 17, 1932, 188.
HASKINS, CHARLES H. The Rise of the Universities.
Holt, 1923. 134 pp.
Rev: Ernest P. Kuhl, MLN, 39, 1924, 381-2; Int
Jour of Ethics, 34, 1924, 204.
HEPPLE, RICHARD B. Mediaeval Education in England.
Hist Assn Leaflet, no. 90. G. Bell, 1932. 30 pp.
HIBBARD, LAURA A. Medieval Romance in England. A
Study of the Sources and Analogues of the Non-cyclic
Metrical Romances. Oxford, 1924. 342 pp.
Rev: G. Binz, AB, 36, 1925, 332-6; Cyril Brett,
MLR, 20, 1925, 339-40; Kemp Malone, MLN, 41,
1926, 406-7; Howard R. Patch, JEGP, 25, 1926, 108-
14; SP, 22, 1925, 554; SRL, 1, 1924, 419.
HOCKING, LORENA W. The Dress of the Canterbury
Pilgrims. Master's Thesis, Columbia Univ, 1917.
HOLMAN, C. HUGH. Courtly Love in the Merchant's
and Franklin's Tales. ELH, 18, 1951, 241-52.
HOLMES, URBAN T. History of Old French Literature
from the Origins to 1300. Univ of North Carolina
Press, 1937.
Courtly love, 170-5.
HOLZKNECHT, KARL J. Literary Patronage in the
Middle Ages. Doctoral Diss, Univ of Pennsylvania,
1923. Banta, 1923. 258 pp.

Rev: Erna Fischer, AB, 36, 1925, 102-7; G. G.
Coulton, MLR, 20, 1925, 478-9.

HOVETON, MARY GALWAY. Medieval Costume in England and France: The Thirteenth, Fourteenth, and
Fifteenth Centuries with 8 plates in color and 300
black and white drawings. A & C Black, 1939.

IMMACULATE, Sister MARY (CHEEK). Robert Grosseteste's Le Chateau d'Amours. Doctoral Diss, Yale,
1941.

JACOBSON, JOHN H. The Church of Love in the Works
of Chaucer and Gower. Unpubl Diss, Yale, 1939.

JARRETT, BEDE. Social Theories of the Middle Ages,
1200-1500. Benn, 1926. 280 pp.
Rev: TLS, Nov 18, 1926, 810.

KAISER, ROLF. Das Evangelium der Armut in Chaucers England. Archiv, 185, 1948, 36-51.

KELLY, AMY. Eleanor of Aquitaine and her Courts of
Love. Spec, 12, 1937, 3-19.

----------. Eleanor of Aquitaine and the Four Kings.
Harvard Univ Press, 1950. 431 pp.
Rev: Jeremiah F. O'Sullivan, Thought, 26, 1951,
634; Loren C. MacKinney, Spec, 26, 1951, 166.

KELLY, FRANCIS M., and RANDOLPH SCHWABE. A
Short History of Costume and Armour, Chiefly in Eng-
land, 1066-1800. Scribner, 1931. Vol. 1, 1066-1485.
Rev: TLS, Mar 17, 1932, 188; F. M. Kelly, TLS,
Mar 24, 1932, 217; O. H. Leeney, TLS, Mar 31, 1932,
229; F. M. Kelly, TLS, April 21, 1932, 291; O. H.
Leeney, TLS, May 12, 1932, 351; E. G. Craig, Obs,
May 29, 1932; Sat Rev, 153, 1932, 378-9; J. G. Mann,
Antiquaries Jour, 12, 1932, 318-20.

KEOUGH, EDNA ALICE. Physical Action in Chaucer as
It Is Related to Individual and Group Behavior. Master's Thesis, Univ of Washington, 1943. 264 pp.

KOELLREUTER, MARIE. Das Privatleben in England
nach den Dichtungen von Chaucer, Gower, und Langland. Züricher Diss; Halle, 1908.

KREBS, KARL. Der Bedeutungswandel von me. Clerk
mit damit zusammenhängenden Probleme. Bonn:
Harnstein, 1933. 162 pp. Bonner Studien zur englisch-
en Philologie, 21.
For reviews, see section: Clerk's Tale.

KUHL, ERNEST P. Chaucer's Burgesses. Trans Wisconsin Acad of Sciences, Arts, and Letters, 18, 1916, 652-75.

Rev: E. Trauschke, NS, 37, 1929, 651; G. G. Coulton, MLR, 12, 1917, 512.

LEACH, ARTHUR F. The Schools of Medieval England. Methuen; Macmillan, 1915. 349 pp.

Rev: AHR, 20, 1915, 910; Athenaeum, 1915, I, 262; A. G. Little, EHR, 30, 1915, 525; Nation, 100, 1915, 603; Sat Rev, 119, 1915, 560; Spect, 114, 1915, 339.

LEH, MYRTLE CLARKE. Town Life in Fourteenth-Century England. Master's Thesis, Univ of Colorado, 1935. Abstract in Univ of Colorado Studies, 23, no. 1, 1935, 44-5.

LEWIS, CLIVE STAPLES. The Allegory of Love: A Study in Medieval Tradition. Oxford, 1936; reprint, 1948.

For reviews, see section: General Criticism.

McMAHON, CLARA P. Education in Fifteenth-Century England. The Johns Hopkins Press, 1947. 179 pp.

MAGOUN, FRANCIS P., Jr. Football in Medieval England and in Middle English Literature. AHR, 35, 1929, 33-45.

"First in Chaucer." See also Wettwer, below in this section.

MALLET, CHARLES E. A History of the University of Oxford. Methuen, 1924. 2 vols.

Vol. 1, The Mediaeval University and Colleges Founded in the Middle Ages.

MATHEW, GERVASE. Marriage and Amour Courtois in Late Fourteenth Century England. In Essays Presented to Charles Williams. Oxford, 1947.

Reviews Lewis, above in this section.

MEAD, WILLIAM EDWARD. The English Medieval Feast. Houghton, 1931. 272 pp.

References to three Chaucer pilgrims.

Rev: AM, 24, 1931, 30; QR, 257, 1931, 408; M. Wallace, AB, 74, 1932, 572-3; Commonweal, 15, 1932, 587; L. F. S., EHR, 47, 1932, 350; J. G. N., Antiquaries Jour, 12, 1932, 90; Brit Archaeol Assoc Jour, 37, 1932, 272.

MEEKINGS, C. A. F. Chaucer, Langland, and Lydgate in Works on History. NQ, 168, 1935, 369.

Asks for information.

MELLER, WALTER CLIFFORD. A Knight's Life in the

Days of Chivalry. T. Werner Laurie, 1924. 316 pp.
Rev: Nation and Athen, 36, 1924, 192; TLS, Aug
21, 1924, 509.

MOTT, LEWIS FREEMAN. The System of Courtly Love:
An Introduction to the Vita Nuova of Dante. Reprint;
Stechert, 1942.
Of value only in the study of concepts of courtly
love before Chaucer.

MUSGRAVE, CLARE A. Household Administration in
the Fourteenth Century with Special Reference to the
Household of Elizabeth de Burgh, Lady of Clare.
Thesis, Univ of London, 1923. Abstract in Bull of
the Institute of Historical Research, 1, 1924, 94.

NORRIS, HERBERT. Costume and Fashion. Vol. 2, Sen-
lac to Bosworth, 1066-1485. Dent, 1927. 485 pp.
Several Canterbury pilgrims discussed or pictured.
Rev: TLS, June 30, 1927, 451.

PAGES, AMADEO, Ed. Andreas Capellani Regii Franco-
rum De Amore. Libri tres. Castellon de la Plana,
1929.
For Andreas, see also Manitius, M., Geschichte
der lat. Lit. des Mittelalters, Munich, 1931; and
Arpad Steiner, The Date of the Composition of Andreas Capellanus' De Amore, Spec, 4, 1929, 92-5.

PAINTER, SIDNEY. French Chivalry: Chivalric Ideas
and Practices in Medieval France. Johns Hopkins
Press, 1940.
For courtly love, see Chapter IV.
Rev: Throop, AHR, 47, 1941, 573-4; H. J., EHR,
56, 1941, 338-9.

PARIS, GASTON. Le Conte de la Charrette. (II, of Lancelot du Lac.) Romania, 12, 1883, 459-534.
L'Esprit du Poème de Chrétien, 516-34, on courtly
love.

----------. Les Cours d'Amour du Moyen Age. Jour
des Savants, ser. 3, 53, 1888, 664-75, 727-36.
Review of above title by E. Trojel, which covers
"whole subject of the authenticity of the courts of
love." Also see Mélanges de Litterature Française du
Moyen Age, Paris, 1912, 473-97.

PARRY, A. W. Education in England in the Middle Ages.
Univ of London Diss. Univ Tutorial Press, 1920.

PARRY, JOHN J. The Art of Courtly Love of Andreas

Capellanus with Introduction, Translation, and Notes.
Columbia Univ Records of Civilization: Sources and
Studies, 33. Columbia Univ Press; London: Milford,
1941. 218 pp. including excellent bibliography.

Rev: Thomas A. Kirby, PQ, 3, 1942, 119-21; Ogle,
JEGP, 41, 1942, 372-4; Painter, MLN, 57, 1942, 315;
Tatlock, Spec, 17, 1942, 305-8; Thompson, Classical
Weekly, 35, 1942, 126-7; Tinker, NYTBR, Nov 9,
1941, 28; Boyce, Thought, 17, 1942, 361-4; Calhoun,
Amer Soc Rev, 7, 1942, 581-2; Olin H. Moore, Italica,
19, 1942, 121-4; G. Morey, History, 27, 1942, 94-5.

PECK, MARGARET ELEANOR. Types of Women in
Chaucer. Master's Thesis, Univ of Washington, 1939.
78 pp.

PENDRILL, CHARLES. London Life in the Fourteenth Century. Allen & Unwin; New York: Adelphi Co, 1925. 287 pp.

Rev: TLS, April 2, 1925.

----------. Wanderings in Medieval London. Macauley,
1928. 256 pp.

PHILIP, Brother C., F.S.C. A Further Note on Old Age
in Chaucer's Day. MLN, 53, 1938, 181-2.

PLIMPTON, GEORGE ARTHUR. The Education of Chaucer, Illustrated from the School-books in Use in his
Time. Oxford Univ Press, 1935. 176 pp.

For reviews and note, see section: Manuscripts.

POTTER, GEORGE RICHARD. Education in the Fourteenth and Fifteenth Centuries with Special Reference
to the Development of the Universities of Northern
Europe. Diss, St. John's College, Cambridge Univ;
Abstracts of Dissertations . . . , 1926-1927, 55-9.

POWER, EILEEN. Medieval People. Houghton, 1924.
216 pp.

See especially, Madame Eglentyne, Chaucer's
Prioress in Real Life, 59-84; and The Ménagier's
Wife, a Paris Housewife in the Fourteenth Century,
85-110.

Rev: Bertrand Russell, Dial, 78, 1925, 295-8.

POWICKE, FREDERICK MAURICE. Medieval Books of
Merton College. Oxford Univ Press, 1931. 287 pp.

RASHDALL, HASTINGS. The Universities of Europe in
the Middle Ages. A new ed in 3 vols, ed by F. M.
Powicke and A. B. Emden. Oxford, 1936.

Vol. 3, English Universities.

Rev: A. G. Little, EHR, 52, 1937, 308-10; Gray C.
Boyce, AHR, 42, 1937, 725-8; Gaines Post, Spec, 12,
1937, 129-35; Edward A. Pace, CHR, 23, 1937, 40-4;
TLS, May 2, 1936, 361; G. M. Young, Spect, 157, 1936,
65; M. Wade, Amer Rev, 7, 1936, 460-7; G. G. Coulton,
Obs, May 3, 1936; H. N. MacCracken, SRL, 14, Aug 8,
1936, 16-17; Louis Halphen, Rev Hist, 180, 1937, 92-3;
R. I. Flewelling, Personalist, 18, 1937, 99-101.

RICKERT, EDITH. The Babees' Book: Medieval Manners
for the Young: Done into Modern English. Chatto &
Windus; Duffield, 1908. 203 pp.

ROBERTSON, D. W., Jr. The Subject of De Amore of
Andreas Capellanus. MP, 50, 1953, 145-61.
The subject is "fornicatio" not courtly love.

ROBERTSON, STUART. Elements of Realism in the
Knight's Tale. JEGP, 14, 1915, 226-55.

ROGERS, LORENA BLANCHE. The May-Day Festival
in Literature. Abstracts of Theses, Univ of Pittsburgh, 1932, 400-1.

ROLLESTON, J. D. Alcoholism in Mediaeval England.
British Jour of Inebriety, 1933, 31.

ROSENBERG, MELRICH V. Eleanor of Aquitaine, Queen
of the Troubadours, and the Courts of Love. Houghton,
1937.
Rev: A. Steiner, Com, 25, 1937, 676-7; L. Hartley,
SAQ, 36, 1937, 348-9; S. Painter, Spec, 12, 1937, 411-2.

ROSLER, M. Die Lebensweise der Auslander in England
im späteren Mittelalter und in der Renaissance. ESt,
68, 1933, 17-56.
See also Weinbaum, in this section.

RUSSELL, JOSIAH COX. Medieval Population. Social
Forces, 14, 1927, 503-11.

SABINE, ERNEST L. Butchering in Mediaeval London.
Spec, 8, 1933, 335-53.

----------. City Cleaning in Mediaeval London. Spec,
12, 1937, 19-43.

----------. City Health and City Utilities of Chaucer's
London. Doctoral Diss, Chicago, 1928. Abstract in Abstracts of Theses, Humanistic Ser, 6, 1927-8, 377-80.

----------. Latrines and Cesspools of Mediaeval London.
Spec, 9, 1934, 303-21.

ST MARIE, LOUIS HAROLD. The Humility Element in
Chaucer's Troilus and Criseyde in Relation to the

Courtly Love Tradition. Master's Thesis, Univ of
Washington, 1946. 97 pp.
SALTER, H. E. Medieval Oxford. Oxford, 1936. 160 pp.
    Rev: B. H. Putnam, AHR, 43, 1937, 100-1; G. G.
    Coulton, EHR, 53, 1938, 120-3.
SAVAGE, ERNEST A. Old English Libraries; the Mak-
    ing, Collection and Use of Books during the Middle
    Ages. Methuen, 1912. 298 pp.
    Rev: Dial, 52, 1912, 287; P. S. A. , EHR, 27, 1912,
    390; Nation, 95, 1912, 85; Spect, 107, 1911, 713.
SAVAGE, HENRY L. Hunting in the Middle Ages. Spec,
    8, 1933, 30-41.
    Discusses beginnings of English hunting tradition.
    See Emerson, above in this section.
SCHLAUCH, MARGARET. Chaucer's Merchant's Tale
    and Courtly Love. ELH, 4, 1937, 201-12.
SCHOECK, R. J. Andreas Capellanus and Saint Bernard
    of Clairvaux: The Twelve Rules of Love and the
    Twelve Steps of Humility. MLN, 66, 1951, 295-300.
    See also Etienne Gilson, The Mystic Theology of
    St. Bernard, 170-7.
SCHOFIELD, WILLIAM H. Chivalry in English Litera-
    ture: Chaucer, Malory, Spenser, Shakespeare. Har-
    vard Univ Press, 1912.
    Rev: Th. Mühe, AB, 30, 1919, 158-61; R. Acker-
    mann, LGRP, 35, 1914, 283-4.
SILVERSTEIN, THEODORE. Andreas, Plato, and the
    Arabs: Remarks on Some Recent Accounts of Courtly
    Love. MP, 47, 1949, 117-26.
    Footnote bibliography; reviews A. J. Denomy's ar-
    ticles on courtly love.
SLAUGHTER, EUGENE E. Love and the Virtues and
    Vices in Chaucer. Bull of Vanderbilt Univ, 47, 1947,
    19-20.
STEARNS, MARSHALL W. A Note on Chaucer's Attitude
    toward Love. Spec, 17, 1942, 570-5.
    Suggests Blanche, the Duchess, as the object of
    Chaucer's eight years' sickness.
STEPHENSON, CARL. Borough and Town; a Study of
    Urban Origins in England. Medieval Academy of
    America, 1933. 236 pp.
    Rev: W. E. Lunt, AHR, 39, 1933, 99; E. H. Byrne,
    Columbia Law Rev, 33, 1933, 940.

STEWART-BROWN, R. The Scrope-Grosvenor Controversy. TLS, June 12, 1937, 447.
    Records cancelling the Grosvenor claim.
STOKES, MARGARET RUTH. The Peasant Rebellion of
1381 in History and Literature. Master's Thesis, Univ
of Washington, 1929. Typewritten, 60 pp.
    Chaucer's reference to rebellion in NPT, 32-3.
TAIT, JAMES. The Medieval English Borough: Studies
on its Origin and Constitutional History. Manchester
Univ Press, 1936. 371 pp.
    Rev: Helen M. Cam, EHR, 52, 1937, 303-6; Carl
    Stephenson, AHR, 43, 1937, 96-99; TLS, Aug 29,
    1936, 694; Sydney K. Mitchell, Spec, 13, 1938, 256-9.
THORNDIKE, LYNN. Mediaeval Sauce-book; with Latin
Text. Spec, 9, 1934, 183-90.
----------. Sanitation, Baths, and Street-Cleaning in the
Middle Ages and Renaissance. Spec, 3, 1928, 192-203.
----------. Elementary and Secondary Education in the
Middle Ages. Spec, 15, 1940, 400-8.
TOWNE, FRANK S. The Active and the Contemplative
Life: A Study of Patterns of Living in Medieval Eng-
land. Doctoral Diss, California (Los Angeles), 1949.
TREVELYAN, G. M. English Social History: A Survey
of Six Centuries: Chaucer to Queen Victoria. Long-
mans, 1944. 628 pp.
    Rev: E. S. de Beer, Hist, 30, 1945, 99-102.
----------. Chaucer's England and the Early Tudors. Stand-
ard English Social History, 1. Longmans, 1950.
TRUMAN, NEVIL. Historic Costuming. Pitman, 1936.
    The Three Edwards, 1272-1377, 24-8; Richard of
    Bordeaux, 1377-1399, 29-33; The Three Henries,
    1399-1401, 34-8.
TUPPER, FREDERICK. The Pardoner's Tavern. JEGP,
13, 1914, 553-65.
----------. Types of Society in Medieval Literature.
Three lectures: Conditions of Men; Sins and Sinners;
The Eternal Womanly. Brown Univ Colver Lectures.
Holt, 1926. 167 pp.
    Several Chaucer references and quotations.
    Rev: George R. Coffman, MLN, 42, 1927, 489-91;
    Dorothy Everett, YWES, 98.
----------. Wilful and Impatient Poverty. Nation, 99,
1914, 41.

UTLEY, FRANCIS LEE. Satire on Women in Greek, Latin, and Middle English. Harvard Summaries of Theses, 1936, 353.

----------. The Crooked Rib: An Analytical Index to the Argument about Women in English and Scots Literature to the End of the Year 1568. Ohio State Univ Press, 1944. 368 pp.

Contains edited materials, discussions of authenticity, and many Chaucer references.

Rev: S. Gibson, YWES, 208; J. W. Spargo, Spec, 20, 1945, 365-7; H. Braddy, MLN, 60, 1945, 421-2; H. Kahin, MLQ, 7, 1946, 357-8; TLS, April 14, 1945, 176; H. D. Taylor, RES, 22, 1946, 63-4; Elizabeth J. Sweeting, MLR, 40, 1945, 316. These reviews contain additional bibliography.

VON STRAUSS und TORNEY, L. Frauenarbeit im Mittelalter. Westermanns Monatshefte, 143, 1927, 173-5.

WALKER, CURTIS HOWE. Eleanor of Aquitaine. Univ of North Carolina Press, 1950. 274 pp.

Rev: Jeremiah F. O'Sullivan, Thought, 26, 1951, 634; Loren C. MacKinney, Spec, 26, 1951, 166.

WALKER, T. A. English and Scottish Education. Universities and Public Schools to the Time of Colet. Vol. 2, 341-71 of Cambridge History of English Literature. 3rd impression. Macmillan, 1920.

WAUGH, M. T. The Lollard Knights. SHR, 11, 1913, 58-63, 88-92.

WEBSTER, K. G. T. Twelfth Century Tourney. Anniversary Papers (Kittredge), 227. Ginn, 1913.

WEINBAUM, M. Zur Stellung des Fremden im mittelalterlichen England. Zeitschrift für vergleichende Rechtswissenschaft, 46, 1931, 360-78.

See Rösler, above in this section.

WEST, C. B. Courtoisie in Anglo-Norman Literature. Medium Aevum Monographs, 3. Blackwell, 1938. 175 pp.

Rev: Howard R. Patch, Spec, 13, 1938, 479-80.

WETTWER, ALBRECHT. Englischer Sport im 14. Jahrhundert. Göttingen Diss, 1933. Süddruck Göttingen-Reinhausen, 1934. 102 pp.

See Magoun, above in this section.

Rev: F. P. Magoun, Jr., Spec, 9, 1934, 346-7.

WHITMORE, Sister MARY ERNESTINE. Medieval Eng-

lish Domestic Life and Amusements in the Works of
Chaucer. Doctoral Diss, 1937. Catholic Univ of America, 1937. 279 pp.

Rev: B. J. Whiting, Spec, 13, 1938, 370-2; M. B.
Ruud, MLN, 54, 1939, 140-2; F. Schubel, ES, 73,
1939, 303-5; Hans Marcus, AB, 49, 1938, 305-6; D.
Everett, YWES, 69-70.

WHITNEY, MARIAN P. The Queen of Mediaeval Virtues:
Largesse. Vassar Mediaeval Studies, 181-215. Yale
Univ Press, 1923.

WILCOX, JOHN. French Courtly Love in English Composite Romances. Papers of the Michigan Acad of
Science, Arts, and Letters, 18, 1933, 575-90.

YOUNG, KARL. Aspects of the Story of Troilus and Criseyde. Univ of Wisconsin Studies in Language and Literature, 2, 1918, 367-94.

Courtly love material; bibliography, 367 n.

----------. Chaucer's Renunciation of Love in Troilus.
MLN, 40, 1925, 270-6.

More courtly love.

ECONOMIC BACKGROUNDS

See also entries in sections: General Backgrounds
and Religious Backgrounds.

ADDY, SIDNEY O. Church and Manor: A Study in English
Economic History. London: Geo. Allen & Co, 1913.
BAKER, J. N. L. Medieval Trade Routes. Historic Society Pamphlet. G. Bell, 1938.
BALDWIN, SUMMERFIELD. Business in the Middle
Ages. Berkshire Lectures in European History. Holt,
1937.
    Rev: E. H. Byrne, AHR, 43, 1937, 185.
BEARDWOOD, ALICE. Alien Merchants in England,
1350-1377; their Legal and Economic Position. Mono-
graph, no. 3. Cambridge, The Mediaeval Academy,
1931. 212 pp.
    Rev: N. Neilson, AHR, 38, 1932, 96-7; L. F. S.,
EHR, 48, 1933, 155; A. H. Thomas, Hist, 18, 1933,
47-9.
BECKER, HOWARD. Unrest, Culture Contact, and Re-
lease during the Middle Ages and the Renaissance.
Southwestern Social Science Quart, 12, 1931, 143-55.
    Culture contacts of the crusades and of trade with
the Levant.
BENNETT, H. S. The Reeve and the Manor in the Four-
teenth Century. EHR, 41, 1926, 358-65.
CAVE, R. C., and H. H. COULSON, Eds. Source Book
for Medieval Economic History. Science and Culture
Texts. St. Paul, Minn: Bruce Publ Co, 1936. 467 pp.
COULTON, GEORGE G. The Meaning of Medieval Mon-
eys. Hist Assoc Leaflet, no. 95. Bell, 1934. 16 pp.
DAVIS, WILLIAM S. Life on a Medieval Barony: A Pic-
ture of a Typical Feudal Community of the Thirteenth
Century. Harpers, 1923.
EDLER, FLORENCE. Glossary of Mediaeval Terms of
Business: Italian Series, 1200-1600. Mediaeval Acad
of America, 1934. 450 pp.

343

Rev: C. J., EHR, 51, 1936, 384; M. M. Postan,
Econ Hist Rev, 6, 1936, 235-6; Dino Bigongiari, AHR,
41, 1936, 521-2; C. F., MA, 6, 1937, 230-2.
GRAS, NORMAN S. B. The Early English Customs Sys-
tem. Harvard Univ Press, 1918.
GRAY, HOWARD L. The Production and Exportation of
English Woolens in the Fourteenth Century. EHR, 39,
1924, 13-35.
HALL, HUBERT, Ed. A Select Bibliography for the
Study, Sources, and Literature of English Medieval
Economic History. P. S. King & Son, 1914.
KNOOP, DOUGLAS, and G. P. JONES. The Medieval
Mason: An Economic History of English Stone Build-
ing in the Later Middle Ages and Early Modern Times.
Manchester Univ Press, 1933. 294 pp.
Rev: H. Heaton, AHR, 40, 1934, 109-10; A. P.
Usher, Spec, 9, 1934, 454-6; M. S. Briggs, Econ
Hist Rev, 5, 1934, 123-4.
KNOTT, THOMAS A. Chaucer's Anonymous Merchant.
PQ, 1, 1922, 1-16.
Banking conditions and trade.
Rev: John Koch, ESt, 57, 1923, 122-3.
KRAMER, STELLA. The English Craft Gilds: Studies in
their Progress and Decline. Columbia Univ Press,
1927. 228 pp.
Rev: Georgiana P. McEntee, Commonweal, 6,
1927, 478-9.
LAMOND, ELIZABETH. Walter of Henley. London, 1890.
Estate management.
LIPSON, E. The Economic History of England. Vol. 1,
The Middle Ages. 7th ed. Black, 1937. 674 pp.
MOFFETT, H. Y. Oswald, the Reeve. PQ, 4, 1925, 208-
23.
Estate management.
MONROE, ARTHUR ELI. Monetary Theory before Adam
Smith. Doctoral Diss, Harvard, 1923? Harvard Eco-
nomic Studies, Vol. 25. Harvard Univ Press, 1923.
312 pp.
POWER, EILEEN. The Wool Trade in English Medieval
History. The Ford Lectures, 1939. Oxford Univ Press,
1941.
Rev: TLS, Sept 20, 1941, 472; DUJ, 3, 1942, 133-4.
RAMSAY, JAMES HENRY. History of the Revenues of

the Kings of England, 1066-1399. Oxford Univ Press, 1925. 2 vols.
Financial history of medieval England.
Rev: J. R. N. Macphail, SHR, 23, 1926, 250-3.
SALZMAN, L. F. English Industries of the Middle Ages. Rev ed. Oxford: Clarendon Press, 1923.
----------. English Trade in the Middle Ages. Oxford Univ Press, 1931. 464 pp.
Rev: J. F. Willard, Hist, 16, 1931, 251; A. E. P., QQ, 38, 1931, 581-3; W. E. Lunt, AHR, 37, 1931, 150-1; N. S. B. Gras, Spec, 7, 1932, 157-9.
THRUPP, SYLVIA L. The Merchant Class in Medieval London: 1300-1500. Univ of Chicago Press, 1948. 401 pp.
Rev: J. de Surles, Moyen Age, 57, 1951, 428-31.
TOUT, THOMAS F. Beginnings of a Modern Capital. Proc of the British Acad, 11, 1923.
UNWIN, GEORGE, Ed. Finance and Trade under Edward III. By members of the History School, Manchester Univ. Manchester Univ Press, 1918. 390 pp.
----------. The Gilds and Companies of London. Methuen, 1908. 416 pp. Rev ed. Antiquary's Books. Methuen, 1925. 413 pp.
WESTLAKE, H. F. Parish Guilds of Medieval England. London, 1919.
WILLARD, JAMES F. Inland Transportation in England during the Fourteenth Century. Spec, 1, 1926, 361-74.

RELIGIOUS BACKGROUNDS

See the section: General Backgrounds, especially
for items that are both philosophic and religious. Also Gerould, 3-32.

ARNOULD, E. J. F. Henry of Lancaster and his Livre
de Seintes Medicines. JRLB, 21, 1937, 352-6.
ATTWATER, DONALD. A Dictionary of the Saints. Lon-
don, 1938.
BALDWIN, SUMMERFIELD. Organization of Medieval
Christianity. Berkshire Studies in European History.
Holt, 1929. 105 pp.
BANNISTER, A. T. Parish Life in the Fourteenth Cen-
tury. Nineteenth Century, 102, 1927, 399-404.
    Outline of a newly discovered MS containing record
of an episcopal visitation in 1397.
BASKERVILLE, GEOFFREY. English Monks. Yale Univ
Press, 1937.
BLAND, C. C. SWINTON, Tr. Miracles of the Blessed
Virgin Mary. Routledge and Sons, 1928.
    Johannes Herolt's Promptuarium Discipuli de Mi-
raculis Beate Marie Virginis. Translation and an ac-
count of 99 miracles of the Virgin.
BLOOMFIELD, MORTON W. The Origin of the Concep-
tion of the Seven Deadly Sins. Harvard Theological
Rev, 34, 1941, 121-8.
----------. The Seven Deadly Sins: An Introduction to the
History of a Religious Concept, with Special Reference
to Medieval English Literature. Michigan State College
Press, 1952. 482 pp. Also abstract, Univ of Wisconsin,
Summaries of Doctoral Dissertations, 3, 1938, 286-8.
    See index for references to Chaucer.
BOURDILLON, A. F. C. The Order of Minoresses in
England. British Society of Franciscan Studies, 12.
Manchester Univ Press, 1926. 107 pp.
    Comprehensive review of activities of minoresses,
to their dissolution in 1539.

346

Rev: AHR, 32, 1927, 912-3; TLS, July 21, 1927, 498.

BOWERS, R. H. A Middle English Treatise on Herme-
neutics: Harley MS 2276, 32^V-35^V. PMLA, 65, 1950,
590-600.

The four interpretations of scripture and story explained in an edited MS.

BREGY, KATHERINE. The Inclusiveness of Chaucer.
CW, 115, 1922, 304-13.

Chaucer's religious attitudes.

BROWN, CARLETON. Chaucer and the Hours of the
Blessed Virgin. MLN, 30, 1915, 231-2.

BYRNE, Sister MARY-OF-THE-INCARNATION. The
Tradition of the Nun in Medieval England. Doctoral
Diss, Catholic Univ of America, 1932. Catholic Univ,
1932. 236 pp.

Several references to Chaucer.

Rev: Dorothy Everett, YWES, 13, 1932, 127; H. R.
Patch, MLN, 49, 1934, 274-5; A. T., MP, 31, 1933,
103; G. W. Wolthius, Neophil, 19, 1934, 125; Legouis,
RAA, 11, 1934, 49; F. Wild, LGRP, 57, 1936, 313-4.

CAPLAN, HARRY. Classical Rhetoric and the Medieval
Theory of Preaching. Classical Philology, 28, 1933,
73-96.

----------. The Four Senses of Scriptural Interpretation
and the Mediaeval Theory of Preaching. Spec, 4, 1929,
282-90.

----------. Mediaeval Artes Praedicandi; a Handlist.
The same, a Supplementary Handlist. Cornell Studies
in Classical Philology, 24, 25. Cornell Univ Press,
1934, 1936. 52, 36 pp.

Rev: A(rcher) T(aylor), MP, 35, 1937, 101-2; G.
R. Owst, MA, 6, 1937, 151-6; Woodburn O. Ross,
MLN, 53, 1938, 473-4.

----------. Rhetorical Invention in Some Mediaeval
Tractates on Preaching. Spec, 2, 1927, 284-95.

----------, and H. H. KING. Latin Tractates on
Preaching: A Book List. Harvard Theological Rev,
42, 1949, 184-206.

Note also Italian Treatises on Preaching and Spanish Treatises on Preaching, Speech Monographs, 16,
1949, 243-52, and 17, 1950, 161-70; and French Tractates on Preaching: A Book List, Quart Jour of
Speech, 36, 1950, 296-325.

CARNEGY, FRANCIS A. R. The Relations between the
    Social and Divine Order in William Langland's "Vision
    of William concerning Piers the Plowman. " Sprache
    und Kultur der germanischen und romanischen Völker,
    Reihe A, Bd XII. Priebatsch, 1934. 48 pp.
CHAPLIN, W. N. Lollardry and the Great Bible. Church
    Quart Rev, 128, 1939, 210-37.
CHAPMAN, COOLIDGE OTIS. Chaucer on Preachers
    and Preaching. PMLA, 44, 1929, 178-85.
        Rev: Dorothy Everett, YWES, 107-8.
CHARLAND, THOMAS M. Les Artes Praedicandi: Con-
    tribution a l'Histoire de la Rhétorique au Moyen Age.
    Publ de l'Inst d'Etudes Médiévales d'Ottawa, 7. Insti-
    tut d'Etudes Médiévales, 1936. 420 pp.
        Rev: Harry Caplan, Spec, 13, 1938, 352-4; Sister
    Angele (Gleason), AHR, 43, 1938, 439-40.
CLINE, RUTH H. Four Chaucer Saints. MLN, 60, 1945,
    480-2.
        The significance of swearing by St. Frideswide,
    St. Cuthbert, St. Yve, and St. Thomas, the Apostle.
    MilT, 3449; Reeve'sT, 4127; MerT, E1230; ShT,
    B1417 (VII, 227).
        Rev: D. Everett, YWES, 49-50.
COULTON, GEORGE GORDON. Five Centuries of Reli-
    gion. Vol. 2, The Friars and the Dead Weight of Tra-
    dition, 1200-1400. Cambridge Univ Press, 1928. 703
    pp. Vol. 3, Getting and Spending, 1936; Vol. 4, Last
    Days of Monachism, 1950.
        Many references to Chaucer and to Canterbury.
        Rev: TLS, Jan 26, 1928, 54; NQ, 154, 1928, 71;
    Sydney M. Brown, AHR, 33, 1928, 633-5; Eileen Pow-
    er, Econ Hist Rev, 7, 1936, 87-92; G. Post, Spec, 11,
    1936, 524-30; A. L. R. Owst, Spect, 156, 1936, 478;
    NQ, 170, 1936, 251-2; TLS, Mar 7, 1936, 196; R. B.
    Lloyd, Obs, April 5, 1936; Claude Jenkins, MA, 20,
    1951, 50-3.
----------. Ten Medieval Studies; with Four Appendices.
    3rd ed. Macmillan, 1930. 297 pp.
        Chapters on medieval religious themes. Several
    Chaucer references.
        Rev: C. Wright, Commonweal, 14, 1931, 22-4; E.
    C. Lodge, Hist, 16, 1931, 154-5.
COX, JOHN CHARLES. English Church Fittings, Furni-

ture and Accessories. With an Introduction by Aymer
Vallance. Putnam, 1923.
CRANAGE, D. H. S. The Home of the Monk: An Account
of English Monastic Life and Buildings in the Middle
Ages. Cambridge Univ Press, 1926. 125 pp. 3rd ed,
1934. 123 pp.
Rev: NQ, 151, 1926, 144.
DAHMUS, JOSEPH H. The Career in Church and State of
William Courtenay, Archbishop of Canterbury: A Typ-
ical Fourteenth Century Bishop. Doctoral Diss, Illi-
nois, 1938.
----------. The Prosecution of John Wyclif. Yale Univ
Press, 1952. 167 pp.
DEANSLEY, MARGARET. A History of the Mediaeval
Church, 590-1500. Methuen, 1925. 288 pp.
----------. The Lollard Bible and Other Medieval Bib-
lical Versions. Cambridge Univ Press, 1920.
    Rev: SP, 18, 1921, 364-5; Charles R. Baskervill,
MP, 18, 1921, 507; E. W. Watson, MLR, 16, 1921,
72-4.
FOAKES-JACKSON, F. J. The Church in the Middle
Ages. Macmillan, 1934.
    Rev: A. C. Wyckoff, SRL, 12, 1935, 18.
GASQUET, Cardinal. Monastic Life in the Middle Ages.
Bell, 1922.
    Rev: TLS, July 6, 1922.
GEROULD, GORDON HALL. Saints' Legends. Houghton,
1916. 393 pp.
    For reviews, see section: Literary Relations.
----------. "Tables" in Mediaeval Churches. Spec, 1,
1926, 439-40.
    Mural displays of verse, common during 14th and
15th centuries.
GWYNN, AUBREY. The English Austin Friars in the
Time of Wyclif. Oxford Univ Press, 1940. 295 pp.
    Rev: DUJ, 2, 1940, 74-5; M. Deansley, Hist, 26,
1941, 75-6; S. Harrison Thompson, AHR, 46, 1941,
620-1.
HEINRICH, Sister MARY P. .The Canonesses and Education in the Early Middle Ages. Washington Univ Diss,
1924. Privately printed.
HELMING, VERNON P. Medieval Pilgrimages and English Literature to 1400. Diss, Yale, 1937.

HERAUCOURT, WILL. Chaucers Vorstellung von den geistigseelischen Kräften des Menschen. Ang, 65, 1941, 255-302.

HORT, GRETA. Piers Plowman and Contemporary Religious Thought. Macmillan, 1938. 178 pp.

HJORT, GRETHE. Piers Plowman as a Work of Moral Theology. Doctoral Diss, Girton College, Cambridge, and Univ of Copenhagen, 1931-2. Abstract in Cambridge Abstracts of Dissertations . . . , 1931-2, 68.

----------. Theological Schools in Medieval England. CQR, 116, 1933, 201-18.

    Reply: G. G. Coulton, CQR, 118, 1934, 98-101.

HORSTMANN, C. Altenglischen Legenden. Neue Folge. Heilbronn: Henninger, 1881.

    A Middle English legend collection, containing Blood of Hayles, St. Martin, St. Cecilia.

HUGHES, HELEN. A Medieval Scholar in Action: Richard Fitz-Ralph, Archbishop of Armagh. Discovery, 10, 1929, 393-6.

HUNTER-BLAIR, A. O. Black Monks at Oxford University. Dublin Rev, 192, 1933, 17-25.

HUTTON, EDWARD. The Franciscans in England, 1224-1538. Constable, 1926. 326 pp.

    Chaucer, 189-98.

    Rev: TLS, Jan 6, 1927, 4.

JESSOPP, AUGUSTUS. The Coming of the Friars and Other Historic Essays. 19th impression. Unwin; Putnam, 1922.

JOHNSON, DUDLEY. Chaucer and the Bible. Doctoral Diss, Yale, 1941.

JONES, H. S. V. The Clerk of Oxenford. PMLA, 27, 1912, 106-15.

JORDAN, E. , Comp. Histoire Ecclésiastique du Moyen Age. Revue Historique, 172, 1933, 473-509.

    Critical bibliography.

KEMP, E. Augustinian Tradition in the Religious Life. Church Quart Rev, 125, 1937, 19-47.

KRUISINGA, E. New Chaucer Word: Cloisterlees. Athenaeum, 1902, II, 722.

KUHL, ERNEST P. Chaucer and the Church. MLN, 40, 1925, 321-38.

LOWES, JOHN LIVINGSTON. Chaucer and the Seven Deadly Sins. PMLA, 30, 1915, 237-371.

    See Tupper, below in this section.

MACAULAY, ROSE. Some Religious Elements in Eng-
lish Literature. Hogarth Lectures, no. 14. Harcourt,
1931. 160 pp.
  Some references to Chaucer.
  For reviews, see section: General Criticism.
McKENNA, Sister MARY BONAVENTURE. Liturgy of
the Canterbury Tales. Cath Educ Rev, 35, 1937, 474-
80.
MADELEVA, Sister MARY (MARY EVALINE WOLFF).
Chaucer's Nuns and Other Essays. Appleton, 1925.
  Rev: D. Everett, YWES, 92.
MAXFIELD, EZRA K. Chaucer and Religious Reform.
PMLA, 39, 1924, 64-74.
MOSSE, F. Chaucer et la Liturgie. Rev Germ, 14, 1923,
283-9.
MULROONEY, Rev. CHARLES RICHARD. The Cultus of
the Blessed Virgin Mary in Middle English Lyrics.
Doctoral Diss, St. John's, 1942.
O'NEILL, BURKE. Certain Theological Matters in Chau-
cer. Diss, Univ of California, 1938.
  A defense of the orthodoxy of Chaucer in regard to
the doctrine of grace, medieval eschatology, and sac-
ramental theology.
OWST, G. R. Literature and the Pulpit in Medieval Eng-
land. A Neglected Chapter in the History of English
Letters and of the English People. Macmillan, 1933.
616 pp.
  Rev: NQ, 164, 1933, 413-4; TLS, May 11, 1933, 327;
  F. J. M. Raby, Antiquaries Jour, 13, 1933, 325-7;
  G. G. Coulton, Obs, May 21, 1933; H. Caplan, Phil
  Rev, 42, 1933, 639-40; Holb Rev, 157, 1933, 416; A.
  G. , Studies, 22, 1933, 700-2; S. Addleshaw, CQR,
  117, 1933, 165-72; V. H. G. , Oxford Mag, Nov 23,
  1933, 274; E. Power, N St, 5, 1933, 576, 578; J. E.
  G. de M. , CR, 144, 1933, 246-50; G. R. Coffman,
  SP, 31, 1934, 104-9; H. R. Patch, Spec, 9, 1934,
  233-4; G. B. Phelan, Commonweal, 19, 1934, 275-6;
  M. R. P. McGuire, CHR, 20, 1934, 67-71; A. G.
  Little, EHR, 49, 1934, 115-6; C. W. David, AHR, 40,
  1934, 107-8; W. A. G. Boyle-Davidson, E Stud, 16,
  1934, 175-83; B. J. Whiting, MLN, 50, 1935, 338-41;
  P. E. T. Widdington, RES, 12, 1936, 337-41.
----------. Preaching in Medieval England: An Intro-

duction to Sermon Manuscripts of the Period, c. 1350-
1450. Cambridge Univ Press, 1926. 382 pp.
    Rev: TLS, July 22, 1926, 489; NQ, 151, 1926, 143;
Eileen Power, Nation-Athen, 40, 1926, 2, 87; Charles
H. Haskins, Spec, 2, 1927, 496; Wm. F. McGinnis,
Commonweal, 5, 1927, 557-8; Alfred H. Sweet, AHR,
32, 1927, 305-6; H. B. Workman, LQR, ser. 5, no.
64, 1926, 229-36; Dorothy Everett, YWES, 96-8.
PALMER, H. P. Excommunication in the Middle Ages.
QR, 251, 1928, 129-43.
    Illustrated from the Diocese registers of Bath and
Wells.
----------. The Troubles of a Mediaeval Bishop. LQR,
152, 1929, 172-84.
    Bishop is Grandisson, Bishop of Exeter in Edward
III's reign. Comparison of Grandisson's archdeacons
with Chaucer's Summoner, 173-4.
PANTIN, WILLIAM ABEL, Ed. Documents Illustrating
the Activities of the General and Provincial Chapters
of English Black Monks: 1215-1540. 2 vols. 1931-3.
PATCH, HOWARD R. Troilus on Predestination. JEGP,
17, 1918, 399-422.
PECHEUX, Mother MARY CHRISTOPHER. Aspects of
the Treatment of Death in Middle English Poetry.
Catholic Univ, 1951.
PFANDER, HOMER G. The Popular Sermon of the Med-
ieval Friar in England. Doctoral Diss, New York
Univ, 1937. Published by the author, 1937. 72 pp.
    Rev: A. B(randl), Arch, 172, 1938, 247-8; C. O.
Chapman, MLN, 53, 1938, 533-6; M. Rösler, ES, 73,
1938, 137-8.
----------. Some Medieval Manuals of Religious In-
struction in England and Observations on Chaucer's
Parson's Tale. JEGP, 35, 1936, 243-58.
    Rev: Dorothy Everett, YWES, 84-5.
POWER, EILEEN. Medieval English Nunneries, c1275-
1535. Cambridge Univ Press, 1922.
    Rev: TLS, Dec 28, 1922; W. B. Workman, LQR,
July, 1923, 19-30; E. B. and E. H. D., Dublin Rev,
July-Sept, 1923, 128-34; E. W. Watson, EHR, 38,
1923, 435-7; NQ, Jan 13, 1923, 39-40; G. G. Coulton,
NQ, Feb 10, 1923, 107; J. H. R., NQ, Mar 3, 1923,
180; W. R. N. Baron, NQ, Mar 17, 1923, 216; Hilda

Johnstone, Hist, 8, 1923, 218-20; R. Ellis Roberts, Mercury, 9, 1923, 220-2.

RAMSAY, J. H. Chaucer and Wycliffe's Bible. Acad, 1891, II, 435-6.

ROBERTSON, D. W. Frequency of Preaching in Thirteenth Century England. Spec, 24, 1949, 376-88.

RUSSELL, JOSIAH COX. The Clerical Population in Medieval England. Traditio, 2, 1944, 177-212.

SMALLEY, B. The Study of the Bible in the Middle Ages. Oxford: Clarendon Press, 1941. 296 pp. 2nd ed, Oxford: Basil Blackwell; New York: The Philosophical Library, 1952. 406 pp.
    Rev: M. L. W. Laistner, Spec, 17, 1942, 146-8; MA, 16, 1947, 34-5; A. G. Little, EHR, 57, 1942, 267-9; M. L. W. Laistner, Spec, 27, 1952, 585; F. G. Sitwell, MA, 21, 1952, 86-8; G. Willcock, YWES, 69-70; TLS, Aug 20, 1941, 416.

SMITH, HERBERT MAYNARD. Lollardry. CQR, 119, 1934, 30-60.

SMITH, LUCY TOULMIN. English Popular Preaching in the Fourteenth Century. EHR, 7, 1892, 25-36.

SPENCER, THEODORE. Chaucer's Hell: A Study in Mediaeval Convention. Spec, 2, 1927, 177-200.

SPIERS, EDWARD HOWARD. Chaucer's References to Old Testament Persons Including Textual Comparison with the Vulgate. Master's Thesis, Univ of Washington, 1950.

STAPLETON, CHRISTOPHER. Chaucer the Catholic. CW, 127, 1928, 186-93.

STARNES, DE WITT T. Our Lady of Walsingham. Texas Rev, 7, 1922, 306-27.
    Pilgrimages and shrines.

STRITTMATTER, EUGENE. Classical Elements in the Roman Liturgy. Classical Jour, 18, 1923, 195-207.

STUCKERT, HOWARD MORRIS. Corrodies in the English Monasteries. Philadelphia, 1923. Privately printed. 54 pp.

TANELLE, PIERRE. Moines et Franciscains dans l'Angleterre du Moyen-Age. RAA, Juin, 1927, 403-16.

TATLOCK, JOHN STRONG PERRY. Chaucer and Wyclif. MP, 14, 1916, 257-68.

----------. Epilog of Chaucer's Troilus. MP, 18, 1921, 625-59.

Chaucer's attitude as a Christian poet toward pagan subject matter.

THOMAS, MARY EDITH. Medieval Skepticism and Chaucer: An Evaluation of the Skepticism of the 13th and 14th Centuries, of Geoffrey Chaucer, and his Immediate Predecessors -- An Era that Looked Back on an Age of Faith and Forward to an Age of Reason. New York: The William-Frederick Press, 1950. 184 pp. Notes and bibliography.

Rev: G. R. Owst, RES, 4 n. s. , 1953, 68-9; H. R. P. , MLN, 67, 1952, 269-71; Dorothy Everett, MLR, 48, 1953, 64-5; Haldeen Braddy, MLQ, 15, 1954, 74-5; A. L. Kellogg, Spec, 27, 1952, 258-60.

THOMPSON, A. HAMILTON. The English Clergy and their Organization in the Later Middle Ages. Oxford, 1947. 327 pp.

Rev: DUJ, 40, 1947, 31-2; Hist, 34, 1949, 126.

TOWNE, FRANK. Wyclif and Chaucer on the Contemplative Life. 3-14, in Essays Critical and Historical Dedicated to Lily B. Campbell. Univ of California: Dept of English: Essays Critical and Historical, 1951.

TUPPER, FREDERICK. Chaucer's Bed's Head. MLN, 30, 1915, 5-12.

Chaucer and the Prymer, 9-11.

----------. Chaucer and the Seven Deadly Sins. PMLA, 29, 1914, 93-128.

See Lowes, above in this section.

Rev: John Koch, AB, 25, 1914, 327-32.

----------. Chaucer's Sinners and Sins. JEGP, 15, 1916, 56-106.

Rev: John Koch, AB, 28, 1917, 152-5.

WATT, FRANCIS. Canterbury Pilgrims and their Ways. Methuen, 1917; Dodd, 1918. 288 pp.

Rev: Athen, 1918, I, 35-6.

WAUGH, M. T. The Lollard Knights. SHR, 11, 1913, 58-63, 88-92.

WHITMORE, NYENLAH O. Medieval Preaching: Canterbury Tales. Master's Thesis, Univ of Iowa, 1934.

WHITNEY, J. P. Religious Movements in the Fourteenth Century. Vol. 2, 43-69, of Cambridge History of English Literature. 3rd impression. Macmillan, 1920.

WILLIAMS, ARNOLD. Chaucer and the Friars. Spec, 28, 1953, 499-513.

WILSON, JAMES M. Monastic Life in England Just before the Reformation. CR, 123, 1923, 488-95.
----------. The Worcester Liber Albus: Glimpses of
Life in a Great Benedictine Monastery in the Fourteenth Century. SPCK, 1920.
WOOD-LEGH, K. L. Studies in Church Life in England
under Edward III. Cambridge Studies in Medieval Life
and Thought. Cambridge Univ Press; Macmillan, 1934.
181 pp.
    Rev: TLS, Aug 9, 1934, 548; NQ, 167, 1934, 125-6;
W. E. Lunt, AHR, 40, 1935, 774-5; C. R. Cheney,
EHR, 50, 1935, 327-9; I. J. Churchill, Hist, 20, 1935,
164-5; Dom B. Heurtebize, Rev Hist Ecclés, 31, 1935,
394-5; J. T. Ellis, CHR, 21, 1936, 453-4; F. M. Pow-
icke, MA, 4, 1935, 123-5.
WORK, JAMES A. Echoes of the Anathema in Chaucer.
PMLA, 47, 1932, 419-30.
    For review, see section: General Criticism.
WORKMAN, H. B. John Wyclif; A Study of the English
Medieval Church. Oxford Univ Press, 1926. 2 vols.
    Rev: TLS, Nov 18, 1926, 809; John A. Faulkner,
Biblical Rev, 12, 1927, 635-8; Shirley J. Case, Na-
tion, 124, 1927, 454-5; Alfred H. Sweet, AHR, 32,
1927, 581-3; W. P. Reeves, JEGP, 27, 1928, 87-92;
J. P. Whitney, EHR, 44, 1929, 466-7.
WYCLIFFE, JOHN. Responsiones ad Radulphum Strodum.
Reproductions of Manuscripts and Rare Printed Books.
Now on deposit in the Library of Congress. Vienna:
Nazionalbibliothek, MS 2603, fols. 1-100.
YOUNG, KARL. Chaucer and the Liturgy. MLN, 30,
1915, 97-9.

SCIENTIFIC BACKGROUNDS

See Manly, 132-44; Wells, CBEL, I, 215, and the
supplements to the Manual since 1933. Also see
Price, in section: Manuscripts.

AIKEN, PAULINE. Vincent of Beauvais and the Green
Yeoman's Lecture on Demonology. SP, 35, 1938, 1-9.
----------. Vincent of Beauvais and Dame Pertelote's
Knowledge of Medicine. Spec, 10, 1935, 281-7.
ANON. Memorabilia. NQ, 169, 1935, 397.
Brief account of Dr. J. D. Rolleston's paper on
Chaucer and Mediaeval Medicine, "contributed a year
or two ago to the International Congress of the Histo-
ry of Medicine, and published in the Comptes Rendus
(Bucarest)."
BASHFORD, H. H. Chaucer's Physician and his Fore-
bears. Nineteenth Century, 104, 1928, 237-48.
BOLDAUN, NILS W. Chaucer and Matters Medical. New
Eng Jour of Medicine, 208, 1933, 1365-8.
BOMBARDIER. Chaucer: Ornithologist. Blackwoods,
256, 1944, 120-5.
Bird lore rather than scientific ornithology.
BRANDL, A. Zur Geographie der Chaucerzeit. Arch,
165, 1934, 81.
BROWNE, WILLIAM H. Notes on Chaucer's Astrology.
MLN, 23, 1908, 53-4.
BRUNET, A. M. La Notion de "Science" au Moyen Age.
Doctoral Diss, Institut d'Etudes Medievales. Listed
as completed in Willard, 11, 1933, 49.
CAMPBELL, ANNA MONTGOMERY. The Black Death
and Men of Learning. History of Science Society Pub-
lications, new ser., no. 1. Columbia Univ Press,
1931. 210 pp.
CAMPBELL, DONALD. Arabian Medicine and its Influ-
ence on the Middle Ages. Trübners Original Series.
Dutton, 1926.
Arabic influence in England, Vol. 1, 175, 198-200.

COLLINS, J. Medicine in England in Chaucer's Time.
Proc of the Charaka Club, 4, 1916, 139.
CURRY, WALTER CLYDE. Astrologizing the Gods. Ang,
47, 1923, 213-43.
----------. Chaucer and the Mediaeval Sciences. Ox-
ford, 1926. 268 pp.
For reviews, see section: General Criticism. This
book incorporates and revises Professor Curry's ar-
ticles listed here following.
----------. Chaucer's Doctor of Phisyk. PQ, 4, 1925,
1-24.
----------. Chaucer's Reeve and Miller. PMLA, 35,
1920, 189-209.
Physiognomical lore.
----------. Chaucer's Science and Art. Texas Rev, 8,
1923, 307-22.
----------. Chauntecleer and Pertelote on Dreams. ESt,
58, 1924, 24-60.
----------. Fortuna Maior. MLN, 38, 1923, 94-6.
Astrology.
----------. More about Chaucer's Wife of Bath. PMLA,
37, 1922, 30-51.
Astrological and physiognomical lore.
----------. The Malady of Chaucer's Summoner. MP,
19, 1922, 395-404.
Chaucer's medical knowledge.
----------. The Middle English Ideal of Personal
Beauty, as Found in the Metrical Romances, Chron-
icles, and Legends of the XIII, XIV, and XV Centuries.
Doctoral Diss, Stanford, 1915. J. H. Furst Co, 1916.
127 pp.
----------. O Mars, O Atazir. JEGP, 22, 1923, 347-68.
Astrology.
----------. The Secret of Chaucer's Pardoner. JEGP,
18, 1919, 593-606.
Physiognomical lore.
DAMON, S. FOSTER. Chaucer and Alchemy. PMLA, 39,
1924, 782-8.
DE GIVRY, GRILLOT. Witchcraft, Magic and Alchemy.
Trans by J. Courtenay Locke. Harrap, 1932. 395 pp.
Rev: TLS, May 5, 1932, 329.
DONOVAN, MORTIMER J. Three Notes on Chaucer's
Marine Life. PQ, 31, 1952, 439-41.

DUNCAN, EDGAR H. The Yeoman's Canon's "Silver
    Citrinacioun." MP, 37, 1940, 241-62.
    Chaucer's knowledge of alchemy, and the operation
    known as citrination of silver.
DUSTOOR, P. E. Chaucer's Astrology in "The Knightes
    Tale." TLS, May 5, 1927, 318.
EMERSON, OLIVER F. Chaucer's Opie of Thebes Fyn.
    MP, 17, 1919, 287-91.
FARNHAM, WILLARD E. The Dayes of the Mone. SP,
    20, 1923, 70-82.
    Astronomical lore. Reference to T&C, II, 74-6; MilT,
    328-32 (A3514-8); FrankT, 208-10; and MLT, 306-8.
FOX, GEORGE GILLESPIE. The Mediaeval Sciences in
    the Works of John Gower. Doctoral Diss, Princeton,
    1926. Princeton Studies in English, no. 6. Princeton
    Univ Press, 1931. 164 pp.
    Many references to Chaucer.
    Rev: Dorothy Everett, YWES, 12, 1931, 92-3.
GOODE, CLEMENT TYSON, and EDGAR FINLEY SHAN-
    NON. An Atlas of English Literature. Century, 1925.
    130 pp.
    One chapter and map, 10-11, on Middle English
    period; one on London, 82-7; one on Italy, in relation
    to English literature, 74-6.
    Rev: Clark S. Northup, Cornell Alumni News, 27,
    1925, 359; Robert Withington, Sewanee Rev, 36, 1928,
    124-6.
GRIMM, FLORENCE MARIE. Astronomical Lore in
    Chaucer. Univ of Nebraska Studies in Language, Lit-
    erature, and Criticism, 1919. 96 pp.
    Rev: John S. P. Tatlock, JEGP, 19, 1920, 129-30;
    Howard R. Patch, MLN, 35, 1920, 128.
HASKINS, CHARLES HOMER. Studies in the History of
    Medieval Science. Harvard Univ Historical Studies,
    Vol. 27. Harvard Univ Press, 1924. 411 pp. 2nd ed,
    Harvard Univ Press, 1927.
    Rev: SHR, 22, 1925, 148; David Eugene Smith, SRL,
    2, 1925, 124; TLS, Dec 4, 1924.
HEATHER, P. J. The Seven Planets. Folk-Lore, 54,
    1943, 338-61.
    Chaucer's references to the planets.
HOUSEMAN, PERCY A. Science in Chaucer. Scientific
    Monthly, 38, 1934, 561-4.

HUME, EDGAR ERSKINE. Medical Work of the Knights
    Hospitallers of St. John of Jerusalem. Johns Hopkins
    Press, 1940.
JOHNSON, FRANCIS R. , and SANFORD V. LARKEY.
    Science. MLQ, 2, 1941, 363-401.
    A survey of research in the field of Renaissance
    science.
LANGE, HUGO. Hat Chaucer den Kompass Gekannt und
    Benützt? Ang, 58, 1934, 333-44.
    See also Lange, Die Deklination, etc. , in section:
    Parlement of Foules.
LENNOX, WILLIAM G. John of Gaddesden on Epilepsy.
    Annals of Medical History, 3rd ser. , 1, 1939, 283-
    307.
LOWES, JOHN LIVINGSTON. The Loveres Maladye of
    Hereos. MP, 11, 1914, 491-546.
    See also Lowes, Hereos, Nation, Sept 11, 1913,
    233, and Hereos Again, MLN, 31, 1916, 185-6.
    For review, see section: Word Study.
LUNN, JOHN. The Black Death, 1348-1349, with Special
    Reference to Cathedral Registers for the Mortality of
    the Clergy. Doctoral Diss, St. John's College, Cam-
    bridge, and the Univ of Manchester, 1930-1. Abstract
    in Cambridge Abstracts of Dissertations, 1930-1, 53.
McCARTNEY, EUGENE. The Plant Almanac and the
    Weather Bureau. Classical Weekly, 17, 1924, 105-8.
MILLER, AMANDA H. Chaucer's "Secte Saturnyn. "
    MLN, 47, 1932, 99-102.
    Medieval astrology.
NICHOLLS, ALBERT G. Medicine in Chaucer's Day.
    Dalhousie Rev, 12, 1932, 218-30.
NOWAK, L. Die Alchemie und die Alchemisten in der
    englischen Literatur. Breslau Diss, 1934. 83 pp.
OGDEN, MARGARET S. , Ed. The Liber de Diversis
    Medicinis in the Thornton MS [MS Lincoln Cathedral,
    A. 5. 2, 1938.] EETS, 207.
POOLE, REGINALD L. The Beginning of the Year in the
    Middle Ages. Oxford Univ Press, 1922.
    Rev: TLS, Jan 5, 1922.
PRICE, DEREK J. Chaucer's Astronomy. Nature, 170,
    Sept 20, 1952, 474-5.
READ, JOHN. Alchemy and Alchemists. Folk-Lore, 44,
    1933, 251-78.
    Development and literature of alchemy.

----------. Prelude to Chemistry; an Outline of Alchemy,
its Literature and Relationships. Macmillan, 1937.
329 pp.
    Rev: T. L. Davis, Amer Chem Soc Jour, 59, 1937,
771; Gerald Wendt, NYHTB, Feb 7, 1937, 22; C. A.
Browne, Ind and Engr Chem, 15, 1937, 215; E. J.
Holmyard, Nature, 139, 1937, 452; N St, 13, 1937, 24;
NYTBR, Feb 7, 1937, 12; John Riordan, SRL, 15, Jan
23, 1937, 6; R. J. Anderson, YR, 26, 1937, 626.
----------. The Alchemist in Life, Literature, and Art.
Thomas Nelson, 1947.
RIESMAN, DAVID. Story of Medicine in the Middle Ages.
Hoeber, 1935. 425 pp.
    Rev: M. P. Ravenel, Amer Jour Public Health, 25,
1935, 1382; NYTBR, July 21, 1935, 10; J. J. Walsh,
Commonweal, 24, 1936, 369.
RUSKA, JULIUS. Chaucer und das Buch Senior. Ang, 61,
1937, 136-7.
SARTON, GEORGE. Introduction to the History of Sci-
ence. Vol. III, Part 2. Carnegie Institution of Wash-
ington, 1949.
SINGER, CHARLES. Early English Magic and Medicine.
British Acad Proc, 1919-20, 341-74. Milford, 1924.
SINGER, DOROTHY WALEY, assisted by ANNIE ANDER-
SON. Catalogue of Latin and Vernacular Alchemical
Manuscripts in Great Britain and Ireland. Brussels:
Lamertin, 1928, 1930. 2 vols.
STOKER, RAY COOKE. Geographical Lore in the Middle
English Metrical Romances. Doctoral Diss, Stanford,
1929. Abstract in Abstracts of Dissertations, 4, 1928-
9, 43-7.
TATLOCK, JOHN STRONG PERRY. Astrology and Magic
in Chaucer's Franklin's Tale. 339-50, in Anniversary
Papers . . . for George Lyman Kittredge. Ginn, 1913.
    Rev: John Koch, AB, 25, 1914, 339-41.
THORNDIKE, LYNN. The Historical Background of Modern Science. Scientific Monthly, 16, 1923, 487-96.
----------. A History of Magic and Experimental Science
during the First Thirteen Centuries of our Era. Macmillan, 1923. 6 vols. 2nd ed, 1929.
    Rev: Alex. Weinstein, The Freeman, 8, 1923, 67-
70; Gordon H. Gerould, Literary Rev, June 9, 1923,
748; Boston Transcript, June 23, 1923, 5; John S. P.

Tatlock, Univ of Calif Chron, 25, 1923, 510-2; Samuel C. Chew, Nation, 116, 1923, 437; Outlook, 133, 1923, 456; George L. Burr, AHR, 29, 1923, 118-20; E. N. da C. Andrade, Mercury, 8, 1923, 333-4; TLS, April 5, 1923; Robert Steele, QR, 240, 1923, 291-307; R. R. Marett, Folk-Lore, 34, 1923, 252-5; Wilfred P. Mustard, AJP, 45, 1924, 93; Allan H. Gilbert, SAQ, 23, 1924, 79-81; A. G. Keller, YR, 13, 1924, 398-401; S. Foster Damon, Dial, 76, 1924, 75-8; Stephen H. Bush, PQ, 3, 1924, 78-9; George R. Coffman, MP, 23, 1925, 115-8.

----------. A History of Magic and Experimental Science. Vols. 3 and 4, Fourteenth and Fifteenth Centuries. Columbia Univ Press, 1934.

   Rev: F. G. Lewis, Crozer Quart, 12, 1935, 198; J. T. McNeill, Jour of Religion, 15, 1935, 342; Harold Ward, NR, 84, 1935, 26; T. Wingate Todd, AHR, 41, 1936, 523-5.

----------. The Latin Pseudo-Aristotle and Medieval Occult Science. JEGP, 21, 1922, 229-58.

----------. Magic and Science in the Fourteenth and Fifteenth Centuries. Columbia Univ Quart, 27, 1935, 132-40.

----------. Peter Abano: A Medieval Scientist. American Historical Association, Annual Report for 1919, 1, 1923, 315-26.

----------. Science and Thought in the Fifteenth Century: Studies in the History of Medicine and Surgery, Natural and Mathematical Science, Philosophy and Politics. Columbia Univ Press, 1929. 387 pp.

   Introduction: Study of Western Science of 14th and 15th Centuries.

   Rev: TLS, Oct 17, 1929, 827.

----------, and PEARL KIBRE. A Catalogue of Incipits of Mediaeval Scientific Writings in Latin. Cambridge, Mass: Mediaeval Academy of America, 1937. Also More Incipits of . . ., Spec, 18, 1942, 342-66; Thorndike, Lynn, Additional Incipits of . . . , Spec, 14, 1939, 93-105; and Thorndike, Lynn, Further Incipits of . . . , Spec, 26, 1951, 673-95.

TUPPER, FREDERICK. Chaucer's Doctour of Phisik. Nation, 96, 1913, 640-1.

VEAZIE, WALTER B. Chaucer's Text-Book of Astron-

omy; Johannes de Sacrobosco. Univ of Colorado
Studies, Series B, Studies in the Humanities, 1, 1940,
169-82.
WAITE, ARTHUR EDWARD. The Secret Tradition in
Alchemy: Its Development and Records. Knopf, 1927.
415 pp.
    Rev: S. Foster Damon, Dial, 83, 1927, 66-9.
WALSH, JAMES J. Medieval Medicine. Black, 1920.
221 pp.
WEDEL, T. O. The Medieval Attitude toward Astrology
Particularly in England. Yale Studies in English.
Yale Univ Press, 1920.
    Rev: Arch, 141, 1921, 316.
WHITE, LYNN, Jr. Technology and Invention in the
Middle Ages. Spec, 15, 1940, 141-59.
    Bibliography, 156-9.
WRIGHT, JOHN K. The Geographical Lore of the Time
of the Crusades: A Study in the History of Medieval
Science. American Geographical Society, 1925.
----------. Notes on the Knowledge of Latitudes and
Longitudes in the Middle Ages. Isis, 5, 1923, 75-98.

ARTISTIC BACKGROUNDS

For costume, see section: Social Backgrounds.

ADDISON, JULIA DE WOLF. Arts and Crafts in the
Middle Ages; a Description of Mediaeval Workman-
ship in Several of the Departments of Applied Art, to-
gether with Some Account of Special Artisans in the
Early Renaissance. Page, 1908. Rev ed, 1933. 364 pp.
ALLEN, HOPE EMILY. Lollards and English Art. TLS,
July 18, 1929, 576.
ANDERSON, M. D. The Medieval Carver, with a Pre-
face by W. G. Constable. Macmillan; Cambridge Univ
Press, 1935. 187 pp.
    Not seen.
    Rev: TLS, April 25, 1935, 269; A. B. Parsons,
NYHTB, June 16, 1935, 18; E. A. Jewell, NYTBR,
Jan 19, 1936, 11; Spect, 154, 1935, 804; Living Church,
92, 1935, 590; NQ, 168, 1935, 234; A. G. , Antiquaries
Jour, 15, 1935, 490-1; G. Woodthorpe, Obs, April 14,
1935; H. E. B. , EHR, 52, 1937, 152-3.
APEL, WILLI. The Notation of Polyphonic Music: 900 to
1500. 4th ed, rev with commentary. 471 pp; 88 plates.
Med Acad of America, 1949.
----------. French Secular Music in the Late Four-
teenth Century. Med Acad, 1950.
ARNOLD, HUGH. Stained Glass of the Middle Ages in
England and France; Painted by Lawrence B. Saint.
Macmillan, 1926. 269 pp.
    Late 14th Century Glass in England, 195-200.
ASHDOWN, CHARLES H. Armour and Weapons in the
Middle Ages. Harrap, 1925. 220 pp.
    Chaucer's period, 78-112.
    Rev: TLS, Oct 15, 1925.
BAKER, CHARLES HENRY COLLINS. British Paintings,
with a Chapter on Primitive Paintings by Montague
R. James. Hale, 1933. 319 pp.
    The Mediaeval Period, 1-25.

BEARD, CHARLES R. Armour Terminology. TLS, May 26, 1932, 390.

BERENSON, BERNHARD. Studies in Medieval Painting. Yale Univ Press, 1930. 148 pp.

Rev: TLS, May 28, 1931, 413.

BESSELER, HEINRICH. Musik der Mittelalters und der Renaissance. Akad Verlags, 1936.

Rev: Isabel Pope, Spec, 13, 1938, 240-1.

BORENIUS, TANCRED, and E. W. TRISTRAM. English Mediaeval Painting. Pegasus Press, 1928. 80 pp.

Rev: C. R. Post, SRL, 6, 1929, 38.

BROWN, G. BALDWIN. The Arts in Early England. Murray, 1930. 91 pp.

Rev: T. D. Kendrick, Antiquity, 5, 1931, 399; H. E. D. Blakiston, EHR, 46, 1931, 663-5; Brit Archaeol Assoc Jour, 36, 1931, 428-9.

BRUYNE, E. de. Etudes d'Esthétique Médiévale. 3 vols. Bruges, 1946.

CARTER, WILLIAM H. Ut Pictura Poesis: A Study of the Parallel between Painting and Poetry from Classical Times through the Seventeenth Century. Doctoral Diss, Harvard, 1951.

CASEY, D. N. An Embroidery of Mediaeval England. Rhode Island School of Design Bull, 22, 1934, 27-30.

14th century chasuble.

CHAPMAN, COOLIDGE OTIS. Musical Training of the Pearl Poet. PMLA, 46, 1931, 177-81.

References to Chaucer's use of music.

COLLINS, FLETCHER. Chaucer's Understanding of Music. Diss, Yale, 1934.

COULTON, G. G. Art and the Reformation. Blackwell, 1928. 622 pp.

Rise and decay of medieval art.

Rev: TLS, July 12, 1928, 515; NQ, 154, 1928, 359-60; LL, 1, 1928, 62-3; F. J. Mather, SRL, 6, 1929, 156.

CRISP, Sir FRANK. Medieval Gardens, "Flowering Medes," and Other Arrangements of Herbs, Flowers, and Shrubs Grown in the Middle Ages with Some Account of Tudor, Elizabethan, and Stuart Gardens. Ed by his daughter, C. Childs Patterson. Ill from the original sources collected by the author. Lane, 1924. 2 vols.

DUNN, WILLIAM P. The De Musica of Boethius, with
Particular Reference to the Music of the Fourteenth
Century as Reflected in Chaucer. Master's Thesis,
Columbia, 1917.

EVANS, JOAN. Chaucer and Decorative Art. RES, 6,
1930, 408-12.

Rev: Dorothy Everett, YWES, 78.

FFOULKES, CHARLES. Some Aspects of the Craft of
the Armourer. Archaeologia, 79, 1929, 13-28.

Description of armor about Chaucer's time.

GALPIN, FRANCIS W. Old English Instruments of Music, their History and Character. Methuen, 1911. 327
pp.

Rev: Dial, 50, 1911, 396; Nation, 92, 1911, 431; Sat
Rev, 110, 1910, 652; Independent, 71, 1911, 431; International Studio, 42, 1911, 257.

GARDINER, S. A Guide to English Gothic Architecture.
Cambridge Univ Press, 1922. Ill.

GARDNER, ARTHUR. A Handbook of English Medieval
Sculpture. Macmillan; Cambridge Univ Press, 1935.
392 pp.

Based on An Account of Medieval Figure Sculpture
in England, by Prior and Gardner, 1912, but consider-
ably revised and rewritten.

Rev: TLS, Oct 10, 1935, 625; N St, 10, 1935, 786;
E. A. Jewell, NYTBR, Jan 19, 1936, 23; Living
Church, 93, 1935, 715.

----------. English Medieval Sculpture. Cambridge
Univ Press, 1951. 351 pp. 683 ill.

Rev: William S. A. Dale, Spec, 27, 1952, 381-3.

GEROULD, T. La Musique au Moyen Age. Les Clas-
siques Français du Moyen Age. H. Champion, 1932.
443 pp.

Early Christian era to 14th century.

Rev: Helen Robbins Bittermann, Spec, 9, 1934,
333-4.

GIBBON, JOHN MURRAY. Melody and the Lyric. From
Chaucer to the Cavaliers. Dent, 1930. 204 pp.

Chaucer's knowledge of music, 1-9.

Rev: TLS, Nov 20, 1930, 968.

HADOW, W. HENRY, Ed. The Oxford History of Music.
2nd ed rev by Percy C. Buck. Oxford Univ Press,
1929. 334 pp.

Theoretical Writers on Music to 1400, by Dom An-
selm Hughes, 117-32; Social Aspects of Music in Mid-
dle Ages, by E. J. Dent, 184-221; Bibliography, by
M. D. Calvocoressi, 223-39.
    Rev: TLS, April 11, 1929, 288.
HARRIS, ELIZABETH L. The Mural as a Decorative
    Device in Mediaeval Literature. Doctoral Diss, Van-
    derbilt. Vanderbilt Univ Press, 1935. 89 pp.
HARRISON, FREDERICK. Treasures of Illumination;
    English Manuscripts of the Fourteenth Century (c.
    1250 to 1400). Studio, 1937. 48 pp. 24 plates.
HEATHER, P. J. Precious Stones in the Middle-English
    Verse of the Fourteenth Century. Folk-Lore, 42, 1931,
    217-64, 345-404.
    Several mentions of Chaucer.
KENNEDY, CLOANTHA COPASS. Story Material in the
    Decorative Art of Chaucer's Time. Doctoral Diss,
    Univ of Chicago, 1933. Published in part (7 pp.),
    Univ of Chicago Libraries, 1933.
KENYON, F. English Paintings in the Middle Ages. Dis-
    covery, 5, 1924, 311-5; 6, 1925, 10-14.
KNOWLES, J. A. Essays in the History of the York
    School of Glass Painting. SPCK, 1936.
    Rev: TLS, Nov 21, 1936, 947; D. H. S. Cranage,
    EHR, 52, 1937, 696-8; C. Woodford, Antiquaries
    Jour, 17, 1937, 453-5.
LETHABY, WILLIAM RICHARD. Medieval Paintings at
    Westminster. Brit Acad: Henriette Hertz Trust. An-
    nual lecture on aspects of art. Oxford Univ Press,
    1927. 32 pp.
MILLAR, ERIC. English Illuminated Manuscripts of the
    Fourteenth and Fifteenth Centuries. Paris and Brus-
    sels, 1928.
MONTMORENCY, J. E. G. de. Gardens in Chaucer and
    Shakespeare. CR, 99, supp. 44, 1911, 1-8; Living Age,
    269, 1911, 625-9.
NORTH, J. N. Medieval Embroideries. International
    Studio, 81, 1925, 362-6.
OLSON, CLAIR C. A Study of Music of the Fourteenth
    Century with Especial Reference to Chaucer. Unprint-
    ed Diss, Univ of Chicago, 1939.
----------. The Minstrels at the Court of Edward III.
    PMLA, 56, 1941, 601-12.

Number, names, compensation, and activities of
court minstrels.
----------. Chaucer and the Music of the Fourteenth
Century. Spec, 16, 1941, 64-92.
An estimation of Chaucer's musical knowledge and
interests.
Rev: D. Everett, YWES, 65.
PATTISON, BRUCE. Music and Poetry in the English
Renaissance. London, 1948.
PRESTON, RAYMOND. Chaucer and the Ballades No-
tées of Guillaume de Machaut. Spec, 26, 1951, 615-23.
PRIOR, E. S. Eight Chapters on English Medieval Art.
Cambridge Univ Press, 1922.
READ, HERBERT. English Stained Glass. Putnam, 1926.
260 pp.
Several excellent illustrations of Canterbury win-
dows.
REESE, GUSTAVE. Music in the Middle Ages: With an
Introduction on Music of Ancient Times. New York:
Norton, 1940. 502 pp.
Rev: TLS, Nov 1, 1941, 545; Erich Herstmann, AHR,
46, 1941, 972-3; Willi Apel, Spec, 20, 1945, 119-22.
RICKERT, MARGARET. Reconstruction of an English
Carmelite Missal. Spec, 16, 1941, 92-102.
Discussion of illumination.
ROHDE, ELEANOUR SINCLAIR. Mediaeval Garden Lit-
erature. Bookman (London), 82, 1932, 98-100.
RUTTER, FRANK. English Medieval Art. Edinburgh Rev,
239, 1924, 130-43.
SAHLIN, MARGIT. Etude sur la Carole Médiévale: L'O-
rigine du Mot et ses Rapports avec l'Eglise. Upsala,
1940.
Rev: Leo Spitzer, MLN, 56, 1941, 222-5.
SAUNDERS, O. ELFRIDA. English Illumination. Pega-
sus Press, 1928. 2 vols. 129 plates.
Rev: TLS, May 10, 1928, 349; Kingsley Porter,
SRL, 5, 1928, 1111.
----------. A History of English Art in the Middle Ages.
With a Preface by Tancred Borenius. Clarendon
Press, 1932. 272 pp.
Rev: TLS, June 2, 1932, 403; J. G. Noppen, Anti-
quaries Jour, 12, 1932, 469-70; H. Eichler, DL, 54,
1933, 1944-5.

SCOTT-GILES, C. WILFRID. The Romance of Heraldry.
    Dent, 1929. 234 pp.
        Rev: TLS, Oct 31, 1929, 862.
TERRY, Sir RICHARD RUNCIMAN, Ed. Medieval Carol
    Book; Melodies Chiefly from MSS in the Bodleian Li-
    brary, Oxford, and in the Library of Trinity College,
    Cambridge. Burns, 1932. 66 pp.
THOMPSON, A. HAMILTON. Song Schools in the Middle
    Ages. Oxford Univ Press, 1942.
        Rev: TLS, July 25, 1942, 369.
THOMPSON, DANIEL V., Jr., and GEORGE HEARD
    HAMILTON, Trans. De Arte Illuminandi. The Tech-
    nique of Manuscript Illumination. An anonymous 14th
    century treatise, translated from the Latin of Naples
    MS. XII. E. 27. Yale Univ Press, 1933. 67 pp.
THOMPSON, DANIEL V., Jr., Trans. Cennino d'Andrea
    Cennini da Colle di Val d'Elsa. Il Libro dell'Arte: The
    Craftsman's Handbook. Yale Univ Press, 1938. 142 pp.
        Instruction book for medieval artists.
----------. The Materials of Medieval Painting. Fore-
    word by Bernhard Berenson. Yale Univ Press, 1936.
    239 pp.
        Rev: TLS, July 4, 1936, 557; E. Harrison, QQ,
    43, 1936, 324-5; SRL, 15, Jan 9, 1936, 16; Philip
    Webster Souers, Spec, 13, 1938, 366-8.
VON REBER, FRANZ. History of Medieval Art. Trans
    by Joseph Thatcher Clarke. Harper, 1887. 422 ill.
WOODFORDE, Rev. CHRISTOPHER. English Stained
    Glass and Glass Painters in the Fourteenth Century.
    Oxford Univ Press, 1939.

ADDENDA

Page 6
ENGLISH ASSOCIATION. Dorothy Everett completed her editorship of the Chaucer section of YWES in 1951. 1952 is edited by Beatrice White.

Page 14
BLAND, D. S. Chaucer and the Inns of Court: A Reexamination. E Stud, 33, 1952, 145-55.
See also his Inns of Court Nomenclature, NQ, 198, 1953, 2-4. Bland questions Manly and Rickert's support of the possibility that Chaucer was a student at one of the Inns.

Page 18
KELLY, REGINA Z. Young Geoffrey Chaucer: His Boyhood Adventures, his Student Days at Oxford, his Romantic Training as a Page at Court. New York: Lothrop, Lee and Shepard, 1952.
An imaginative interpretation.

Page 32
CHEWNING, HARRIS. The Text of the Envoy to Alison. Stud in Bibl, 5, 1952.
Discussion of the technique of MS classification.

Page 38
PRICE, DEREK J. Also Jour of the SW Essex Tech Coll, Dec, 1952, 154-68.

Page 49
ANON. Gentle Blurber. Publishers' Weekly, 164, 1953, 2228.
BECKER, W. Chaucer Made New. NR, 127, 1952, 19-20.

Page 60
BREWER, DEREK STANLEY. Chaucer. Longmans, Green, 1953.
I. A Young Squire; II. The Literary Tradition; III. A Working Courtier; IV. Diplomat and Civil Servant; V. The Intellectual Background: Boethius and Venus; VI. A Philosophical Poet; VII. The Romances; VIII. The Legend of Good Women; IX. Prologue to the

Canterbury Tales; X. The Canterbury Tales; XI. The
Last Years.
Page 67
HOLLIS, C. Voice of Catholic England. The Tablet, 200,
1952, 417.
Page 78
STEPHENSON, HAROLD. Chaucer Explored. Use of
English, 4, 1952, 91-3.
SWART, J. Het Probleem van Chaucers Poëzie. Gronin-
gen, 1951. 23 pp.
Page 108
LLEWELLYN, R. H. "The Wright's Chaste Wife" Disin-
terred. Southern Folklore Quart, 16, 1952, 251-4.
LYLES, ALBERT M. A Note on Sidney's Use of Chaucer.
NQ, 198, 1953, 99-100.
Page 111
SCHLAUCH, MARGARET. Chaucer in Iceland: A Supple-
ment. Spec, 28, 1953, 363-70.
Page 213
WHITE, BEATRICE. Two Notes on Middle English. Neo-
phil, 37, 1953, 113-5.
On "camaille" and "aventaille," 1195 ff.
Page 245
KELLOGG, ALFRED L. Seith Moyses by the Devel: A
Problem in Chaucer's Parson's Tale. Rev Belg de
Phil et d'Hist, 31, 1953, 61-4.
Page 261
KENDALL, LYLE H. Melt with Ruth. NQ, 198, 1953,
145.
Page 267
BRUNNER, KARL. Chaucer's House of Fame. Rivista di
Letterature Moderne, 2, 1951, 344-50.
Page 282
WICKERT, MARIA. Chaucers Konstanze und die Legende
der Guten Frauen. Ang, 69, 1950, 89-104.
Page 284
BRADDY, HALDEEN. Chaucer's Comic Valentine. MLN,
68, 1953, 232-4.
Page 323
MOHAN, GAUDENS E. Incipits of Logical Writings of
the XIIIth-XVth Centuries. Franciscan Studies, 12,
1952, 349-89.

Page 353

POWICKE, Sir MAURICE. Robert Grosseteste, Bishop of Lincoln. JRLB, 35, 1953, 482-507.

INDEX

This index does not include the names of the authors of the reviews as these references are always to be considered only in relation to the book or article to which they are appended. Review articles, however, have been given independent listing when they are part of a controversy. In order to avoid duplication of classifications in the bibliography, such references as those to saints, to writers who influenced Chaucer, to chronology, to the order of the Canterbury Tales, to courtly love, and to Chaucer's associates have been given a full listing.